The Writer's Journey

Mythic Structure for Writers

~

Third Edition

Christopher Vogler

Illustrated by Michele Montez

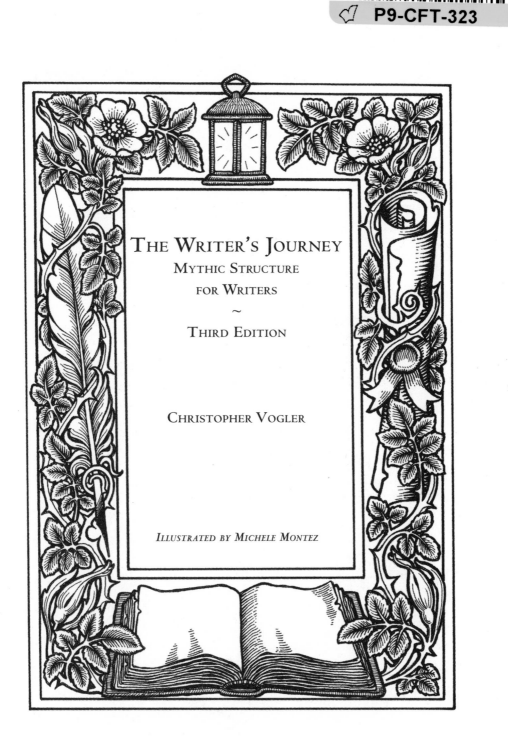

MIX
Paper from responsible sources
FSC® C014174
FSC
www.fsc.org

Published by Michael Wiese Productions
12400 Ventura Blvd., # 1111
Studio City, CA 91604
tel. 818.379.8799
fax 818.986.3408
mw@mwp.com
www.mwp.com

Cover Design: Michael Wiese Productions
Illustrations: Fritz Springmeyer & Michele Montez
Book Layout: Gina Mansfield Design
Editor: Paul Norlen

Printed by Sheridan Books, Ann Arbor, Michigan
Manufactured in the United States of America
Printed on Recycled Stock

First Printing October 1998

Library of Congress Cataloging-in-Publication Data

Vogler, Christopher, 1949-
The writer's journey : mythic structure for writers / Christopher Vogler. -- 3rd ed.
p. cm.
Includes bibliographical references and index.
ISBN 978-1-932907-36-0
1. Motion picture authorship. 2. Narration (Rhetoric) 3. Myth in literature. 4. Creative writing. I. Title.
PN1996.V64 2007
808.2'3--dc22

2007026844

"This book is like having the smartest person in the story meeting come home with you and whisper what to do in your ear as you write a screenplay. Insight for insight, step for step, Chris Vogler takes us through the process of connecting theme to story and making a script come alive."

— Lynda Obst, Producer,
How to Lose a Guy in 10 Days, Sleepless in Seattle, One Fine Day, Contact; Author, *Hello, He Lied*

"*The Writer's Journey* is an insightful and even inspirational guide to the craft of storytelling. An approach to structure that is fresh and contemporary, while respecting our roots in mythology."

— Charles Russell, Writer, Director, Producer, *Dreamscape, The Mask, Eraser*

"*The Writer's Journey* should be on anyone's bookshelf who cares about the art of storytelling at the movies. Not just some theoretical tome filled with development clichés of the day, this book offers sound and practical advice on how to construct a story that works."

— David Friendly, Producer, *Little Miss Sunshine, Daylight, Courage Under Fire, Out to Sea, My Girl*

"A classic of its kind full of insight and inspiration that every writer, both amateur and professional, must read."

— Richard D. Zanuck, The Zanuck Company
Charlie and the Chocolate Factory, Big Fish, Reign of Fire, Driving Miss Daisy, Cocoon, The Verdict, Sting

"The basis for a great movie is a great screenplay, and the basis for a great screenplay should be *The Writer's Journey*."

— Adam Fields,
Donnie Darko, Money Train, Great Balls of Fire

"One of the most valuable tools in understanding and appreciating the structure of a plot that's available today. *The Writer's Journey* is an essential tool to any writer at any stage of their career."

— Debbie Macomber, Best-selling Author, *Montana*

"A valuable tool for any creative writer, *The Writer's Journey* is consistently among our top-selling books each month. Christopher Vogler's narrative helps writers construct well-developed characters that enrich their stories."

— The Writer's Computer Store

"There's not a better book to read if you want to write movies, or anything else for that matter. I keep it on my desk, always within reach, knowing that when I get lost — and I always do — I have somebody close by to help show me the way. Chris Vogler is a (bleep)ing genius."

— Scott Silver, Writer, *Eight Mile*

"*The Writer's Journey* provides both fiction and nonfiction writers with powerful tools and guidelines to create remarkable stories. It is the best book of its kind."

— John Tullius, Director, Maui Writers Conference and Writer's Retreat

"This is a book about the stories we write, and perhaps more importantly, the stories we live. It is the most influential work I have yet encountered on the art, nature, and the very purpose of storytelling."

— Bruce Joel Rubin, Screenwriter, *Ghost, Jacob's Ladder*

"This book should come with a warning: You're going to learn about more than just writing movies–you're going to learn about life! *The Writer's Journey* is the perfect manual for developing, pitching and writing stories with universal human themes that will forever captivate a global audience. It's the secret weapon I hope every writer finds out about."

— Jeff Arch, Screenwriter, *Sleepless in Seattle*

"Vogler was the genius behind *The Writer's Journey,* which should be on the shelf of every screenwriter. Studies classical mythology and its use in moviemaking for stories."

— *Fade In* Magazine 1996 (From Article "The Top 100 People in Hollywood You Need to Know")

"The Katzenberg memo has joined the show-biz vernacular. But there's another, lesser-known Disney memo whose influence arguably exceeded Katzenberg's. This seven-page memo distills myth-master Joseph Campbell's storytelling theories into an algorithm for screenplays."

— *Los Angeles Times* Magazine, 1994

"The current industry bible ...

— *Spy* Magazine, Holiday Issue, 1997

"A seven-page memo by Christopher Vogler is now the stuff of Hollywood legend. ... The idea of a "mythic structure" has been quickly accepted by Hollywood, and Vogler's book now graces the bookshelves of many studio heads."

— *The London Times,* 1994

"I tell every story teller who asks, it all starts with this book. Vogler conjures up ancient tools and teaches readers how to wield them — unlocking solutions to every story problem."

— Darren Aronofsky, Director, *Pi, Requiem for a Dream,* and *The Fountain for*

Mom and Dad

TABLE OF CONTENTS

INTRODUCTION

Third Edition

The waves are still rolling in from the pebbles in the pond that were the original *Writer's Journey* and its second edition. Since almost a decade has gone by since the second edition was launched, the ideas in that volume have been strenuously tested in a number of story-making laboratories around the world. Concepts I had developed as a story consultant for the Disney company and as a teacher of story construction have been through a fresh battery of challenges in the real world that I hope have made them stronger. The new chapters of this book will, I hope, reflect some of the ideas that have continued to evolve around the Hero's Journey concept. There are new chapters on the life force operating in stories, on the mechanism of polarity that rules in storytelling, on the wisdom of the body, catharsis, and other concepts that I have developed in recent years in my lectures and in practical work in Hollywood and in Europe. I have gathered together this new material near the end of the book, in an appendix following "Looking Back on the Journey."

In the nine years since the last edition, I have traveled widely, applied my ideas to writing, publishing, and producing projects of my own, and done a few more "tours of duty" as it were for major Hollywood studios. The first of these jobs, commencing just after the publishing of the second edition, was a four-year return to 20th Century Fox, where I had been a story analyst at the beginning of my career. This time around I was operating at a slightly higher level, as a development executive for the Fox 2000 feature film label, with more responsibility and pressure. I was involved in the research and development aspects of films like *Courage*

Under Fire, Volcano, Anna and the King, Fight Club, and *The Thin Red Line.* My concepts of storytelling, shaped by the patterns of mythology and the thinking of Joseph Campbell and Carl Jung, were now being tested not only on animated features but on big-budget, live-action movies for adult audiences.

The office atmosphere of Fox 2000 was a fascinating place to study the ways of power. In the past I had been aware of places like it, but as a story analyst I had not been inside those meeting rooms where the decisions were taken about the writers, the stories, and the movies made from them. Power flows in those rooms like hot lava, and until I worked at Fox 2000 I had only heard it rumbling. Now I was standing hip deep in it.

It was the most adult environment I had ever been in, run on unspoken but rigorous principles of personal responsibility. No whining allowed, no excuses. And the same fierce intensity was applied to the stories. Every concept, every comment, every suggestion had to pass the most stringent tests of common sense, logic, and show business instinct. I had the good fortune to work with some of the best story brains in the business, foremost among them being Fox 2000's founder Laura Ziskin, but also many talented executives, writers, directors, and producers. In this exacting laboratory I learned useful techniques for analyzing stories, ways of looking at characters and describing story situations that I hope will inform the new sections of this revised edition.

Among the things I learned at Fox 2000 was to listen to my body as a judge of a story's effectiveness. I realized that the good stories were affecting the organs of my body in various ways, and the really good ones were stimulating more than one organ. An effective story grabs your gut, tightens your throat, makes your heart race and your lungs pump, brings tears to your eyes or an explosion of laughter to your lips. If I wasn't getting some kind of physiological reaction from a story, I knew it was only affecting me on an intellectual level and therefore it would probably leave audiences cold. You will find my thoughts about this in a new chapter on the wisdom of the body.

When my job at Fox 2000 came to an end, as all good things must do, I wanted to write and produce some projects of my own. I soon found myself writing the screenplay for an animated feature, the result of a lecture trip to Munich. I was approached by producer Eberhard

Junkersdorf to write the script for his version of the merry adventures of Till Eulenspiegel, Europe's favorite medieval clown. I knew of Till's colorful character from stories I had read as a child and was delighted to take up the challenge. I enjoyed working with the energetic and charming Herr Junkersdorf and his international team of artists. Eberhard is so persuasive he even got me to contribute lyrics for two songs on the film's soundtrack, which really was a challenge. The film was released in Germany as *Till Eulenspiegel,* and I am hopeful it will be released in English one day under its English title, *Jester Till.* The experience taught me a multitude of lessons that I have tried to incorporate into the present edition.

Next up, I got involved as an executive producer of an independent feature, *P.S. Your Cat Is Dead,* actor/director/writer Steve Guttenberg's adaptation of the play and novel by James Kirkwood. This took me deep into the editing room for a period of months, another of the sacred temples of the movie business and for me, a place of intense joy. I loved sitting in the dark staring at images all day long and making the pictures dance. I called it going into the submarine, a blissful world of concentration that called on every cell of my creativity and forced me to articulate my ideas in order to communicate with my creative partners. I could see many ways in which the editing process echoes the writing process, and imagined new possibilities for combining the two. I learned new principles and gave the old theories a good workout.

The process of editing seemed to me to be a lot like making a wooden boat, like one of those sleek dragon-ships the Vikings made. The spine of the story is like the keel, the major plot points are the ribs, and the individual scenes and lines of dialogue are the planks and rigging that complete the vessel, a vehicle for your vision that you hope will sail on the seas of public attention.

Another insight from the editing room was a greater appreciation of the importance of focus. I realized that focused attention is one of the rarest things in the world, and that an audience is giving a lot when they devote their full attention to your work for two hours. There is only so much focus available in a given work, and it seems the more elements you take out of a composition, the more focus is poured into those that remain. Cutting lines, pauses, and entire scenes sharpened the focus on the elements that were left, as if a large number of diffuse spotlights had been concentrated into a few bright beams aimed at select important points.

P.S. Your Cat Is Dead enjoyed a brief theatrical run and then was distributed on DVD. After that adventure I concentrated for a time on traveling to give seminars for various international cinema and television training programs. Most recently I have gone back to the Hollywood studio world with a tour of duty at Paramount Pictures and a number of consulting jobs for other studios. I tried my hand at a new form, writing the first installment of *Ravenskull,* a story for a "manga," a highly stylized kind of comic book from Japan. This is a highly cinematic form, much like writing a screenplay and with a great deal of emphasis on the visual.

I hope something of what I have learned from collaborating with artists has found its way into this latest edition. It has been an intense pleasure to work with my artist friends Michele Montez and Fritz Springmeyer, whose illustrations provide the chapter headings in this volume.

And while I'm cataloguing the influences of recent years that inform the changes in the present volume, some of my most valuable time was spent walking the beach and thinking about why things are as they are and how they got to be that way. I tried to understand how the sun and stars move across the sky and how the moon got there. I saw that it's all waves, all of the Universe, just echoes and counter-echoes of the original cosmic sound, not the Big Bang, that's the wrong sound effect. It was more like a gong, that's it, the Great Gong, the original creative vibration that rolled out from a single pinpoint of concentration and unraveled and echoed and collided to create everything that is, and the Hero's Journey is part of that. I watch the sunsets march up and down the horizon, creating my own Stonehenge from the islands and ridge peaks that mark solstice and equinox, inviting me to puzzle out the place of stories and my own place in the story of everything. I hope you find your own place in that design. For those to whom the concept is new, bon voyage, and for those who are familiar with earlier versions, I hope you find some new surprises and connections in this work, and that it serves you on your own creative journeys.

Christopher Vogler
Venice, California
February 26, 2007

PREFACE
Second Edition

"I'm not trying to copy Nature. I'm trying to find the principles she's using."
— R. Buckminster Fuller

A book goes out like a wave rolling over the surface of the sea. Ideas radiate from the author's mind and collide with other minds, triggering new waves that return to the author. These generate further thoughts and emanations, and so it goes. The concepts described in *The Writer's Journey* have radiated and are now echoing back interesting challenges and criticisms as well as sympathetic vibrations. This is my report on the waves that have washed back over me from publication of the book, and on the new waves I send back in response.

In this book I described the set of concepts known as "The Hero's Journey," drawn from the depth psychology of Carl G. Jung and the mythic studies of Joseph Campbell. I tried to relate those ideas to contemporary storytelling, hoping to create a writer's guide to these valuable gifts from our innermost selves and our most distant past. I came looking for the design principles of storytelling, but on the road I found something more: a set of principles for living. I came to believe that the Hero's Journey is nothing less than a handbook for life, a complete instruction manual in the art of being human.

The Hero's Journey is not an invention, but an observation. It is a recognition of a beautiful design, a set of principles that govern the conduct of life and the world of storytelling the way physics and chemistry govern the physical world. It's difficult to avoid the sensation that the Hero's Journey exists somewhere, somehow, as an eternal reality, a Platonic ideal form, a divine model. From this model, infinite and highly varied copies can be produced, each resonating with the essential spirit of the form.

The Hero's Journey is a pattern that seems to extend in many dimensions, describing more than one reality. It accurately describes, among other things, the process of making a journey, the necessary working parts of a story, the joys and despairs of being a writer, and the passage of a soul through life.

A book that explores such a pattern naturally partakes of this multi–dimensional quality. *The Writer's Journey* was intended as a practical guidebook for writers, but can also be read as a guide to the life lessons that have been carefully built into the stories of all times. Some people have even used it as a kind of travel guide, predicting the inevitable ups and downs of making a physical journey.

A certain number of people say the book has affected them on a level that may have nothing to do with the business of telling a story or writing a script. In the description of the Hero's Journey they might have picked up some insight about their own lives, some useful metaphor or way of looking at things, some language or principle that defines their problem and suggests a way out of it. They recognize their own problems in the ordeals of the mythic and literary heroes, and are reassured by the stories that give them abundant, time-tested strategies for survival, success, and happiness.

Other people find validation of their own observations in the book. From time to time I meet people who know the Hero's Journey well although they may never have heard it called by that name. When they read about it or hear it described, they experience the pleasurable shock of recognition as the patterns resonate with what they've seen in stories and in their own lives. I had the same reaction when I first encountered these concepts in Campbell's book, *The Hero with a Thousand Faces,* and heard him speak about them with passion. Campbell himself felt it when he first heard his mentor, Heinrich Zimmer, speak about mythology. In Zimmer he recognized a shared attitude about myths — that they are not abstract theories or the quaint beliefs of ancient peoples, but practical models for understanding how to live.

A PRACTICAL GUIDE

The original intent of this book was to make an accessible, down-to-earth writing manual from these high-flying mythic elements. In that practical spirit, I am gratified to hear from so many readers that the book can be a useful writing guide. Professional writers as well as novices and students report that it has been an effective design tool, validating their instincts and providing new concepts and principles to apply to their stories. Movie and television executives, producers, and directors have told me the book influenced their projects and helped them solve story problems. Novelists, playwrights, actors, and writing teachers have put the ideas to use in their work.

Happily, the book has won acceptance as one of the standard Hollywood guidebooks for the screenwriting craft. *Spy* magazine called it "the new industry Bible." Through the various international editions (U.K., German, French, Portuguese, Italian, Icelandic, etc.) it has radiated to greater Hollywood, the world community of storytellers. Filmmakers and students from many countries have reported their interest in the Hero's Journey idea and their appreciation for the book as a practical guide for designing and troubleshooting stories.

The Writer's Journey, meanwhile, has been put to work in many ways, not only by writers in many forms and genres, but by teachers, psychologists, advertising executives, prison counselors, video game designers, and scholars of myth and pop culture.

I am convinced the principles of the Hero's Journey have had a deep influence over the shaping of stories in the past and will reach even deeper in the future as more storytellers become consciously aware of them. Joseph Campbell's great accomplishment was to articulate clearly something that had been there all along — the life principles embedded in the structure of stories. He wrote down the unwritten rules of storytelling, and that seems to be stimulating authors to challenge, test, and embellish the Hero's Journey. I see signs that writers are playing with the ideas and even introducing "Campbellian" language and terms into their dramas.

The conscious awareness of its patterns may be a mixed blessing, for it's easy to generate thoughtless clichés and stereotypes from this matrix. The self-conscious, heavy-handed use of this model can be boring and predictable. But if writers absorb its ideas and re-create them with fresh insights and surprising combinations, they can make amazing new forms and original designs from the ancient, immutable parts.

QUESTIONS AND CRITICISMS

"It takes a great enemy to make a great airplane."
— Air Force saying

Inevitably, aspects of the book have been questioned or criticized. I welcome this as a sign the ideas are worthy of argument. I'm sure I've learned more from the challenges than from the positive feedback. Writing a book may be, as the historian Paul Johnson says, "the only way to study a subject systematically, purposefully and retentively." Harvesting the response, both positive and negative, is part of that study.

Since the book came out in 1993 I have continued to work in the story end of the movie business, at Disney, Fox, and Paramount. I've had the chance to try out the Hero's Journey concepts with the big toys. I saw where it works but also where my understanding of it fell short and needed to be adjusted. My beliefs about what makes a good story were tested in the toughest arenas on earth — Hollywood story conferences and the world marketplace — and I hope my understanding has grown from the objections, doubts, and questions of my esteemed colleagues, and from the reaction of the audience.

At the same time, I kept up a schedule of lecturing about *The Writer's Journey* that took me far afield from the literal, geographic bounds of Hollywood, into the greater-world Hollywood, the international film community. I had the fortune to see how the ideas of the Hero's Journey unfold in cultures different from the one I grew up in, as I traveled to Barcelona, Maui, Berlin, Rome, London, Sydney, and so on.

Local tastes and thinking challenged many facets of the Hero's Journey idea severely. Each culture has a unique orientation to the Hero's Journey, with something in each local character resisting some terms, defining them differently, or giving them different emphasis. My theoretical framework has been shaken from every angle, and I think is the richer for it.

A FORM, NOT A FORMULA

First, I must address a significant objection about the whole idea of *The Writer's Journey* — the suspicion of artists and critics that it is formulaic, leading to stale repetition. We come to a great divide in theory and practice about these principles. Some professional writers don't like the idea of analyzing the creative process at all, and urge students to ignore all books and teachers and "Just do it." Some artists make the choice to avoid systematic thinking, rejecting all principles, ideals, schools of thought, theories, patterns, and designs. For them, art is an entirely intuitive process that can never be mastered by rules of thumb and should not be reduced to formula. And they aren't wrong. At the core of every artist is a sacred place where all the rules are set aside or deliberately forgotten, and nothing matters but the instinctive choices of the heart and soul of the artist.

But even that is a principle, and those who say they reject principles and theories can't avoid subscribing to a few of them: Avoid formula, distrust order and pattern, resist logic and tradition.

Artists who operate on the principle of rejecting all form are themselves dependent on form. The freshness and excitement of their work comes from its contrast to the pervasiveness of formulas and patterns in the culture. However, these artists run the risk of reaching a limited audience because most people can't relate to totally unconventional art. By definition it doesn't intersect with commonly held patterns of experience. Their work might only be appreciated by other artists, a small part of the community in any time or place. A certain amount of form is necessary to reach a wide audience. People expect it and enjoy it, so long as it's varied by some innovative combination or arrangement and doesn't fall into a completely predictable formula.

At the other extreme are the big Hollywood studios who use conventional patterns to appeal to the broadest cross-section of the public. At the Disney studios, I saw the application of simple story principles, such as making the main character a "fish out of water," that became tests of a story's power to appeal to a mass audience. The minds guiding Disney at that time believed that there were proper questions to ask of a story and its characters: Does it have conflict? Does it have a theme? Is it about something that can be expressed as a well-known statement of folk wisdom like "Don't judge a book by its cover" or "Love conquers all"? Does it present the story as a series of broad movements or acts, allowing audiences to orient and pace themselves in the narrative? Does it take viewers someplace they've never been, or make them see familiar places in new ways? Do the characters have relevant backstories and plausible motivations to make them relatable to the audience? Do they pass through realistic stages of emotional reaction and growth (character arcs)? And so on.

Studios have to use design principles and apply some kind of standards to evaluating and developing stories, if only because they produce so many of them. The average studio or division in Hollywood has bought and is developing one hundred fifty to two hundred stories at a time. They must spend more resources evaluating thousands of potential projects submitted by agents each year. To handle the large number of stories, some of the techniques of mass production, such as standardization, have to be employed. But they should be employed sparingly and with great sensitivity for the needs of the particular story.

STANDARD LANGUAGE

A most important tool is a standardized language that makes possible the thousands of communications necessary to tell so many stories. No one dictates this language, but it becomes part of everyone's education in the unwritten rules of the business. Newcomers quickly learn the lingo, concepts, and assumptions that have been passed down by generations of storytellers and filmmakers. This provides everyone with a shorthand for the rapid communication of story ideas.

Meanwhile new terms and concepts are always being created to reflect changing conditions. Junior studio executives listen carefully for signs of insight, philosophy, or ordering principle from their bosses. People take their lead from the leader. Any terms of art, any aphorisms or rules of thumb are seized upon and passed down, becoming part of the corporate culture of that studio and the general knowledge of the industry. It's especially true when those bits of received wisdom lead to successful, popular entertainments.

The Hero's Journey language is clearly becoming part of the storytelling common knowledge and its principles have been used consciously to create hugely popular films. But there is danger in this self-awareness. Overreliance on traditional language or the latest buzzwords can lead to thoughtless, cookie-cutter products. Lazy, superficial use of Hero's Journey terms, taking this metaphorical system too literally, or arbitrarily imposing its forms on every story can be stultifying. It should be used as a form, not a formula, a reference point and a source of inspiration, not a dictatorial mandate.

CULTURAL IMPERIALISM

Another of the dangers of standardized language and methods is that local differences, the very things that add zest and spice to journeys to faraway places, will get hammered into blandness by the machinery of mass production. Artists around the world are on guard against "cultural imperialism," the aggressive export of Hollywood storytelling techniques and the squeezing out of local accents. American values and the cultural assumptions of Western society threaten to smother the unique flavors of other cultures. Many observers have remarked that American culture is becoming world culture, and what a loss it would be if the only flavorings available were sugar, salt, mustard, and ketchup.

This problem is much on the minds of European storytellers as many countries with distinct cultures are drawn into a union. They are striving to create stories that are somewhat universal, that can travel beyond their national borders, for local audiences may not be numerous enough to support the always-growing cost of production. They are up against intensely competitive American companies that aggressively courts the world market. Many are studying and applying American techniques, but they also worry that their unique regional traditions will be lost.

Is the Hero's Journey an instrument of cultural imperialism? It could be, if naively interpreted, blindly copied, or unquestioningly adopted. But it can also be a useful tool for the storyteller in any culture, if adapted thoughtfully to reflect the unique, inimitable qualities of the local geography, climate, and people.

I found that artists in Australia were acutely conscious of cultural imperialism, perhaps because that country's people have had to struggle to create their own society. They have forged something distinct from England, independent of America and Asia, influenced by all of them but uniquely Australian, and humming with the mysterious energy of the land and the Aboriginal people. They pointed out to me hidden cultural assumptions in my understanding of the Hero's Journey. While it is universal and timeless, and its workings can be found in every culture on earth, a Western or American reading of it may carry subtle biases. One instance is the Hollywood preference for happy endings and tidy resolutions, the tendency to show admirable, virtuous heroes overcoming evil by individual effort. My Australian teachers helped me see that such elements might make good stories for the world market but may not reflect the views of all cultures. They made me aware of what assumptions were being carried by Hollywood-style films, and of what was not being expressed.

In my travels I learned that Australia, Canada, and many countries in Europe subsidize their local filmmakers, in part to help preserve and celebrate local differences. Each region, department, or state operates as a small-scale movie studio, developing scripts, putting artists to work, and producing feature films and television shows. For America, I like to imagine a version of a decentralized Hollywood in which every state in the Union functions like a movie studio, evaluating the stories of its citizens and advancing money to produce regional films that represent and enhance the culture of the locality while supporting the local artists.

HEROPHOBIC CULTURES

Here and there in my travels I learned that some cultures are not entirely comfortable with the term "hero" to begin with. Australia and Germany are two cultures that seem slightly "herophobic."

The Australians distrust appeals to heroic virtue because such concepts have been used to lure generations of young Australian males into fighting Britain's battles. Australians have their heroes, of course, but they tend to be unassuming and self-effacing, and will remain reluctant for much longer than heroes in other cultures. Like most heroes, they resist calls to adventure but continue demurring and may never be comfortable with the hero mantle. In Australian culture it's unseemly to seek out leadership or the limelight, and anyone who does is a "tall poppy," quickly cut down. The most admirable hero is one who denies his heroic role as long as possible and who, like Mad Max, avoids accepting responsibility for anyone but himself.

German culture seems ambivalent about the term "hero." The hero has a long tradition of veneration in Germany, but two World Wars and the legacy of Hitler and the Nazis have tainted the concept. Nazism and German militarism manipulated and distorted the powerful symbols of the hero myth, invoking its passions to enslave, dehumanize, and destroy. Like any archetypal system, like any philosophy or creed, the heroic form can be warped and used with great effect for ill intention.

In the post-Hitler period the idea of hero has been given a rest as the culture re-evaluates itself. Dispassionate, cold-blooded anti-heroes are more in keeping with the current German spirit. A tone of unsentimental realism is more popular at present, although there will always be a strain of romanticism and love of fantasy. Germans can enjoy imaginative hero tales from other cultures but don't seem comfortable with home-grown romantic heroes for the time being.

THE HERO AS WARRIOR

More generally, the Hero's Journey has been criticized as an embodiment of a male-dominated warrior culture. Critics say it is a propaganda device invented to encourage young males to enlist in armies, a myth that glorifies death and foolish self-sacrifice. There is some truth in this charge, for many heroes of legend and story are warriors and the patterns of the Hero's Journey have certainly been used for propaganda and recruitment. However, to condemn and dismiss these patterns because they can be put to military use is shortsighted and narrow-minded. The warrior is only one of the faces of the hero, who can also be pacifist, mother, pilgrim, fool, wanderer, hermit, inventor, nurse, savior, artist, lunatic, lover, clown, king, victim, slave, worker, rebel, adventurer, tragic failure, coward, saint, monster, etc. The many creative possibilities of the form far outweigh its potential for abuse.

GENDER PROBLEMS

The Hero's Journey is sometimes critiqued as a masculine theory, cooked up by men to enforce their dominance, and with little relevance to the unique and quite different journey of womanhood. There may be some masculine bias built into the description of the hero cycle since many of its theoreticians have been male, and I freely admit it: I'm a man and can't help seeing the world through the filter of my gender. Yet I have tried to acknowledge and explore the ways in which the woman's journey is different from the man's.

I believe that much of the journey is the same for all humans, since we share many realities of birth, growth, and decay, but clearly being a woman imposes distinct cycles, rhythms, pressures, and needs. There may be a real difference in the form of men's and women's journeys. Men's journeys may be in some sense more linear, proceeding from one outward goal to the next, while women's journeys may spin or spiral inward and outward. The spiral may be a more accurate analogue for the woman's journey than a straight line or a simple circle. Another possible model might be a series of concentric rings, with the woman making a journey inward towards the center and then expanding out again. The masculine need to go out and overcome obstacles, to achieve, conquer, and possess, may be replaced in the woman's journey by the drives to preserve the family and the species, make a home, grapple with emotions, come to accord, or cultivate beauty.

Good work has been done by women to articulate these differences, and I recommend books such as Merlin Stone's *When God Was a Woman,* Clarissa Pinkola Estes' *Women Who Run with the Wolves,* Jean Shinoda Bolen's *Goddesses in Everywoman,* Maureen Murdock's *The Heroine's Journey,* and *The Woman's Dictionary of Myth and Symbols* as starting points for a more balanced understanding of the male and female aspects of the Hero's Journey. (Note to men: If in doubt on this point, consult the nearest woman.)

THE COMPUTER CHALLENGE

Shortly after the first edition of this book came out, a few people (threshold guardians) jumped up to say the technology of the Hero's Journey is already obsolete, thanks to the advent of the computer and its possibilities of interactivity and nonlinear narrative. According to this batch of critics, the ancient ideas of the Journey are hopelessly mired in the conventions of beginning, middle, and end, of cause and effect, of one event after another. The new wave, they said, would dethrone the old linear storyteller, empowering people to tell their own stories in any sequence they chose, leaping from point to point, weaving stories more like spider webs than linear strings of events.

It's true that exciting new possibilities are created by computers and the nonlinear thinking they encourage. However, there will always be pleasure in "Tell me a story." People will always enjoy going into a story trance and allowing themselves to be led through a tale by a masterful story weaver. It's fun to drive a car, but it can also be fun to be driven, and as passengers we might see more sights than if we were forced to concentrate on choosing what happens next.

Interactivity has always been with us — we all make many nonlinear hypertext links in our own minds even as we listen to a linear story. In fact, the Hero's Journey lends itself extremely well to the world of computer games and interactive experiences. The thousands of variations on the paradigm, worked out over the centuries, offer endless branches from which infinite webs of story can be built.

THE CYNIC'S RESPONSE

Another of my deep cultural assumptions that was challenged as I traveled is the idea that one person can make a difference, that heroes are needed to make change, and that change is generally a good thing. I encountered artists from Eastern Europe who pointed out that in their cultures, there is deep cynicism about heroic efforts to change the world. The world is as it is, any efforts to change it are a foolish waste of time, and any so-called heroes who try to change it are doomed to fail. This point of view is not necessarily an antithesis of the Hero's Journey — the pattern is flexible enough to embrace the cynical or pragmatic philosophies, and many of its principles are still operative in stories that reflect them. However, I must acknowledge that not every person or culture sees the model as optimistically as I do, and they might be right.

BUT WHAT ABOUT . . .

It's exciting to see that there is no end to what can be learned from the Hero's Journey concepts. I find surprising and delightful turns of the path every time I pick up a new story, and life itself keeps teaching new angles.

My understanding of the Shadow archetype, for example, continues to evolve. I have been impressed all over again by the power of this pattern, especially as it operates within the individual as a repository for unexpressed feelings and desires. It is a force that accumulates when you fail to honor your gifts, follow the call of your muses, or live up to your principles and ideals. It has great but subtle power, operating on deep levels to communicate with you, perhaps sabotaging your efforts, upsetting your balance until you realize the message these events bring — that you must express your creativity, your true nature, or die. A car accident a few years ago taught me the rebellious power of the Shadow,

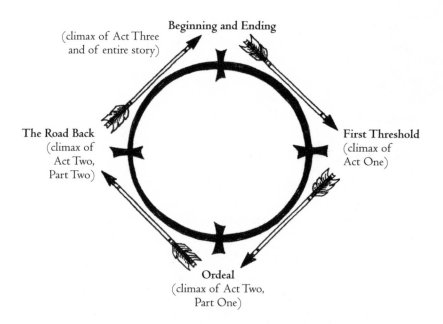

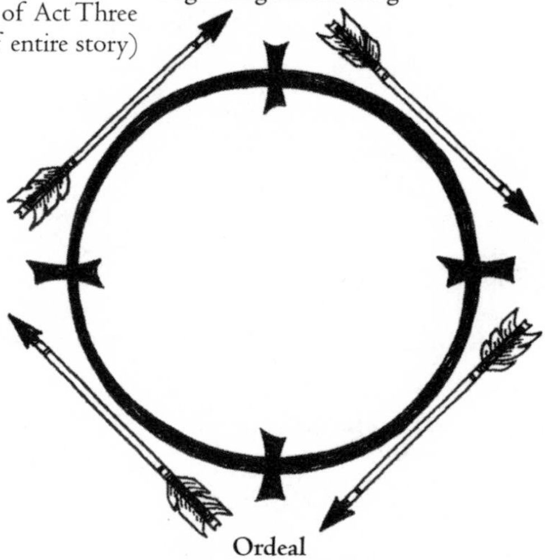

showed me that I was distracted, out of harmony, heading for even greater disasters if I didn't find a way to express my personal creative side.

Occasional puzzled looks on the faces of students taught me that I hadn't completely thought through some aspects of the pattern. Some people were confused by the various turning points and ordeals of the model, particularly by the distinction between the midpoint, which I call the Ordeal, and the climax of the second act, which I call The Road Back. Trying to explain this led me to a new realization. Each act is like a movement of a symphony, with its own beginning, middle, and end, and with its own climax (the highest point of tension) coming just before the ending of the act. These act climaxes are the major turning points on the circular diagram:

Lecturing in Rome, I came upon a further development of this idea, an alternate way of graphing the Hero's Journey: not as a circle, but as a diamond. I was explaining that each act sends the hero on a certain track with a specific aim or goal, and that the climaxes of each act change the hero's direction, assigning a new goal. The hero's first act goal, for instance, might be to seek treasure, but after meeting a potential lover at the first threshold crossing, the goal might change to pursuing that love. If the ordeal at the midpoint has the villain capturing the hero and lover, the goal in the next movement could become trying to escape. And if the

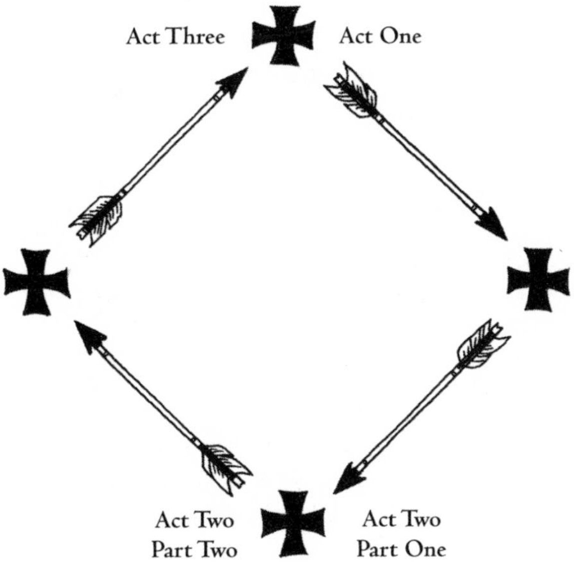

villain kills the lover at The Road Back, the new goal of the final movement might be to get revenge. The original objective might be achieved as well, or there might be some overall goal (to learn self-reliance or come to terms with past failures, for example) that continues to be served in all movements as the hero pursues changing superficial goals.

To illustrate this concept I drew the hero's goals in each movement as straight lines, vectors of intention, rather than curves. Straightening out the curves of the circle created sharp, 90-degree turns at the quarter points and revealed the drastic changes that may occur in the hero's objectives. Each straight line represents the hero's aim in that act — to escape the constraints of the ordinary world, to survive in a strange land, to win the boon and escape the strange land, to return home safely with something to share that revives the world.

I was amused to realize I had just drawn a baseball diamond (in reverse.) I've often felt that the layout of game-playing fields produces patterns that overlap with the design of the Hero's Journey. Baseball can be read as another metaphor of life, with the base runner as the hero making his way around the stages of the journey.

Perhaps the best way to explore the endless possibilities of the Hero's Journey is to apply it to a number of films or stories. To that end Michael Wiese Productions has prepared a book and CD-ROM entitled *Myth in the Movies.* These examine a large number of popular movies through the lens of the Hero's Journey. It's a way to test the idea and see for yourself if it's valid and useful. One can see how it operates in a general way and how it transforms in specific cases. And from the comparison of many examples and from the interesting exceptions, one can find more of the principles, values, and relationships that give the craftsperson command of the form.

At the end of this second edition I have added a few new elements in a section called "Looking Back at the Journey." Here I have used the tools of mythology and the Hero's Journey to analyze some key films, including *Titanic, The Lion King, Pulp Fiction, The Full Monty,* and the *Star Wars* saga. I hope these will demonstrate some of the ways that the mythic principles continue to be explored in popular entertainment.

Unlike the stories of heroes, which eventually come to an end, the journey to understand and articulate these ideas is truly endless. Although certain human conditions will never change, new situations are always arising, and the Hero's Journey will adapt to reflect them. New waves will roll out, and so it will go, on and on forever.

INTRODUCTION

Second Edition

PREPARING FOR THE JOURNEY

"This is the tale I pray the divine Muse to unfold to us. Begin it, goddess, at whatever point you will."
—*The Odyssey* of Homer

I invite you to join me on a Writer's Journey, a mission of discovery to explore and map the elusive borderlands between myth and modern storytelling. We will be guided by a simple idea: **All stories consist of a few common structural elements found universally in myths, fairy tales, dreams, and movies.** They are known collectively as **The Hero's Journey.** Understanding these elements and their use in modern writing is the object of our quest. Used wisely, these ancient tools of the storyteller's craft still have tremendous power to heal our people and make the world a better place.

My own Writer's Journey begins with the peculiar power storytelling has always had over me. I got hooked on the fairy tales and Little Golden Books read out loud by my mother and grandmother. I devoured the cartoons and movies pouring out of TV in the 1950s, the thrilling adventures on the drive-in screens, the lurid comic books and mind-stretching science fiction of the day. When I was laid up with a sprained ankle, my father went to the local library and brought back wonder stories of Norse and Celtic mythology that made me forget the pain.

A trail of stories eventually led me to reading for a living as a story analyst for Hollywood studios. Though I evaluated thousands of novels and screenplays, I never got tired of exploring the labyrinth of story with its stunningly repeated patterns, bewildering variants, and puzzling questions.

Where do stories come from? How do they work? What do they tell us about ourselves? What do they mean? Why do we need them? How can we use them to improve the world?

Above all, how do storytellers manage to make the story mean something? Good stories make you feel you've been through a satisfying, complete experience. You've cried or laughed or both. You finish the story feeling you've learned something about life or about yourself. Perhaps you've picked up a new awareness, a new character or attitude to model your life on. How do storytellers manage to pull that off? What are the secrets of this ancient trade? What are its rules and design principles?

Over the years I began to notice some common elements in adventure stories and myths, certain intriguingly familiar characters, props, locations, and situations. I became vaguely aware there was a pattern or a template of some sort guiding the design of stories. I had some pieces of the puzzle but the overall plan eluded me.

Then at the USC film school I was fortunate enough to cross paths with the work of the mythologist Joseph Campbell. The encounter with Campbell was, for me and many other people, a life-changing experience. A few days of exploring the labyrinth of his book *The Hero with a Thousand Faces* produced an electrifying reorganization of my life and thinking. Here, fully explored, was the pattern I had been sensing. Campbell had broken the secret code of story. His work was like a flare suddenly illuminating a deeply shadowed landscape.

I worked with Campbell's idea of the Hero's Journey to understand the phenomenal repeat business of movies such as *Star Wars* and *Close Encounters*. People were going back to see these films as if seeking some kind of religious experience. It seemed to me these films drew people in this special way because they reflected the universally satisfying patterns Campbell found in myths. They had something people needed.

The Hero with a Thousand Faces was a lifesaver when I began to work as a story analyst for major movie studios. In my first jobs I was deeply grateful for Campbell's work, which became a reliable set of tools for diagnosing story problems and prescribing solutions. Without the guidance of Campbell and mythology, I would have been lost.

It seemed to me the Hero's Journey was exciting, useful story technology which could help filmmakers and executives eliminate some of the guesswork and expense of developing stories for film. Over the years, I ran into quite a few people who had been affected by encounters with Joe Campbell. We were like a secret society of true believers, commonly putting our faith in "the power of myth."

Shortly after going to work as a story analyst for the Walt Disney Company, I wrote a seven-page memo called "A Practical Guide to *The Hero with a Thousand Faces*" in which I described the idea of the Hero's Journey, with examples from classic and current movies. I gave the memo to friends, colleagues, and several Disney executives to test and refine the ideas through their feedback. Gradually I expanded the "Practical Guide" into a longer essay and began teaching the material through a story analysis class at the UCLA Extension Writers' Program.

At writers' conferences around the country I tested the ideas in seminars with screenwriters, romance novelists, children's writers, and all kinds of storytellers. I found many others were exploring the intertwined pathways of myth, story, and psychology.

The Hero's Journey, I discovered, is more than just a description of the hidden patterns of mythology. It is a useful guide to life, especially the writer's life. In the perilous adventure of my own writing, I found the stages of the Hero's Journey showing up just as reliably and usefully as they did in books, myths, and movies. In my personal life, I was thankful to have this map to guide my quest and help me anticipate what was around the next bend.

The usefulness of the Hero's Journey as a guide to life was brought home forcefully when I first prepared to speak publicly about it in a large seminar at UCLA. A couple of weeks before the seminar two articles appeared in the Los Angeles *Herald-Examiner,* in which a film critic attacked filmmaker George Lucas and his movie *Willow.* Somehow the critic had got hold of the "Practical Guide" and claimed it had deeply influenced and corrupted Hollywood storytellers. The critic blamed the "Practical Guide" for every flop from *Ishtar* to *Howard the Duck,* as well as for the hit *Back to the Future.* According to him, lazy, illiterate studio executives, eager to find a quick-bucks formula, had seized upon the "Practical Guide" as a cure-all and were busily stuffing it down the throats of writers, stifling their creativity with a technology the executives hadn't bothered to understand.

While flattered that someone thought I had such a sweeping influence on the collective mind of Hollywood, I was also devastated. Here, on the threshold of a new phase of working with these ideas, I was shot down before I even started. Or so it seemed.

Friends who were more seasoned veterans in this war of ideas pointed out that in being challenged I was merely encountering an **archetype**, one of the familiar characters who people the landscape of the Hero's Journey, namely a **Threshold Guardian**.

That information instantly gave me my bearings and showed me how to handle the situation. Campbell had described how heroes often encounter these "unfamiliar yet strangely intimate forces, some of which severely threaten" them. The Guardians seem to pop up at the various **thresholds** of the journey, the narrow and dangerous passages from one stage of life to the next. Campbell showed the many ways in which heroes can deal with Threshold Guardians. Instead of attacking these seemingly hostile powers head-on, journeyers learn to outwit them or join forces with them, absorbing their energy rather than being destroyed by it.

I realized that this Threshold Guardian's apparent attack was potentially a blessing, not a curse. I had thought of challenging the critic to a duel (laptops at twenty paces) but now reconsidered. With a slight change in attitude I could turn his hostility to my benefit. I contacted the critic and invited him to talk over our differences of opinion at the seminar. He accepted and joined a panel discussion which turned into a lively and entertaining debate, illuminating corners of the story world that I had never glimpsed before. The seminar was better and my ideas were stronger for being challenged. Instead of fighting my Threshold Guardian, I had absorbed him into my adventure. What had seemed like a lethal blow had turned into something useful and healthy. The mythological approach had proven its worth in life as well as story.

Around this time I realized the "Practical Guide" and Campbell's ideas *did* have an influence on Hollywood. I began to get requests from studio story departments for copies of the "Practical Guide". I heard that executives at other studios were giving the pamphlet to writers, directors, and producers as guides to universal, commercial story patterns. Apparently Hollywood was finding the Hero's Journey useful.

Meanwhile Joseph Campbell's ideas exploded into a wider sphere of awareness with the Bill Moyers interview show on PBS, *The Power of Myth*. The show was a hit, cutting across lines of age, politics, and religion to speak directly to people's spirits. The book version, a transcript of the interviews, was on the *New York Times* bestseller list for over a year. *The Hero with a Thousand Faces,* Campbell's venerable warhorse of a textbook, suddenly became a hot bestseller after forty years of slow but steady backlist sales.

The PBS show brought Campbell's ideas to millions and illuminated the impact of his work on filmmakers such as George Lucas, John Boorman, Steven Spielberg, and George Miller. Suddenly I found a sharp increase in awareness and acceptance of Campbell's ideas in Hollywood. More executives and writers were versed in these concepts and interested in learning how to apply them to moviemaking and screenwriting.

The Hero's Journey model continued to serve me well. It got me through reading and evaluating over ten thousand screenplays for half a dozen studios. It was my atlas, a book of maps for my own writing journeys. It guided me to a new role in the Disney company, as a story consultant for the Feature Animation division at the time *The Little Mermaid* and *Beauty and the Beast* were being conceived. Campbell's ideas were of tremendous value as I researched and developed stories based on fairy tales, mythology, science fiction, comic books, and historical adventure.

Joseph Campbell died in 1987. I met him briefly a couple of times at seminars. He was still a striking man in his eighties, tall, vigorous, eloquent, funny, full of energy and enthusiasm, and utterly charming. Just before his passing, he told me, "Stick with this stuff. It'll take you a long way."

I recently discovered that for some time the "Practical Guide" has been required reading for Disney development executives. Daily requests for it, as well as countless letters and calls from novelists, screenwriters, producers, writers, and actors, indicate that the Hero's Journey ideas are being used and developed more than ever.

And so I come to the writing of this book, the descendant of the "Practical Guide." The book is designed somewhat on the model of the *I Ching,* with an introductory overview followed by commentaries that expand on the typical stages of the Hero's Journey. Book One, **Mapping the Journey**, is a quick survey of the territory. Chapter 1 is a revision of the "Practical Guide" and a concentrated presentation of the twelve-stage Hero's Journey. You might think of this as the map of a journey we are about to take together through the special world of story. Chapter 2 is an introduction to the archetypes, the *dramatis personae* of myth and story. It describes eight common character types or psychological functions found in all stories.

Book Two, **Stages of the Journey**, is a more detailed examination of the twelve elements of the Hero's Journey. Each chapter is followed by suggestions for your further exploration, **Questioning the Journey**. An Epilogue, **Looking Back on the Journey**, deals with the special adventure of the Writer's Journey and some pitfalls to avoid on the road. It includes Hero's Journey analyses of some influential films including *Titanic, Pulp Fiction, The Lion King, The Full Monty,* and *Star Wars.* In one case, *The Lion King,* I had the opportunity to apply the Hero's Journey ideas as a story consultant during the development process, and saw firsthand how useful these principles can be.

Throughout the book I make reference to movies, both classic and current. You might want to view some of these films to see how the Hero's Journey works in practice. A representative list of films appears in Appendix I.

You might also select a single movie or story of your choice and keep it in mind as you take the Writer's Journey. Get to know the story of your choice by reading or viewing it several times, taking brief notes on what happens in each scene and how it functions in the drama. Running a movie on a VCR is ideal, because you can stop to write down the content of each scene while you grasp its meaning and relation to the rest of the story.

I suggest you go through this process with a story or movie and use it to test out the ideas in this book. See if your story reflects the stages and archetypes of the Hero's Journey. (A sample worksheet for the Hero's Journey can be found in Appendix 3.) Observe how the stages are adapted to meet the needs of the story or the particular culture for which the story was written. Challenge these ideas, test them in practice, adapt them to your needs, and make them yours. Use these concepts to challenge and inspire your own stories.

The Hero's Journey has served storytellers and their listeners since the very first stories were told, and it shows no signs of wearing out. Let's begin the Writer's Journey together to explore these ideas. I hope you find them useful as magic keys to the world of story and the labyrinth of life.

BOOK ONE:

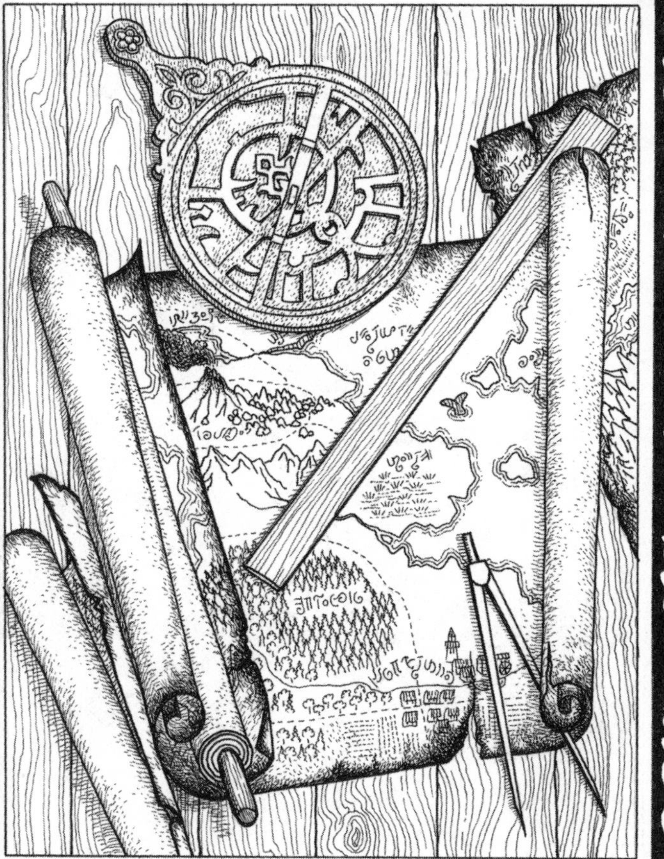

MAPPING THE JOURNEY

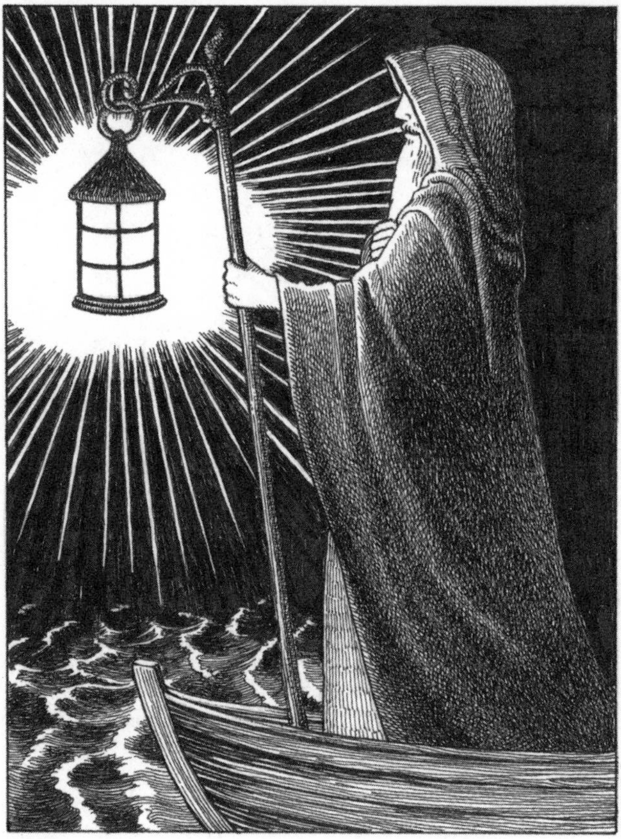

A PRACTICAL GUIDE

A PRACTICAL GUIDE

"There are only two or three human stories, and they go on repeating themselves as fiercely as if they had never happened before."
—Willa Cather, in *O Pioneers!*

In the long run, one of the most influential books of the 20th century may turn out to be Joseph Campbell's *The Hero with a Thousand Faces.*

The ideas expressed in Campbell's book are having a major impact on storytelling. Writers are becoming more aware of the ageless patterns which Campbell identifies, and are enriching their work with them.

Inevitably Hollywood has caught on to the usefulness of Campbell's work. Filmmakers like George Lucas and George Miller acknowledge their debt to Campbell and his influence can be seen in the films of Steven Spielberg, John Boorman, Francis Coppola, and others.

It's little wonder that Hollywood is beginning to embrace the ideas Campbell presents in his books. For the writer, producer, director, or designer his concepts are a welcome tool kit, stocked with sturdy instruments ideal for the craft of storytelling. With these tools you can construct a story to meet almost any situation, a story that will be dramatic, entertaining, and psychologically true. With this equipment you can diagnose the problems of almost any ailing plot line, and make the corrections to bring it to its peak of performance.

These tools have stood the test of time. They are older than the Pyramids, older than Stonehenge, older than the earliest cave paintings.

Joseph Campbell's contribution to the tool kit was to gather the ideas together, recognize them, articulate them, name them, organize them. He exposed for the first time the pattern that lies behind every story ever told.

The Hero with a Thousand Faces is his statement of the most persistent theme in oral tradition and recorded literature: the myth of the hero. In his study of world hero myths Campbell discovered that they are all basically the same story, retold endlessly in infinite variation.

He found that all storytelling, consciously or not, follows the ancient patterns of myth and that all stories, from the crudest jokes to the highest flights of literature, can be understood in terms of the Hero's Journey: the "monomyth" whose principles he lays out in the book.

The pattern of the Hero's Journey is universal, occurring in every culture, in every time. It is as infinitely varied as the human race itself and yet its basic form remains constant. The Hero's Journey is an incredibly tenacious set of elements that springs endlessly from the deepest reaches of the human mind; different in its details for every culture, but fundamentally the same.

Campbell's thinking runs parallel to that of the Swiss psychologist Carl G. Jung, who wrote about the **archetypes**: constantly repeating characters or energies which occur in the dreams of all people and the myths of all cultures. Jung suggested that these archetypes reflect different aspects of the human mind — that our personalities divide themselves into these characters to play out the drama of our lives. He noticed a strong correspondence between his patients' dream figures and the common archetypes of mythology. He suggested that both were coming from a deeper source, in the **collective unconscious** of the human race.

The repeating characters of world myth such as the young hero, the wise old man or woman, the shapeshifter, and the shadowy antagonist are the same as the figures who appear repeatedly in our dreams and fantasies. That's why myths and most stories constructed on the mythological model have the ring of psychological truth.

Such stories are accurate models of the workings of the human mind, true maps of the psyche. They are psychologically valid and emotionally realistic even when they portray fantastic, impossible, or unreal events.

This accounts for the universal power of such stories. Stories built on the model of the Hero's Journey have an appeal that can be felt by everyone, because they well up from a universal source in the shared unconscious and reflect universal concerns.

They deal with the childlike universal questions: Who am I? Where did I come from? Where will I go when I die? What is good and what is evil? What must I do about it? What will tomorrow be like? Where did yesterday go? Is there anybody else out there?

The ideas embedded in mythology and identified by Campbell in *The Hero with a Thousand Faces* can be applied to understanding almost any human problem. They are a great key to life as well as a major instrument for dealing more effectively with a mass audience.

If you want to understand the ideas behind the Hero's Journey, there's no substitute for actually reading Campbell's work. It's an experience that has a way of changing people.

It's also a good idea to read a lot of myths, but reading Campbell's work amounts to the same thing since Campbell is a master storyteller who delights in illustrating his points with examples from the rich storehouse of mythology.

Campbell gives an outline of the Hero's Journey in Chapter IV, "The Keys," of *The Hero with a Thousand Faces*. I've taken the liberty of amending the outline slightly, trying to reflect some of the common themes in movies with illustrations drawn from contemporary films and a few classics. You can compare the two outlines and terminology by examining Table One.

TABLE ONE
COMPARISON OF OUTLINES AND TERMINOLOGY

The Writer's Journey	*The Hero with a Thousand Faces*
ACT ONE	DEPARTURE, SEPARATION
Ordinary World	World of Common Day
Call to Adventure	Call to Adventure
Refusal of the Call	Refusal of the Call
Meeting with the Mentor	Supernatural Aid
Crossing the First Threshold	Crossing the First Threshold
	Belly of the Whale
ACT TWO	DESCENT, INITIATION, PENETRATION
Tests, Allies, Enemies	Road of Trials
Approach to the Inmost Cave	
Ordeal	Meeting with the Goddess
	Woman as Temptress
	Atonement with the Father
	Apotheosis
Reward	The Ultimate Boon
ACT THREE	RETURN
The Road Back	Refusal of the Return
	The Magic Flight
	Rescue from Within
	Crossing the Threshold
	Return
Resurrection	Master of the Two Worlds
Return with the Elixir	Freedom to Live

I'm retelling the hero myth in my own way, and you should feel free to do the same. Every storyteller bends the mythic pattern to his or her own purpose or the needs of a particular culture.

That's why the hero has a thousand faces.

A note about the term "hero": As used here, the word, like "doctor" or "poet," may refer to a woman or a man.

THE HERO'S JOURNEY

At heart, despite its infinite variety, the hero's story is always a journey. A hero leaves her comfortable, ordinary surroundings to venture into a challenging, unfamiliar world. It may be an outward journey to an actual place: a labyrinth, forest or cave, a strange city or country, a new locale that becomes the arena for her conflict with antagonistic, challenging forces.

But there are as many stories that take the hero on an inward journey, one of the mind, the heart, the spirit. In any good story the hero grows and changes, making a journey from one way of being to the next: from despair to hope, weakness to strength, folly to wisdom, love to hate, and back again. It's these emotional journeys that hook an audience and make a story worth watching.

The stages of the Hero's Journey can be traced in all kinds of stories, not just those that feature "heroic" physical action and adventure. The protagonist of every story is the hero of a journey, even if the path leads only into his own mind or into the realm of relationships.

The way stations of the Hero's Journey emerge naturally even when the writer is unaware of them, but some knowledge of this most ancient guide to storytelling is useful in identifying problems and telling better stories. Consider these twelve stages as a map of the Hero's Journey, one of many ways to get from here to there, but one of the most flexible, durable and dependable.

THE STAGES OF THE HERO'S JOURNEY

1. Ordinary World
2. Call to Adventure
3. Refusal of the Call
4. Meeting with the Mentor
5. Crossing the First Threshold
6. Tests, Allies, Enemies
7. Approach to the Inmost Cave
8. Ordeal
9. Reward (Seizing the Sword)
10. The Road Back
11. Resurrection
12. Return with the Elixir

THE HERO'S JOURNEY MODEL

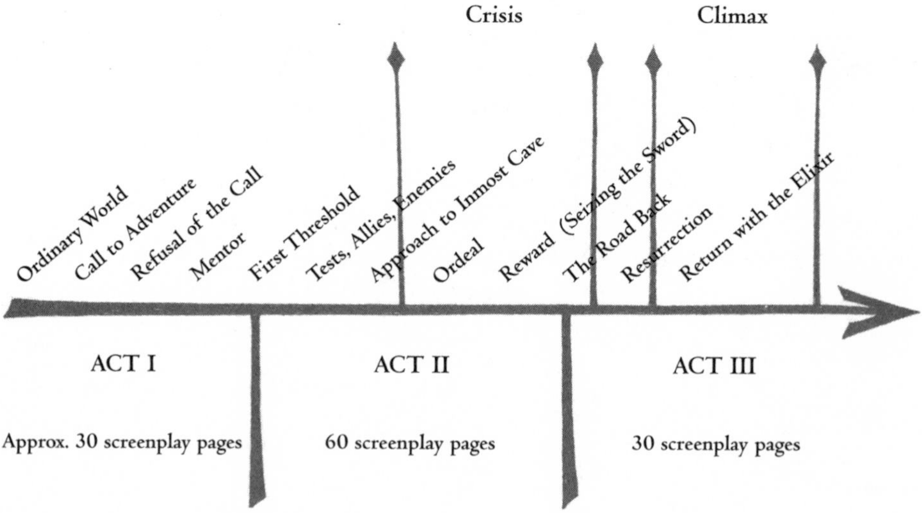

THE HERO'S JOURNEY

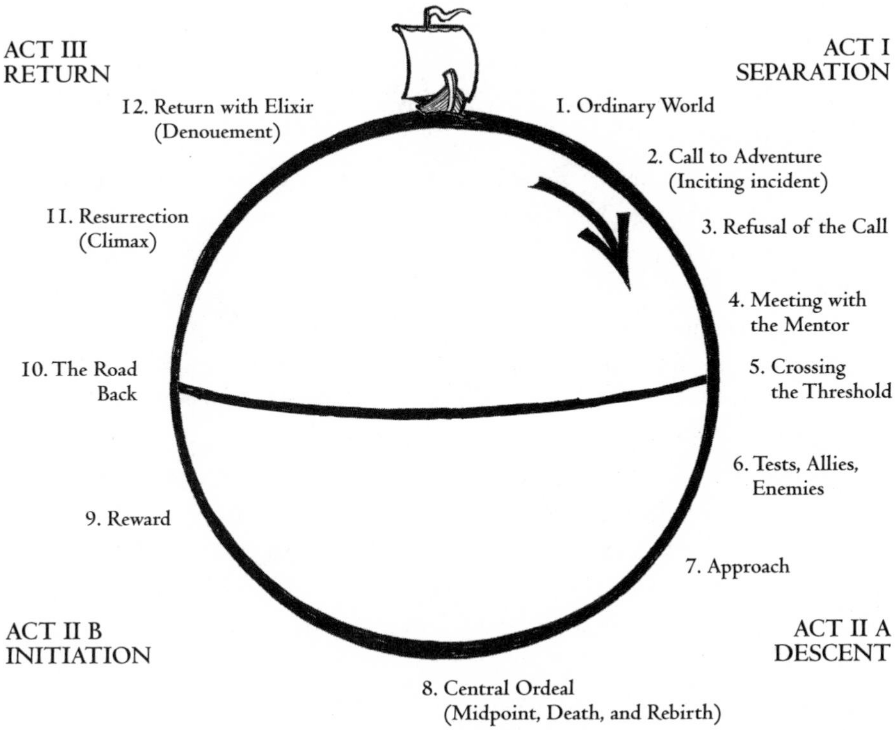

1. THE ORDINARY WORLD

Most stories take the hero out of the ordinary, mundane world and into a Special World, new and alien. This is the familiar "fish out of water" idea which has spawned countless films and TV shows ("The Fugitive," "The Beverly Hillbillies," *Mr. Smith Goes to Washington, A Connecticut Yankee in King Arthur's Court, The Wizard of Oz, Witness, 48 Hours, Trading Places, Beverly Hills Cop,* etc.).

If you're going to show a fish out of his customary element, you first have to show him in that **Ordinary World** to create a vivid contrast with the strange new world he is about to enter.

In *Witness* you see both the city policeman and the Amish mother and son in their normal worlds before they are thrust into totally alien environments: the Amish being overwhelmed by the city, and the city cop encountering the 19th-century world of the Amish. You first see Luke Skywalker, hero of *Star Wars,* being bored to death as a farmboy before he sets out to tackle the universe.

Likewise in *The Wizard of Oz,* considerable time is spent to establish Dorothy's drab normal life in Kansas before she is blown to the wonderworld of Oz. Here the contrast is heightened by shooting the Kansas scenes in stern black and white while the Oz scenes are shot in vibrant Technicolor.

An Officer and a Gentleman sketches a vivid contrast between the Ordinary World of the hero — that of a tough Navy brat with a drunken, whore-chasing father — and the Special World of the spit-and-polish Navy flight school which the hero enters.

2. THE CALL TO ADVENTURE

The hero is presented with a problem, challenge, or adventure to undertake. Once presented with a **Call to Adventure**, she can no longer remain indefinitely in the comfort of the Ordinary World.

Perhaps the land is dying, as in the King Arthur stories of the search for the Grail, the only treasure that can heal the wounded land. In *Star Wars,* the Call to Adventure is Princess Leia's desperate holographic message to wise old Obi Wan Kenobi, who asks Luke to join in the quest. Leia has been snatched by evil Darth Vader, like the Greek springtime goddess Persephone, who was kidnapped to the underworld by Pluto, lord of the dead. Her rescue is vital to restoring the normal balance of the universe.

In many detective stories, the Call to Adventure is the private eye being asked to take on a new case and solve a crime which has upset the order of things. A good detective should right wrongs as well as solve crimes.

In revenge plots, the Call to Adventure is often a wrong which must be set right, an offense against the natural order of things. In *The Count of Monte Cristo,* Edmond Dantes is unjustly imprisoned and is driven to escape by his desire for revenge. The plot of *Beverly Hills Cop* is set in motion by the murder of the hero's best friend. *In First Blood* Rambo is motivated by his unfair treatment at the hands of an intolerant sheriff.

In romantic comedies, the Call to Adventure might be the first encounter with the special but annoying someone the hero or heroine will be pursuing and sparring with.

The Call to Adventure establishes the stakes of the game, and makes clear the hero's goal: to win the treasure or the lover, to get revenge or right a wrong, to achieve a dream, confront a challenge, or change a life.

What's at stake can often be expressed as a question posed by the call. Will E.T. or Dorothy in *The Wizard of Oz* get home again? Will Luke rescue Princess Leia and defeat Darth Vader? In *An Officer and a Gentleman,* will the hero be driven out of Navy flight school by his own selfishness and the needling of a fierce Marine drill instructor, or will he earn the right to be called an officer and a gentleman? Boy meets girl, but does boy get girl?

3. REFUSAL OF THE CALL (THE RELUCTANT HERO)

This one is about fear. Often at this point the hero balks at the threshold of adventure, **Refusing the Call** or expressing reluctance. After all, she is facing the greatest of all fears, terror of the unknown. The hero has not yet fully committed to the journey and may still be thinking of turning back. Some other influence — a change in circumstances, a further offense against the natural order of things, or the encouragement of a Mentor — is required to get her past this turning point of fear.

In romantic comedies, the hero may express reluctance to get involved (maybe because of the pain of a previous relationship). In a detective story, the private eye may at first turn down the case, only to take it on later against his better judgment.

At this point in *Star Wars,* Luke refuses Obi Wan's Call to Adventure and returns to his aunt and uncle's farmhouse, only to find they have been barbecued by the Emperor's stormtroopers. Suddenly Luke is no longer reluctant and is eager to undertake the quest. The evil of the Empire has become personal to him. He is motivated.

4. Mentor (The Wise Old Man or Woman)

By this time many stories will have introduced a Merlin-like character who is the hero's **Mentor**. The relationship between hero and Mentor is one of the most common themes in mythology, and one of the richest in its symbolic value. It stands for the bond between parent and child, teacher and student, doctor and patient, god and man.

The Mentor may appear as a wise old wizard (*Star Wars*), a tough drill sergeant (*An Officer and a Gentleman*), or a grizzled old boxing coach (*Rocky*). In the mythology of "The Mary Tyler Moore Show", it was Lou Grant. In *Jaws* it's the crusty Robert Shaw character who knows all about sharks.

The function of Mentors is to prepare the hero to face the unknown. They may give advice, guidance or magical equipment. Obi Wan in *Star Wars* gives Luke his father's light-saber, which he will need in his battles with the dark side of the Force. In *The Wizard of Oz,* Glinda the Good Witch gives Dorothy guidance and the ruby slippers that will eventually get her home again.

However, the Mentor can only go so far with the hero. Eventually the hero must face the unknown alone. Sometimes the Mentor is required to give the hero a swift kick in the pants to get the adventure going.

5. Crossing the First Threshold

Now the hero finally commits to the adventure and fully enters the Special World of the story for the first time by **Crossing the First Threshold**. He agrees to face the consequences of dealing with the problem or challenge posed in the Call to Adventure. This is the moment when the story takes off and the adventure really gets going. The balloon goes up, the ship sails, the romance begins, the plane or the spaceship soars off, the wagon train gets rolling.

Movies are often built in three acts, which can be regarded as representing 1) the hero's decision to act, 2) the action itself, and 3) the consequences of the action. The First Threshold marks the turning point between Acts One and Two. The hero, having overcome fear, has decided to confront the problem and take action. She is now committed to the journey and there's no turning back.

This is the moment when Dorothy sets out on the Yellow Brick Road. The hero of *Beverly Hills Cop,* Axel Foley, decides to defy his boss's order, leaving his Ordinary World of the Detroit streets to investigate his friend's murder in the Special World of Beverly Hills.

6. TESTS, ALLIES, AND ENEMIES

Once across the First Threshold, the hero naturally encounters new challenges and **Tests**, makes **Allies and Enemies**, and begins to learn the rules of the Special World.

Saloons and seedy bars seem to be good places for these transactions. Countless Westerns take the hero to a saloon where his manhood and determination are tested, and where friends and villains are introduced. Bars are also useful to the hero for obtaining information, for learning the new rules that apply to the Special World.

In *Casablanca,* Rick's Cafe is the den of intrigue in which alliances and enmities are forged, and in which the hero's moral character is constantly tested. In *Star Wars,* the cantina is the setting for the creation of a major alliance with Han Solo and the making of an important enmity with Jabba the Hutt, which pays off two movies later in *Return of the Jedi.* Here in the giddy, surreal, violent atmosphere of the cantina swarming with bizarre aliens, Luke also gets a taste of the exciting and dangerous Special World he has just entered.

Scenes like these allow for character development as we watch the hero and his companions react under stress. In the *Star Wars* cantina, Luke gets to see Han Solo's way of handling a tight situation, and learns that Obi Wan is a warrior wizard of great power.

There are similar sequences in *An Officer and a Gentleman* at about this point, in which the hero makes allies and enemies and meets his "love interest." Several aspects of the hero's character — aggressiveness and hostility, knowledge of street fighting, attitudes about women — are revealed under pressure in these scenes, and sure enough, one of them takes place in a bar.

Of course not all Tests, Alliances, and Enmities are confronted in bars. In many stories, such as *The Wizard of Oz,* these are simply encounters on the road. At this stage on the Yellow Brick Road, Dorothy acquires her companions the Scarecrow, Tin Woodsman and Cowardly Lion, and makes enemies such as an orchard full of grumpy talking trees. She passes a number of Tests such as getting Scarecrow off the nail, oiling the Tin Woodsman, and helping the Cowardly Lion deal with his fear.

In *Star Wars* the Tests continue after the cantina scene. Obi Wan teaches Luke about the Force by making him fight blindfolded. The early laser battles with the Imperial fighters are another Test which Luke successfully passes.

7. APPROACH TO THE INMOST CAVE

The hero comes at last to the edge of a dangerous place, sometimes deep underground, where the object of the quest is hidden. Often it's the headquarters of the hero's greatest enemy, the most dangerous spot in the Special World, the **Inmost Cave.** When the hero enters that fearful place he will cross the second major threshold. Heroes often pause at the gate to prepare, plan, and outwit the villain's guards. This is the phase of **Approach.**

In mythology the Inmost Cave may represent the land of the dead. The hero may have to descend into hell to rescue a loved one (Orpheus), into a cave to fight a dragon and win a treasure (Sigurd in Norse myth), or into a labyrinth to confront a monster (Theseus and the Minotaur).

In the Arthurian stories the Inmost Cave is the Chapel Perilous, the dangerous chamber where the seeker may find the Grail.

In the modern mythology of *Star Wars* the Approach to the Inmost Cave is Luke Skywalker and company being sucked into the Death Star where they will face Darth Vader and rescue Princess Leia. In *The Wizard of Oz* it's Dorothy being kidnapped to the Wicked Witch's baleful castle, and her companions slipping in to save her. The title of *Indiana Jones and the Temple of Doom* reveals the Inmost Cave of that film.

Approach covers all the preparations for entering the Inmost Cave and confronting death or supreme danger.

8. The Ordeal

Here the fortunes of the hero hit bottom in a direct confrontation with his greatest fear. He faces the possibility of death and is brought to the brink in a battle with a hostile force. **The Ordeal** is a "black moment" for the audience, as we are held in suspense and tension, not knowing if he will live or die. The hero, like Jonah, is "in the belly of the beast."

In *Star Wars* it's the harrowing moment in the bowels of the Death Star when Luke, Leia, and company are trapped in the giant trashmasher. Luke is pulled under by the tentacled monster that lives in the sewage and is held down so long that the audience begins to wonder if he's dead. In *E.T.*, the lovable alien momentarily appears to die on the operating table. In *The Wizard of Oz* Dorothy and her friends are trapped by the Wicked Witch, and it looks like there's no way out. At this point in *Beverly Hills Cop* Axel Foley is in the clutches of the villain's men with a gun to his head.

In *An Officer and a Gentleman*, Zack Mayo endures an Ordeal when his Marine drill instructor launches an all-out drive to torment and humiliate him into quitting the program. It's a psychological life-or-death moment, for if he gives in, his chances of becoming an officer and a gentleman will be dead. He survives the Ordeal by refusing to quit, and the Ordeal changes him. The drill sergeant, a foxy Wise Old Man, has forced him to admit his dependency on others, and from this moment on he is more cooperative and less selfish.

In romantic comedies the death faced by the hero may simply be the temporary death of the relationship, as in the second movement of the old standard plot, "Boy meets girl, boy loses girl, boy gets girl." The hero's chances of connecting with the object of affection look their bleakest.

This is a critical moment in any story, an Ordeal in which the hero must die or appear to die so that she can be born again. It's a major source of the magic of the heroic myth. The experiences of the preceding stages have led us, the audience, to identify with the hero and her fate. What happens to the hero happens to us. We are encouraged to experience the brink-of-death moment with her. Our emotions are temporarily depressed so that they can be revived by the hero's return from death. The result of this revival is a feeling of elation and exhilaration.

The designers of amusement park thrill rides know how to use this principle. Roller coasters make their passengers feel as if they're going to die, and there's a great thrill that comes from brushing up against death and surviving it. You're never more alive than when you're looking death in the face.

This is also the key element in rites of passage or rituals of initiation into fraternities and secret societies. The initiate is forced to taste death in some terrible experience, and then is allowed to experience resurrection as he is reborn as a new member of the group. The hero of every story is an initiate being introduced to the mysteries of life and death.

Every story needs such a life-or-death moment in which the hero or his goals are in mortal jeopardy.

9. REWARD (SEIZING THE SWORD)

Having survived death, beaten the dragon, or slain the Minotaur, hero and audience have cause to celebrate. The hero now takes possession of the treasure she has come seeking, her **Reward**. It might be a special weapon like a magic sword, or a token like the Grail or some elixir which can heal the wounded land.

Sometimes the "sword" is knowledge and experience that leads to greater understanding and a reconciliation with hostile forces.

In *Star Wars,* Luke rescues Princess Leia and captures the plans of the Death Star, keys to defeating Darth Vader.

Dorothy escapes from the Wicked Witch's castle with the Witch's broomstick and the ruby slippers, keys to getting back home.

At this point the hero may also settle a conflict with a parent. *In Return of the Jedi,* Luke is reconciled with Darth Vader, who turns out to be his father and not such a bad guy after all.

The hero may also be reconciled with the opposite sex, as in romantic comedies. In many stories the loved one is the treasure the hero has come to win or rescue, and there is often a love scene at this point to celebrate the victory.

From the hero's point of view, members of the opposite sex may appear to be **Shapeshifters**, an archetype of change. They seem to shift constantly in form or age, reflecting the confusing and constantly changing aspects of the opposite sex. Tales of vampires, werewolves and other shapechangers are symbolic echoes of this shifting quality which men and women see in each other.

The hero's Ordeal may grant a better understanding of the opposite sex, an ability to see beyond the shifting outer appearance, leading to a reconciliation.

The hero may also become more attractive as a result of having survived the Ordeal. He has earned the title of "hero" by having taken the supreme risk on behalf of the community.

10. The Road Back

The hero's not out of the woods yet. We're crossing into Act Three now as the hero begins to deal with the consequences of confronting the dark forces of the Ordeal. If she has not yet managed to reconcile with the parent, the gods, or the hostile forces, they may come raging after her. Some of the best chase scenes spring up at this point, as the hero is pursued on **The Road Back** by the vengeful forces she has disturbed by Seizing the sword, the elixir, or the treasure.

Thus Luke and Leia are furiously pursued by Darth Vader as they escape the Death Star. The Road Back in *E.T.* is the moonlight bicycle flight of Elliott and E.T. as they escape from "Keys" (Peter Coyote), who represents repressive governmental authority.

This stage marks the decision to return to the Ordinary World. The hero realizes that the Special World must eventually be left behind, and there are still dangers, temptations, and tests ahead.

11. Resurrection

In ancient times, hunters and warriors had to be purified before they returned to their communities, because they had blood on their hands. The hero who has been to the realm of the dead must be reborn and cleansed in one last Ordeal of death and **Resurrection** before returning to the Ordinary World of the living.

This is often a second life-and-death moment, almost a replay of the death and rebirth of the Ordeal. Death and darkness get in one last, desperate shot before being finally defeated. It's a kind of final exam for the hero, who must be tested once more to see if he has really learned the lessons of the Ordeal.

The hero is transformed by these moments of death-and-rebirth, and is able to return to ordinary life reborn as a new being with new insights.

The Star Wars films play with this element constantly. The films of the "original trilogy" feature a final battle scene in which Luke is almost killed, appears to be dead for a moment, and then miraculously survives. Each Ordeal wins him new knowledge and command over the Force. He is transformed into a new being by his experience.

Axel Foley in the climactic sequence of *Beverly Hills Cop* once again faces death at the hands of the villain, but is rescued by the intervention of the Beverly Hills police force. He emerges from the experience with a greater respect for cooperation, and is a more complete human being.

An Officer and a Gentleman offers a more complex series of final ordeals, as the hero faces death in a number of ways. Zack's selfishness dies as he gives up the chance for a personal athletic trophy in favor of helping another cadet over an obstacle. His relationship with his girlfriend seems to be dead, and he must survive the crushing blow of his best friend's suicide. As if that weren't enough, he also endures a final hand-to-hand, life-or-death battle with his drill instructor, but survives it all and is transformed into the gallant "officer and gentleman" of the title.

12. Return with the Elixir

The hero Returns to the Ordinary World, but the journey is meaningless unless she brings back some **Elixir**, treasure, or lesson from the Special World. The Elixir is a magic potion with the power to heal. It may be a great treasure like the Grail that magically heals the wounded land, or it simply might be knowledge or experience that could be useful to the community someday.

Dorothy returns to Kansas with the knowledge that she is loved, and that "There's no place like home." E.T. returns home with the experience of friendship with humans. Luke Skywalker defeats Darth Vader (for the time being) and restores peace and order to the galaxy.

Zack Mayo wins his commission and leaves the Special World of the training base with a new perspective. In the sparkling new uniform of an officer (with a new attitude to match) he literally sweeps his girlfriend off her feet and carries her away.

Sometimes the Elixir is treasure won on the quest, but it may be love, freedom, wisdom, or the knowledge that the Special World exists and can be survived. Sometimes it's just coming home with a good story to tell.

Unless something is brought back from the Ordeal in the Inmost Cave, the hero is doomed to repeat the adventure. Many comedies use this ending, as a foolish character refuses to learn his lesson and embarks on the same folly that got him in trouble in the first place.

To recap the Hero's Journey:

1. Heroes are introduced in the ORDINARY WORLD, where
2. they receive the CALL TO ADVENTURE.
3. They are RELUCTANT at first or REFUSE THE CALL, but
4. are encouraged by a MENTOR to
5. CROSS THE FIRST THRESHOLD and enter the Special World, where
6. they encounter TESTS, ALLIES, AND ENEMIES.
7. They APPROACH THE INMOST CAVE, crossing a second threshold
8. where they endure the ORDEAL.
9. They take possession of their REWARD and
10. are pursued on THE ROAD BACK to the Ordinary World.
11. They cross the third threshold, experience a RESURRECTION, and are transformed by the experience.
12. They RETURN WITH THE ELIXIR, a boon or treasure to benefit the Ordinary World.

The Hero's Journey is a skeletal framework that should be fleshed out with the details and surprises of the individual story. The structure should not call attention to itself, nor should it be followed too precisely. The order of the stages given here is only one of many possible variations. The stages can be deleted, added to, and drastically shuffled without losing any of their power.

The values of the Hero's Journey are what's important. The images of the basic version — young heroes seeking magic swords from old wizards, maidens risking death to save loved ones, knights riding off to fight evil dragons in deep caves, and so on — are just symbols of universal life experiences. The symbols can be changed infinitely to suit the story at hand and the needs of the society.

The Hero's Journey is easily translated to contemporary dramas, comedies, romances, or action-adventures by substituting modern equivalents for the symbolic figures and props of the hero's story. The wise old man or woman may be a real shaman or wizard, but may also be any kind of Mentor or teacher, doctor or therapist, "crusty but benign" boss, tough but fair top sergeant, parent, grandparent, or guiding, helping figure.

Modern heroes may not be going into caves and labyrinths to fight mythical beasts, but they do enter a Special World and an Inmost Cave by venturing into space, to the bottom of the sea, into the depths of a modern city, or into their own hearts.

The patterns of myth can be used to tell the simplest comic book story or the most sophisticated drama. The Hero's Journey grows and matures as new experiments are tried within its framework. Changing the traditional sex and relative ages of the archetypes only makes it more interesting, and allows ever more complex webs of understanding to be spun among them. The basic figures can be combined, or each can be divided into several characters to show different aspects of the same idea.

The Hero's Journey is infinitely flexible, capable of endless variation without sacrificing any of its magic, and it will outlive us all.

Now that we've looked over the map, let's meet the characters who populate the landscape of storytelling: the **Archetypes**.

THE ARCHETYPES

THE ARCHETYPES

"Summoned or not, the god will come."
— Motto over the door of Carl Jung's house

As soon as you enter the world of fairy tales and myths, you become aware of recurring character types and relationships: questing heroes, heralds who call them to adventure, wise old men and women who give them magical gifts, threshold guardians who seem to block their way, shapeshifting fellow travelers who confuse and dazzle them, shadowy villains who try to destroy them, tricksters who upset the status quo and provide comic relief. In describing these common character types, symbols, and relationships the Swiss psychologist Carl G. Jung employed the term archetypes, meaning ancient patterns of personality that are the shared heritage of the human race.

Jung suggested there may be a collective unconscious, similar to the personal unconscious. Fairy tales and myths are like the dreams of an entire culture, springing from the collective unconscious. The same character types seem to occur on both the personal and the collective scale. The archetypes are amazingly constant throughout all times and cultures, in the dreams and personalities of individuals as well as in the mythic imagination of the entire world. An understanding of these forces is one of the most powerful elements in the modern storyteller's bag of tricks.

The concept of archetypes is an indispensable tool for understanding the purpose or function of characters in a story. If you grasp the function of the archetype which a particular character is expressing, it can help you determine if the character is pulling her full weight in the story. The archetypes are part of the universal language of storytelling, and a command of their energy is as essential to the writer as breathing.

Joseph Campbell spoke of the archetypes as biological: as expressions of the organs of the body, built into the wiring of every human being. The universality of these patterns makes possible the shared experience of storytelling. Storytellers instinctively choose characters and relationships that resonate to the energy of the archetypes, to create dramatic experiences that are recognizable to everyone. Becoming aware of the archetypes can only expand your command of your craft.

ARCHETYPES AS FUNCTIONS

When I first began working with these ideas I thought of an archetype as a fixed role which a character would play exclusively throughout a story. Once I identified a character as a mentor, I expected her to remain a mentor and only a mentor. However, as I worked with fairy tale motifs as a story consultant for Disney Animation, I encountered another way of looking at the archetypes — not as rigid character roles but as functions performed temporarily by characters to achieve certain effects in a story. This observation comes from the work of the Russian fairy tale expert Vladimir Propp, whose book, *Morphology of the Folktale*, analyzes motifs and recurrent patterns in hundreds of Russian tales.

Looking at the archetypes in this way, as flexible character functions rather than as rigid character types, can liberate your storytelling. It explains how a character in a story can manifest the qualities of more than one archetype. The archetypes can be thought of as masks, worn by the characters temporarily as they are needed to advance the story. A character might enter the story performing the function of a herald, then switch masks to function as a trickster, a mentor, and a shadow.

FACETS OF THE HERO'S PERSONALITY

Another way to look at the classic archetypes is that they are facets of the hero's (or the writer's) personality. The other characters represent possibilities for the hero, for good or ill. A hero sometimes proceeds through the story gathering and incorporating the energy and traits of the other characters. She learns from the other characters, fusing them into a complete human being who has picked up something from everyone she has met along the way.

THE ARCHETYPES AS EMANATIONS OF THE HERO

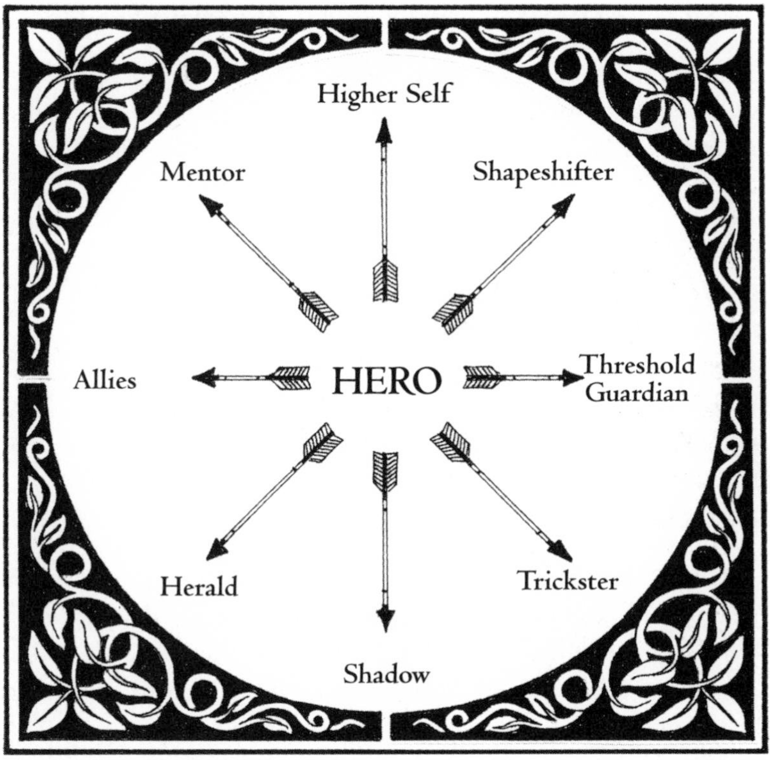

The archetypes can also be regarded as personified symbols of various human qualities. Like the major arcana cards of the Tarot, they stand for the aspects of a complete human personality. Every good story reflects the total human story, the universal human condition of being born into this world, growing, learning, struggling to become an individual, and dying. Stories can be read as metaphors for the general human situation, with characters who embody universal, archetypal qualities, comprehensible to the group as well as the individual.

THE MOST COMMON AND USEFUL ARCHETYPES

For the storyteller, certain character archetypes are indispensable tools of the trade. You can't tell stories without them. The archetypes that occur most frequently in stories, and that seem to be the most useful for the writer to understand, are:

HERO
MENTOR (Wise Old Man or Woman)
THRESHOLD GUARDIAN
HERALD
SHAPESHIFTER
SHADOW
ALLY
TRICKSTER

There are, of course, many more archetypes; as many as there are human qualities to dramatize in stories. Fairy tales are crowded with archetypal figures: the Wolf, the Hunter, the Good Mother, the Wicked Stepmother, the Fairy Godmother, the Witch, the Prince or Princess, the Greedy Innkeeper, and so forth, who perform highly specialized functions. Jung and others have identified many psychological archetypes, such as the *Puer Aeternus* or eternal boy, who can be found in myths as the ever-youthful Cupid, in stories as characters such as Peter Pan, and in life as men who never want to grow up.

Particular genres of modern stories have their specialized character types, such as the "Whore with the Heart of Gold" or the "Arrogant West Point Lieutenant" in Westerns, the "Good Cop/Bad Cop" pairing in buddy pictures, or the "Tough but Fair Sergeant" in war movies.

However, these are only variants and refinements of the archetypes discussed in the following chapters. The archetypes we will discuss are the most basic patterns, from which all others are shaped to fit the needs of specific stories and genres.

Two questions are helpful for a writer trying to identify the nature of an archetype: 1) What psychological function or part of the personality does it represent? and 2) What is its dramatic function in a story?

Keep these questions in mind as we look at eight of the basic archetypes, the people or energies we are likely to meet on the Hero's Journey.

HERO

HERO

"We're on a mission from God."
— from *The Blues Brothers* screenplay
by Dan Aykroyd and John Landis

The word **hero** is Greek, from a root that means "to protect and to serve" (incidentally the motto of the Los Angeles Police Department). A Hero is someone who is willing to sacrifice his own needs on behalf of others, like a shepherd who will sacrifice to protect and serve his flock. At the root the idea of **Hero** is connected with self-sacrifice. (Note that I use the word Hero to describe a central character or protagonist of either sex.)

PSYCHOLOGICAL FUNCTION

In psychological terms, the archetype of the Hero represents what Freud called the ego — that part of the personality that separates from the mother, that considers itself distinct from the rest of the human race. Ultimately, a Hero is one who is able to transcend the bounds and illusions of the ego, but at first, Heroes are all ego: the I, the one, that personal identity which thinks it is separate from the rest of the group. The journey of many Heroes is the story of that separation from the family or tribe, equivalent to a child's sense of separation from the mother.

The Hero archetype represents the ego's search for identity and wholeness. In the process of becoming complete, integrated human beings, we are all Heroes facing internal guardians, monsters, and helpers. In the quest to explore our own minds we find teachers, guides, demons, gods, mates, servants, scapegoats, masters, seducers, betrayers, and allies, as aspects of our personalities and characters in our dreams. All the villains, tricksters, lovers, friends, and foes of the Hero can be found inside ourselves. The psychological task we all face is to integrate these separate parts into one complete, balanced entity. The ego, the Hero thinking she is separate from all these parts of herself, must incorporate them to become the Self.

DRAMATIC FUNCTIONS

AUDIENCE IDENTIFICATION

The dramatic purpose of the Hero is to give the audience a window into the story. Each person hearing a tale or watching a play or movie is invited, in the early stages of the story, to **identify** with the Hero, to merge with him and see the world of the story through his eyes. Storytellers do this by giving their Heroes a combination of qualities, a mix of universal and unique characteristics.

Heroes have qualities that we all can identify with and recognize in ourselves. They are propelled by universal drives that we can all understand: the desire to be loved and understood, to succeed, survive, be free, get revenge, right wrongs, or seek self-expression.

Stories invite us to invest part of our personal identity in the Hero for the duration of the experience. In a sense we become the Hero for a while. We project ourselves into the Hero's psyche, and see the world through her eyes. Heroes need some admirable qualities, so that we want to be like them. We want to experience the self-confidence of Katharine Hepburn, the elegance of Fred Astaire, the wit of Cary Grant, the sexiness of Marilyn Monroe.

Heroes should have universal qualities, emotions, and motivations that everyone has experienced at one time or another: revenge, anger, lust, competition, territoriality, patriotism, idealism, cynicism, or despair. But Heroes must also be unique human beings, rather than stereotypical creatures or tin gods without flaws or unpredictability. Like any effective work of art they need both universality and originality. Nobody wants to see a movie or read a story about abstract qualities in human form. We want stories about real people. A real character, like a real person, is not just a single trait but a unique combination of many qualities and drives, some of them conflicting. And the more conflicting, the better. A character torn by warring allegiances to love and duty is inherently interesting to an audience. A character who has a unique combination of contradictory impulses, such as trust and suspicion or hope and despair, seems more realistic and human than one who displays only one character trait.

A well-rounded Hero can be determined, uncertain, charming, forgetful, impatient, and strong in body but weak at heart, all at the same time. It's the particular combination of qualities that gives an audience the sense that the Hero is one of a kind, a real person rather than a type.

GROWTH

Another story function of the Hero is learning or growth. In evaluating a script sometimes it's hard to tell who is the main character, or who should be. Often the best answer is: the one who learns or grows the most in the course of the story. Heroes overcome obstacles and achieve goals, but they also gain new knowledge and wisdom. The heart of many stories is the learning that goes on between a Hero and a mentor, or a Hero and a lover, or even between a Hero and a villain. We are all each other's teachers.

ACTION

Another heroic function is acting or doing. The Hero is usually the most active person in the script. His will and desire is what drives most stories forward. A frequent flaw in screenplays is that the Hero is fairly active throughout the story, but at the most critical moment becomes passive and is rescued by the timely arrival of some outside force. At this moment above all, a Hero should be fully active, in control of his own fate. The Hero should perform the decisive action of the story, the action that requires taking the most risk or responsibility.

SACRIFICE

People commonly think of Heroes as strong or brave, but these qualities are secondary to **sacrifice** — the true mark of a Hero. Sacrifice is the Hero's willingness to give up something of value, perhaps even her own life, on behalf of an ideal or a group.

Sacrifice means "making holy." In ancient times people made sacrifices, even of human beings, to acknowledge their debt to the spirit world, the gods, or nature, to appease those mighty forces, and to make holy the processes of daily life. Even death became sanctified, a holy act.

DEALING WITH DEATH

At the heart of every story is a confrontation with death. If the Hero doesn't face actual death, then there is the threat of death or symbolic death in the form of a high-stakes game, love affair, or adventure in which the Hero may succeed (live) or fail (die).

Heroes show us how to deal with death. They may survive it, proving that death is not so tough. They may die (perhaps only symbolically) and be reborn, proving that death can be transcended. They may die a Hero's death, transcending death by offering up their lives willingly for a cause, an ideal, or a group.

True heroism is shown in stories when Heroes offer themselves on the altar of chance, willing to take the risk that their quest for adventure may lead to danger, loss, or death. Like soldiers who know that by enlisting they have agreed to give their lives if their country asks them to, Heroes accept the possibility of sacrifice.

The most effective Heroes are those who experience sacrifice. They may give up a loved one or friend along the way. They may give up some cherished vice or eccentricity as the price of entering into a new way of life. They may return some of their winnings or share what they have gained in the Special World. They may return to their starting point, the tribe or village, and bring back boons, elixirs, food, or knowledge to share with the rest of the group. Great cultural Heroes like Martin Luther King or Gandhi gave their lives in pursuit of their ideals.

HEROISM IN OTHER ARCHETYPES

Sometimes the Hero archetype is not just manifested in the main character, the protagonist who bravely fights the bad guys and wins. The archetype can be manifested in other characters, when they act heroically. An unheroic character can grow to be heroic. The title character of *Gunga Din* begins as another archetype altogether, a trickster or clown, but by striving to be a Hero, and by sacrificing himself at a crucial moment on behalf of his friends, he earns the right to be called a Hero. In *Star Wars,* Obi Wan Kenobi clearly manifests the archetype of the mentor through most of the story. However, he **acts** heroically and temporarily wears the mask of the Hero when he sacrifices himself to allow Luke to escape the Death Star.

It can be very effective to have a villainous or antagonistic character unexpectedly manifest heroic qualities. On the sitcom level, when a character like Danny DeVito's despicable "Taxi" dispatcher Louie suddenly reveals he has a soft heart or has done something noble, the episode wins an Emmy. A gallant villain, heroic in some ways and despicable in others, can be very appealing. Ideally, every well-rounded character should manifest a touch of every archetype, because the archetypes are expressions of the parts that make up a complete personality.

CHARACTER FLAWS

Interesting flaws humanize a character. We can recognize bits of ourselves in a Hero who is challenged to overcome inner doubts, errors in thinking, guilt or trauma from the past, or fear of the future. Weaknesses, imperfections, quirks, and vices immediately make a Hero or any character more real and appealing. It seems the more neurotic characters are, the more the audience likes them and identifies with them.

Flaws also give a character somewhere to go — the so-called "character arc" in which a character develops from condition A to condition Z through a series of steps. Flaws are a starting point of imperfection or incompleteness from which a character can grow. They may be deficiencies in a character. Perhaps a Hero has no romantic partner, and is looking for the "missing piece" to complete her life. This is often symbolized in fairy tales by having the Hero experience a loss or a death in the family. Many fairy tales begin with the death of a parent or the kidnapping of a brother or sister. This subtraction from the family unit sets the nervous energy of the story in motion, not to stop until the balance has been restored by the creation of a new family or the reuniting of the old.

In most modern stories it is the Hero's personality that is being recreated or restored to wholeness. The missing piece may be a critical element of personality such as the ability to love or trust. Heroes may have to overcome some problem such as lack of patience or decisiveness. Audiences love watching Heroes grapple with personality problems and overcome them. Will Edward, the rich but cold-hearted businessman of *Pretty*

Woman, warm up under the influence of the life-loving Vivian and become her Prince Charming? Will Vivian gain some self-respect and escape her life of prostitution? Will Conrad, the guilt-ridden teenager in *Ordinary People,* regain his lost ability to accept love and intimacy?

VARIETIES OF HERO

Heroes come in many varieties, including willing and unwilling Heroes, group-oriented and loner Heroes, Anti-heroes, tragic Heroes, and catalyst Heroes. Like all the other archetypes, the Hero is a flexible concept that can express many kinds of energy. Heroes may combine with other archetypes to produce hybrids like the Trickster Hero, or they may temporarily wear the mask of another archetype, becoming a Shapeshifter, a Mentor to someone else, or even a Shadow.

Although usually portrayed as a positive figure, the Hero may also express dark or negative sides of the ego. The Hero archetype generally represents the human spirit in positive action, but may also show the consequences of weakness and reluctance to act.

WILLING AND UNWILLING HEROES

It seems Heroes are of two types: 1) willing, active, gung-ho, committed to the adventure, without doubts, always bravely going ahead, self-motivated, or 2) unwilling, full of doubts and hesitations, passive, needing to be motivated or pushed into the adventure by outside forces. Both make equally entertaining stories, although a Hero who is passive throughout may make for an uninvolving dramatic experience. It's usually best for an unwilling Hero to change at some point, to become committed to the adventure after some necessary motivation has been supplied.

ANTI-HEROES

Anti-hero is a slippery term that can cause a lot of confusion. Simply stated, an Anti-hero is not the opposite of a Hero, but a specialized kind of Hero, one who may be an outlaw or a villain from the point of view of society, but with whom the audience is basically in sympathy. We identify with these outsiders because we have all felt like outsiders at one time or another.

Anti-Heroes may be of two types: 1) characters who behave much like conventional Heroes, but are given a strong touch of cynicism or have a wounded quality, like Bogart's characters in *The Big Sleep* and *Casablanca,* or 2) tragic Heroes, central figures of a story who may not be likeable or admirable, whose actions we may even deplore, like Macbeth or Scarface or the Joan Crawford of *Mommie Dearest.*

The wounded Anti-hero may be a heroic knight in tarnished armor, a loner who has rejected society or been rejected by it. These characters may win at the end and may have the audience's full sympathy at all times, but in society's eyes they are outcasts, like Robin Hood, roguish pirate or bandit Heroes, or many of Bogart's characters. They are often honorable men who have withdrawn from society's corruption, perhaps ex-cops or soldiers who became disillusioned and now operate in the shadow of the law as private eyes, smugglers, gamblers, or soldiers of fortune. We love these characters because they are rebels, thumbing their noses at society as we would all like to do. Another archetype of this kind is personified in James Dean in *Rebel Without a Cause* and *East of Eden,* or the young Marlon Brando, whose character in *The Wild One* acted out a new and quite different generation's dissatisfaction with the old. Actors like Mickey Rourke, Matt Dillon, and Sean Penn carry on the tradition today.

The second type of Anti-hero is more like the classical idea of the tragic Hero. These are flawed Heroes who never overcome their inner demons and are brought down and destroyed by them. They may be charming, they may have admirable qualities, but the flaw wins out in the end. Some tragic Anti-heroes are not so admirable, but we watch their downfall with fascination because "there, but for the grace of God, go I." Like the ancient Greeks who watched Oedipus fall, we are purged of our emotions and we learn to avoid the same pitfalls as we watch the destruction of Al Pacino's character in *Scarface,* Sigourney Weaver as Dian Fossey in *Gorillas in the Mist,* or Diane Keaton's character in *Looking for Mr. Goodbar.*

GROUP-ORIENTED HEROES

Another distinction must be made about Heroes with respect to their orientation to society. Like the first storytellers, the earliest humans who went out hunting and gathering on the plains of Africa, most Heroes are group-oriented: They are part of a society at the beginning of the story, and their journey takes them to an unknown land far from home. When we first meet them, they are part of a clan, tribe, village, town, or family. Their story is one of separation from that group (Act One); lone adventure in the wilderness away from the group (Act Two); and usually, eventual reintegration with the group (Act Three).

Group-oriented Heroes often face a choice between returning to the Ordinary World of the first act, or remaining in the Special World of the second act. Heroes who choose to remain in the Special World are rare in Western culture but fairly common in classic Asian and Indian tales.

LONER HEROES

In contrast to the group-oriented Hero is the loner Western Hero such as *Shane,* Clint Eastwood's Man with No Name, John Wayne's Ethan in *The Searchers,* or The Lone Ranger. With this Hero type, the stories begin with the Heroes estranged from society. Their natural habitat is the wilderness, their natural state is solitude. Their journey is one of re-entry into the group (Act One); adventure within the group, on the group's normal turf (Act Two); and return to isolation in the wilderness (Act Three). For them the Special World of Act Two is the tribe or village, which they visit briefly but in which they are always uncomfortable. The wonderful shot of John Wayne at the end of *The Searchers* sums up the energy of this Hero type. Wayne is framed in a cabin doorway as an outsider forever cut off from the joys and comforts of the family. This kind of Hero need not be limited to Westerns. It can be used effectively in dramas or action movies where a loner detective is tempted back into adventure, where a hermit or retired person is called back into society, or where an emotionally isolated person is challenged to re-enter the world of relationships.

As with group-oriented Heroes, the loner Heroes have the final choice of returning to their initial state (solitude), or remaining in the Special World of Act Two. Some Heroes begin as loners and end as group-oriented Heroes who elect to stay with the group.

CATALYST HEROES

A certain class of Hero is an exception to the rule that the Hero is usually the character who undergoes the most change. These are catalyst Heroes, central figures who may act heroically, but who do not change much themselves because their main function is to bring about transformation in others. Like a true catalyst in chemistry, they bring about a change in a system without being changed themselves.

A good example is Eddie Murphy's character Axel Foley from *Beverly Hills Cop*. His personality is already fully formed and distinctive at the story's beginning. He doesn't have much of a character arc because he has nowhere to go. He doesn't learn or change much in the course of the story, but he does bring about change in his Beverly Hills cop buddies, Taggart and Rosewood. By comparison they have relatively strong character arcs, from being uptight and by-the-book to being hip and streetwise, thanks to Axel's influence. In fact, although Axel is the central figure, the villain's main opponent, and the character with the best lines and the most screen time, it could be argued that he is not the true Hero, but the Mentor of the piece, while young Rosewood (Judge Reinhold) is the actual Hero because he learns the most.

Catalyst Heroes are especially useful in continuing stories such as episodic TV shows and sequels. Like The Lone Ranger or Superman, these Heroes undergo few internal changes, but primarily act to help others or guide them in their growth. Of course it's a good idea once in a while to give even these characters some moments of growth and change to help keep them fresh and believable.

THE ROAD OF HEROES

Heroes are symbols of the soul in transformation, and of the journey each person takes through life. The stages of that progression, the natural stages of life and growth, make up the Hero's Journey. The Hero archetype is a rich field for exploration by writers and spiritual seekers. Carol S. Pearson's book *Awakening the Heroes* Within further breaks down the idea of the Hero into useful archetypes (Innocent, Orphan, Martyr, Wanderer, Warrior, Caregiver, Seeker, Lover, Destroyer, Creator, Ruler, Magician, Sage, and Fool) and graphs the emotional progress of each. It's a good guide to a deeper psychological understanding of the Hero in its many facets. The special avenues traveled by some female heroes are described in *The Heroine's Journey: Woman's Quest for Wholeness* by Maureen Murdock.

MENTOR

MENTOR: WISE OLD MAN OR WOMAN

"May the Force be with you!"
— from *Star Wars* by George Lucas

An archetype found frequently in dreams, myths, and stories is the Mentor, usually a positive figure who aids or trains the hero. Campbell's name for this force is the **Wise Old Man** or **Wise Old Woman.** This archetype is expressed in all those characters who teach and protect heroes and give them gifts. Whether it's God walking with Adam in the Garden of Eden, Merlin guiding King Arthur, the Fairy Godmother helping Cinderella, or a veteran sergeant giving advice to a rookie cop, the relationship between hero and Mentor is one of the richest sources of entertainment in literature and film.

The word "Mentor" comes to us from *The Odyssey.* A character named Mentor guides the young hero, Telemachus, on his Hero's Journey. In fact it's the goddess Athena who helps Telemachus, by assuming the form of Mentor. (See Chapter 4 in book two for a fuller discussion of Mentor's role.) Mentors often speak in the voice of a god, or are inspired by divine wisdom. Good teachers and Mentors are **enthused**, in the original sense of the word. "Enthusiasm" is from the Greek **en theos,** meaning god-inspired, having a god in you, or being in the presence of a god.

PSYCHOLOGICAL FUNCTION

In the anatomy of the human psyche, Mentors represent the Self, the god within us, the aspect of personality that is connected with all things. This higher Self is the wiser, nobler, more godlike part of us. Like Jiminy Cricket in the Disney version of *Pinocchio,* the Self acts as a conscience to guide us on the road of life when no Blue Fairy or kindly Gepetto is there to protect us and tell us right from wrong.

Mentor figures, whether encountered in dreams, fairy tales, myths, or screenplays, stand for the hero's highest aspirations. They are what the hero may become if she persists on the Road of Heroes. Mentors are often former heroes who have survived life's early trials and are now passing on the gift of their knowledge and wisdom.

The Mentor archetype is closely related to the image of the parent. The fairy godmother in stories such as "Cinderella" can be interpreted as the protecting spirit of the girl's dead mother. Merlin is a surrogate parent to the young King Arthur, whose father is dead. Many heroes seek out Mentors because their own parents are inadequate role models.

DRAMATIC FUNCTIONS

TEACHING

Just as learning is an important function of the hero, teaching or training is a key function of the Mentor. Training sergeants, drill instructors, professors, trail bosses, parents, grandparents, crusty old boxing coaches, and all those who teach a hero the ropes, are manifesting this archetype. Of course the teaching can go both ways. Anyone who has taught knows that you learn as much from your students as they do from you.

GIFT-GIVING

Giving gifts is also an important function of this archetype. In Vladimir Propp's analysis of Russian fairy tales, *Morphology of the Folktale,* he identifies this function as that of a "donor" or provider: one who temporarily aids the hero, usually by giving some gift. It may be a magic weapon, an important key or clue, some magical medicine or food, or a life-saving piece of advice. In fairy tales the donor might be a witch's cat, grateful for a little girl's kindness, who gives her a towel and a comb. Later when the girl is being chased by the witch, the towel turns into a raging river and the comb turns into a forest to block the witch's pursuit.

Examples of these gifts are abundant in movies, from the small-time mobster Puttynose giving James Cagney his first gun in *The Public Enemy* to Obi Wan Kenobi giving Luke Skywalker his father's light-saber. Nowadays the gift is as likely to be a computer code as the key to a dragon's lair.

GIFTS IN MYTHOLOGY

Gift-giving, the donor function of the Mentor, has an important role in mythology. Many heroes received gifts from their Mentors, the gods. Pandora, whose name means "all-gifted," was showered with presents, including Zeus' vindictive gift of the box which she was not supposed to open. Heroes such as Hercules were given some gifts by their Mentors, but among the Greeks the most gifted of heroes was Perseus.

PERSEUS

The Greek ideal of heroism was expressed in Perseus, the monster-slayer. He has the distinction of being one of the best equipped of heroes, so loaded down with gifts from higher powers that it's a wonder he could walk. In time, with the help of Mentors such as Hermes and Athena, he acquired winged sandals, a magic sword, a helmet of invisibility, a magic sickle, a magic mirror, the head of Medusa that turned all who look upon it to stone, and a magic satchel to stow the head in. As if this were not enough, the movie version of the Perseus tale, *Clash of the Titans*, gives him the flying horse Pegasus as well.

In most stories, this would be overdoing it a bit. But Perseus is meant to be a paragon of heroes, so it's fitting he should be so well provided for by the gods, his Mentors in the quest.

GIFTS SHOULD BE EARNED

In Propp's dissection of Russian fairy tales, he observes that donor characters give magical presents to heroes, but usually only after the heroes have passed a test of some kind. This is a good rule of thumb: **The gift or help of the donor should be earned, by learning, sacrifice, or commitment.** Fairy-tale heroes eventually earn the aid of animals or magical creatures by being kind to them in the beginning, sharing food with them, or protecting them from harm.

MENTOR AS INVENTOR

Sometimes the Mentor functions as a scientist or inventor, whose gifts are his devices, designs, or inventions. The great inventor of classical myth is Daedalus, who designed the Labyrinth and other wonders for the rulers of Crete. As the master artisan of the Theseus and the Minotaur story, he had a hand in creating the monster Minotaur and designed the Labyrinth as a cage for it. As a Mentor, Daedalus gave Ariadne the ball of thread that allowed Theseus to get in and out of the Labyrinth alive.

Imprisoned in his own maze as punishment for helping Theseus, Daedalus also invented the famous wax-and-feather wings that allowed him and his son Icarus to escape. As a Mentor to Icarus, he advised his son not to fly too close to the sun. Icarus, who had grown up in the pitch dark of the Labyrinth, was irresistibly attracted to the sun, ignored his father's advice, and fell to his death when the wax melted. The best advice is worthless if you don't take it.

THE HERO'S CONSCIENCE

Some Mentors perform a special function as a conscience for the hero. Characters like Jiminy Cricket in *Pinocchio* or Walter Brennan's Groot in *Red River* try to remind an errant hero of an important moral code. However, a hero may rebel against a nagging conscience. Would-be Mentors should remember that in the original Collodi story Pinocchio squashed the cricket to shut him up. The angel on a hero's shoulder can never offer arguments as colorful as those of the devil on the opposite side.

MOTIVATION

Another important function of the Mentor archetype is to motivate the hero, and help her overcome fear. Sometimes the gift alone is sufficient reassurance and motivation. In other cases the Mentor shows the hero something or arranges things to motivate her to take action and commit to the adventure.

The Mentor may act as a conscience for the Hero.

In some cases a hero is so unwilling or fearful that he must be pushed into the adventure. A Mentor may need to give a hero a swift kick in the pants in order to get the adventure rolling.

PLANTING

A function of the Mentor archetype is often to *plant* information or a prop that will become important later. The James Bond films have a mandatory scene in which the weapons master "Q," one of Bond's recurring Mentors, describes the workings of some new briefcase gadget to a bored 007. This information is a **plant**, meant for the audience to note but forget about until the climactic moment where the gadget becomes a lifesaver. Such constructions help tie the beginning and end of the story together, and show that at some point everything we've learned from our Mentors comes in handy.

SEXUAL INITIATION

In the realm of love, the Mentor's function may be to initiate us into the mysteries of love or sex. In India they speak of the *shakti* — a sexual initiator, a partner who helps you experience the power of sex as a vehicle of higher consciousness. A shakti is a manifestation of God, a Mentor leading the lover to experience the divine.

Seducers and thieves of innocence teach heroes lessons the hard way. There may be a shadow side to Mentors who lead a hero down a dangerous road of obsessive love or loveless, manipulative sex. There are many ways to learn.

TYPES OF MENTOR

Like heroes, Mentors may be willing or unwilling. Sometimes they teach in spite of themselves. In other cases they teach by their bad example. The downfall of a weakened, tragically flawed Mentor can show the hero pitfalls to avoid. As with heroes, dark or negative sides may be expressed through this archetype.

DARK MENTORS

In certain stories the power of the Mentor archetype can be used to mislead the audience. In thrillers the mask of a Mentor is sometimes a decoy used to lure the hero into danger. Or in an anti-heroic gangster picture such as *The Public Enemy* or *Goodfellas,* where every conventional heroic value is inverted, an anti-Mentor appears to guide the anti-hero on the road to crime and destruction.

Another inversion of this archetype's energy is a special kind of **Threshold Guardian** (an archetype discussed in the next chapter). An example is found in *Romancing the Stone,* where Joan Wilder's witchy, sharp-tongued agent is to all appearances a Mentor, guiding her career and giving her advice about men. But when Joan is about to cross the threshold to adventure, the agent tries to stop her, warning her of the dangers and casting doubt in her mind. Rather than motivating her like a true Mentor, the agent becomes an obstacle in the hero's path. This is psychologically true to life, for often we must overcome or outgrow the energy of our best teachers in order to move to the next stage of development.

FALLEN MENTORS

Some Mentors are still on a Hero's Journey of their own. They may be experiencing a crisis of faith in their calling. Perhaps they are dealing with the problems of aging and approaching the threshold of death, or have fallen from the hero's road. The hero needs the Mentor to pull himself together one more time, and there's serious doubt that he can do it. Tom

Hanks in *A League of Their Own* plays a former sports hero sidelined by injury and making a poor transition into Mentor-hood. He has fallen far from grace, and the audience is rooting for him to straighten up and honor his task of helping the heroes. Such a Mentor may go through all the stages of a hero's journey, on his own path to redemption.

CONTINUING MENTORS

Mentors are useful for giving assignments and setting stories in motion. For this reason they are often written into the cast of continuing stories. Recurring Mentors include Mr. Waverly on "The Man from U.N.C.L.E.," "M" in the Bond pictures, The Chief on "Get Smart," Will Geer and Ellen Corby as the grandparents on "The Waltons," Alfred in "Batman," James Earl Jones' CIA official in *Patriot Games* and *The Hunt for Red October*, etc.

MULTIPLE MENTORS

A hero may be trained by a series of Mentors who teach specific skills. Hercules is surely among the best trained of heroes, mentored by experts on wrestling, archery, horsemanship, weapon-handling, boxing, wisdom, virtue, song, and music. He even took a driver-training course in charioteering from one Mentor. All of us have learned from a series of Mentors, including parents, older brothers and sisters, friends, lovers, teachers, bosses, co-workers, therapists, and other role models.

Multiple Mentors may be needed to express different functions of the archetype. In the James Bond movies, 007 always returns to his home base to confer with his main Wise Old Man or Woman, the spymaster "M" who gives him assignments, advice, and warnings. But the Mentor function of giving gifts to the hero is delegated to "Q," the weapons and gadget master. A certain amount of emotional support as well as advice and critical information is provided by Miss Moneypenny, representing another aspect of the Mentor.

COMIC MENTORS

A special type of Mentor occurs in romantic comedies. This person is often the friend or fellow office worker of the hero, and is usually of the same sex as the hero. She gives the hero some advice about love: go out more to forget the pain of a lost love; pretend to have an affair to make your husband jealous; feign interest in the beloved's hobbies; impress the beloved with gifts, flowers, or flattery; be more aggressive; and so on. The advice often seems to lead the hero into temporary disaster, but it all turns out right in the end. These characters are a feature of romantic comedies, especially those of the 1950s when movies like *Pillow Talk* and *Lover Come Back* gave plenty of work for character actors like Thelma Ritter and Tony Randall who could portray this wise-cracking, sarcastic version of a Mentor.

MENTOR AS SHAMAN

Mentor figures in stories are closely related to the idea of the **shaman**: the healer, the medicine man or woman, of tribal cultures. Just as Mentors guide the hero through the Special World, shamans guide their people through life. They travel to other worlds in dreams and visions and bring back stories to heal their tribes. It's often the function of a Mentor to help the hero seek a guiding vision for a quest to another world.

FLEXIBILITY OF THE MENTOR ARCHETYPE

Like the other archetypes, the Mentor or donor is not a rigid character type, but rather a **function**, a job which several different characters might perform in the course of a story. A character primarily manifesting one archetype — the hero, the shapeshifter, the trickster, even the villain — may temporarily slip on the mask of the Mentor in order to teach or give something to the hero.

In Russian fairy tales, the wonderful character of the witch Baba Yaga is a Shadow figure who sometimes wears the Mentor mask. On the surface she's a horrible, cannibalistic witch representing the dark side of the forest, its power to devour. But like the forest, she can be appeased and can shower gifts on the traveler. Sometimes if Prince Ivan is kind and complimentary to her, Baba Yaga gives him the magical treasure he needs to rescue the Princess Vasilisa.

Although Campbell called these Mentor figures Wise Old Men or Women, they are sometimes neither wise nor old. The young, in their innocence, are often wise and capable of teaching the old. The most foolish person in a story might be the one we learn the most from. As with the other archetypes, the function of a Mentor is more important than mere physical description. What the character **does** will often determine what archetype is being manifested at the moment.

Many stories have no specific character who can be identified as a Mentor. There's no white-bearded, wizardly figure who wanders around acting like a Wise Old Man. Nevertheless, almost every story calls on the energy of this archetype at some point.

INNER MENTORS

In some Westerns or film noir stories the hero is an experienced, hardened character who has no need for a Mentor or guide. He has internalized the archetype and it now lives within him as an inner code of behavior. The Mentor may be the unspoken code of the gunfighter, or the secret notions of honor harbored by Sam Spade or Philip Marlowe. A code of ethics may be a disembodied manifestation of the Mentor archetype guiding the hero's actions. It's not uncommon for a hero to make reference to a Mentor who meant something to him earlier in life, even if there's no actual Mentor character in the story. A hero may remember, "My mother/father/ grandfather/drill sergeant used to say...," and then call to mind the bit of wisdom that will become critical in solving the problem of the story. The energy of the Mentor archetype also may be invested in a prop such as a book or other artifact that guides the hero in the quest.

PLACEMENT OF MENTORS

Although the Hero's Journey often finds the Mentor appearing in Act One, the placement of a Mentor in a story is a practical consideration. A character may be needed at any point who knows the ropes, has the map to the unknown country, or can give the hero key information at the right time. Mentors may show up early in a story, or wait in the wings until needed at a critical moment in Act Two or Act Three.

Mentors provide heroes with motivation, inspiration, guidance, training, and gifts for the journey. Every hero is guided by something, and a story without some acknowledgement of this energy is incomplete. Whether expressed as an actual character or as an internalized code of behavior, the Mentor archetype is a powerful tool at the writer's command.

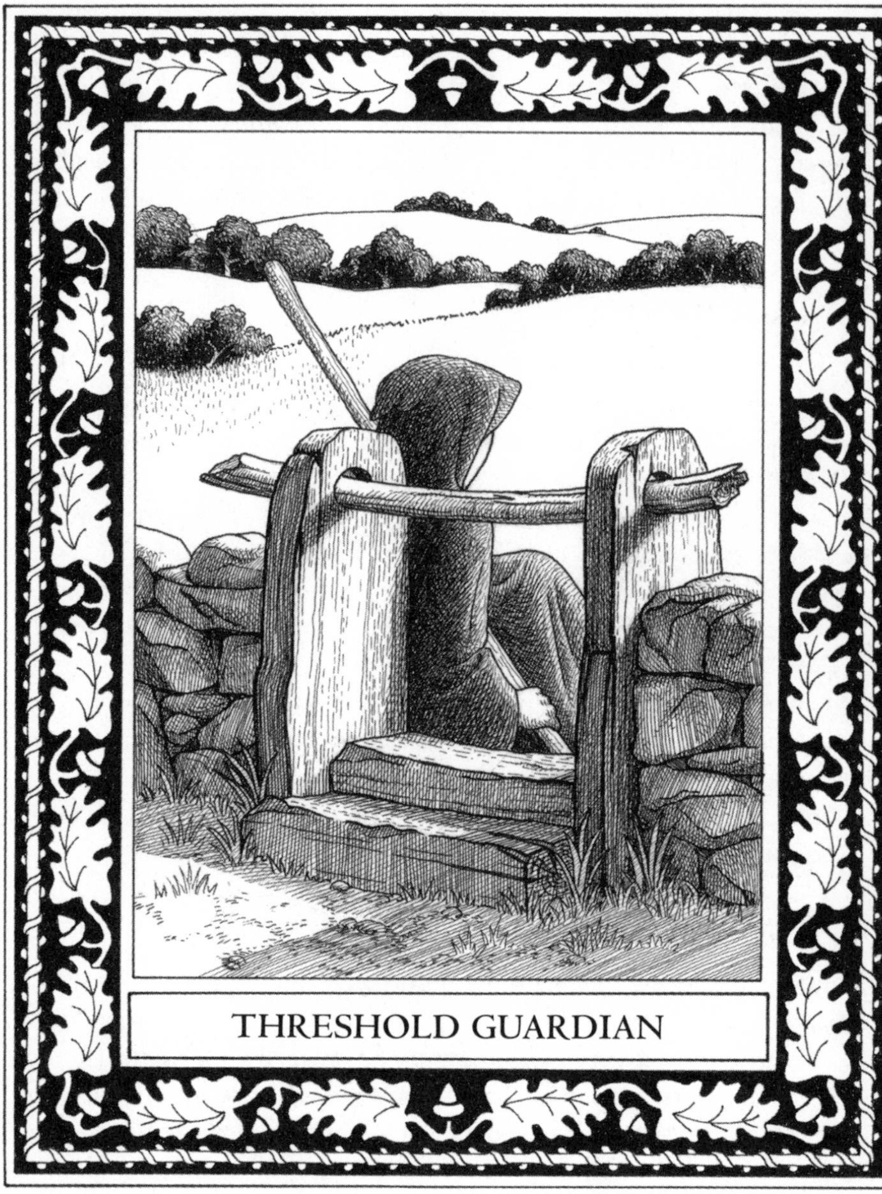

THRESHOLD GUARDIAN

THRESHOLD GUARDIAN

"I, for one, have an idea that he will never bring this journey off..."
— *The Odyssey* of Homer

All heroes encounter obstacles on the road to adventure. At each gateway to a new world there are powerful guardians at the threshold, placed to keep the unworthy from entering. They present a menacing face to the hero, but if properly understood, they can be overcome, bypassed, or even turned into allies. Many heroes (and many writers) encounter **Threshold Guardians**, and understanding their nature can help determine how to handle them.

Threshold Guardians are usually not the main villains or antagonists in stories. Often they will be lieutenants of the villain, lesser thugs or mercenaries hired to guard access to the chief's headquarters. They may also be neutral figures who are simply part of the landscape of the Special World. In rare cases they may be secret helpers placed in the hero's path to test her willingness and skill.

There is often a symbiotic relationship between a villain and a Threshold Guardian. In nature, a powerful animal such as a bear will sometimes tolerate a smaller animal such as a fox nesting at the entrance of its lair. The fox, with its strong smell and sharp teeth, tends to keep other animals from wandering into the cave while the bear is sleeping. The fox also serves as an early warning system for the bear by making a racket if something tries to enter the cave. In similar fashion, villains of stories often rely on underlings such as doorkeepers, bouncers, bodyguards, sentries, gunslingers, or mercenaries to protect and warn them when a hero approaches the Threshold of the villain's stronghold.

PSYCHOLOGICAL FUNCTION: NEUROSES

These Guardians may represent the ordinary obstacles we all face in the world around us: bad weather, bad luck, prejudice, oppression, or hostile people like the waitress who refuses to grant Jack Nicholson's simple request in *Five Easy Pieces*. But on a deeper psychological level they stand for our internal demons: the neuroses, emotional scars, vices, dependencies, and self-limitations that hold back our growth and progress. It seems that every time you try to make a major change in your life, these inner demons rise up to their full force, not necessarily to stop you, but to test if you are really determined to accept the challenge of change.

DRAMATIC FUNCTION: TESTING

Testing of the hero is the primary dramatic function of the Threshold Guardian. When heroes confront one of these figures, they must solve a puzzle or pass a test. Like the Sphinx who presents Oedipus with a riddle before he can continue his journey, Threshold Guardians challenge and test heroes on the path.

How to deal with these apparent obstacles? Heroes have a range of options. They can turn around and run, attack the opponent head-on, use craft or deceit to get by, bribe or appease the Guardian, or make an **Ally** of a presumed enemy. (Heroes are aided by a variety of archetypes known collectively as Allies, which will be discussed in a separate chapter.)

One of the most effective ways of dealing with a Threshold Guardian is to "get into the skin" of the opponent, like a hunter entering into the mind of a stalked animal. The Plains Indians wore buffalo skins to sneak within bow-shot of the bison herd. The hero may get past a Threshold Guardian by entering into its spirit or taking on its appearance. A good example is in Act Two of *The Wizard of Oz*, when the Tin Woodsman, Cowardly Lion, and Scarecrow come to the Wicked Witch's castle to rescue the kidnapped Dorothy. The situation looks bleak. Dorothy's inside a strong castle defended by a regiment of fierce-looking soldiers who march up and down singing "Oh-Ee-Oh." There's no possible way for the three friends to defeat such a large force.

However, our heroes are ambushed by three sentries and overcome them, taking their uniforms and weapons. Disguised as soldiers, they join the end of a column and march right into the castle. They have turned an attack to their advantage by literally climbing into the skins of their opponents. Instead of uselessly trying to defeat a superior enemy, they have temporarily **become** the enemy.

It's important for a hero to recognize and acknowledge these figures as Threshold Guardians. In daily life, you have probably encountered resistance when you try to make a positive change in your life. People around you, even those who love you, are often reluctant to see you change. They are used to your neuroses and have found ways to benefit from them. The idea of your changing may threaten them. If they resist you, it's important to realize they are simply functioning as Threshold Guardians, testing you to see if you are really resolved to change.

SIGNALS OF NEW POWER

Successful heroes learn to recognize Threshold Guardians not as threatening enemies, but as useful Allies and early indicators that new power or success is coming. Threshold Guardians who appear to be attacking may in fact be doing the hero a huge favor.

Heroes also learn to recognize resistance as a source of strength. As in bodybuilding, the greater the resistance, the greater the strength. Rather than attacking the power of Threshold Guardians head-on, heroes learn to use it so it doesn't harm them. In fact it makes them stronger. The martial arts teach that an opponent's strength can be used against him. Ideally, Threshold Guardians are not to be defeated but **incorporated** (literally, taken into the body). Heroes learn the Guardians' tricks, absorb them, and go on. Ultimately, fully evolved heroes feel compassion for their apparent enemies and transcend rather than destroy them.

Heroes must learn to read the signals of their Threshold Guardians. In *The Power of Myth*, Joseph Campbell illustrated this idea beautifully with an example from Japan. Ferocious-looking demon statues sometimes guard the entrances to Japanese temples. The first thing you notice is one hand held up like that of a policeman gesturing "Stop!" But when you look more closely, you see that the other hand invites you to enter. The message is: Those who are put off by outward appearances cannot enter the Special World, but those who can see past surface impressions to the inner reality are welcome.

In stories, Threshold Guardians take on a fantastic array of forms. They may be border guards, sentinels, night watchmen, lookouts, bodyguards, bandidos, editors, doormen, bouncers, entrance examiners, or anyone whose function is to temporarily block the way of the hero and test her powers. The energy of the Threshold Guardian may not be embodied as a character, but may be found as a prop, architectural feature, animal, or force of nature that blocks and tests the hero. Learning how to deal with Threshold Guardians is one of the major tests of the Hero's Journey.

HERALD

HERALD

"If you build it, they will come."
—The Voice in *Field of Dreams,* screenplay by Phil Alden Robinson from the novel *Shoeless Joe* by W.P. Kinsella

Often a new force will appear in Act One to bring a challenge to the hero. This is the energy of the **Herald** archetype. Like the heralds of medieval chivalry, Herald characters issue challenges and announce the coming of significant change.

The heralds of knighthood were responsible for keeping track of lineages and coats of arms, and had an important role in identifying people and relationships in battle, tournaments, and on great state occasions such as weddings. They were the protocol officers of their day. At the commencement of war a herald might be called upon to recite the causes of the conflict; in effect, to provide the motivation. In Shakespeare's *Henry V,* the Ambassadors from the Dauphin (crown prince) of France act as Heralds when they bring the young English king an insulting gift of tennis balls, which implies King Henry is fit for nothing but a frivolous game of tennis. The appearance of these Heralds is the spark that sets off a war. Later the character of Mountjoy, the Dauphin's Herald, bears messages between King Henry and his master during the crucial battle of Agincourt.

Typically, in the opening phase of a story, heroes have "gotten by" somehow. They have handled an imbalanced life through a series of defenses or coping mechanisms. Then all at once some new energy enters the story that makes it impossible for the hero to simply get by any longer. A new person, condition, or information shifts the hero's balance, and nothing will ever be the same. A decision must be made, action taken, the conflict faced. A Call to Adventure has been delivered, often by a character who manifests the archetype of the Herald.

Heralds are so necessary in mythology that the Greek god Hermes (Roman Mercury) is devoted to expressing this function. Hermes appears everywhere as the messenger or Herald of the gods, performing some errand or bearing a message from Zeus. At the beginning of *The Odyssey* Hermes, at Athena's urging, bears a message from Zeus to the nymph Calypso that she must release Odysseus. The appearance of Hermes as Herald gets the story rolling.

PSYCHOLOGICAL FUNCTION: CALL FOR CHANGE

Heralds have the important psychological function of announcing the need for change. Something deep inside us knows when we are ready to change and sends us a messenger. This may be a dream figure, a real person, or a new idea we encounter. In *Field of Dreams* it's the mysterious Voice that the hero hears saying, "If you build it, they will come." The Call might come from a book we read, or a movie we see. But something inside us has been struck like a bell, and the resulting vibrations spread out through our lives until change is inevitable.

DRAMATIC FUNCTION: MOTIVATION

Heralds provide motivation, offer the hero a challenge, and get the story rolling. They alert the hero (and the audience) that change and adventure are coming.

An example of the Herald archetype as a motivator in movies can be found in Alfred Hitchcock's *Notorious.* Cary Grant plays a secret agent trying to enlist Ingrid Bergman, the playgirl daughter of a Nazi spy, in a noble cause. He offers her both a challenge and an opportunity: She can overcome her bad reputation and the family shame by dedicating herself to Cary's noble cause. (The cause turns out to be not so noble later on, but that's another story.)

Like most heroes, Bergman's character is fearful of change and reluctant to accept the challenge, but Grant, like a medieval herald, reminds her of the past and gives her motivation to act. He plays her a recording of an argument she had with her father, in which she renounced his spying and declared her loyalty to the United States. Confronted by the evidence of her own patriotism, she accepts the call to adventure. She is motivated.

The Herald may be a person or a force. The coming of a storm or the first tremors of the earth, as in *Hurricane* or *Earthquake,* may be the Herald of adventure. The crash of the stock market or the declaration of war have set many a story in motion.

Often the Herald is simply a means of bringing news to the hero of a new energy that will change the balance. It could be a telegram or a phone call. In *High Noon,* the Herald is a telegraph clerk who brings Gary Cooper word that his enemies are out of jail and headed for town to kill him. In *Romancing the Stone,* the Herald for Joan Wilder is a treasure map that arrives in the mail, and a phone call from her sister, who is being held hostage in Colombia.

TYPES OF HERALD

The Herald may be a positive, negative, or neutral figure. In some stories the Herald is the villain or his emissary, perhaps issuing a direct challenge to the hero, or trying to dupe the hero into getting involved. In the thriller *Arabesque,* the Herald is the private secretary of the villain who tries to lure the hero, a college professor of modest means, into danger with a tempting offer of work. In some cases, a villainous Herald may announce the challenge not to the hero but to the audience. In *Star Wars* the first appearance of Darth Vader, as he captures Princess Leia, proclaims to the audience that something is out of balance before the hero, Luke Skywalker, has even appeared.

In other stories the Herald is an agent of the forces of good, calling the hero to a positive adventure. The Herald's mask may be worn temporarily by a character who mainly embodies some other archetype. A Mentor frequently acts as a Herald who issues a challenge to the hero. The Herald may be a hero's loved one or Ally, or someone neutral to the hero, such as a Trickster or Threshold Guardian.

The Herald archetype may come into play at almost any point in a story, but is most frequently employed in Act One to help bring the hero into the adventure. Whether it is an inner call, an external development, or a character bringing news of change, the energy of the Herald is needed in almost every story.

SHAPESHIFTER

SHAPESHIFTER

"You can expect the unexpected."
— publicity for the film *Charade*

People often have trouble grasping the elusive archetype of the **Shapeshifter**, perhaps because its very nature is to be shifting and unstable. Its appearance and characteristics change as soon as you examine it closely. Nonetheless, the Shapeshifter is a powerful archetype and understanding its ways can be helpful in storytelling and in life.

Heroes frequently encounter figures, often of the opposite sex, whose primary characteristic is that they appear to change constantly from the hero's point of view. Often the hero's love interest or romantic partner will manifest the qualities of a Shapeshifter. We have all experienced relationships in which our partner is fickle, two-faced, or bewilderingly changeable. In *Fatal Attraction* the hero is confronted with a Shapeshifting woman who changes from a passionate lover to an insane, murderous harpy.

Shapeshifters change appearance or mood, and are difficult for the hero and the audience to pin down. They may mislead the hero or keep her guessing, and their loyalty or sincerity is often in question. An Ally or friend of the same sex as the hero may also act as a Shapeshifter in a buddy comedy or adventure. Wizards, witches, and ogres are traditional Shapeshifters in the world of fairy tales.

PSYCHOLOGICAL FUNCTION

An important psychological purpose of the Shapeshifter archetype is to express the energy of the **animus** and **anima**, terms from the psychology of Carl Jung. The animus is Jung's name for the male element in the female unconscious, the bundle of positive and negative images of masculinity in a woman's dreams and fantasies. The anima is the corresponding female element in the male unconscious. In this theory, people have a complete set of both male and female qualities which are necessary for survival and internal balance.

Historically, the female characteristics in men and the male characteristics in women have been sternly repressed by society. Men learn at an early age to show only the macho, unemotional side of themselves. Women are taught by society to play down their masculine qualities. This can lead to emotional and even physical problems. Men are now working to regain some of their suppressed feminine qualities — sensitivity, intuition, and the ability to feel and express emotion. Women sometimes spend their adult lives trying to reclaim the male energies within them which society has discouraged, such as power and assertiveness.

These repressed qualities live within us and are manifested in dreams and fantasies as the animus or anima. They may take the form of dream characters such as opposite-sex teachers, family members, classmates, gods or monsters who allow us to express this unconscious but powerful force within. An encounter with the anima or animus in dreams or fantasy is considered an important step in psychological growth.

PROJECTION

We may also confront the animus and anima in reality. By nature we look for people who match our internal image of the opposite sex. Often we imagine the resemblance and **project** onto some unsuspecting person our desire to join with the anima or animus. We may fall into relationships in which we have not seen the partner clearly. Instead we have seen the anima or animus, our own internal notion of the ideal partner, projected onto the other person. We often go through relationships trying to force the partner to match our **projection**. Hitchcock created a powerful expression of this phenomenon in *Vertigo*. James Stewart forces Kim Novak to change her hair and clothing to match the image of his feminine ideal Carlota, a woman who ironically never existed in the first place.

It's natural for each sex to regard the other as ever-changing, mysterious. Many of us don't understand our own sexuality and psychology very well, let alone that of the opposite sex. Often our main experience of the opposite sex is their changeability and their tendency to shift attitudes, appearances, and emotions for no apparent reason.

Women complain that men are vague, vacillating, and unable to commit. Men complain that women are moody, flighty, fickle, and unpredictable. Anger can turn gentle men into beasts. Women change dramatically during their monthly cycle, shifting with the phases of the moon. During pregnancy they drastically shift shape and mood. At some time most of us have been perceived by others as "two-faced" Shapeshifters.

The animus and anima may be positive or negative figures who may be helpful to the hero or destructive to him. In some stories it's the task of the hero to figure out which side, positive or negative, he is dealing with.

The Shapeshifter archetype is also a catalyst for change, a symbol of the psychological urge to transform. Dealing with a Shapeshifter may cause the hero to change attitudes about the opposite sex or come to terms with the repressed energies that this archetype stirs up.

These projections of our hidden opposite sides, these images and ideas about sexuality and relationships, form the archetype of the Shapeshifter.

DRAMATIC FUNCTION

The Shapeshifter serves the dramatic function of bringing doubt and suspense into a story. When heroes keep asking, "Is he faithful to me? Is she going to betray me? Does he truly love me? Is he an ally or an enemy?" a Shapeshifter is generally present.

Shapeshifters appear with great frequency and variety in the film noir and thriller genres. *The Big Sleep, The Maltese Falcon,* and *Chinatown* feature detectives confronting Shapeshifting women whose loyalty and motives are in doubt. In other stories such as Hitchcock's *Suspicion* or *Shadow of a Doubt,* a good woman must figure out if a Shapeshifting man is worthy of her trust.

A common type of Shapeshifter is called the **femme fatale**, the woman as temptress or destroyer. The idea is as old as the Bible, with its stories of Eve in the Garden of Eden, the scheming Jezebel, and Delilah cutting off Samson's hair to rob him of his strength. The femme fatale finds expression today in stories of cops and detectives betrayed by killer women, such as Sharon Stone's character in *Basic Instinct* or Kathleen Turner's in *Body Heat. Black Widow* and *Single White Female* are interesting variants in which a female hero confronts a deadly, Shapeshifting femme fatale.

The Shapeshifter, like the other archetypes, can be manifested by male or female characters. There are as many **hommes fatales** in myth, literature, and movies as there are femmes. In Greek mythology, Zeus was a great Shapeshifter, changing forms to cavort with human maidens who usually ended up suffering for it. *Looking for Mr. Goodbar* is about a woman seeking a perfect lover, but finding instead a Shapeshifting man who brings her death. The film *The Stranger* depicts a good woman (Loretta Young) who is about to marry a monstrous Shapeshifter, a closet Nazi played by Orson Welles.

The *fatale* aspect is not always essential to this archetype. Shapeshifters may only dazzle and confuse the hero, rather than try to kill her. Shapeshifting is a natural part of romance. It's common to be blinded by love, unable to see the other person clearly through the many masks they wear. The character played by Michael Douglas in *Romancing the Stone* appears to be a Shapeshifter to hero Kathleen Turner, who is kept guessing until the last moment about the loyalty of her male counterpart.

Shapeshifting may manifest in changes of appearance. In many films a woman's change of costume or hairstyle indicates that her identity is shifting and her loyalty is in doubt. This archetype may also be expressed through changes in behavior or speech, such as assuming different accents or telling a succession of lies. In the thriller *Arabesque*, Shapeshifter Sophia Loren tells unwilling hero Gregory Peck a bewildering series of stories about her background, all of which turn out be untrue. Many heroes have to deal with Shapeshifters, male and female, who assume disguises and tell lies to confuse them.

A famous Shapeshifter from *The Odyssey* is the sea god Proteus, "the Old Man of the Sea." Menelaus, one of the heroes returning from the Trojan War, traps Proteus to force information out of him. Proteus changes into a lion, a snake, a panther, a boar, running water, and a tree in his attempt to escape. But Menelaus and his men hold on tight until Proteus returns to his true form and yields up the answers to their questions. The story teaches that if heroes are patient with Shapeshifters the truth may eventually come out. "Protean," our adjective meaning "readily taking many forms," comes from the story of Proteus.

MASK OF THE SHAPESHIFTER

As with the other archetypes, Shapeshifting is a function or a mask that may be worn by any character in a story. A hero may wear the mask in a romantic situation. Richard Gere, in *An Officer and a Gentleman,* puts on airs and tells a hat-full of lies to impress Debra Winger. He temporarily acts as a Shapeshifter although he is the hero of the piece.

Sometimes a hero must become a Shapeshifter to escape a trap or get past a Threshold Guardian. In *Sister Act,* Whoopi Goldberg's character, a Las Vegas lounge singer, disguises herself as a Catholic nun to keep from being killed as a witness to a mob murder.

Villains or their allies may wear the Shapeshifter mask to seduce or confuse a hero. The wicked queen in *Snow White* assumes the form of an old crone to trick the hero into eating a poisoned apple.

Shapeshifting is also a natural attribute of other archetypes such as Mentors and Tricksters. Merlin, Mentor of the King Arthur stories, frequently changes shape to aid Arthur's cause. The goddess Athena in *The Odyssey* assumes the appearance of many different humans to help Odysseus and his son.

Shapeshifters can also be found in so-called "buddy movies" in which the story centers on two male or two female characters who share the role of hero. Often one is more conventionally heroic and easier for the audience to identify with. The second character, while of the same sex as the main hero, will often be a Shapeshifter, whose loyalty and true nature are always in question. In the comedy *The In-Laws,* the "straight" hero, Alan Arkin, is nearly driven crazy by the Shapeshifting of his buddy, Peter Falk, a CIA agent.

The Shapeshifter is one of the most flexible archetypes and serves a protean variety of functions in modern stories. It's found most often in male-female relationships, but it may also be useful in other situations to portray characters whose appearance or behavior changes to meet the needs of the story.

SHADOW

SHADOW

"You can't keep a good monster down!"
— publicity for *Ghost of Frankenstein*

The archetype known as the **Shadow** represents the energy of the dark side, the unexpressed, unrealized, or rejected aspects of something. Often it's the home of the suppressed monsters of our inner world. Shadows can be all the things we don't like about ourselves, all the dark secrets we can't admit, even to ourselves. The qualities we have renounced and tried to root out still lurk within, operating in the Shadow world of the unconscious. The Shadow can also shelter positive qualities that are in hiding or that we have rejected for some reason.

The negative face of the Shadow in stories is projected onto characters called villains, antagonists, or enemies. Villains and enemies are usually dedicated to the death, destruction, or defeat of the hero. Antagonists may not be quite so hostile — they may be Allies who are after the same goal but who disagree with the hero's tactics. Antagonists and heroes in conflict are like horses in a team pulling in different directions, while villains and heroes in conflict are like trains on a head-on collision course.

PSYCHOLOGICAL FUNCTION

The Shadow can represent the power of repressed feelings. Deep trauma or guilt can fester when exiled to the darkness of the unconscious, and emotions hidden or denied can turn into something monstrous that wants to destroy us. If the Threshold Guardian represents neuroses, then the Shadow archetype stands for psychoses that not only hamper us, but threaten to destroy us. The Shadow may simply be that shady part of ourselves that we are always wrestling with in struggles over bad habits and old fears. This energy can be a powerful internal force with a life of its own and its own set of interests and priorities. It can be a destructive force, especially if not acknowledged, confronted, and brought to light.

Thus in dreams, Shadows may appear as monsters, demons, devils, evil aliens, vampires, or other fearsome enemies. Note that many Shadow figures are also shapeshifters, such as vampires and werewolves.

DRAMATIC FUNCTION

The function of the Shadow in drama is to challenge the hero and give her a worthy opponent in the struggle. Shadows create conflict and bring out the best in a hero by putting her in a life-threatening situation. It's often been said that a story is only as good as its villain, because a strong enemy forces a hero to rise to the challenge.

The challenging energy of the Shadow archetype can be expressed in a single character, but it may also be a mask worn at different times by any of the characters. Heroes themselves can manifest a Shadow side. When the protagonist is crippled by doubts or guilt, acts in self-destructive ways, expresses a death wish, gets carried away with his success, abuses his power, or becomes selfish rather than self-sacrificing, the Shadow has overtaken him.

MASK OF THE SHADOW

The Shadow can combine in powerful ways with other archetypes. Like the other archetypes, the Shadow is a **function** or **mask** which can be worn by any character. The primary Mentor of a story may wear the Shadow mask at times. In *An Officer and a Gentleman* the drill sergeant played by Louis Gossett, Jr. wears the masks of both Mentor and Shadow. He is Richard Gere's Mentor and second father, guiding him through the rigorous Navy training. But in terms of the life-and-death heart of the story, Gossett is also a Shadow who is trying to destroy Gere by driving him out of the program. He tests the young man to the limit to find out if he has what it takes, and almost kills him in the process of bringing out the best in him.

Another strong combination of archetypes is found in the fatal Shapeshifter figures discussed earlier. In some stories, the person who starts out as the hero's love interest shifts shape so far that she becomes the Shadow, bent on the hero's destruction. Femmes fatales are often called "shady ladies." This might represent a struggle between a person's male and female sides, or obsession with the opposite sex turned into a psychotic state of mind. Orson Welles created a classic story on this theme in *The Lady from Shanghai,* in which Rita Hayworth dazzles Welles' character, shifts shape, and tries to destroy him.

A Shadow may also wear the masks of other archetypes. Anthony Hopkins' "Hannibal the Cannibal" character from *The Silence of the Lambs* is primarily a Shadow, a projection of the dark side of human nature, but he also functions as a helpful Mentor to Jodie Foster's FBI agent, providing her with information that helps her catch another insane killer.

Shadows may become seductive Shapeshifters to lure the hero into danger. They may function as Tricksters or Heralds, and may even manifest heroic qualities. Villains who fight bravely for their cause or experience a change of heart may even be redeemed and become heroes themselves, like the Beast in *Beauty and the Beast.*

HUMANIZING THE SHADOW

Shadows need not be totally evil or wicked. In fact, it's better if they are humanized by a touch of goodness, or by some admirable quality. The Disney animated cartoons are memorable for their villains, such as Captain Hook in *Peter Pan,* the demon in *Fantasia,* the beautiful but wicked queen from *Snow White,* the glamorous fairy Maleficent in *The Sleeping Beauty,* and Cruelle D'Eville in *One Hundred and One Dalmatians.* They are even more deliciously sinister because of their dashing, powerful, beautiful, or elegant qualities.

Shadows can also be humanized by making them vulnerable. The novelist Graham Greene masterfully makes his villains real, frail people. He often has the hero on the verge of killing a villain, only to discover the poor fellow has a head cold or is reading a letter from his little daughter.

Suddenly the villain is not just a fly to be swatted but a real human being with weaknesses and emotions. Killing such a figure becomes a true moral choice rather than a thoughtless reflex.

It's important to remember in designing stories that most Shadow figures do not think of themselves as villains or enemies. From his point of view, a villain is the hero of his own myth, and the audience's hero is his villain. A dangerous type of villain is "the right man," the person so convinced his cause is just that he will stop at nothing to achieve it. Beware the man who believes the end justifies the means. Hitler's sincere belief that he was right, even heroic, allowed him to order the most villainous atrocities to achieve his aims.

A Shadow may be a character or force external to the hero, or it may be a deeply repressed part of the hero. *Dr. Jekyll and Mr. Hyde* vividly depicts the power of the dark side in a good man's personality.

External Shadows must be vanquished or destroyed by the hero. Shadows of the internal kind may be disempowered like vampires, simply by bringing them out of the Shadows and into the light of consciousness. Some Shadows may even be redeemed and turned into positive forces. One of the most impressive Shadow figures in movie history, Darth Vader of the *Star Wars* series, is revealed in *Return of the Jedi* to be the hero's father. All his wickedness is finally forgiven, making him a benign, ghostly figure, watching over his son. The Terminator also grows from being a killing machine bent on destroying the heroes in *The Terminator* to being a protective Mentor to the heroes in *Terminator 2: Judgment Day.*

Like the other archetypes, Shadows can express positive as well as negative aspects. The Shadow in a person's psyche may be anything that has been suppressed, neglected, or forgotten. The Shadow shelters the healthy, natural feelings we believe we're not supposed to show. But healthy anger or grief, if suppressed in the territory of the Shadow, can turn to harmful energy that strikes out and undermines us in unexpected ways. The Shadow may also be unexplored potential, such as affection, creativity, or psychic ability, that goes unexpressed. "The roads not taken," the possibilities of life that we eliminate by making choices at various stages, may collect in the Shadow, biding their time until brought into the light of consciousness.

The psychological concept of the Shadow archetype is a useful metaphor for understanding villains and antagonists in our stories, as well as for grasping the unexpressed, ignored, or deeply hidden aspects of our heroes.

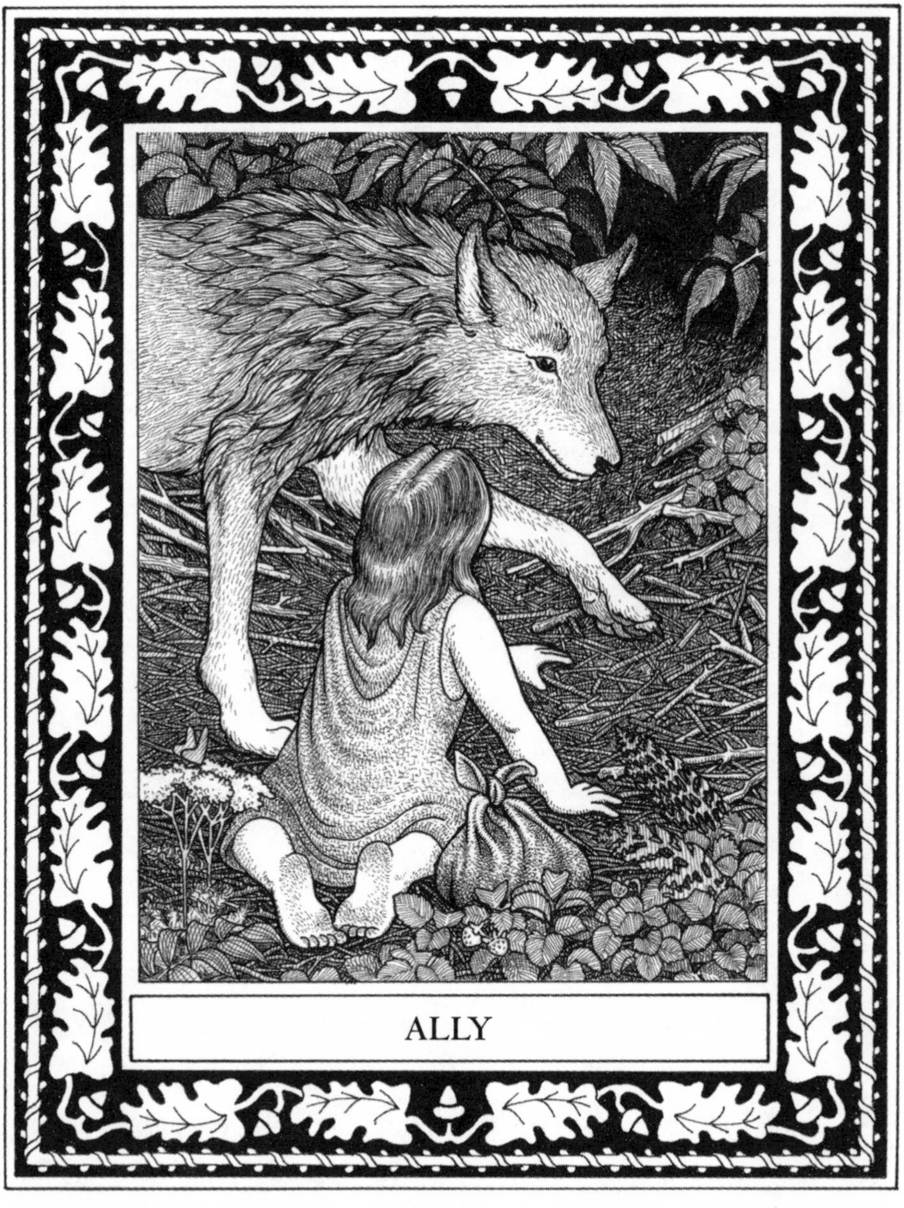

ALLY

ALLY

"From quiet homes and first beginning,
Out to the undiscovered ends,
There's nothing worth the wear of winning
But laughter and the love of friends."
— From "Dedicatory Ode" by Hilaire Belloc

Heroes on their journeys may need someone to travel with them, an **Ally** who can serve a variety of necessary functions, such as companion, sparring partner, conscience, or comic relief. It's useful to have someone to send on errands, to carry messages, to scout locations. It's convenient to have someone for the hero to talk to, to bring out human feelings or reveal important questions in the plot. Allies do many mundane tasks but also serve the important function of humanizing the heroes, adding extra dimensions to their personalities, or challenging them to be more open and balanced.

From the dawn of storytelling, heroes have been paired with friendly figures who fight at their sides, advise and warn them, and sometimes challenge them. In one of the first great stories ever recorded, the tale of Gilgamesh, the Babylonian hero-king is linked by the gods with a mighty wild man of the forest, Enkidu, who at first mistrusts and opposes him, but soon wins his respect and becomes his trusted Ally. Hercules had a valuable ally in his charioteer Iolaus, an Olympic champion who cauterized the necks of the Hydra to keep the heads from growing back after Hercules knocked them off with his club.

MULTIPLE ALLIES

Heroes on great epic journeys may acquire whole ship-loads of Allies, building up a team of adventurers, each with his or her different skill. Odysseus has his shipmates and Jason has his Argonauts. In the British Isles, King Arthur, beginning with his foster-brother Sir Kay, attracts a small army of Allies, the Knights of the Round Table. In France, Charlemagne gathers a similar band of Ally knights from all the nations of his empire who become known as his Paladins. Dorothy picks up a series of Allies on her quest, starting with her animal Ally Toto.

GREAT ALLIES IN LITERATURE

Some great stories have been woven from the relationship between a hero and an Ally. Don Quixote and his reluctant squire Sancho Panza form one such pair, representing two extremes of society and very different ways of viewing the world. Shakespeare often employs Allies like Lear's Fool or Prince Hal's riotous companion Falstaff to explore his heroes more deeply, providing the heroes with comic foils or challenging them to look more deeply into their own souls. Sherlock Holmes and Doctor Watson are another example, where the amazing intellect of Holmes is unfolded for the reader through the admiring eyes of his Ally, Watson, narrator of the tales.

INTRODUCTION TO THE SPECIAL WORLD

Dr. Watson illustrates a useful function for Allies of introducing us to an unfamiliar world. Like Watson, they can ask the questions we would be asking. When the hero is tight-lipped or where it would be awkward and unrealistic for him or her to explain things that are second nature to the hero but very exotic to us, an Ally can do the work of explaining everything as needed. The Ally is sometimes an "audience character," someone who sees the Special World of the story with fresh eyes as we would do if we were there.

Novelist Patrick O'Brian employed this device in his long series of books about the British Navy in the *Napoleonic Wars.* His hero, Jack Aubrey, is similar to heroes of other seafaring books like C. S. Forester's *Horatio Hornblower,* but O'Brian's books are distinguished by the introduction of a strong, life-long Ally for the dashing sea captain, in the character of Stephen

Maturin, a doctor, naturalist, and secret agent who remains a stranger to the ways of the sea despite decades of sailing with his friend. O'Brian provides much comedy with Stephen's lame attempts to understand the jargon of the sailor, but also gives a good reason for the exasperated Jack to explain details of battle and sailing that we, the readers, want to know about.

WESTERN ALLIES: SIDEKICKS

In the rich tradition of Hollywood Western movie serials and TV shows, the Ally is called a "sidekick," a term from early nineteenth-century pickpocket's slang for a side pants pocket. In other words, a sidekick is someone you keep as close to you as your side pocket. Every TV Western hero had to have his Ally, from the Lone Ranger's "faithful Indian companion" Tonto to Wild Bill Hickock's "comical sidekick" Jingles, played by character actor Andy Devine, who also filled the Ally's role in many Western movies going back to *Stagecoach*. The Cisco Kid had his comic foil Pancho, Zorro had his silent but very useful accomplice Bernardo. Walter Brennan played a gallery of sidekicks, notably supporting John Wayne in *Red River*. There he goes beyond the usual roles of Ally as provider of comic relief and someone for the hero to talk to. He also serves as a conscience, muttering every time John Wayne's character makes a moral error and rejoicing when Wayne's surrogate son finally stands up to him.

The relationship with the Ally can be quite complex, sometimes becoming dramatic material in its own right. A vast body of story has been written and filmed about self-righteous Western lawman Wyatt Earp and his unruly, alcoholic, sickly, but very dangerous Ally, Doc Holliday. In some versions of the tale, like director John Sturges' thundering *Gunfight at the O.K. Corral*, the two men are nearly equally matched, and while joining together to fight the external threat of the Clanton gang, they are also two horns of a great debate in American culture, between the rigid moral universe of the Puritans, represented by law-abiding Wyatt Earp, and the wilder rebel side represented by Holliday, a gambler from the old South.

NON-HUMAN ALLIES

Allies need not be human. In some religions of the world, each person is assigned a spirit protector, a lifelong sidekick or Ally. This may be an angel, the guardian angel who is supposed to look out for the person and keep them on the right path, or a minor deity of some kind. The Egyptians taught that Khnemu, the ram-headed builder god, fashioned each person out of clay on his potter's wheel and at the same time made a "ka" or spirit protector in the exact same shape. The ka accompanied each person throughout life and on into the afterlife as long as the person's body was preserved. Its job was to encourage the person to lead a good and useful life.

The Romans also believed that every man had a guardian spirit or Ally, his "genius," and that every woman had a "juno." Originally these were ghosts of the family's distinguished ancestors, but later came to be personal guardian deities. Each person made offerings to the genius or juno on his or her birthday, in return for guidance and protection or a little extra brain power. Not only individuals but also families, households, the Senate, cities, provinces, and entire empires could have such protective supernatural Allies.

The play and movie *Harvey* show a man who relies on an imaginary friend, a kind of psychic Ally who helps him cope with reality. Woody Allen's character in *Play It Again, Sam* conjures up the spirit of Humphrey Bogart's movie persona to guide him through the subtleties of love. *It's a Wonderful Life* depicts a desperate man being helped by an angel Ally.

ANIMAL ALLIES

Animals as Allies are common in the history of storytelling. Goddesses especially are accompanied by animal Allies, like Athena and her companion owl, or Artemis and the deer who is often seen running at her side. The jester of European folktale, Till Eulenspiegel, was always associated with two symbols, an owl and a mirror. His name "Eulenspiegel" means "Owl-Mirror" and suggests that he is wise as an owl and that he holds up a mirror to the hypocrisy of society. The owl became Till's reluctant Ally in the animated film *Till Eulenspiegel.* The heroes of Westerns are often supported by animal Allies like Roy Rogers' elegant steed Trigger and dog Bullet.

ALLIES FROM BEYOND THE GRAVE

Ancient folktales tell of Allies even among the dead. The name for the band "The Grateful Dead" had its origins in a folktale term for the dead who give aid to living people in gratitude for doing something to set their souls at rest, such as paying a debt to give them decent burial. *The Helpful Ghost* is the title of a romance novel by Sheila Rosalind Allen in which a ghost sorts out romantic matters in an old house.

HELPFUL SERVANTS

Another folktale Ally motif is the "helpful servant," a stock character in tales of romance who helps the hero achieve his or her goal by carrying love letters and messages or providing disguises, hideaways, escape routes, and alibis. D'Artagnan's long-suffering valet Planchet is one of the helpful servants in *The Three Musketeers* and Dudley Moore's butler, played by stately John Gielgud, performs the role in *Arthur*. Batman's butler Alfred serves many roles and it should be noted that the Ally function can easily overlap with that of the Mentor, as Allies occasionally step up to the higher function of guiding the hero in spiritual or emotional matters.

PSYCHOLOGICAL FUNCTION

The Ally in dreams and fiction might represent the unexpressed or unused parts of the personality that must be brought into action to do their jobs. In stories, Allies remind us of these under-utilized parts and bring to mind actual friends or relationships that may be helpful to us in the journey of our lives. Allies may represent powerful internal forces that can come to our aid in a spiritual crisis.

MODERN ALLIES

Allies thrive in the modern world of storytelling. Allies in fiction suggest alternate paths for problem-solving and help to round out the personalities of heroes, allowing expression of fear, humor, or ignorance that might not be appropriate for the hero. James Bond relies on his loyal Ally Miss Moneypenny and occasionally needs the help of his American Ally, CIA man Felix Leiter. Comic book writers, aiming to expand the appeal of their stories to younger readers, will often add young Allies for their superheroes, like Batman's ward Robin. Simba, the young lion hero of *The Lion King*, has his comical Allies Timon and Pumbaa. One vision of the future is provided by the *Star Wars* universe where machines, animals, alien beings, and spirits of the dead all can serve as Allies. Increasingly, computer intelligences and robots will be seen as natural Allies as we move on to new journeys into space and other uncharted realms.

TRICKSTER

TRICKSTER

"That makes no sense and so do I."
— Daffy Duck

The **Trickster** archetype embodies the energies of mischief and desire for change. All the characters in stories who are primarily clowns or comical sidekicks express this archetype. The specialized form called the Trickster Hero is the leading figure in many myths and is very popular in folklore and fairy tales.

PSYCHOLOGICAL FUNCTION

Tricksters serve several important psychological functions. They cut big egos down to size, and bring heroes and audiences down to earth. By provoking healthy laughter they help us realize our common bonds, and they point out folly and hypocrisy. Above all, they bring about healthy change and transformation, often by drawing attention to the imbalance or absurdity of a stagnant psychological situation. They are the natural enemies of the status quo. Trickster energy can express itself through impish accidents or slips of the tongue that alert us to the need for change. When we are taking ourselves too seriously, the Trickster part of our personalities may pop up to bring back needed perspective.

DRAMATIC FUNCTION: COMIC RELIEF

In drama, Tricksters serve all these psychological functions, plus the dramatic function of **comic relief**. Unrelieved tension, suspense, and conflict can be emotionally exhausting, and in even the heaviest drama an audience's interest is revived by moments of laughter. An old rule of drama points out the need for balance: **Make 'em cry a lot; let 'em laugh a little.**

Tricksters may be servants or Allies working for the hero or Shadow, or they may be independent agents with their own skewed agendas.

The Tricksters of mythology provide many examples of the workings of this archetype. One of the most colorful is Loki, the Norse god of trickery and deceit. A true Trickster, he serves the other gods as legal counselor and advisor, but also plots their destruction, undermining the status quo. He is fiery in nature, and his darting, elusive energy helps heat up the petrified, frozen energy of the gods, moving them to action and change. He also provides much-needed comic relief in the generally dark Norse myths.

Loki is sometimes a comical sidekick character in stories featuring the gods Odin or Thor as heroes. In other stories he is a hero of sorts, a **Trickster Hero** who survives by his wits against physically stronger gods or giants. At last he turns into a deadly adversary or Shadow, leading the hosts of the dead in a final war against the gods.

TRICKSTER HEROES

Trickster Heroes have bred like rabbits in the folktales and fairy tales of the world. Indeed, some of the most popular Tricksters are rabbit heroes: the Br'er Rabbit of the American South, the Hare of African tales, the many rabbit heroes from Southeast Asia, Persia, India, etc. These stories pit the defenseless but quick-thinking rabbit against much larger and more dangerous enemies: folktale Shadow figures like wolves, hunters, tigers, and bears. Somehow the tiny rabbit always manages to outwit his hungry opponent, who usually suffers painfully from dealing with a Trickster Hero.

The modern version of the rabbit Trickster is of course Bugs Bunny. The Warner Brothers animators made use of folktale plots to pit Bugs against hunters and predators who didn't stand a chance against his quick wits. Other cartoon Tricksters of this type include Warner's Daffy

Duck, Speedy Gonzales, the Roadrunner, and Tweety Bird; Walter Lantz's Woody Woodpecker and Chilly Willy the penguin; and MGM's ubiquitous dog Droopy, who always outwits the befuddled Wolf. Mickey Mouse started as an ideal animal Trickster, although he has matured into a sober master of ceremonies and corporate spokesman.

Native Americans have a particular fondness for Tricksters such as Coyote and Raven. The clown Kachina gods of the Southwest are Tricksters of great power as well as comic ability.

Once in a while it's fun to turn the tables and show that Tricksters themselves can be outwitted. Sometimes a Trickster like the Hare will try to take advantage of a weaker, slower animal like Mr. Tortoise. In folktales and fables such as "The Tortoise and the Hare," the slowest outwits the fastest by dogged persistence or by cooperating with others of its kind to outwit the faster animal.

Tricksters like to stir up trouble for its own sake. Joseph Campbell relates a Nigerian story in which the Trickster god Edshu walks down a road in a hat that's red on one side and blue on the other. When people comment, "Who was that going by in a red hat?" they get into fights with people on the other side of the road who insist the hat was blue. The god takes credit for the trouble, saying, "Spreading strife is my greatest joy."

Tricksters are often **catalyst characters**, who affect the lives of others but are unchanged themselves. Eddie Murphy in *Beverly Hills Cop* displays Trickster energy as he stirs up the existing system without changing much himself.

The heroes of comedy, from Charlie Chaplin to the Marx Brothers to the cast of "In Living Color," are Tricksters who subvert the status quo and make us laugh at ourselves. Heroes of other genres must often put on the Trickster mask in order to outwit a Shadow or get around a Threshold Guardian.

The archetypes are an infinitely flexible language of character. They offer a way to understand what function a character is performing at a given moment in a story. Awareness of the archetypes can help to free writers from stereotyping, by giving their characters greater psychological verity and depth. The archetypes can be used to make characters who are both unique individuals and universal symbols of the qualities that form a complete human being. They can help make our characters and stories psychologically realistic and true to the ancient wisdom of myths.

Now that we've met the denizens of the story world, let's return to the Road of Heroes for a closer look at the twelve stages and how the archetypes play their parts in the Hero's Journey.

BOOK TWO:

STAGES OF THE JOURNEY

THE ORDINARY WORLD

Stage One: THE ORDINARY WORLD

"A beginning is a very delicate time."
— from *Dune*, screenplay by David Lynch, based on the novel by Frank Herbert

In *The Hero with a Thousand Faces*, Joseph Campbell describes the beginning of the typical hero's journey. "A hero ventures forth from the world of common day into a region of supernatural wonder..." In this chapter, we'll explore that "world of common day," the **Ordinary World**, and see how it frames the hero and sets modern-day stories in motion.

The opening of any story, be it myth, fairy tale, screenplay, novel, short story, or comic book, has some special burdens to bear. It must hook the reader or viewer, set the tone of the story, suggest where it's going, and get across a mass of information without slowing the pace. A beginning is, indeed, a delicate time.

A GUIDE TO THE JOURNEY

As a guide through the labyrinth of story, let's imagine ourselves as a tribe of people who live by hunting and gathering, as our ancestors did a hundred thousand years ago, or as people still do in remote parts of the world today. We'll check in with these Seekers at each stage of the hero's journey, and try to put ourselves in their skins.

Look around, sister, brother of the Home Tribe. You can see the people are barely getting by, surviving on a dwindling supply of last season's food. Times are bad and the country all around seems lifeless. The people grow weak before our eyes, but a few of us are filled with restless energy.

Like you. You're uncomfortable, feeling you no longer fit in with this drab, exhausted place. You may not know it, but you're soon to be selected as a hero, to join the select company of the Seekers, those who have always gone out to face the unknown. You'll undertake a journey to restore life and health to the entire Home Tribe, an adventure in which the only sure thing is that you'll be changed. You're uneasy, but there's a thrill running through you. You're poised to break free from this world, ready to enter the world of adventure.

BEFORE THE BEGINNING

Before a story even begins, a storyteller faces creative choices. What's the first thing your audience will experience? The title? The first line of dialogue? The first image? Where in the lives of your characters will the story actually begin? Do you need a prologue or introduction, or should you jump right into the middle of the action? The opening moments are a powerful opportunity to set the tone and create an impression. You can conjure up a mood, an image, or a metaphor that will give the audience a frame of reference to better experience your work. **The mythological approach to story boils down to using metaphors or comparisons to get across your feelings about life.**

The great German stage and film director Max Reinhardt believed that you can create an atmosphere in a theatre well before an audience sits down or the curtain goes up. A carefully selected title can strike a metaphor that intrigues the audience and attunes them to the coming experience. Good promotion can engage them with images and slogans that are metaphors for the world of your story. By controlling music and lighting as the audience enters the space, and consciously directing such details as the attitudes and costumes of the ushers, a specific mood can be created. The audience can be put in the ideal frame of mind for the experience they will share, prepared for comedy, romance, horror, drama, or whatever effect you wish to create.

Oral storytellers begin their tales with ritualized phrases ("Once upon a time") and personalized gestures to get the attention of the audience. These signals can cue the listeners to the funny, sad, or ironic mood of the story they will hear.

Today many elements go into making those first impressions before the book or the movie ticket is bought; the title, the book cover art, publicity and advertising, posters and trailers, and so forth. The story is cooked down to a few symbols or metaphors that begin to put the audience in the right mood for the journey.

TITLE

A title is an important clue to the nature of the story and the writer's attitude. A good title can become a multi-leveled metaphor for the condition of the hero or his world. The title of *The Godfather,* for example, suggests that Don Corleone is both god and father to his people. The graphic design of the logo for the novel and movie lays out another metaphor, the hand of a puppeteer working the strings of an unseen marionette. Is Don Corleone the puppeteer, or is he the puppet of a higher force? Are we all puppets of God, or do we have free will? The metaphoric title and imagery allow many interpretations and help to make the story a coherent design.

OPENING IMAGE

The opening image can be a powerful tool to create mood and suggest where the story will go. It can be a visual metaphor that, in a single shot or scene, conjures up the Special World of Act Two and the conflicts and dualities that will be confronted there. It can suggest the theme, alerting the audience to the issues your characters will face. The opening shot of Clint Eastwood's *Unforgiven* shows a man outside a farmhouse, digging a grave for his wife who has just died. His relationship with his wife and the way she changed him are major themes in the story. The image of a man digging a grave outside his house can be read as an apt metaphor for the plot: The hero leaves home and journeys to the land of death, where he witnesses death, causes death, and almost dies himself. Eastwood the director returns to the same setup at the end of the film, using the image to give a sense of closure as we see the man leave the grave and return to his home.

PROLOGUE

Some stories begin with a prologue section that precedes the main body of the story, perhaps before the introduction of the main characters and their world. The fairy tale of "Rapunzel" begins with a scene before the birth of the hero, and Disney's *Beauty and the Beast* begins with a prologue illustrated in stained glass, giving the backstory of the Beast's enchantment. Myths take place within a context of mythical history that goes back to the Creation, and events leading up to the entrance of the main character may have to be portrayed first. Shakespeare and the Greeks often gave their plays a prologue, spoken by a narrator or a chorus, to set the tone and give the context of the drama. Shakespeare's *Henry V* begins with an eloquent passage, intoned by a Chorus character who invites us to use our "imaginary forces" to create the kings, horses, and armies of his story. "Admit me Chorus to this history," he requests, "Who, prologue-like, your humble patience pray/Gently to hear, kindly to judge, our play."

A prologue can serve several useful functions. It may give an essential piece of backstory, cue the audience to what kind of movie or story this is going to be, or start the story with a bang and let the audience settle into their seats. In *Close Encounters of the Third Kind,* a prologue shows the discovery of a mysterious squadron of World War II airplanes, perfectly preserved in the desert. This precedes the introduction of the hero, Roy Neary, and his world. It serves to intrigue the audience with a host of riddles, and gives a foretaste of the thrills and wonder ahead.

In *The Last Boy Scout* a prologue shows a pro football player going berserk and shooting his teammates under the pressure of drugs and gambling. The sequence precedes the first appearance of the hero and intrigues or "hooks" the audience. It signals that this is going to be an exciting action story involving life-and-death matters.

This prologue and the one in *Close Encounters* are a little disorienting. They hint that these movies are going to be about extraordinary events that may strain credibility. In secret societies, an old rule of initiation is: **Disorientation leads to suggestibility**. That's why initiates are often blindfolded and led around in the dark, so they will be more psychologically open to suggestion from the rituals staged by the group. In storytelling, getting the audience a little off-base and upsetting their normal perceptions can put them into a receptive mood. They begin to suspend their disbelief and enter more readily into a Special World of fantasy.

Some prologues introduce the villain or threat of the story before the hero appears. In *Star Wars,* the evil Darth Vader is shown kidnapping Princess Leia before the hero, Luke Skywalker, is introduced in his mundane world. Some detective films begin with a murder before the hero is introduced in his office. Such prologues cue the audience that the balance of a society has been disturbed. A chain of events is set in motion, and the forward drive of the story cannot cease until the wrong has been righted and the balance restored.

A prologue is not necessary or desirable in every case. **The needs of the story will always dictate the best approach to structure.** You may want to begin, as many stories do, by introducing the hero in her normal environment: the "Ordinary World."

THE ORDINARY WORLD

Because so many stories are journeys that take heroes and audiences to Special Worlds, most begin by establishing an Ordinary World as a baseline for comparison. The Special World of the story is only special if we can see it in contrast to a mundane world of everyday affairs from which the hero issues forth. The Ordinary World is the context, home base, and background of the hero.

The Ordinary World in one sense is the place you came from last. In life we pass through a succession of Special Worlds which slowly become ordinary as we get used to them. They evolve from strange, foreign territory to familiar bases from which to launch a drive into the next Special World.

CONTRAST

It's a good idea for writers to make the Ordinary World as different as possible from the Special World, so audience and hero will experience a dramatic change when the threshold is finally crossed. In *The Wizard of Oz* the Ordinary World is depicted in black and white, to make a stunning contrast with the Technicolor Special World of Oz. In the thriller *Dead Again*, the Ordinary World of modern day is shot in color to contrast with the nightmarish black-and-white Special World of the 1940s flashbacks. *City Slickers* contrasts the drab, restrictive environment of the city with the more lively arena of the West where most of the story takes place.

Compared to the Special World, the Ordinary World may seem boring and calm, but the seeds of excitement and challenge can usually be found there. The hero's problems and conflicts are already present in the Ordinary World, waiting to be activated.

FORESHADOWING: A MODEL OF THE SPECIAL WORLD

Writers often use the Ordinary World section to create a small model of the Special World, **foreshadowing** its battles and moral dilemmas. In *The Wizard of Oz,* Dorothy clashes with ornery Miss Gulch and is rescued from danger by three farmhands. These early scenes foretell Dorothy's battles with the Witch and her rescue by the Tin Woodsman, Cowardly Lion, and Scarecrow.

Romancing the Stone begins with a clever foreshadowing technique. The first thing the audience sees is an elaborate fantasy of a noble heroine battling sleazy villains and finally riding off to romance with a comically idealized hero. The scene is a model of the Special World Joan Wilder will encounter in the second act. The fantasy is revealed to be the conclusion of Joan Wilder's romance novel, which she is writing in her cluttered New York apartment. The opening fantasy sequence serves a dual purpose. It tells us a great deal about Joan Wilder and her unrealistic notions of romance, and also predicts the problems and situations she will face in the Special World of Act Two, when she encounters real villains and a less than ideal man. Foreshadowing can help unify a story into a rhythmic or poetic design.

RAISING THE DRAMATIC QUESTION

Another important function of the Ordinary World is to suggest the dramatic question of the story. **Every good story poses a series of questions about the hero.** Will she achieve the goal, overcome her flaw, learn the lesson she needs to learn? Some questions relate primarily to the action or plot. Will Dorothy get home from Oz? Will E.T. get home to his planet? Will the hero get the gold, win the game, beat the villains?

Other questions are dramatic and have to do with the hero's emotions and personality. Will Patrick Swayze's character in *Ghost* learn to express love? In *Pretty Woman,* will the uptight businessman Edward learn from the prostitute Vivian how to relax and enjoy life? The action questions may propel the plot, but the dramatic questions hook the audience and involve them with the emotions of the characters.

INNER AND OUTER PROBLEMS

Every hero needs both an inner and an outer problem. In developing fairy tales for Disney Feature Animation, we often find that writers can give the heroes a good outer problem: Can the princess manage to break an enchantment on her father who has been turned to stone? Can the hero get to the top of a glass mountain and win a princess' hand in marriage? Can Gretel rescue Hansel from the Witch? But sometimes writers neglect to give the characters a compelling inner problem to solve as well.

Characters without inner challenges seem flat and uninvolving, however heroically they may act. They need an inner problem, a personality flaw or a moral dilemma to work out. They need to learn something in the course of the story: how to get along with others, how to trust themselves, how to see beyond outward appearances. Audiences love to see characters learning, growing, and dealing with the inner and outer challenges of life.

MAKING AN ENTRANCE

How the audience first experiences your hero is another important condition you control as a storyteller. What is he doing the first time we see him, when he makes his **entrance**? What is he wearing, who is around him, and how do they react to him? What is his attitude, emotion, and goal at the moment? Does he enter alone or join a group, or is he already on stage when the story begins? Does he narrate the story, is it told through the eyes of another character, or is it seen from the objective eye of conventional narrative?

Every actor likes to "make an entrance," an important part of building a character's relationship with the audience. Even if a character is written as already on stage when the lights come up, the actor will often make an entrance out of it by how she first impresses an audience with her appearance and behavior. As writers we can give our heroes an entrance by thinking about how the audience first experiences them. What are they doing, saying, feeling? What is their context when we first see them? Are they at peace or in turmoil? Are they at full emotional power or are they holding back for a burst of expression later?

Most important is: What is the character *doing* at the moment of entrance? The character's first action is a wonderful opportunity to speak volumes about his attitude, emotional state, background, strengths, and problems. The first action should be a model of the hero's characteristic attitude and the future problems or solutions that will result. The first behavior we see should be characteristic. It should define and reveal character, unless your intent is to mislead the audience and conceal the character's true nature.

Tom Sawyer makes a vivid entrance into our imaginations because Samuel Clemens has painted such a character-revealing first look at his Missouri boy hero. The first time we see Tom he is performing a characteristic action, turning the rotten job of whitewashing the fence into a wonderful mind game. Tom is a con artist, but the con is thoroughly enjoyed by his victims. Tom's character is revealed through all his actions, but most clearly and definitively in his entrance, which defines his attitude toward life.

Actors stepping onto a stage and writers introducing a character are also trying to *entrance* the audience, or produce in them a trance-like state of identification and recognition. One of the magic powers of writing is its ability to lure each member of the audience into projecting a part of their ego into the character on the page, screen, or stage.

As a writer you can build up an atmosphere of anticipation or provide information about an important character by having other characters talk about her before she shows up. But more important and memorable will be her own first action upon entering the story — her entrance.

INTRODUCING THE HERO TO THE AUDIENCE

Another important function of the Ordinary World is to **introduce** the hero to the audience. Like a social introduction, the Ordinary World establishes a bond between people and points out some common interests so that a dialogue can begin. In some way we should recognize that the hero is like us. In a very real sense, a story invites us to step into the hero's shoes, to see the world through his eyes. As if by magic we project part of our consciousness into the hero. To make this magic work you must establish a strong bond of sympathy or common interest between the hero and the audience.

This is not to say that heroes must always be good or wholly sympathetic. They don't even have to be likeable, but they must be *relatable,* a word used by movie executives to describe the quality of compassion and understanding that an audience must have for a hero. Even if the hero is underhanded or despicable, we can still understand her plight and imagine ourselves behaving in much the same way, given the same background, circumstances, and motivation.

IDENTIFICATION

The opening scenes should create an **identification** between audience and hero, a sense that they are equals in some ways.

How do you achieve this? Create identification by giving heroes universal goals, drives, desires, or needs. We can all relate to basic drives such as the need for recognition, affection, acceptance, or understanding. The screenwriter Waldo Salt, speaking of his script for *Midnight Cowboy,* said that his hero Joe Buck was driven by a universal human need to be touched. Even though Joe Buck engaged in some pretty sleazy behavior, we sympathize with his need because we have all experienced it at some time. Identification with universal needs establishes a bond between audience and hero.

THE HERO'S LACK

Fairy tale heroes have a common denominator, a quality that unites them across boundaries of culture, geography, and time. They are **lacking** something, or something is taken away from them. Often they have just lost a family member. A mother or father has died, or a brother or sister has been kidnapped. Fairy tales are about searching for completeness and striving for wholeness, and often it's a subtraction from the family unit that sets the story in motion. The need to fill in the missing piece drives the story toward the final perfection of "They lived happily ever after."

Many movies begin by showing an incomplete hero or family. Joan Wilder in *Romancing the Stone* and Roger Thornhill in *North by Northwest* are incomplete because they need ideal mates to balance their lives. Fay Wray's character in *King Kong* is an orphan who knows only "There's supposed to be an uncle someplace."

These missing elements help to create sympathy for the hero, and draw the audience into desiring her eventual wholeness. Audiences abhor the vacuum created by a missing piece in a character.

Other stories show the hero as essentially complete until a close friend or relative is kidnapped or killed in the first act, setting in motion a story of rescue or revenge. John Ford's *The Searchers* begins with news that a young woman has been kidnapped by Indians, launching a classic saga of search and rescue.

Sometimes the hero's family may be complete, but something is missing from the hero's personality — a quality such as compassion, forgiveness, or the ability to express love. The hero of *Ghost* is unable to say "I love you" at the beginning of the film. Only after he has run the course of the journey from life to death is he able to say those magic words.

It can be very effective to show that a hero is unable to perform some simple task at the beginning of the story. In *Ordinary People* the young hero Conrad is unable to eat French toast his mother has prepared for him. It signifies, in symbolic language, his inability to accept being loved and cared for, because of the terrible guilt he bears over the accidental death of his brother. It's only after he undertakes an emotional hero's journey, and relives and processes the death through therapy, that he is able to accept love. At the end of the story Conrad's girlfriend offers to make him breakfast, and this time he finds he has an appetite. In symbolic language, his appetite for life has returned.

TRAGIC FLAWS

The Greek theory of tragedy, expressed twenty-four centuries ago by Aristotle, describes a common fault of tragic heroes. They may possess many admirable qualities, but among them is one tragic flaw or *hamartia* that puts them at odds with their destiny, their fellow men, or the gods. Ultimately it leads to their destruction.

Most commonly this tragic flaw was a kind of pride or arrogance called *hubris*. Tragic heroes are often superior people with extraordinary powers but they tend to see themselves as equal to or better than the gods. They ignore fair warnings or defy the local moral codes, thinking they are above the laws of gods and men. This fatal arrogance inevitably unleashes a force called *Nemesis,* originally a goddess of retribution. Her job was to set things back into balance, usually by bringing about the destruction of the tragic hero.

Every well-rounded hero has a trace of this tragic flaw, some weakness or fault that makes him thoroughly human and real. Perfect, flawless heroes aren't very interesting, and are hard to relate to. Even Superman has weak spots which humanize him and make him sympathetic: his vulnerability to Kryptonite, his inability to see through lead, and his secret identity which is always in danger of being exposed.

WOUNDED HEROES

Sometimes a hero may seem to be well-adjusted and in control, but that control masks a deep psychic **wound**. Most of us have some old pain or hurt that we don't think about all the time, but which is always vulnerable on some level of awareness. These wounds of rejection, betrayal, or disappointment are personal echoes of a universal pain that everyone has suffered from: the pain of the child's physical and emotional separation from its mother. In a larger sense, we all bear the wound of separation from God or the womb of existence — that place from which we are born and to which we will return when we die. Like Adam and Eve cast out of Eden, we are forever separate from our source, isolated and wounded.

To humanize a hero or any character, give her a wound, a visible, physical injury or a deep emotional wound. The hero of *Lethal Weapon,* played by Mel Gibson, is sympathetic because he has lost a loved one. The wound makes him edgy, suicidal, unpredictable, and interesting. Your hero's wounds and scars mark the areas in which he is guarded, defensive, weak, and vulnerable. A hero may also be extra-strong in some areas as a defense for the wounded parts.

The movie *The Fisher King* is a thorough study of two men and their psychic wounds. The story is inspired by the Arthurian legend of the Holy Grail and the Fisher King, whose physical wound symbolized a wound of the spirit. This legend tells of a king who was wounded in the thigh and was therefore unable to rule his land or find any pleasure in life. Under his weakened kingship, the land was dying, and only the powerful spiritual magic of the Holy Grail could revive it. The quest by the Knights of the Round Table to find the Grail is the great adventure to restore health and wholeness to a system that has been almost fatally wounded. The Jungian psychologist Robert A. Johnson brings insight to the meaning of the Fisher King wound in his book on masculine psychology, *He.*

The Hero Refuses a Call of the heart with tragic consequences.

Another wounded, almost tragic hero is Tom Dunson, played by John Wayne in the classic Western *Red River*. Dunson makes a terrible moral error early in his career as a cattleman, by choosing to value his mission more than his love, and following his head rather than his heart. This choice leads to the death of his lover, and for the rest of the story he bears the psychic scars of that wound. His suppressed guilt makes him more and more harsh, autocratic, and judgmental, and almost brings him and his adopted son to destruction before the wound is healed by letting love back into his life.

A hero's wounds may not be visible. People put a great deal of energy into protecting and hiding these weak and vulnerable spots. But in a fully developed character they will be apparent in the areas where she is touchy, defensive, or a little too confident. The wound may never be openly expressed to the audience — it can be a secret between the writer and the character. But it will help give the hero a sense of personal history and realism, for we all bear some scars from past humiliations, rejections, disappointments, abandonments, and failures. Many stories are about the journey to heal a wound and to restore a missing piece to a broken psyche.

ESTABLISHING WHAT'S AT STAKE

For readers and viewers to be involved in the adventure, to care about the hero, they have to know at an early stage exactly what's at stake. In other words, what does the hero stand to gain or lose in the adventure? What will be the consequences for the hero, society, and the world if the hero succeeds or fails?

Myths and fairy tales are good models for establishing what's at stake. They often set up a threatening condition that makes the stakes of the game very clear. Perhaps the hero must pass a series of tests or his head will be cut off. The Greek hero Perseus, portrayed in the movie *Clash of the Titans*, must undergo many ordeals or his beloved princess Andromeda will be devoured by a sea monster. Other tales put family members in jeopardy like the father who is threatened in *Beauty and the Beast*. The hero Belle has a strong motivation to put herself in a dangerous position at the mercy of the Beast. Her father will languish and die unless she does the Beast's bidding. The stakes are high and clear.

Scripts often fail because the stakes simply aren't high enough. A story in which the hero will only be slightly embarrassed or inconvenienced if he fails is likely to get the "So what?" reaction from readers. Make sure the stakes are high — life and death, big money, or the hero's very soul.

BACKSTORY AND EXPOSITION

The Ordinary World is the most appropriate place to deal with exposition and backstory. **Backstory** is all the relevant information about a character's history and background — what got her to the situation at the beginning of the story. **Exposition** is the art of gracefully revealing the backstory and any other pertinent information about the plot: the hero's social class, upbringing, habits, experiences, as well as the prevailing social conditions and opposing forces that may affect the hero. Exposition is everything the audience needs to know to understand the hero and the story. Backstory and exposition are among the hardest writing skills to master. Clumsy exposition tends to stop the story cold. Blunt exposition draws attention to itself, giving the backstory in the form of a voiceover or a "Harry the Explainer" character who comes on solely for the purpose of telling the audience what the author wants them to know. It's usually better to put the audience right into the action and let them figure things out as the story unfolds.

The audience will feel more involved if they have to work a little to piece together the backstory from visual clues or exposition blurted out while characters are emotionally upset or on the run. Backstory can be doled out gradually over the course of the story or yielded up grudgingly. Much is revealed by what people **don't** do or say.

Many dramas are about secrets being slowly and painfully revealed. Layer by layer the defenses protecting a hurtful secret are torn away. This makes the audience participants in a detective story, an emotional puzzle.

THEME

The Ordinary World is the place to state the theme of your story. What is the story really about? If you had to boil down its essence to a single word or phrase, what would it be? What single idea or quality is it about? Love? Trust? Betrayal? Vanity? Prejudice? Greed? Madness? Ambition? Friendship? What are you trying to say? Is your theme "Love conquers all," "You can't cheat an honest man," "We must work together to survive," or "Money is the root of all evil"?

Theme, a word derived from Greek, is close in meaning to the Latin-based **premise**. Both words mean "something set before," something laid out in advance that helps determine a future course. The theme of a story is an underlying statement or assumption about an aspect of life. Usually it's set out somewhere in Act One, in the Ordinary World. It could be an offhand remark by one of the characters, expressing a belief which is then rigorously tested in the course of the story. The real theme of the piece may not emerge or announce itself until you have worked with the story for a while, but sooner or later you must become aware of it. Knowing the theme is essential to making the final choices in dialogue, action, and set dressing that turn a story into a coherent design. In a good story, everything is related somehow to the theme, and the Ordinary World is the place to make the first statement of the main idea.

THE WIZARD OF OZ

I refer often to *The Wizard of Oz* because it's a classic movie that most people have seen, and because it's a fairly typical hero's journey with clearly delineated stages. It also has a surprising degree of psychological depth, and can be read not only as a fairy story of a little girl trying to get back home, but also as a metaphor of a personality trying to become complete.

> *As the story unfolds, the hero Dorothy has a clear outer problem. Her dog Toto has dug up Miss Gulch's flowerbed and Dorothy is in trouble. She tries to elicit sympathy for her problem from her aunt and uncle, but they are too busy preparing for a coming storm. Like the heroes of myth and legend before her, Dorothy is restless, out of place, and doesn't know where to light.*
>
> *Dorothy also has a clear inner problem. She doesn't fit in anymore, she doesn't feel "at home." Like the incomplete heroes of fairy tales, she has a big piece missing from her life — her parents are dead. She doesn't yet know it, but she's about to set out on a quest for completion: not through a marriage and the beginning of a new ideal family, but through meeting a series of magical forces that represent parts of a complete and perfect personality.*
>
> *To foreshadow these meetings, Dorothy encounters a small model of the Special World adventure. Bored, she tries to balance on the thin railing of a pig pen, and falls in. Three friendly farmhands rescue her from danger, predicting the roles the same actors will play in the Special World. The scene says, in the language of symbol, that Dorothy has been walking a tightrope between warring sides of her personality, and sooner or later she will need all the help she can get, from every part of her being, to survive the inevitable fall into conflict.*

Heroes may have no obvious missing piece, flaw, or wound. They may merely be restless, uneasy, and out of sync with their environment or culture. They may have been getting by, trying to adjust to unhealthy conditions by using various coping mechanisms or crutches such as emotional or chemical dependencies. They may have deluded themselves that everything is all right. But sooner or later, some new force enters the story to make it clear they can no longer mark time. That new energy is the Call to Adventure.

QUESTIONING THE JOURNEY

1. What is the Ordinary World of *Big*? *Fatal Attraction*? *The Fisher King*? Look at a film, play, or story of your choice. How does the author introduce the hero? Reveal character? Give exposition? Suggest the theme? Does the author use an image to foreshadow or suggest where the story is going?

2. In your own writing, how well do you know your hero? Do a complete biographical sketch, specifying personal history, physical description, education, family background, job experiences, romances, dislikes and prejudices, preferences in food, clothes, hair, cars, etc.

3. Do a timeline, specifying what the character was doing and where he was at every stage of life. Find out what was going on in the world at these times. What ideas, events, and people have been the greatest influences on your character?

4. How is your story's hero incomplete? Get specific about the character's needs, desires, goals, wounds, fantasies, wishes, flaws, quirks, regrets, defenses, weaknesses, and neuroses. What single characteristic could lead to your hero's destruction or downfall? What single characteristic could save her? Does your character have both an inner and an outer problem? Does she have a universal human need? How does she characteristically go about getting that need met?

5. Make a list of all the points of backstory and exposition that the audience needs to know to get the story started. How can those be revealed indirectly, visually, on the run, or through conflict?

6. Do different cultures need different kinds of stories? Do men and women need different kinds of stories? How are the heroic journeys of men and women different?

THE CALL TO ADVENTURE

STAGE TWO: THE CALL TO ADVENTURE

"It's money and adventure and fame! It's the thrill of a lifetime!...and a long sea voyage that starts at six o'clock tomorrow!"

— from *King Kong,* screenplay by James Creelman and Ruth Rose

The Ordinary World of most heroes is a static but unstable condition. The seeds of change and growth are planted, and it takes only a little new energy to germinate them. That new energy, symbolized in countless ways in myths and fairy tales, is what Joseph Campbell termed the **Call to Adventure.**

Trouble shadows the Home Tribe. You hear its call, in the grumbling of our stomachs and the cries of our hungry children. The land for miles around is tapped out and barren and clearly someone must go out beyond the familiar territory. That unknown land is strange and fills us with fear, but pressure mounts to do something, to take some risks, so that life can continue.

A figure emerges from the campfire smoke, an elder of the Home Tribe, pointing to you. Yes, you have been chosen as a Seeker and called to begin a new quest. You'll venture your life so that the greater life of the Home Tribe may go on.

GET THE STORY ROLLING

Various theories of screenwriting acknowledge the Call to Adventure by other names such as the inciting or initiating incident, the catalyst, or the trigger. All agree that some event is necessary to get a story rolling, once the work of introducing the main character is done.

The Call to Adventure may come in the form of a message or a messenger. It may be a new event like a declaration of war, or the arrival of a telegram reporting that the outlaws have just been released from prison and will be in town on the noon train to gun down the sheriff. Serving a writ or warrant and issuing a summons are ways of giving Calls in legal proceedings.

The Call may simply be a stirring within the hero, a messenger from the unconscious, bearing news that it's time for change. These signals sometimes come in the form of dreams, fantasies, or visions. Roy Neary in *Close Encounters of the Third Kind* gets his Call in the form of haunting images of Devil's Tower drifting up from his subconscious. Prophetic or disturbing dreams help us prepare for a new stage of growth by giving us metaphors that reflect the emotional and spiritual changes to come.

The hero may just get fed up with things as they are. An uncomfortable situation builds up until that one last straw sends him on the adventure. Joe Buck in *Midnight Cowboy* has simply had enough of washing dishes in a diner and feels the Call building up inside him to hit the road of adventure. In a deeper sense, his universal human need is driving him, but it takes that one last miserable day in the diner to push him over the edge.

SYNCHRONICITY

A string of accidents or coincidences may be the message that calls a hero to adventure. This is the mysterious force of **synchronicity** which C. G. Jung explored in his writings. The coincidental occurrence of words, ideas, or events can take on meaning and draw attention to the need for action and change. Many thrillers such as Hitchcock's *Strangers on a Train* get rolling because an accident throws two people together as if by the hand of fate.

TEMPTATION

The Call to Adventure may summon a hero with **temptation**, such as the allure of an exotic travel poster or the sight of a potential lover. It could be the glint of gold, the rumor of treasure, the siren song of ambition. In the Arthurian legend of Percival (aka Parsifal), the innocent young hero is summoned to adventure by the sight of five magnificent knights in armor, riding off on some quest. Percival has never seen such creatures, and is stirred to follow them. He is compelled to find out what they are, not realizing it is his destiny to soon become one of them.

HERALDS OF CHANGE

The Call to Adventure is often delivered by a character in a story who manifests the archetype of the Herald. A character performing the function of Herald may be positive, negative, or neutral, but will always serve to get the story rolling by presenting the hero with an invitation or challenge to face the unknown. In some stories the Herald is also a Mentor for the hero, a wise guide who has the hero's best interests at heart. In others the Herald is an enemy, flinging a gauntlet of challenge in the hero's face or tempting the hero into danger.

Initially heroes often have trouble distinguishing whether a Enemy or an Ally lies behind the Herald's mask. Many a hero has mistaken a well-meaning mentor's Call for that of an enemy, or misinterpreted the overtures of a villain as a friendly invitation to an enjoyable adventure. In the thriller and film noir genres, writers may deliberately obscure the reality of the Call. Shadowy figures may make ambiguous offers, and heroes must use every skill to interpret them correctly.

Often heroes are unaware there is anything wrong with their Ordinary World and don't see any need for change. They may be in a state of denial. They have been just barely getting by, using an arsenal of crutches, addictions, and defense mechanisms. The job of the Herald is to kick away these supports, announcing that the world of the hero is unstable and must be put back into healthy balance by action, by taking risks, by undertaking the adventure.

RECONNAISSANCE

The Russian fairy-tale scholar Vladimir Propp identified a common early phase in a story, called **reconnaissance**. A villain makes a survey of the hero's territory, perhaps asking around the neighborhood if there are any children living there, or seeking information about the hero. This information-gathering can be a Call to Adventure, alerting the audience and the hero that something is afoot and the struggle is about to begin.

DISORIENTATION AND DISCOMFORT

The Call to Adventure can often be unsettling and disorienting to the hero. Heralds sometimes sneak up on heroes, appearing in one guise to gain a hero's confidence and then shifting shape to deliver the Call. Alfred Hitchcock provides a potent example in *Notorious*. Here the hero is playgirl Ingrid Bergman, whose father has been sentenced as a Nazi spy. The Call to Adventure comes from a Herald in the form of Cary Grant, who plays an American agent trying to enlist her aid in infiltrating a Nazi spy ring.

First he charms his way into her life by pretending to be a playboy interested only in booze, fast cars, and her. But after she accidentally discovers he's a "copper," he shifts to the mask of Herald to deliver a deeply challenging Call to Adventure.

Bergman wakes up in bed, hung over from their night of partying. Grant, standing in the doorway, orders her to drink a bubbly bromide to settle her stomach. It doesn't taste good but he makes her drink it anyway. It symbolizes the new energy of the adventure, which tastes like poison compared to the addictions she's been used to, but which ultimately will be good medicine for her.

In this scene Grant leans in a doorway, silhouetted like some dark angel. From Bergman's point of view, this Herald could be an angel or a devil. The devilish possibility is suggested by his name, revealed for the first time as "Devlin." As he advances into the room to deliver the Call to Adventure, Hitchcock follows him in a dizzying point-of-view shot that reflects the hung-over state of the hero, Bergman, as she lies in bed. Grant seems to walk on the ceiling. In the symbolic language of film the shot expresses his change of position from playboy to Herald, and its disorienting effect on the hero. Grant gives the Call, a patriotic invitation to infiltrate a Nazi spy ring. As it is delivered, Grant is seen right side up and in full light for the first time, representing the Call's sobering effect on Bergman's character.

As they talk, a crown-like, artificial hairpiece slides from Bergman's head, showing that her fairy tale existence as a deluded, addicted princess must now come to an end. Simultaneously on the soundtrack can be heard the distant call of a train leaving town, suggesting the beginning of a long journey. In this sequence Hitchcock has used every symbolic element at his command to signal that a major threshold of change is approaching. The Call to Adventure is disorienting and distasteful to the hero, but necessary for her growth.

LACK OR NEED

A Call to Adventure may come in the form of a loss or subtraction from the hero's life in the Ordinary World. The adventure of the movie *Quest for Fire* is set in motion when a Stone Age tribe's last scrap of fire, preserved in a bone fire-cage, is extinguished. Members of the tribe begin to die of cold and hunger because of this loss. The hero receives his Call to Adventure when one of the women puts the fire-cage in front of him, signalling without words that the loss must be made up by undertaking the adventure.

The Call could be the kidnapping of a loved one or the loss of anything precious, such as health, security, or love.

NO MORE OPTIONS

In some stories, the Call to Adventure may be the hero simply running out of options. The coping mechanisms no longer work, other people get fed up with the hero, or the hero is placed in increasingly dire straits until the only way left is to jump into the adventure. In *Sister Act,* Whoopi Goldberg's character witnesses a mob murder and has to go into hiding as a nun. Her options are limited — pretend to be a nun or die. Other heroes don't even get that much choice — they are simply "shanghaied" into adventure, conked on the head to wake up far out at sea, committed to adventure whether they like it or not.

WARNINGS FOR TRAGIC HEROES

Not all Calls to Adventure are positive summonses to high adventure. They may also be dire warnings of doom for tragic heroes. In Shakespeare's *Julius Caesar,* a character cries out the warning, "Beware the Ides of March." In *Moby Dick,* the crew is warned by a crazy old man that their adventure will turn into a disaster.

MORE THAN ONE CALL: CALL WAITING

Since many stories operate on more than one level, a story can have more than one Call to Adventure. A sprawling epic such as *Red River* has a need for several scenes of this type. John Wayne's character Tom Dunson receives a Call of the heart, when his lover urges him to stay with her or take her with him on his quest. Dunson himself issues another Call to physical adventure when he invites his cowboys to join him on the first great cattle drive after the Civil War.

Romancing the Stone issues a complex Call to Adventure to its hero Joan Wilder when she receives a phone call from her sister who has been kidnapped by thugs in Colombia. The simple Call of physical adventure is set up by the need to rescue the sister, but another Call is being made on a deeper level in this scene. Joan opens an envelope which her sister's husband has mailed to her and finds a map to the treasure mine of *El Corazon*, "The Heart," suggesting that Joan is also being called to an adventure of the heart.

THE WIZARD OF OZ

> *Dorothy's vague feelings of unease crystallize when Miss Gulch arrives and spitefully takes away Toto. A conflict is set up between two sides struggling for control of Dorothy's soul. A repressive Shadow energy is trying to bottle up the good-natured intuitive side. But the instinctive Toto escapes. Dorothy follows her instincts, which are issuing her a Call to Adventure, and runs away from home. She feels painted into a corner by a lack of sympathy from Aunt Em, her surrogate mother, who has scolded her. She sets out to respond to the Call, under a sky churning with the clouds of change.*

The Call to Adventure is a process of selection. An unstable situation arises in a society and someone volunteers or is chosen to take responsibility. Reluctant heroes have to be called repeatedly as they try to avoid responsibility. More willing heroes answer to inner calls and need no external urging. They have selected themselves for adventure. These gung-

gung-ho heroes are rare, and most heroes must be prodded, cajoled, wheedled, tempted, or shanghaied into adventure. Most heroes put up a good fight and entertain us by their efforts to escape the Call to Adventure. These struggles are the work of the reluctant hero or as Campbell called it, the Refusal of the Call.

QUESTIONING THE JOURNEY

1. What is the Call to Adventure in *Citizen Kane*? *High Noon*? *Fatal Attraction*? *Basic Instinct*? *Moby Dick*? Who or what delivers the Call? What archetypes are manifested by the deliverer?

2. What Calls to Adventure have you received, and how did you respond to them? Have you ever had to deliver a Call to Adventure to someone else?

3. Can a story exist without some kind of Call to Adventure? Can you think of stories that don't have a Call?

4. In your own story, would it make a difference if the Call were moved to another point in the script? How long can you delay the Call and is this desirable?

5. What is the ideal place for the Call? Can you do without it?

6. Have you found an interesting way to present the Call or twist it around so it's not a cliche?

7. Your story may require a succession of Calls. Who is being called to what level of adventure?

Stage Three: REFUSAL OF THE CALL

"You're not cut out for this, Joan, and you know it."
— from *Romancing the Stone*, screenplay by Diane Thomas

The problem of the hero now becomes how to respond to the Call to Adventure. Put yourself in the hero's shoes and you can see that it's a difficult passage. You're being asked to say yes to a great unknown, to an adventure that will be exciting but also dangerous and even life-threatening. It wouldn't be a real adventure otherwise. You stand at a threshold of fear, and an understandable reaction would be to hesitate or even refuse the Call, at least temporarily.

Gather your gear, fellow Seeker. Think ahead to possible dangers, and reflect on past disasters. The specter of the unknown walks among us, halting our progress at the threshold. Some of us turn down the quest, some hesitate, some are tugged at by families who fear for our lives and don't want us to go. You hear people mutter that the journey is foolhardy, doomed from the start. You feel fear constricting your breathing and making your heart race. Should you stay with the Home Tribe, and let others risk their necks in the quest? Are you cut out to be a Seeker?

This halt on the road before the journey has really started serves an important dramatic function of signalling the audience that the adventure is risky. It's not a frivolous undertaking but a danger-filled, high-stakes gamble in which the hero might lose fortune or life. The pause to weigh the consequences makes the commitment to the adventure a real choice in which the hero, after this period of hesitation or refusal, is willing to stake her life against the possibility of winning the goal. It also forces the hero to examine the quest carefully and perhaps redefine its objectives.

AVOIDANCE

It's natural for heroes to first react by trying to dodge the adventure. Even Christ, in the Garden of Gethsemane on the eve of the Crucifixion, prayed "Let this cup pass from me." He was simply checking to see if there was any way of avoiding the ordeal. Is this trip really necessary?

Even the most heroic of movie heroes will sometimes hesitate, express reluctance, or flatly refuse the Call. Rambo, Rocky, and innumerable John Wayne characters turn away from the offered adventure at first. A common grounds for Refusal is past experience. Heroes claim to be veterans of past adventures which have taught them the folly of such escapades. You won't catch them getting into the same kind of trouble again. The protest continues until the hero's Refusal is overcome, either by some stronger motivation (such as the death or kidnapping of a friend or relative) which raises the stakes, or by the hero's inborn taste for adventure or sense of honor.

Detectives and lovers may refuse the Call at first, referring to experiences which have made them sadder but wiser. There is charm in seeing a hero's reluctance overcome, and the stiffer the Refusal, the more an audience enjoys seeing it worn down.

EXCUSES

Heroes most commonly Refuse the Call by stating a laundry list of weak excuses. In a transparent attempt to delay facing their inevitable fate, they say they *would* undertake the adventure, if not for a pressing series of engagements. These are temporary roadblocks, usually overcome by the urgency of the quest.

PERSISTENT REFUSAL LEADS TO TRAGEDY

Persistent Refusal of the Call can be disastrous. In the Bible, Lot's wife is turned to a pillar of salt for denying God's Call to leave her home in Sodom and never look back. Looking backward, dwelling in the past, and denying reality are forms of Refusal.

Continued denial of a high Calling is one of the marks of a tragic hero. At the beginning of *Red River,* Tom Dunson refuses a Call to an adventure of the heart and begins a slide into almost certain doom. He continues to refuse Calls to open his heart, and is on the path of a tragic hero. It's only when he finally accepts the Call in Act Three that he is redeemed and spared the tragic hero's fate.

CONFLICTING CALLS

Actually Tom Dunson faces two Calls to Adventure at once. The Call to the heart's adventure comes from his sweetheart, but the one he answers is the Call of his male ego, telling him to strike out alone on a macho path. Heroes may have to choose between conflicting Calls from different levels of adventure. The Refusal of the Call is a time to articulate the hero's difficult choices.

POSITIVE REFUSALS

Refusal of the Call is usually a negative moment in the hero's progress, a dangerous moment in which the adventure might go astray or never get off the ground at all. However, there are some special cases in which refusing the Call is a wise and positive move on the part of the hero. When the Call is a temptation to evil or a summons to disaster, the hero is smart to say no. The Three Little Pigs wisely refused to open the door to the Big Bad Wolf's powerful arguments. *In Death Becomes Her,* Bruce Willis' character receives several powerful Calls to drink a magic potion of immortality. Despite an alluring sales pitch by Isabella Rossellini, he Refuses the Call and saves his own soul.

ARTIST AS HERO

Another special case in which Refusal of the Call can be positive is that of the artist as hero. We writers, poets, painters, and musicians face difficult, contradictory Calls. We must fully immerse ourselves in the world to find the material for our art. But we must also at times withdraw from the world, going alone to actually make the art. Like many heroes of story, we receive conflicting Calls, one from the outer world, one from our own insides, and we must choose or make compromises. To answer a higher Call to express ourselves, we artists may have to refuse the Call of what Joseph Campbell terms "the blandishments of the world."

When you are getting ready to undertake a great adventure, the Ordinary World knows somehow and clings to you. It sings its sweetest, most insistent song, like the Sirens trying to draw Odysseus and his crew onto the rocks. Countless distractions tempt you off track as you begin to work. Odysseus had to stop up the ears of his men with wax so they wouldn't be lured onto the rocks by the Sirens' bewitching song.

However, Odysseus first had his men tie him to the mast, so he could hear the Sirens but would be unable to steer the ship into danger. Artists sometimes ride through life like Odysseus lashed to the mast, with all senses deeply experiencing the song of life, but also voluntarily bound to the ship of their art. They are refusing the powerful Call of the world, in order to follow the wider Call of artistic expression.

WILLING HEROES

While many heroes express fear, reluctance, or refusal at this stage, others don't hesitate or voice any fear. They are **willing heroes** who have accepted or even sought out the Call to Adventure. Propp calls them "seekers" as opposed to "victimized heroes." However, the fear and doubt represented by the Refusal of the Call will find expression even in the stories of willing heroes. Other characters will express the fear, warning the hero and the audience of what may happen on the road ahead.

A willing hero like John Dunbar from *Dances with Wolves* may be past the fear of personal death. He has already sought out death in the first sequence of the movie as he rides suicidally in front of Rebel rifles and is miraculously spared. He seeks out the adventure of the West willingly, without refusal or reluctance. But the danger and harshness of the prairie is made clear to the audience through the fate of other characters who represent Refusal of the Call. One is the mad, pathetic Army officer who gives Dunbar his scribbled "orders." He shows a possible fate for

Dunbar. The frontier is so strange and challenging that it can drive some people insane. The officer has been unable to accept the reality of this world, has retreated into denial and fantasy, and refuses the frontier's Call by shooting himself.

The other character who bears the energy of Refusal is the scroungy wagon driver who escorts Dunbar to his deserted post. He expresses nothing but fear of the Indians and the prairie, and wants Dunbar to Refuse the Call, abandon his enterprise, and return to civilization. The driver ends up being brutally killed by the Indians, showing the audience another possible fate for Dunbar. Though there is no Refusal by the hero himself, the danger of the adventure is acknowledged and dramatized through another character.

THRESHOLD GUARDIANS

Heroes who overcome their fear and commit to an adventure may still be tested by powerful figures who raise the banner of fear and doubt, questioning the hero's very worthiness to be in the game. They are Threshold Guardians, blocking the heroes before the adventure has even begun.

In *Romancing the Stone,* Joan Wilder accepts the Call and is totally committed to the adventure for the sake of her sister in Colombia. However, the moment of fear, the way station of Refusal, is still elaborately acknowledged in a scene with her agent, who wears the fearful mask of a Threshold Guardian. A tough, cynical woman, she forcefully underlines the dangers and tries to talk Joan out of going. Like a witch pronouncing a curse, she declares that Joan is not up to the task of being a hero. Joan even agrees with her, but is now motivated by the danger to her sister. She is committed to the adventure. Though Joan herself does not Refuse the Call, the fear, doubt, and danger have still been made clear to the audience.

Joan's agent demonstrates how a character may switch masks to show aspects of more than one archetype. She appears at first to be a Mentor and friend to Joan, an ally in her profession and her dealings with men. But this Mentor turns into a fierce Threshold Guardian, blocking the way into the adventure with stern warnings. She's like an overprotective parent, not allowing the daughter to learn through her own mistakes. Her function at this point is to test the hero's commitment to the adventure.

This character serves another important function. She poses a dramatic question for the audience. Is Joan truly heroic enough to face and survive the adventure? This doubt is more interesting than knowing that the hero will rise to every occasion. Such questions create emotional suspense for the audience, who watch the hero's progress with uncertainty hanging in the back of their minds. Refusal of the Call often serves to raise such doubts.

It's not unusual for a Mentor to change masks and perform the function of a Threshold Guardian. Some Mentors guide the hero deeper into the adventure; others block the hero's path on an adventure society might not approve of — an illicit, unwise, or dangerous path. Such a Mentor/Threshold Guardian becomes a powerful embodiment of society or culture, warning the hero not to go outside the accepted bounds. In *Beverly Hills Cop,* Eddie Murphy's Detroit police boss stands in his way, orders him off the case, and draws a line which Murphy is not supposed to cross. Of course Murphy does cross the line, immediately.

THE SECRET DOOR

Heroes inevitably violate limits set by Mentors or Threshold Guardians, due to what we might call the Law of the Secret Door. When Belle in *Beauty and the Beast* is told she has the run of the Beast's household, except for one door which she must never enter, we know that she will be compelled at some point to open that secret door. If Pandora is told she must not open the box, she won't rest until she's had a peek inside. If Psyche is told she must never look upon her lover Cupid, she will surely find a way to lay eyes on him. These stories are symbols of human curiosity, the powerful drive to know all the hidden things, all the secrets.

THE WIZARD OF OZ

Dorothy runs away from home and gets as far as the carnival wagon of Professor Marvel, a Wise Old Man whose function, in this incarnation, is to block her at the threshold of a dangerous journey. At this point Dorothy is a willing hero, and it's left for the Professor to express the danger of the road for the audience. With a bit of shamanic magic, he convinces her to return home. He has convinced her to Refuse the Call, for now.

But in effect Professor Marvel is issuing a higher Call to go home, make peace with her embattled feminine energy, reconnect with Aunt Em's love, and deal with her feelings rather than run away from them.

Although Dorothy turns back for the time being, powerful forces have been set in motion in her life. She finds that the frightful power of the tornado, a symbol of the feelings she has stirred up, has driven her loved ones and allies underground, out of reach. No one can hear her. She is alone except for Toto, her intuition. Like many a hero she finds that once started on a journey, she can never go back to the way things were. Ultimately, Refusal is pointless. She has already burned some bridges behind her and must live with the consequences of taking the first step on the Road of Heroes.

Dorothy takes refuge in the empty house, the common dream symbol for an old personality structure. But the whirling forces of change, which she herself has stirred up, come sweeping towards her and no structure can protect against its awesome power.

Refusal may be a subtle moment, perhaps just a word or two of hesitation between receiving and accepting a Call. (Often several stages of the journey may be combined in a single scene. Folklorists call this "conflation.") Refusal may be a single step near the beginning of the journey, or it may be encountered at every step of the way, depending on the nature of the hero.

Refusal of the Call can be an opportunity to redirect the focus of the adventure. An adventure taken on a lark or to escape some unpleasant consequence may be nudged into a deeper adventure of the spirit.

A hero hesitates at the threshold to experience the fear, to let the audience know the formidability of the challenges ahead. But eventually fear is overcome or set aside, often with the help of wise, protective forces or magical gifts, representing the energy of the next stage, Meeting with the Mentor.

QUESTIONING THE JOURNEY

1. How does the hero Refuse the Call in *Fatal Attraction*? *Pretty Woman*? *A League of Their Own*? Is Refusal of the Call or reluctance a necessary stage for every story? For every hero?

2. What are the heroes of your story afraid of? Which are false fears or paranoia? Which are real fears? How are they expressed?

3. In what ways have they refused Calls to Adventure, and what are the consequences of Refusal?

4. If the protagonists are willing heroes, are there characters or forces that make the dangers clear for the audience?

5. Have you refused Calls to Adventure, and how would your life be different if you had accepted them?

6. Have you accepted Calls to Adventure that you wish you had refused?

MEETING WITH THE MENTOR

Stage Four: MEETING WITH THE MENTOR

"She (Athena) assumed the appearance of Mentor
and seemed so like him as to deceive both eye and ear..."
— *The Odyssey* of Homer

Sometimes it's not a bad idea to refuse a Call until you've had time to prepare for the "zone unknown" that lies ahead. In mythology and folklore that preparation might be done with the help of the wise, protective figure of the **Mentor**, whose many services to the hero include protecting, guiding, teaching, testing, training, and providing magical gifts. In his study of Russian folktales, Vladimir Propp calls this character type the "donor" or "provider" because its precise function is to supply the hero with something needed on the journey. Meeting with the Mentor is the stage of the Hero's Journey in which the hero gains the supplies, knowledge, and confidence needed to overcome fear and commence the adventure.

> *You Seekers, fearful at the brink of adventure, consult with the elders of the Home Tribe. Seek out those who have gone before. Learn the secret lore of watering holes, game trails, and berry patches, and what badlands, quicksand, and monsters to avoid. An old one, too feeble to go out again, scratches a map for us in the dirt. The shaman of the tribe presses something into your hand, a magic gift, a potent talisman that will protect us and guide us on the quest. Now we can set out with lighter hearts and greater confidence, for we take with us the collected wisdom of the Home Tribe.*

HEROES AND MENTORS

Movies and stories of all kinds are constantly elaborating the relationship between the two archetypes of hero and Mentor.

The *Karate Kid* films, *The Prime of Miss Jean Brodie,* and *Stand and Deliver* are stories devoted entirely to the process of mentors teaching students. Countless films such as *Red River, Ordinary People, Star Wars,* and *Fried Green Tomatoes* reveal the vital force of Mentors at key moments in the lives of heroes.

SOURCES OF WISDOM

Even if there is no actual character performing the many functions of the Mentor archetype, heroes almost always make contact with some source of wisdom before committing to the adventure. They may seek out the experience of those who have gone before, or they may look inside themselves for wisdom won at great cost in former adventures. Either way, they are smart to consult the map of the adventure, looking for the records, charts, and ship's logs of that territory. It's only prudent for wayfarers to stop and check the map before setting out on the challenging, often disorienting, Road of Heroes.

For the storyteller, Meeting with the Mentor is a stage rich in potential for conflict, involvement, humor, and tragedy. It's based in an emotional relationship, usually between a hero and a Mentor or advisor of some kind, and audiences seem to enjoy relationships in which the wisdom and experience of one generation is passed on to the next. Everyone has had a relationship with a Mentor or role model.

MENTORS IN FOLKLORE AND MYTH

Folklore is filled with descriptions of heroes meeting magical protectors who bestow gifts and guide them on the journey. We read of the elves who help the shoemaker; the animals who help and protect little girls in Russian fairy tales; the seven dwarfs who give Snow White shelter; or Puss-in-Boots, the talking cat who helps his poor master win a kingdom. All are projections of the powerful archetype of the Mentor, helping and guiding the hero.

Heroes of mythology seek the advice and help of the witches, wizards, witch doctors, spirits, and gods of their worlds. The heroes of Homer's stories are guided by patron gods and goddesses who give them magical aid. Some heroes are raised and trained by magical beings that are somewhere between gods and men, such as centaurs.

CHIRON: A PROTOTYPE

Many of the Greek heroes were mentored by the centaur Chiron, a prototype for all Wise Old Men and Women. A strange mix of man and horse, Chiron was foster-father and trainer to a whole army of Greek heroes including Hercules, Actaeon, Achilles, Peleus, and Aesculapius, the greatest surgeon of antiquity. In the person of Chiron, the Greeks stored many of their notions about what it means to be a Mentor.

As a rule, centaurs are wild and savage creatures. Chiron was an unusually kind and peaceful one, but he still kept some of his wild horse nature. As a half man/half animal creature, he is linked to the shamans of many cultures who dance in the skins of animals to get in touch with animal power. Chiron is the energy and intuition of wild nature, gentled and harnessed to teaching. Like the shamans, he is a bridge between humans and the higher powers of nature and the universe. Mentors in stories often show that they are connected to nature or to some other world of the spirit.

As a Mentor, Chiron led his heroes-in-training through the thresholds of manhood by patiently teaching them the skills of archery, poetry, surgery, and so on. He was not always well rewarded for his efforts. His violence-prone pupil Hercules wounded him with a magic arrow which made Chiron beg the gods for the mercy of death. But in the end, after a truly heroic sacrifice in which he rescued Prometheus from the underworld by taking his place, Chiron received the highest distinction the Greeks could bestow. Zeus made him a constellation and a sign of the zodiac — Sagittarius, a centaur firing a bow. Clearly the Greeks had a high regard for teachers and Mentors.

MENTOR HIMSELF

The term **Mentor** comes from the character of that name in *The Odyssey*. Mentor was the loyal friend of Odysseus, entrusted with raising his son

Telemachus while Odysseus made his long way back from the Trojan War. Mentor has given his name to all guides and trainers, but it's really Athena, the goddess of wisdom, who works behind the scenes to bring the energy of the Mentor archetype into the story.

"The goddess with the flashing eyes" has a big crush on Odysseus, and an interest in getting him home safely. She also looks out for his son Telemachus. She finds the son's story stuck in the opening scenes (the Ordinary World) of *The Odyssey* when the household is overrun by arrogant young suitors for his mother's hand. Athena decides to unstick the situation by taking human form. An important function of the Mentor archetype is to get the story rolling.

First she assumes the appearance of a traveling warrior named Mentes, to issue a stirring challenge to stand up to the suitors and seek his father (Call to Adventure). Telemachus accepts the challenge but the suitors laugh him off and he is so discouraged he wants to abandon the mission (Refusal of the Call). Once again the story seems stuck, and Athena unsticks it by taking the form of Telemachus' teacher Mentor. In this disguise she drums some courage into him and helps him assemble a ship and crew. Therefore, even though Mentor is the name we give to wise counselors and guides, it is really the goddess Athena who acts here.

Athena is the full, undiluted energy of the archetype. If she appeared in her true form, it would probably blast the skin off the bones of the strongest hero. The gods usually speak to us through the filter of other people who are temporarily filled with a godlike spirit. A good teacher or Mentor is **enthused** about learning. The wonderful thing is that this feeling can be communicated to students or to an audience.

The names Mentes and Mentor, along with our word "mental," stem from the Greek word for mind, *menos*, a marvelously flexible word that can mean intention, force, or purpose as well as mind, spirit, or remembrance. Mentors in stories act mainly on the mind of the hero, changing her consciousness or redirecting her will. Even if physical gifts are given, Mentors also strengthen the hero's mind to face an ordeal with confidence. *Menos* also means courage.

AVOIDING MENTOR CLICHÉS

The audience is extremely familiar with the Mentor archetype. The behaviors, attitudes, and functions of Wise Old Women and Men are well known from thousands of stories, and it's easy to fall into clichés and stereotypes — kindly fairy godmothers and white-bearded wizards in tall Merlin hats. To combat this and keep your writing fresh and surprising, defy the archetypes! Stand them on their heads, turn them inside out, purposely do without them altogether to see what happens. The absence of a Mentor creates special and interesting conditions for a hero. But be aware of the archetype's existence, and the audience's familiarity with it.

MISDIRECTION

Audiences don't mind being misled about a Mentor (or any character) from time to time. Real life is full of surprises about people who turn out to be nothing like we first thought. The mask of the Mentor can be used to trick a hero into entering a life of crime. This is how Fagin enlists little boys as pickpockets in *Oliver Twist.* The mask of Mentor can be used to get a hero involved in a dangerous adventure, unknowingly working for the villains. In *Arabesque,* Gregory Peck is tricked into helping a ring of spies by a fake Wise Old Man. You can make the audience think they are seeing a conventional, kindly, helpful Mentor, and then reveal that the character is actually something quite different. Use the audience's expectations and assumptions to surprise them.

MENTOR-HERO CONFLICTS

The Mentor-hero relationship can take a tragic or deadly turn if the hero is ungrateful or violence-prone. Despite the reputation of Hercules as a peerless hero, he has an alarming tendency to do harm to his Mentors. In addition to painfully wounding Chiron, Hercules got so frustrated at music lessons that he bashed in the head of his music teacher Lycus with the first lyre ever made.

Sometimes a Mentor turns villain or betrays the hero. The movie *The Eiger Sanction* shows an apparently benevolent Mentor (George Kennedy) who surprisingly turns on his student hero (Clint Eastwood) and tries to kill him. The dwarf Regin, in Nordic myth, is at first a Mentor to Sigurd the Dragonslayer and helpfully reforges his broken sword. But in the long run the helper turns out to be a doublecrosser. After the dragon is slain, Regin plots to kill Sigurd and keep the treasure for himself.

Rumpelstiltskin is initially a fairy-tale Mentor who helps the heroine by making good on her father's boast that she can spin straw into gold. But the price he demands for his gift is too high — he wants her baby. These stories teach us that not all Mentors are to be trusted, and that it's healthy to question a Mentor's motives. It's one way to distinguish good from bad advice.

Mentors sometimes disappoint the heroes who have admired them during apprenticeship. In *Mr. Smith Goes to Washington,* Jimmy Stewart learns that his Mentor and role model, the noble Senator played by Claude Rains, is as crooked and cowardly as the rest of Congress.

Mentors, like parents, may have a hard time letting go of their charges. An overprotective Mentor can lead to a tragic situation. The character of Svengali from the novel *Trilby* is a chilling portrait of a Mentor who becomes so obsessed with his student that he dooms them both.

MENTOR-DRIVEN STORIES

Once in a while an entire story is built around a Mentor. *Goodbye, Mr. Chips,* the novel and film, is a whole story built on teaching. Mr. Chips is the Mentor of thousands of boys *and* the hero of the story, with his own series of Mentors.

The movie *Barbarossa* is a wise and funny look at a Mentor relationship sustained throughout the story. Its focus is the training of a country boy (Gary Busey) by a legendary Western desperado (Willie Nelson). The young man's learning is so complete that when the movie ends, he is ready to take Barbarossa's place as a larger-than-life folk hero.

MENTOR AS EVOLVED HERO

Mentors can be regarded as heroes who have become experienced enough to teach others. They have been down the Road of Heroes one or more times, and they have acquired knowledge and skill which can be passed on. The progression of images in the Tarot deck shows how a hero evolves to become a Mentor. A hero begins as a Fool and at various stages of the adventure rises through ranks of magician, warrior, messenger, conqueror, lover, thief, ruler, hermit, and so on. At last the hero becomes a Hierophant, a worker of miracles, a Mentor and guide to others, whose experience comes from surviving many rounds of the Hero's Journey.

CRITICAL INFLUENCE

Most often, teaching, training, and testing are only transient stages of a hero's progress, part of a larger picture. In many movies and stories the Wise Old Woman or Man is a passing influence on the hero. But the Mentor's brief appearance is critical to get the story past the blockades of doubt and fear. Mentors may appear only two or three times in a story. Glinda the Good Witch appears only three times in *The Wizard of Oz*: 1) giving Dorothy the red shoes and a yellow path to follow, 2) intervening to blanket the sleep-inducing poppies with pure white snow, and 3) granting her wish to return home, with the help of the magic red shoes. In all three cases her function is to get the story unstuck by giving aid, advice, or magical equipment.

Mentors spring up in amazing variety and frequency because they are so useful to storytellers. They reflect the reality that we all have to learn the lessons of life from someone or something. Whether embodied as a person, a tradition, or a code of ethics, the energy of the archetype is present in almost every story, to get things rolling with gifts, encouragement, guidance, or wisdom.

THE WIZARD OF OZ

Dorothy, like many heroes, encounters a series of Mentors of varying shades. She learns something from almost everyone she meets, and all the characters from whom she learns are in a sense Mentors.

Professor Marvel is the Mentor who reminds her that she is loved, and sends her on her quest for "home," a term that means far more than a Kansas farmhouse. Dorothy has to learn to feel at home in her own soul, and going back to face her problems is a step in that direction.

But the tornado flings her to Oz, where Dorothy encounters Glinda, the good witch, a new Mentor for a new land. Glinda acquaints her with the unfamiliar rules of Oz, gives her the magic gift of the ruby slippers, and points her on the way of the Yellow Brick Road, the golden Road of Heroes. She gives Dorothy a positive feminine role model to balance the negativity of the Wicked Witch.

The three magical figures that Dorothy meets along the way, a man of straw, a man of tin, and a talking lion, are allies and Mentors who teach her lessons about brains, heart, and courage. They are different models of masculine energy that she must incorporate in building her own personality.

The Wizard himself is a Mentor, giving her a new Call to Adventure, the impossible mission of fetching the witch's broomstick. He challenges Dorothy to face her greatest fear — the hostile feminine energy of the Witch.

The little dog Toto is a Mentor, too, in a way. Acting entirely on instinct, he is her intuition, guiding her deeper into the adventure and back out again.

The concept of the Mentor archetype has many uses for the writer. In addition to offering a force that can propel the story forward and supply the hero with necessary motivation or equipment for the journey, Mentors can provide humor or deep, tragic relationships. Some stories don't need a special character solely dedicated to perform the functions of this archetype, but at some point in almost any story, the Mentor functions of helping the hero are performed by some character or force, temporarily wearing the mask of the Mentor.

When writers get stuck, they may seek the help of Mentors just as heroes do. They may consult writing teachers or seek inspiration from the works of great writers. They may delve deep inside themselves to the real sources of inspiration in the Self, the dwelling place of the Muses. The best Mentor advice may be so simple: Breathe. Hang in there. You're doing fine. You've got what it takes to handle any situation, somewhere inside you.

Writers should bear in mind that they are Mentors of a kind to their readers, shamans who travel to other worlds and bring back stories to heal their people. Like Mentors, they teach with their stories and give of their experience, passion, observation, and enthusiasm. Writers, like shamans and Mentors, provide metaphors by which people guide their lives — a most valuable gift and a grave responsibility for the writer.

It's often the energy of the Mentor archetype that gets a hero past fear and sends her to the brink of adventure, at the next stage of the Hero's Journey, the First Threshold.

QUESTIONING THE JOURNEY

1. Who or what is the Mentor in *Fatal Attraction*? *Pretty Woman*? *The Silence of the Lambs*?

2. Think of three long-running TV series. Are there Mentors in these shows? What functions do these characters serve?

3. Is there a character in your story who is a full-blown Mentor? Do other characters wear the mask of the Mentor at some point?

4. Would it benefit the story to develop a Mentor character if there is none?

5. What Mentor functions can be found or developed in your story? Does your hero need a Mentor?

6. Does your hero have some inner code of ethics or model of behavior? Does your hero have a conscience and how does it manifest itself?

7. *Raiders of the Lost Ark* and *Indiana Jones and the Temple of Doom* portray a hero who has no apparent Mentor. He learns things from people along the way, but there is no special character set aside for that task. The third film in the series, *Indiana Jones and the Last Crusade,* introduces the character of Indy's father, played by Sean Connery. Is he a Mentor? Are all parents Mentors? Are yours? In your stories, what is the attitude of your hero to the Mentor energy?

CROSSING THE FIRST THRESHOLD

Stage Five:
CROSSING THE FIRST THRESHOLD

"Just follow the Yellow Brick Road."
— from *The Wizard of Oz*, screenplay by Noel Langley, Florence Ryerson, and Edgar Allan Woolf

Now the hero stands at the very threshold of the world of adventure, the Special World of Act Two. The call has been heard, doubts and fears have been expressed and allayed, and all due preparations have been made. But the real movement, the most critical action of Act One, still remains. **Crossing the First Threshold** is an act of the will in which the hero commits wholeheartedly to the adventure.

The ranks of the Seekers are thinner now. Some of us have dropped out, but the final few are ready to cross the threshold and truly begin the adventure. The problems of the Home Tribe are clear to everyone, and desperate — something must be done, now! Ready or not, we lope out of the village leaving all things familiar behind. As you pull away you feel the jerk of the invisible threads that bind you to your loved ones. It's difficult to pull away from everything you know but with a deep breath you go on, taking the plunge into the abyss of the unknown.

We enter a strange no-man's-land, a world between worlds, a zone of crossing that may be desolate and lonely, or in places, crowded with life. You sense the presence of other beings, other forces with sharp thorns or claws, guarding the way to the treasure you seek. But there's no turning back now, we all feel it; the adventure has begun for good or ill.

APPROACHING THE THRESHOLD

Heroes typically don't just accept the advice and gifts of their Mentors and then charge into the adventure. Often their final commitment is brought about through some external force which changes the course or intensity of the story. This is equivalent to the famous "plot point" or "turning point" of the conventional three-act movie structure. A villain may kill, harm, threaten, or kidnap someone close to the hero, sweeping aside all hesitation. Rough weather may force the sailing of a ship, or the hero may be given a deadline to achieve an assignment. The hero may run out of options, or discover that a difficult choice must be made. Some heroes are "shanghaied" into the adventure or pushed over the brink, with no choice but to commit to the journey. In *Thelma & Louise,* Louise's impulsive killing of a man who is assaulting Thelma is the action that pushes the women to Cross the First Threshold into a new world of being on the run from the law.

An example of the externally imposed event is found in Hitchcock's *North by Northwest.* Advertising man Roger Thornhill, mistaken for a daring secret agent, has been trying his best to avoid his Call to Adventure all through the first act. It takes a murder to get him committed to the journey. A man he's questioning at the U.N. building is killed in front of witnesses in such a way that everyone thinks Roger did it. Now he is truly a "man on the run," escaping both from the police and from the enemy agents who will stop at nothing to kill him. The murder is the external event that pushes the story over the First Threshold into the Special World, where the stakes are higher.

Internal events might trigger a Threshold Crossing as well. Heroes come to decision points where their very souls are at stake, where they must decide "Do I go on living my life as I always have, or will I risk everything in the effort to grow and change?" In *Ordinary People* the deteriorating life of the young hero Conrad gradually pressures him into making a choice, despite his fears, to see a therapist and explore the trauma of his brother's death.

Often a combination of external events and inner choices will boost the story towards the second act. In *Beverly Hills Cop* Axel Foley sees a childhood friend brutally executed by thugs, and is motivated to find the man who hired them. But it takes a separate moment of decision for him to overcome resistance and fully commit to the adventure. In a brief scene in which his boss warns him off the case, you see him make the inner choice to ignore the warning and enter the Special World at any cost.

THRESHOLD GUARDIANS

As you approach the threshold you're likely to encounter beings who try to block your way. They are called Threshold Guardians, a powerful and useful archetype. They may pop up to block the way and test the hero at any point in a story, but they tend to cluster around the doorways, gates, and narrow passages of threshold crossings. Axel Foley's Detroit police captain, who firmly forbids him from getting involved in the investigation of the murder, is one such figure.

Threshold Guardians are part of the training of any hero. In Greek myth, the three-headed monster dog Cerberus guards the entrance to the underworld, and many a hero has had to figure out a way past his jaws. The grim ferryman Charon who guides souls across the River Styx is another Threshold Guardian who must be appeased with a gift of a penny.

The task for heroes at this point is often to figure out some way around or through these guardians. Often their threat is just an illusion, and the solution is simply to ignore them or to push through them with faith. Other Threshold Guardians must be absorbed or their hostile energy must be reflected back onto them. The trick may be to realize that what seems like an obstacle may actually be the means of climbing over the threshold. Threshold Guardians who seem to be enemies may be turned into valuable allies.

Sometimes the guardians of the First Threshold simply need to be acknowledged. They occupy a difficult niche and it wouldn't be polite to pass through their territory without recognizing their power and their important role of keeping the gate. It's a little like tipping a doorman or paying a ticket-taker at a theatre.

THE CROSSING

Sometimes this step merely signifies we have reached the border of the two worlds. We must take the leap of faith into the unknown or else the adventure will never really begin.

Countless movies illustrate the border between two worlds with the crossing of physical barriers such as doors, gates, arches, bridges, deserts, canyons, walls, cliffs, oceans, or rivers. In many Westerns thresholds are clearly marked by river or border crossings. In the adventure *Gunga Din*, the heroes must leap off a high cliff to escape a horde of screaming cult members at the end of Act One. They are bonded by this leap into the unknown, a Threshold Crossing signifying their willingness to explore the Special World of Act Two together.

In the olden days of film, the transition between Act One and Act Two was often marked by a brief fade-out, a momentary darkening of the screen which indicated passage of time or movement in space. The fade-out was equivalent to the curtain coming down in the theatre so the stagehands can change the set and props to create a new locale or show elapse of time.

Nowadays it's common for editors to cut sharply from Act One to Act Two. Nevertheless the audience will still experience a noticeable shift in energy at the Threshold Crossing. A song, a music cue or a drastic visual contrast may help signal the transition. The pace of the story may pick up. Entering a new terrain or structure may signal the change of worlds. In *A League of Their Own* the Crossing is the moment the women enter a big-league baseball stadium, a marked contrast from the country ball fields where they've been playing.

The actual Crossing of the Threshold may be a single moment, or it may be an extended passage in a story. In *Lawrence of Arabia*, T. E. Lawrence's ordeals in crossing "the Sun's Anvil," a treacherous stretch of desert, are an elaboration of this stage into a substantial sequence.

The Crossing takes a certain kind of courage from the hero. He is like the Fool in the Tarot deck: one foot out over a precipice, about to begin free-fall into the unknown.

That special courage is called making the **leap of faith.** Like jumping out of an airplane, the act is irrevocable. There's no turning back now. The leap is made on faith, the trust that somehow we'll land safely.

ROUGH LANDING

Heroes don't always land gently. They may crash in the other world, literally or figuratively. The leap of faith may turn into a crisis of faith as romantic illusions about the Special World are shattered by first contact with it. A bruised hero make pick herself up and ask, "Is that all there is?" The passage to the Special World may be exhausting, frustrating, or disorienting.

THE WIZARD OF OZ

A tremendous natural force rises up to hurl Dorothy over the First Threshold. She is trying to get home but the tornado sends her on a detour to a Special World where she will learn what "home" really means. Dorothy's last name, Gale, is a wordplay that links her to the storm. In symbolic language, it's her own stirred-up emotions that have generated this twister. Her old idea of home, the house, is wrenched up by the tornado and carried to a far-off land where a new personality structure can be built.

As she passes through the transition zone, Dorothy sees familiar sights but in unfamiliar circumstances. Cows fly through the air, men row a boat through the storm, and Miss Gulch on her bicycle turns into the Wicked Witch. Dorothy has nothing she can count on now but Toto — her instincts.

The house comes down with a crash. Dorothy emerges to find a world startlingly different from Kansas, populated by the Little Men and Women of fairy tales. A Mentor appears magically when Glinda floats onto the scene in a transparent bubble. She begins to teach Dorothy about the strange ways of the new land, and points out that the crash of Dorothy's house has killed a bad witch. Dorothy's old personality has been shattered by the uprooting of her old notion of home.

Glinda gives a mentor's gifts, the ruby slippers, and new direction for the quest. To get home, Dorothy must first see the Wizard, that is, get in touch with her own higher Self. Glinda gives a specific path, the Yellow Brick Road, and sends her over another threshold, knowing she will have to make friends, confront foes, and be tested before she can reach her ultimate goal.

The First Threshold is the turning point at which the adventure begins in earnest, at the end of Act One. According to a corporate metaphor in use at Disney, a story is like an airplane flight, and Act One is the process of loading, fueling, taxiing, and rumbling down the runway towards takeoff. The First Threshold is the moment the wheels leave the ground and the plane begins to fly. If you've never flown before, it may take awhile to adjust to being in the air. We'll describe that process of adjustment in the next phase of the Hero's Journey: Tests, Allies, Enemies.

QUESTIONING THE JOURNEY

1. What is the First Threshold of *City Slickers*? *Rain Man*? *Dances with Wolves*? How does the audience know we've gone from one world to another? How does the energy of the story feel different?

2. Is your hero willing to enter the adventure or not? How does this affect the Threshold Crossing?

3. Are there guardian forces at the Threshold and how do they make the hero's leap of faith more difficult?

4. How does the hero deal with Threshold Guardians? What does the hero learn by Crossing the Threshold?

5. What have been the Thresholds in your own life? How did you experience them? Were you even aware you were crossing a threshold into a Special World at the time?

6. By Crossing a Threshold, what options is a hero giving up? Will these unexplored options come back to haunt the hero later?

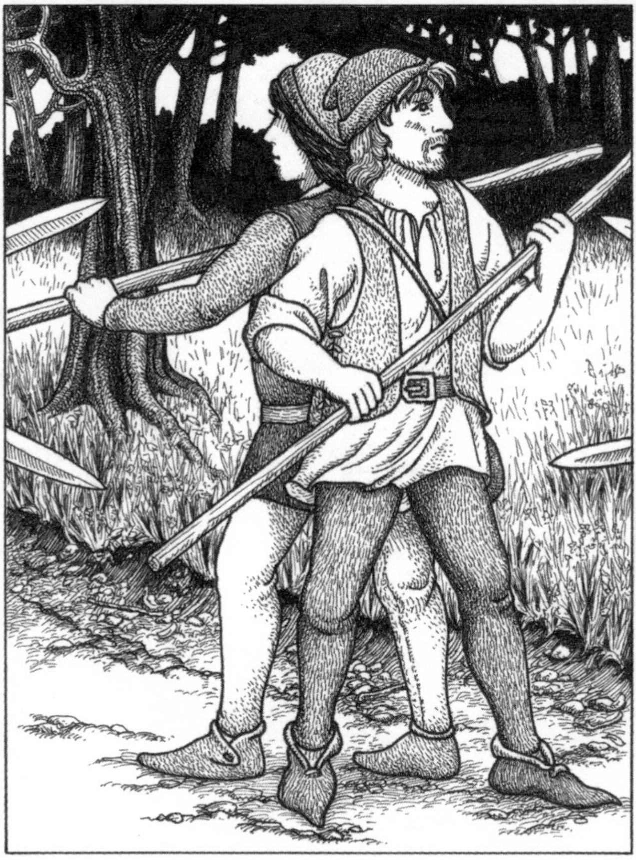

TESTS, ALLIES, ENEMIES

Stage Six:
TESTS, ALLIES, ENEMIES

"See, you got three or four good pals, why then you got yourself a tribe — there ain't nothin' stronger than that."

— from *Young Guns,* screenplay by John Fusco

Now the hero fully enters the mysterious, exciting Special World which Joseph Campbell called "a dream landscape of curiously fluid, ambiguous forms, where he must survive a succession of trials." It's a new and sometimes frightening experience for the hero. No matter how many schools he has been through, he's a freshman all over again in this new world.

We Seekers are in shock — this new world is so different from the home we've always known. Not only are the terrain and the local residents different, the rules of this place are strange as they can be. Different things are valued here and we have a lot to learn about the local currency, customs, and language. Strange creatures jump out at you! Think fast! Don't eat that, it could be poison!

Exhausted by the journey across the desolate threshold zone, we're running out of time and energy. Remember our people back in the Home Tribe are counting on us. Enough sight-seeing, let's concentrate on the goal. We must go where the food and game and information are to be found. There our skills will be tested, and we'll come one step closer to what we seek.

CONTRAST

The audience's first impressions of the Special World should strike a sharp contrast with the Ordinary World. Think of Eddie Murphy's first look at the Special World of *Beverly Hills Cop,* which makes such a drastic contrast to his former world of Detroit. Even if the hero remains physically in the same place throughout the story, there is movement and change as new emotional territory is explored. A Special World, even a figurative one, has a different feel, a different rhythm, different priorities and values, and different rules. In *Father of the Bride* or *Guess Who's Coming to Dinner,* while there is no physical threshold, there's definitely a crossing into a Special World with new conditions.

When a submarine dives, a wagon train leaves St. Louis, or the starship Enterprise leaves the earth, the conditions and rules of survival change. Things are often more dangerous, and the price of mistakes is higher.

TESTING

The most important function of this period of adjustment to the Special World is **testing.** Storytellers use this phase to test the hero, putting her through a series of trials and challenges that are meant to prepare her for greater ordeals ahead.

Joseph Campbell illustrates this stage with the tale of Psyche, who is put through a fairy-tale-like series of Tests before winning back her lost love, Cupid (Eros). This tale has been wisely interpreted by Robert A. Johnson in his book on feminine psychology, *She.* Psyche is given three seemingly impossible tasks by Cupid's jealous mother Venus and passes the Tests with the help of beings to whom she has been kind along the way. She has made Allies.

The Tests at the beginning of Act Two are often difficult obstacles, but they don't have the maximum life-and-death quality of later events. If the adventure were a college learning experience, Act One would be a series of entrance exams, and the Test stage of Act Two would be a series of pop quizzes, meant to sharpen the hero's skill in specific areas and prepare her for the more rigorous midterm and final exams coming up.

The Tests may be a continuation of the Mentor's training. Many Mentors accompany their heroes this far into the adventure, coaching them for the big rounds ahead.

The Tests may also be built into the architecture or landscape of the Special World. This world is usually dominated by a villain or Shadow who is careful to surround his world with traps, barricades, and checkpoints. It's common for heroes to fall into traps here or trip the Shadow's security alarms. How the hero deals with these traps is part of the Testing.

ALLIES AND ENEMIES

Another function of this stage is the making of Allies or Enemies. It's natural for heroes just arriving in the Special World to spend some time figuring out who can be trusted and relied upon for special services, and who is not to be trusted. This too is a kind of Test, examining if the hero is a good judge of character.

ALLIES

Heroes may walk into the Test stage looking for information, but they may walk out with new friends or Allies. In *Shane*, a shaky partnership between the gunfighter Shane (Alan Ladd) and the farmer (Van Heflin) is cemented into a real friendship by the shared ordeal of a saloon-shattering brawl. When John Dunbar in *Dances with Wolves* crosses the threshold into the Special World of the frontier, he gradually makes alliances with Kicking Bear (Graham Greene) and the wolf he names Two Socks.

SIDEKICKS

Westerns frequently make use of a long-standing bond between a hero and a **sidekick**, an Ally who generally rides with the hero and supports his adventures. The Lone Ranger has Tonto, Zorro has the servant Bernardo, the Cisco Kid has Pancho. These pairings of hero and sidekick can be found throughout myth and literature: Sherlock Holmes and Dr. Watson, Don Quixote and Sancho Panza, Prince Hal and Falstaff, or the Sumerian hero Gilgamesh and his wild companion Enkidu.

These close Allies of the hero may provide comic relief as well as assistance. **Comical sidekicks**, played by character actors such as Walter Brennan, Gabby Hayes, Fuzzy Knight, and Slim Pickens, provide humor lacking in their stalwart, serious heroes they accompany. Such figures may freely cross the boundaries between Mentor and Trickster, sometimes aiding the hero and acting as his conscience, sometimes comically goofing up or causing mischief.

TEAMS

The Testing stage may also provide the opportunity for the forging of a team. Many stories feature multiple heroes or a hero backed up by a team of characters with special skills or qualities. The early phases of Act Two may cover the recruiting of a team, or give an opportunity for the team to make plans and rehearse a difficult operation. The World War II adventure films *The Dirty Dozen* and *The Great Escape* show the heroes bonding into a coherent team before tackling the main event of the story. In the Testing stage the hero may have to struggle against rivals for control of the group. The strengths and flaws of the team members are revealed during Testing.

In a romance, the Testing stage might be the occasion for a first date or for some shared experience that begins to build the relationship, such as the tennis match between Diane Keaton and Woody Allen in *Annie Hall.*

ENEMIES

Heroes can also make bitter enmities at this stage. They may encounter the Shadow or his servants. The hero's appearance in the Special World may tip the Shadow to his arrival and trigger a chain of threatening events. The cantina sequence in *Star Wars* sets up a conflict with the villain Jabba the Hutt which culminates in *The Empire Strikes Back.*

Enemies include both the villains or antagonists of stories and their underlings. Enemies may perform functions of other archetypes such as the Shadow, the Trickster, the Threshold Guardian, and sometimes the Herald.

THE RIVAL

A special type of Enemy is the rival, the hero's competition in love, sports, business, or some other enterprise. The rival is usually not out to kill the hero, but is just trying to defeat him in the competition. In the film *The Last of the Mohicans,* Major Duncan Hayward is the rival of hero Nathaniel Poe because they both want the same woman, Cora Munro. The plot of *Honeymoon in Vegas* revolves around a similar rivalry between the hapless hero (Nicolas Cage) and his gambler opponent (James Caan).

NEW RULES

The new rules of the Special World must be learned quickly by the hero and the audience. As Dorothy enters the land of Oz, she is bewildered when Glinda the Good asks, "Are you a good witch or a bad witch?" In Dorothy's Ordinary World of Kansas, there are only bad witches, but in the Special World of Oz, witches can also be good, and fly in pink bubbles instead of on broomsticks. Another Test of the hero is how quickly she can adjust to the new rules of the Special World.

At this stage a Western may impose certain conditions on people entering a town or a bar. In *Unforgiven*, guns cannot be worn in the sheriff's territory. This restriction can draw the hero into conflicts. A hero may enter a bar to discover that the town is totally polarized by two factions: the cattlemen vs. the farmers, the Earps vs. the Clantons, the bounty hunters vs. the sheriff, and so on. In the pressure cooker of the saloon, people size each other up and take sides for the coming showdown. The cantina sequence in *Star Wars* draws on the images we all have of Western saloons as places for reconnaissance, challenges, alliances, and the learning of new rules.

WATERING HOLES

Why do so many heroes pass through bars and saloons at this point in the stories? The answer lies in the hunting metaphor of the Hero's Journey. Upon leaving the Ordinary World of village or den, hunters will often head straight for a watering hole to look for game. Predators sometimes follow the muddy tracks left by game who come down to drink. The watering hole is a natural congregating place and a good spot to observe and get information. It's no accident that we call neighborhood saloons and cocktail lounges our "local watering holes."

The crossing of the First Threshold may have been long, lonely, and dry. Bars are natural spots to recuperate, pick up gossip, make friends, and confront Enemies. They also allow us to observe people under pressure, when true character is revealed. How Shane handles himself in a bar fight convinces a farmer to become his Ally and stand up to the bullying cattlemen. In the tense bar-room confrontations in *Star Wars*, Luke Skywalker sees flashes of Obi Wan Kenobi's spiritual power and Han Solo's "look out for Number One" mentality. The bar can be a microcosm of the Special World, a place through which everyone must pass, sooner or later, like the saloon in *The Life and Times of Judge Roy Bean.* "Everybody Comes to Rick's," says the title of the play on which *Casablanca* is based.

Bars also play host to a number of other activities including music, flirting, and gambling. This stage in a story, whether it takes place in a bar or not, is a good place for a musical sequence that announces the mood of the Special World. A nightclub act may allow the introduction of a romantic interest, as in Jessica Rabbit's sensational torch song in *Who Framed Roger Rabbit?* Music can express the dualities of the Special World as well. At this stage in *Casablanca* the polarities are movingly presented in a musical duel between the passionate "Marsellaise" sung by the French patriots and the brutal "Deutschland uber Alles" sung by the Nazis.

In the lonely outposts of adventure, saloons or their equivalent may be the only places for sexual intrigue. Bars can be the arena for flirting, romance, or prostitution. A hero may strike up a relationship in a bar to get information, and incidentally acquire an Ally or a lover.

Gambling and saloons go together, and games of chance are a natural feature of the Testing stage. Heroes may want to consult the oracles to see how luck will favor them. They want to learn about the wheel of fortune, and how luck can be coaxed their way. Through a game the stakes can be raised or a fortune can be lost. In the Hindu epic *The Mahabharata,* a cosmic family feud is set in motion by a rigged game of chance between two sets of brothers. (The bad guys cheat.)

THE WIZARD OF OZ

Of course not all heroes go to bars at this stage of the journey. Dorothy encounters her Tests, Allies, and Enemies on the Yellow Brick Road. Like Psyche or the heroes of many fairy tales she is wise enough to know that requests for aid on the road should be honored with an open heart. She earns the loyalty of the Scarecrow by getting him unhooked from his post and by helping him learn to walk. Meanwhile she learns that her Enemy, the Wicked Witch, shadows her at every turn and waits for the chance to strike. The Witch influences some grumpy apple trees to become Enemies to Dorothy and the Scarecrow. The Scarecrow proves his worthiness to be on the team by outwitting the trees. He taunts them into throwing apples, which he and Dorothy pick up to eat.

Dorothy wins the affection of another Ally, the Tin Woodsman, by oiling his joints and listening sympathetically to his sad story of having no heart. The

Witch appears again, showing her enmity for Dorothy and her Allies by hurling a fireball at them.

To protect her dog Toto, Dorothy stands up to the blustering of the Cowardly Lion, a potential Enemy or Threshold Guardian, and ends up making him an Ally.

The battlelines are clearly drawn. Dorothy has learned the rules of the Special World and has passed many Tests. Protected by Allies and on guard against declared Enemies, she is ready to approach the central source of power in the land of Oz.

The phase of Tests, Allies, and Enemies in stories is useful for "getting to know you" scenes where the characters get acquainted with each other and the audience learns more about them. This stage also allows the hero to accumulate power and information in preparation for the next stage: Approach to the Inmost Cave.

QUESTIONING THE JOURNEY

1. What is the Testing phase of *Sister Act*? *A League of Their Own*? *Big*? Why do heroes pass through a period of Tests? Why don't they just go right to the main event after entering Act Two?

2. How does your story's Special World differ from the Ordinary World? How can you increase the contrast?

3. In what ways is your hero Tested, and when does she make Allies or Enemies? Keep in mind there is no "right" way. The needs of the story may dictate when alliances are made.

4. Are there loner heroes who have no Allies?

5. Is your hero a single character or a group such as a platoon, a crew, a family, or a gang? If it is an "ensemble piece" like *The Breakfast Club* or *The Big Chill*, when does the team become a coherent group?

6. How does your hero react to the Special World with its strange rules and unfamiliar people?

APPROACH TO THE INMOST CAVE

Stage Seven: APPROACH TO THE INMOST CAVE

COWARDLY LION: *There's only one thing more I'd like you fellows to do.*
TIN WOODSMAN, SCARECROW: *What's that?*
COWARDLY LION: *Talk me out of it!*
— from *The Wizard of Oz*

Heroes, having made the adjustment to the Special World, now go on to seek its heart. They pass into an intermediate region between the border and the very center of the Hero's Journey. On the way they find another mysterious zone with its own Threshold Guardians, agendas, and tests. This is the **Approach to the Inmost Cave**, where soon they will encounter supreme wonder and terror. It's time to make final preparations for the central ordeal of the adventure. Heroes at this point are like mountaineers who have raised themselves to a base camp by the labors of Testing, and are about to make the final assault on the highest peak.

Our band of Seekers leaves the oasis at the edge of the new world, refreshed and armed with more knowledge about the nature and habits of the game we're hunting. We're ready to press on to the heart of the new world where the greatest treasures are guarded by our greatest fears.

Look around at your fellow Seekers. We've changed already and new qualities are emerging. Who's the leader now? Some who were not suited for life in the Ordinary World are now thriving. Others who seemed ideal for adventure are turning out to be the least able. A new perception of yourself and others is forming. Based on this new awareness, you can make plans and direct yourself towards getting what you want from the Special World. Soon you will be ready to enter the Inmost Cave.

FUNCTIONS OF APPROACH

In modern storytelling, certain special functions naturally fall into this zone of **Approach.** As heroes near the gates of a citadel deep within the Special World, they may take time to make plans, do reconnaissance on the enemy, reorganize or thin out the group, fortify and arm themselves, and have a last laugh and a final cigarette before going over the top into no-man's-land. The student studies for the midterm. The hunter stalks the game to its hiding place. Adventurers squeeze in a love scene before tackling the central event of the movie.

COURTSHIP

The Approach can be an arena for elaborate courtship rituals. A romance may develop here, bonding hero and beloved before they encounter the main ordeal. In *North by Northwest,* Cary Grant meets a beautiful woman (Eva Marie Saint) on a train as he escapes from the police and the enemy spies. He doesn't know she works for the evil spies and has been assigned to lure him into their trap. However, her seduction backfires and she finds herself actually falling in love with him. Later, thanks to this scene of bonding, she becomes his Ally.

THE BOLD APPROACH

Some heroes boldly stride up to the castle door and demand to be let in. Confident, committed heroes will take this Approach. Axel Foley in *Beverly Hills Cop* crashes into the precincts of his enemy a number of times at the Approach phase, conning his way past Threshold Guardians and flaunting his intention to upset his opponent's world. Cary Grant in *Gunga Din* marches into the Inmost Cave of his antagonists, a cult of assassins, singing an English drinking song at the top of his lungs. His bold Approach is not pure arrogance: He puts on the outrageous show to buy time for his friend Gunga Din to slip away and summon the British army. In true heroic fashion Grant's character is sacrificing himself and tempting death on behalf of the group.

The Approach of Clint Eastwood's character in *Unforgiven* is not so much arrogant as ignorant. He rides into the Inmost Cave of the town during a rainstorm, and is unable to see a sign forbidding firearms. This brings him to an ordeal, a beating by the sheriff (Gene Hackman) that almost kills him.

PREPARATION FOR THE ORDEAL

Approach may be a time of further reconnaissance and information-gathering, or a time of dressing and arming for an ordeal. Gunfighters check their weapons, bullfighters dress carefully in their suits of lights.

THE WIZARD OF OZ

The Wizard of Oz has such a well-developed Approach section that we'll use it throughout this chapter to illuminate some of the functions of this stage.

OBSTACLES

Having made some Allies in the Testing stage, Dorothy and friends leave the woods on the border of Oz and immediately see the glittering Emerald City of their dreams. They Approach in joy, but before they reach their goal, they face a series of obstacles and challenges that will bond them as a group, and prepare them for the life-and-death struggle yet to come.

BEWARE OF ILLUSIONS

First they are put to sleep by a field of poppies sown by the Wicked Witch's magic. They are brought back to consciousness by a blanket of snow, courtesy of Glinda the Good.

The message for the hero is clear: Don't be seduced by illusions and perfumes, stay alert, don't fall asleep on the march.

THRESHOLD GUARDIANS

Dorothy and friends reach the City, only to find their way blocked by a rude sentry, a perfect Threshold Guardian (who looks suspiciously like Professor Marvel from Act One). He is a satirical figure, an exaggerated image of a bureaucrat whose job is to enforce stupid, pointless rules. Dorothy identifies herself as the one who dropped a house on the Wicked Witch of the East, and she has the Ruby Slippers to prove it. This wins the respect of the sentry who admits them immediately, saying, "Well that's a horse of a different color!"

Message: Past experience on the journey may be the hero's passport to new lands. Nothing is wasted, and every challenge of the past strengthens and informs us for the present. We win respect for having made it this far.

The satire of bureaucratic nonsense reminds us that few heroes are exempt from the tolls and rituals of the Special World. Heroes must either pay the price of admission or find a way around the obstacles, as Dorothy does.

ANOTHER SPECIAL WORLD

Dorothy and company enter the wonderland of the City, where everything is green except for a horse pulling a carriage, the famous Horse of a Different Color who changes hue every time you look at him. The Driver also looks like Professor Marvel.

Message: You've entered yet another little Special World, with different rules and values. You may encounter a series of these like Chinese boxes, one inside the other, a series of shells protecting some central source of power. The multi-colored horse is a signal that rapid change is coming. The detail of several characters looking alike, or the same character taking a variety of roles, is a reminder we are in a dream world ruled by forces of comparison, association, and transformation. The protean changes of Professor Marvel suggest that a single powerful mind is at work in Oz, or that Dorothy's dream, if that's what it is, has been deeply influenced by his personality. Professor Marvel has become an animus figure for Dorothy: a focus for her projections about mature male energy. Her father is dead or absent and the male figures around the farm, Uncle Henry and the three farmhands, are weak. She is seeking an image of what a father can be, and projects Professor Marvel's paternal energy onto every authority figure she sees. If the Good Witch Glinda is a surrogate mother or positive anima for her, these variations of Professor Marvel are surrogate fathers.

BE PREPARED

Dorothy and friends are primped, pampered, and prepared for their meeting with the Wizard, in the beauty parlors and machine shops of the Emerald City.

Message: Heroes know they are facing a great ordeal, and are wise to make themselves as ready as they'll ever be, like warriors polishing and sharpening their weapons, or students doing final drills before a big exam.

WARNING

Our heroes, feeling pretty good now, go out singing about how the day is laughed away in the merry old land of Oz. Just then the Witch screeches over the city, skywriting from her broomstick, "Surrender Dorothy!" The people back away in terror, leaving our heroes alone outside the Wizard's door.

Message: It's good for heroes to go into the main event in a state of balance, with confidence tempered by humility and awareness of the danger. No matter how hysterical the celebrations in Oz, they always seem to be damped by an appearance of the Witch, a real party pooper. She is a deep disturbance in Dorothy's psyche which will ruin every pleasurable moment until dealt with decisively. The isolation of the heroes is typical. Like Gary Cooper trying to line up support from cowardly townspeople in *High Noon,* heroes may find good-time companions fading away when the going gets tough.

ANOTHER THRESHOLD

Our heroes knock at the Wizard's door and an even ruder sentry, another ringer for Professor Marvel, sticks his head out. His orders are "Not nobody, not nohow" is to get in to see the Wizard. Only the information that he's dealing with "the Witch's Dorothy" convinces him to go confer with the Wizard. While he's gone, the Lion sings "If I Were King of the Forest," expressing his aspirations.

Message: The credentials of experience may have to be presented repeatedly at successive rungs of power. When delayed by obstacles, heroes do well to get acquainted with their fellow adventurers and learn of their hopes and dreams.

EMOTIONAL APPEAL TO A GUARDIAN

The Sentry returns to report that the Wizard says, "Go away." Dorothy and her companions break down and lament. Now they'll never have their wishes met and Dorothy will never get home. The sad story brings floods of tears to the Sentry's eyes, and he lets them in.

Message: Sometimes, when the passport of experience no longer works to get you past a gate, an emotional appeal can break down the defenses of Threshold Guardians. Establishing a bond of human feeling may be the key.

AN IMPOSSIBLE TEST

Our heroes cross yet another threshold, being ushered into the throne room of Oz by the Sentry, now their friend. Oz himself is one of the most terrifying images ever put on film — the gigantic head of an angry old man, surrounded by flames and thunder. He can grant your wish, but like the kings of fairy-tales, is miserly with his power. He imposes impossible tests in hopes that you will go away and leave him alone. Dorothy and friends are given the apparently unachievable task of fetching the broomstick of the Wicked Witch.

Message: It's tempting to think you can just march into foreign territory, take the prize, and leave. The awesome image of Oz reminds us that heroes are challenging a powerful status quo, which may not share their dreams and goals. That status quo may even live inside them in strong habits or neuroses that must be overcome before facing the main ordeal. Oz, Professor Marvel in his most powerful and frightening form, is a negative animus figure, the dark side of Dorothy's idea of a father. Dorothy must deal with her confused feelings about male energy before she can confront her deeper feminine nature.

The status quo might be a aging generation or ruler, reluctant to give up power, or a parent unwilling to admit the child is grown. The Wizard at this point is like a harassed father, grouchy about being interrupted and having demands put on him by youth. This angry parental force must be appeased or dealt with in some way before the adventure can proceed. We must all pass tests to earn the approval of parental forces.

Parents sometimes set impossible conditions on winning their love and acceptance. You can't ever seem to please them. Sometimes the very people you naturally turn to in a crisis will push you away. You may have to face the big moment alone.

SHAMANIC TERRITORY

The heroes pass on to the eerie region surrounding the Wicked Witch's castle. Here they encounter more Threshold Guardians, in the witch's creepy servants, the flying monkeys. Dorothy is kidnapped and flown away by the monkeys, and her companions are beaten and scattered. Tin Woodsman is dented and Scarecrow is torn limb from limb.

Message: As heroes Approach the Inmost Cave, they should know they are in shaman's territory, on the edge between life and death. The Scarecrow being torn to pieces and scattered by the monkeys recalls the visions and dreams that signal selection as a shaman. Shamans-to-be often dream of being dismembered by heavenly spirits and reassembled into the new form of a shaman. Dorothy being flown away by the monkeys is just the sort of thing that happens to shamans when they travel to other worlds.

COMPLICATIONS

The terrorized heroes are discouraged and confused after the monkey attack. Scarecrow's scattered limbs are reassembled by the Tin Woodsman and Cowardly Lion.

Heroes may have disheartening setbacks at this stage while approaching the supreme goal. Such reversals of fortune are called *dramatic complications.* Though they may seem to tear us apart, they are only a further test of our willingness to proceed. They also allow us to put ourselves back together in a more effective form for traveling in this unfamiliar terrain.

HIGHER STAKES

Dorothy is now trapped in the castle. The Witch, mirroring the action of her look-alike Miss Gulch, crams Toto into a basket and threatens to throw him in the river unless Dorothy turns over the Ruby Slippers. Dorothy agrees to hand them over but the Witch is zapped by Glinda's protective spell when she tries to take the shoes. The Witch realizes she'll never get the shoes while Dorothy's alive and sets before her the hourglass with its rushing red sand like dried blood. When the last grain runs out, Dorothy will die.

Message: Another function of the Approach stage is to up the stakes and rededicate the team to its mission. The audience may need to be reminded of the "ticking clock" or the "time bomb" of the story. The urgency and life-and-death quality of the issue need to be underscored.

Toto in the basket is a repeated symbol of intuition stifled by the negative anima of the Witch/Miss Gulch. Dorothy's fear of her own intuitive side keeps stuffing away her creativity and confidence, but it keeps popping up again, like Toto.

The Ruby Slippers are a deep dream symbol, representing both Dorothy's means of getting around in Oz and her identity, her unassailable integrity. The shoes are a reassuring Mentor's gift, the knowledge that you are a unique being with a core that cannot be shaken by outside events. They are like Ariadne's Thread in the story of Theseus and the Minotaur, a connection with a positive, loving anima that gets you through the darkest of labyrinths.

REORGANIZATION

Toto escapes from the basket as he did in Act One and runs out of the castle to join forces with the three friends who are still piecing together the Scarecrow. Toto leads them to the castle, where they are daunted at the task of getting the helpless Dorothy out of the forbidding, well-defended place. The responsibility of moving the adventure forward has fallen to Dorothy's three Allies; this place is so terrible that there's no help here from kindly wizards and witches. They have gotten by as clowns; now they must become heroes.

Message: Toto again acts as Dorothy's intuition, sensing that it's time to call on Allies and lessons learned to get her out of a trap. The Approach stage is also a time to reorganize a group: to promote some members, sort out living, dead, and wounded, assign special missions, and so on. Archetypal masks may need to be changed as characters are made to perform new functions.

With her freedom of action removed, Dorothy has switched archetypal masks here, trading the Hero mask for that of the Victim, the archetype of helplessness. The three companions have also traded masks, being promoted from Trickster clowns or Allies, to full-fledged Heroes who will carry the action for a while. The audience may find that assumptions about the characters are being overturned as surprising new qualities emerge under the pressure of Approach.

The sense that the heroes must face some things without the help of protective spirits is reminiscent of many mythic tales of trips to the underworld. Human heroes often have to go it alone on a mission from the gods. They must travel to the land of the dead where the gods themselves are afraid to walk. We may consult doctors or therapists, friends or advisors, but there are some places where our Mentors can't go and we are on our own.

HEAVY DEFENSES

Scarecrow, Lion, and Tin Woodsman now creep up to observe the threshold of the Inmost Cave itself, the drawbridge of the Wicked Witch's castle, defended by a whole army of ferocious-looking Threshold Guardians, wearing bearskin hats and gloves and growling their grim marching song.

Message: Heroes can expect the villain's headquarters to be defended with animal-like ferocity. The castle itself, with its barred gate and drawbridge like a devouring mouth and tongue, is a symbol of the elaborate fortifications around an all-consuming neurosis. The defenses around the Witch's negative anima make the Wizard's guards and palace look inviting by comparison.

WHO IS THE HERO AT THIS POINT?

The three reluctant heroes evaluate the situation. The Lion wants to run, but the Scarecrow has a plan which requires Lion to be the leader. This makes sense since he is the most ferocious-looking, but he still wants to be talked out of it.

Message: The Approach is a good time to recalibrate your team, express misgivings, and give encouragement. Team members make sure all are in agreement about goals, and determine that the right people are in the right jobs. There may even be bitter battles for dominance among the group at this stage, as pirates or thieves fight for control of the adventure.

However, here the Cowardly Lion's efforts to escape responsibility are comic, and point up another function of the Approach: comic relief. This may be the last chance to relax and crack a joke because things are about to get deadly serious in the Supreme Ordeal phase.

GET INTO YOUR OPPONENT'S MIND

As part of their Approach, the three heroes try to cook up a plan as they move closer to the gate. Three sentries attack them, and after a struggle in which costumes fly through the air, our heroes emerge wearing the uniforms and bearskin hats of their enemies. In this disguise, they join the platoon of marching sentries and stride right into the castle.

Message: Here the heroes employ the device of "getting into the skin" of the Threshold Guardians before them. Like the Plains Indians donning buffalo robes to creep close to their prey, the heroes literally put on the skins of their opponents and slip in among them. When in Rome, do as the Romans do. This aspect of the Approach teaches that we must get into the minds of those who seem to stand in our way. If we understand or empathize with them, the job of getting past them or absorbing their energy is much easier. We can turn their attacks into opportunities to get into their skin. Heroes may also put on disguises to conceal their real intentions as they get close to the Inmost Cave of the opponent.

BREAKTHROUGH

The three heroes now discard their disguises and make their way to the chamber of the castle where Dorothy is imprisoned. The Tin Woodsman uses his axe to chop through the door.

Message: At some point it may be necessary to use force to break through the final veil to the Inmost Cave. The hero's own resistance and fear may have to be overcome by a violent act of will.

NO EXIT

With Dorothy rescued, and the foursome united again, they now turn their attention to escape. But they are blocked in all directions by the witch's guards.

Message: No matter how heroes try to escape their fate, sooner or later the exits are closed off and the life-and-death issue must be faced. With Dorothy and companions "trapped like rats," the Approach to the Inmost Cave is complete.

The Approach encompasses all the final preparations for the Supreme Ordeal. It often brings heroes to a stronghold of the opposition, a defended center where every lesson and Ally of the journey so far comes into play. New perceptions are put to the test, and the final obstacles to reaching the heart are overcome, so that the Supreme Ordeal may begin.

QUESTIONING THE JOURNEY

1. Campbell says that in myths, the crossing of the First Threshold is often followed by the hero passing through "the belly of the whale." He cites stories from many cultures of heroes being swallowed by giant beasts. In what sense are the heroes "in the belly of the whale" in the early stages of Act Two in *Thelma & Louise*? *Fatal Attraction*? *Unforgiven*?

2. Campbell describes several ideas or actions surrounding the major ordeal of a myth: "Meeting with the Goddess," "Woman as Temptress," "Atonement with the Father." In what ways are these ideas part of Approaching the Inmost Cave?

3. In your own story, what happens between entering the Special World and reaching a central crisis in that world? What special preparations lead up to the crisis?

4. Does conflict build, and do the obstacles get more difficult or interesting?

5. Do your heroes want to turn back at this stage, or are they fully committed to the adventure now?

6. In what ways is the hero, in facing external challenges, also encountering inner demons and defenses?

7. Is there a physical Inmost Cave or headquarters of the villain which the heroes Approach? Or is there some emotional equivalent?

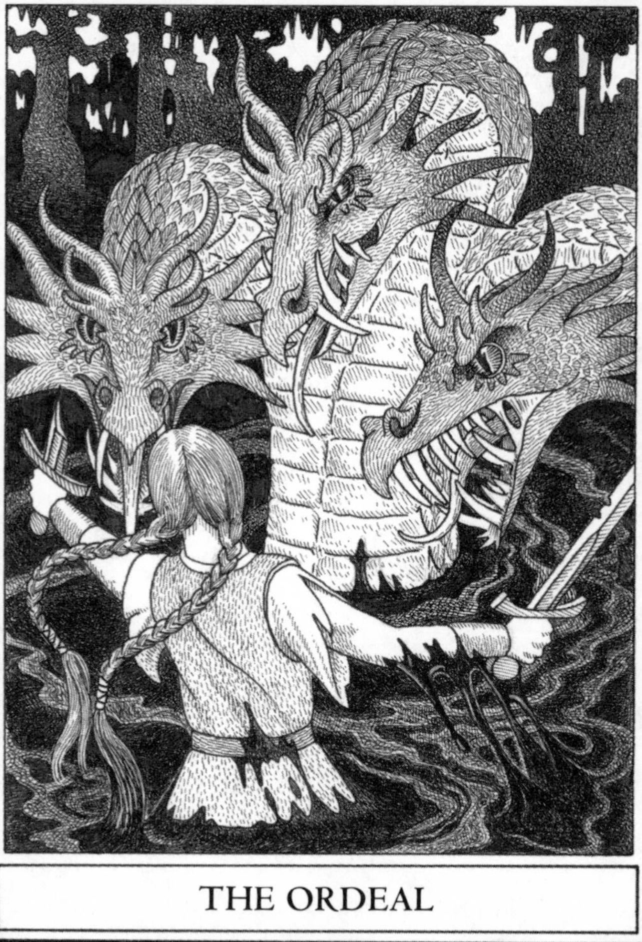

THE ORDEAL

Stage Eight: THE ORDEAL

JAMES BOND: *What do you expect me to do, Goldfinger?*
GOLDFINGER: *Why Mr. Bond, I expect you to die.*
— from *Goldfinger,* screenplay by Richard Maibaum and Paul Dehn

Now the hero stands in the deepest chamber of the Inmost Cave, facing the greatest challenge and the most fearsome opponent yet. This the real heart of the matter, what Joseph Campbell called the **Ordeal.** It is the mainspring of the heroic form and the key to its magic power.

Seeker, enter the Inmost Cave and look for that which will restore life to the Home Tribe. The way grows narrow and dark. You must go alone on hands and knees and you feel the earth press close around you. You can hardly breathe. Suddenly you come out into the deepest chamber and find yourself face-to-face with a towering figure, a menacing Shadow composed of all your doubts and fears and well armed to defend a treasure. Here, in this moment, is the chance to win all or die. No matter what you came for, it's Death that now stares back at you. Whatever the outcome of the battle, you are about to taste death and it will change you.

DEATH AND REBIRTH

The simple secret of the Ordeal is this: **Heroes must die so that they can be reborn.** The dramatic movement that audiences enjoy more than any other is death and rebirth. In some way in every story, heroes face death or something like it: their greatest fears, the failure of an enterprise, the end of a relationship, the death of an old personality. Most of the time, they magically survive this death and are literally or symbolically reborn to reap the consequences of having cheated death. They have passed the main test of being a hero.

Spielberg's E.T. dies before our eyes but is reborn through alien magic and a boy's love. Sir Lancelot, remorseful over having killed a gallant knight, prays him back to life. Clint Eastwood's character in *Unforgiven* is beaten senseless by a sadistic sheriff and hovers at the edge of death, thinking he's seeing angels. Sherlock Holmes, apparently killed with Professor Moriarity in the plunge over Reichenbach Falls, defies death and returns transformed and ready for more adventures. Patrick Swayze's character, murdered in *Ghost*, learns how to cross back through the veil to protect his wife and finally express his true love for her.

CHANGE

Heroes don't just visit death and come home. They return changed, transformed. No one can go through an experience at the edge of death without being changed in some way. In the center of *An Officer and a Gentleman*, Richard Gere survives a death-and-rebirth ordeal of the ego at the hands of drill instructor Lou Gossett. It dramatically changes Gere's character, making him more sensitive to the needs of others and more conscious that he's part of a group.

Axel Foley, with a villain's gun to his head in *Beverly Hills Cop*, seems sure to die, but is rescued by the bumbling, naive white detective Rosewood (Judge Reinhold). After this rescue from death, Foley is more cooperative and willing to submerge his gigantic ego in the group.

THE CRISIS, NOT THE CLIMAX

The Ordeal is a major nerve ganglion of the story. Many threads of the hero's history lead in, and many threads of possibility and change lead out the other side. It should not be confused with the climax of the Hero's Journey — that's another nerve center further down near the end of the story (like the brain at the base of a dinosaur's tail). The Ordeal is usually the central event of the story, or the main event of the second act. Let's call it the **crisis** to differentiate it from the **climax** (the big moment of Act Three and the crowning event of the whole story).

A crisis is defined by *Webster's* as "the point in a story or drama at which hostile forces are in the tensest state of opposition." We also speak of a crisis in an illness: a point, perhaps a high spike of fever, after which the patient either gets worse or begins to recover. The message: Sometimes things have to get worse before they can get better. An Ordeal crisis, however frightening to the hero, is sometimes the only way to recovery or victory.

PLACEMENT OF THE ORDEAL

The placement of the crisis or Ordeal depends on the needs of the story and the tastes of the storyteller. The most common pattern is for the death-and-rebirth moment to come near the middle of the story, as shown in the Central Crisis diagram.

CENTRAL CRISIS

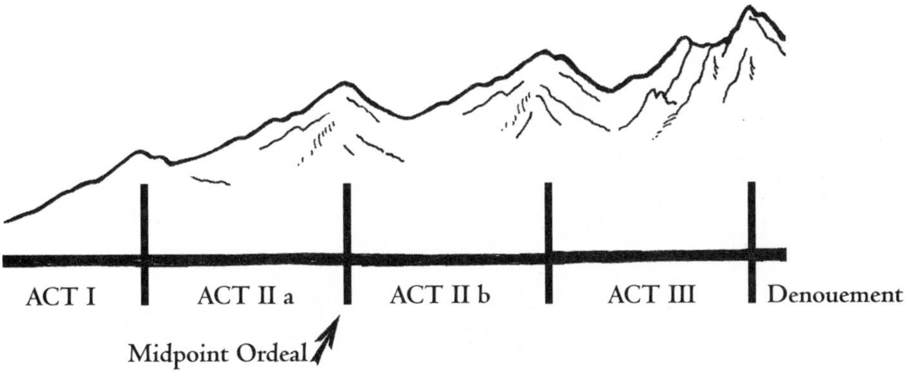

Dramatic high points in a story with a *Central* Crisis (vertical lines represent the high point of each act)

A **central crisis** has the advantage of symmetry, and leaves plenty of time for elaborate consequences to flow from the ordeal. Note that this structure allows for another critical moment or turning point at the end of Act Two.

DELAYED CRISIS

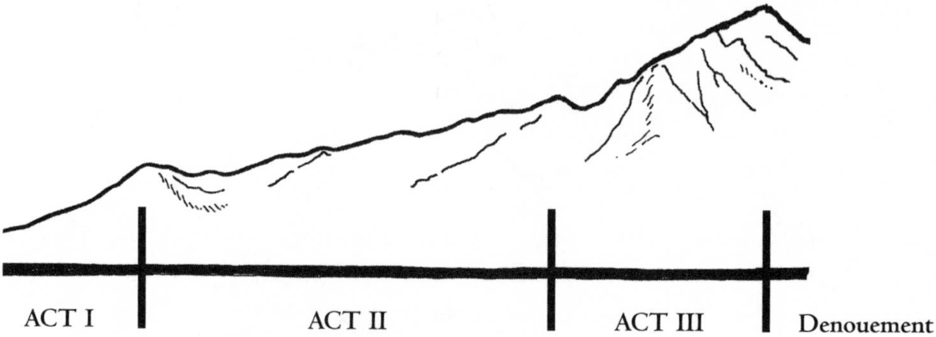

(no central ordeal; instead a long build-up to end of Act II)

Dramatic high points in a story with a *Delayed* Crisis

However, an equally effective structure can be built with a **delayed** crisis that comes near the end of Act Two, about two-thirds to three-quarters of the way into the story.

The delayed-crisis structure matches closely with the ideal of the Golden Mean, that elegant proportion (approximately three to five) that seems to produce the most pleasing artistic results. A delayed crisis leaves more room for preparation and Approach and allows a slow buildup to a big moment at the end of Act Two.

Whether the crisis is at the center of the story or nearer the end of Act Two, it's safe to say every story needs a crisis moment that conveys the Ordeal's sense of death and revival.

POINTS OF TENSION

Act Two is a long stretch for the writer and the audience, up to an hour in an average feature film. You can look at the three-act structure as a dramatic line stretched across two major points of tension, the act breaks. Like a circus tent hanging on its poles, structure is subject to gravity — the waning of the audience's attention in the time between these peaks of tension. A story that has no central moment of tension may sag like a circus tent that needs an extra support pole in the middle. Act Two is an hour-long chunk of your movie, or a hundred pages of your novel. It needs some kind of structure to hold it in tension.

The crisis at the halfway point is a watershed, a continental divide in the hero's journey, that acknowledges the traveler has reached the middle of the trip. Journeys naturally arrange themselves around a central event: getting to the top of the mountain, the depth of the cave, the heart of the forest, the most intimate interior of a foreign country, or the most secret place in your own soul. Everything in the trip has been leading up to this moment, and everything after it will be just going home. There may be even greater adventures to come — the final moments of a trip may be the most exciting or memorable — but every journey seems to have a center: a bottom or a peak, somewhere near the middle.

The words crisis, critic, and critical come from a Greek word that means "to separate." A crisis is an event that separates the two halves of the story. After crossing this zone, which is often the borderland of death, the hero is literally or metaphorically reborn and nothing will ever be the same.

WITNESS TO SACRIFICE

The reality of a death-and-rebirth crisis may depend upon point of view. A witness is often an important part of this stage, someone standing nearby who sees the hero *appear* to die, momentarily mourns the death, and is elated when the hero is revived. Some of the death-and-resurrection effects in *Star Wars* depend on the presence of witnesses, such as the two robot Allies, R2D2 and C3PO. In an elaborate Supreme Ordeal sequence, they are listening by intercom to the progress of their heroes, Skywalker and company. The robots are horrified to hear what sounds like the heroes being crushed to death in a giant trashmasher deep in the Inmost Cave of the Death Star.

These witnesses stand for the audience, who are identifying with the heroes and feeling the pain of death with them. It's not that audiences are sadistic and enjoy seeing their heroes killed. It's that we all relish a little taste of death every now and then. Its bitter flavor makes life taste sweeter. Anyone who has survived a true near-death experience, a sudden close call in a car or plane, knows that for a while afterward colors seem sharper, family and friends are more important, and time is more precious. The nearness of death makes life more real.

A TASTE OF DEATH

People pay good money for a taste of death. Bungee-jumping, skydiving, and terrifying amusement park rides give people the jolt that awakens fuller appreciation of life. Adventure films and stories are always popular because they offer a less risky way to experience death and rebirth, through heroes we can identify with.

But wait a minute, we left poor Luke Skywalker being crushed to death in the heart, or rather the stomach, of the Death Star. He's in the belly of the whale. The robot witnesses are distraught at hearing what sounds like their master's death. They grieve and the audience grieves with them, tasting death. All of the filmmaker's artful technique is dedicated to making the audience think their heroes are being ground to a paste.

I have a bad feeling about this.

But then the robots realize that what they thought were screams of death were in fact cries of relief and triumph. The robots managed to shut off the trashmasher and the heroes have miraculously survived. The grief of the robots and of the audience suddenly, explosively, turns to joy.

THE ELASTICITY OF EMOTION

Human emotions, it seems, have certain elastic properties, rather like basketballs. When thrown down hard, they bounce back high. In any story you are trying to lift the audience, raise their awareness, heighten their emotions. The structure of a story acts like a pump to increase the involvement of the audience. Good structure works by alternately lowering and raising the hero's fortunes and, with them, the audience's emotions. Depressing an audience's emotions has the same effect as holding an inflated basketball under water: When the downward pressure is released, the ball flies up out of the water. Emotions depressed by the presence of death can rebound in an instant to a higher state than ever before. This can become the base on which you build to a still higher level. The Ordeal is one of the deepest "depressions" in a story and therefore leads to one of its highest peaks.

In an amusement park ride you are hurled around in darkness or on the edge of space until you think you're going to die, but somehow you come out elated that you have survived. A story without some hint of this experience is missing its heart. Screenwriters sometimes have a lot of trouble with the length of Act Two. It can seem monotonous, episodic, or aimless. This may be because they've conceived of it as simply a series of obstacles to the hero's final goal, rather than as a dynamic series of events leading up to and trailing away from a central moment of death and rebirth. Even in the silliest comedy or most light-hearted romance, Act Two needs a central life–or–death crisis, a moment when the hero is experiencing death or maximum danger to the enterprise.

HERO APPEARS TO DIE

The long second act of *Star Wars* is kept from sagging by a central crisis section in which the borders of death are thoroughly explored in not one, but a series of ordeals. At another point in the giant trash compactor sequence, Luke is pulled under the sewage by the tentacle of an unseen monster. It was this scene that really made me understand the mechanism of the Ordeal.

First, the audience and the witnesses at hand (Han Solo, Princess Leia, the Wookiee) see a few bubbles come up, a sign that Luke is still struggling, alive, and breathing. So far, so good. But then the bubbles stop coming. The witnesses begin reacting as if he were dead. In a few seconds you begin to wonder if he's ever coming up. You know George Lucas is not going to kill off his hero halfway through the film and yet you begin to entertain the possibility.

I remember seeing a preview screening of *Star Wars* on the Fox lot and being completely taken in by the critical few seconds of this scene. I had invested something of myself in Luke Skywalker and when he appeared to be dead, I instantly became a disembodied presence in the screen. I began flitting from surviving character to character, wondering who I could identify with next. Would I ride through the rest of the story as the spoiled Princess Leia, the selfish opportunist Han Solo, or the beastly Wookiee? I didn't feel comfortable in any of their skins. In these few seconds I experienced something like panic. The hero, for me, was truly in the belly of the whale, inaccessible, effectively dead. With the hero dead, who was I in this movie? What was my point of view? My emotions, like the basketball held under water, were depressed.

Just then Luke Skywalker explodes to the surface, slimy but alive. He has died to our eyes, but now he lives again, rebirthed by the companions who help him to his feet. At once the audience feels elated. The emotions ride higher for having been brought down so far. Experiences like this are the key to the popularity of the *Star Wars* movies. They fling heroes and audiences over the brink of death and snatch them back repeatedly. It's more than great special effects, funny dialogue, and sex that people are paying for. They love to see heroes cheat death. In fact they love to cheat death themselves. Identifying with a hero who bounces back from death is bungee-jumping in dramatic form.

HERO WITNESSES DEATH

Star Wars has not given us enough of a taste of death yet. Before the Ordeal section is over, Luke witnesses the physical death of his Mentor, Obi Wan, in a laser duel with the villain Darth Vader. Luke is devastated and feels the death as keenly as if it were his own. But in this mythical world, the borders of life and death are deliberately fuzzy. Obi Wan's body vanishes, raising the possibility he may survive somewhere to return when needed, like King Arthur and Merlin.

To a shaman like Obi Wan, death is a familiar threshold that can be crossed back and forth with relative ease. Obi Wan lives within Luke and the audience through his teachings. Despite physical death he is able to give Luke crucial advice at later points in the story: "Trust the Force, Luke."

HERO CAUSES DEATH

The hero doesn't have to die for the moment of death to have its effect. The hero may be a witness to death or the cause of death. In *Body Heat* the central event, William Hurt's Ordeal, is murdering Kathleen Turner's husband and disposing of his body. But it's a death for Hurt too, deep in his soul. His innocence has died, a victim of his own lust.

FACING THE SHADOW

By far the most common kind of Ordeal is some sort of battle or confrontation with an opposing force. It could be a deadly enemy villain, antagonist, opponent, or even a force of nature. An idea that comes close to encompassing all these possibilities is the archetype of the Shadow. A villain may be an external character, but in a deeper sense what all these words stand for is the negative possibilities of the hero himself. In other words, the hero's greatest opponent is his own Shadow.

As with all the archetypes, there are negative and positive manifestations of the Shadow. A dark side is needed sometimes to polarize a hero or a system, to give the hero some resistance to push against. Resistance can be your greatest source of strength. Ironically, what seem to be villains fighting for our death may turn out to be forces ultimately working for our good.

DEMONIZATION

Generally the Shadow represents the hero's fears and unlikeable, rejected qualities: all the things we don't like about ourselves and try to project onto other people. This form of projection is called **demonizing**. People in emotional crisis will sometimes project all their problems in a certain area onto another person or group who become the symbol of everything they hate and fear in themselves. In war and propaganda, the enemy becomes an inhuman devil, the dark Shadow of the righteous, angelic image we are trying to maintain for ourselves. The Devil himself is God's Shadow, a projection of all the negative and rejected potential of the Supreme Being.

Sometimes we need this projection and polarization in order to see an issue clearly. A system can stay in unhealthy imbalance for a long time if the conflicts are not categorized, polarized, and made to duke it out in some kind of dramatic confrontation. Usually the Shadow can be brought out into the light. The unrecognized or rejected parts are acknowledged and made conscious despite all their struggling to remain in darkness. Dracula's abhorrence of sunlight is a symbol of the Shadow's desire to remain unexplored.

Villains can be looked at as the hero's Shadow in human form. No matter how alien the villain's values, in some way they are the dark reflection of the hero's own desires, magnified and distorted, her greatest fears come to life.

DEATH OF A VILLAIN

Sometimes the hero comes close to death at the Ordeal, but it is the villain who dies. However, the hero may have other forces, other Shadows, to deal with before the adventure is over. The action may move from the physical arena to a moral, spiritual, or emotional plane. Dorothy kills the Wicked Witch in Act Two, but faces an ordeal of the spirit: the death of her hopes of getting home in Act Three.

A villain's death should not be too easy for the hero to accomplish. In an Ordeal scene in Hitchcock's *Torn Curtain*, the hero tries to kill a spy in a farmhouse with no real weapons at hand. Hitchcock makes the point that killing someone can be much harder than the movies usually make it seem. Anyone's death has an emotional cost, as well, as the movie *Unforgiven* repeatedly shows. Clint Eastwood's bounty hunter kills but is painfully aware his targets are men just like him. Death should be real, and not a mere plot convenience.

THE VILLAIN ESCAPES

The hero may wound the villain at the Ordeal or kill the villain's underling. The chief villain escapes to be confronted once again in Act Three. Axel Foley has a death-and-rebirth confrontation with the criminal mastermind's lieutenants in Act Two of *Beverly Hills Cop,* but the final showdown with the main Shadow is held back for Act Three.

VILLAINS ARE HEROES OF THEIR OWN STORIES

Keep in mind that while some villains or Shadows exult in being bad, many don't think of themselves as evil at all. In their own minds they are right, the heroes of their own stories. A dark moment for the hero is a bright one for a Shadow. The arcs of their stories are mirror images: When the hero is up, the villain is down. It depends on point of view. By the time you are done writing a screenplay or novel, you should know your characters well enough that you can tell the story from the point of view of everyone: heroes, villains, sidekicks, lovers, allies, guardians, and lesser folk. Each is the hero of his own story. It's a good exercise to walk through the story at least once in the Shadow's skin.

HOW HEROES CHEAT DEATH

In the classic hero myths the Ordeal is set up as a moment in which the hero is expected to die. Many have come to this point before and none have survived. Perseus' Approach to the monster Medusa is choked with statues of heroes turned to stone by her glance. The labyrinth which Theseus enters is littered with the bones of those who were eaten by the monster inside or who starved trying to find their way out.

These mythic heroes face certain death but survive where others have failed because they have wisely sought supernatural aid in the earlier stages. They cheat death, usually with the help of the Mentor's gifts. Perseus uses the magic mirror, Athena's gift, to approach Medusa and avoid her direct gaze. He cuts off her head with his magic sword and keeps it from doing further harm by stowing it in his magic pouch, another Mentor's gift.

In the story of Theseus, the hero has won the love of Ariadne, daughter of the tyrant Minos of Crete, in the Approach phase. Now, when Theseus must go into the uncertain, deadly depths of the Labyrinth, he turns to Ariadne for aid. The princess goes to the Mentor of the story, the great inventor and architect Daedalus, designer of the Labyrinth. His magical help is of the simplest kind: a ball of thread. Ariadne holds one end while Theseus winds through the Labyrinth. He is able to find his way back from the house of death because of his connection to her — because of love, the thread that binds them.

ARIADNE'S THREAD

Ariadne's Thread is a potent symbol of the power of love, of the almost telepathic wiring that joins people in an intense relationship. It can tug at you like a physical connector at times. It's close kin to the "apron strings" that bind even adult children to their mothers — invisible wires but with greater tensile strength than steel.

Ariadne's Thread is an elastic band that connects a hero with loved ones. A hero may venture far out into madness or death, but is usually pulled back by such bonds. My mother tells me she had a medical emergency when I was a child that almost killed her. Her spirit left her body and flew around the room, feeling free and ready to leave, and only the sight of my sisters and me snapped her back into life. She had a reason to go on living, to take care of us.

The Old English word for a ball of thread is a "clew." That's where we get our word clue. A clue is a thread that a seeker traces back to a center, looking for answers or order. The skeins of thread that connect one heart to another may be the vital clue that solves a mystery or resolves a conflict.

CRISIS OF THE HEART

The Ordeal can be a crisis of the heart. In a story of romance it might be the moment of greatest intimacy, something we all desire and yet fear. Perhaps what's dying here is a hero's defensiveness. In another story it might be a dark moment in the romance when the hero experiences betrayal or the apparent death of the relationship.

Joseph Campbell describes what we might call the romantic branches of the Ordeal in two chapters of *The Hero with a Thousand Faces* called "Meeting with the Goddess" and "Woman as Temptress." As he says, "the ultimate adventure... is commonly represented as a mystical marriage... the crisis at the nadir, the zenith, or at the uttermost edge of the earth, at the central point of the cosmos, in the cosmos, in the tabernacle of the temple, or within the darkness of the deepest chamber of the heart." In stories of love, the crisis may be either a love scene or a separation from a loved one. Crisis, remember, comes from a Greek word meaning "to separate."

In *Romancing the Stone* the crisis is both a physical Ordeal and a separation of loved ones. Joan Wilder and her shapeshifting companion Jack Colton enter a literal Inmost Cave where they take possession of the giant emerald, *El Corazon*. But that's much too easy and a few moments later they go through a real Supreme Ordeal as their car plunges over a waterfall and they dive out. Joan Wilder disappears under the water for several shots. The audience sees Jack Colton struggle ashore, and for scant seconds we are left wondering if Joan has died. Those few seconds are sufficient for the magic of the Supreme Ordeal to work. Joan then appears, struggling onto a rock in the foreground. That she has died and been reborn is clearly acknowledged in the dialogue. On the opposite bank, Colton cries out, "I thought you drowned." Joan acknowledges, "I did."

Colton is elated by their physical survival, but now the focus of the crisis for Joan shifts to the emotional plane. The untrustworthy Colton is on the opposite side of the raging river with the jewel. A real test of their love is coming. Will he keep his promise to meet her in the next town, or will he simply run away with *El Corazon* and break her heart? Will she be able to survive in the jungle of the Special World without him?

SACRED MARRIAGE

In stories with emotional and psychological depth, the Ordeal may bring a moment of mystic marriage within a person, a balancing of opposing inner forces. The fear and death aspect of the Ordeal may haunt the wedding: What if this doesn't work out? What if the part of myself I am walking to the altar with turns and overwhelms me? But despite these fears, heroes may acknowledge their hidden qualities, even their Shadows, and join with them in a sacred marriage. Heroes are ultimately seeking a confrontation with their anima, their soul, or the unrecognized feminine or intuitive parts of their personality.

Women may be seeking the animus, the masculine powers of reason and assertion that society has told them to hide. They may be trying to get back in touch with a creative drive or a maternal energy they've rejected. In a moment of crisis, a hero may get in touch with all sides of her personality as her many selves are called forth en masse to deal with her life-and-death issues.

BALANCE

In a Sacred Marriage both sides of the personality are acknowledged to be of equal value. Such a hero, in touch with all the tools of being a human, is in a state of balance, centered, and not easily dislodged or upset. Campbell says the Sacred Marriage "represents the hero's total mastery of life," a balanced marriage between the hero and life itself.

Therefore the Ordeal may be a crisis in which the hero is joined with the repressed feminine or masculine side in a Sacred Marriage. But there may also be a Sacred Breakup! Open, deadly war may be declared by the dueling male and female sides.

THE LOVE THAT KILLS

Campbell touches on this destructive conflict in "The Woman as Temptress." The title is perhaps misleading — as with "The Meeting with the Goddess," the energy of this moment could be male or female. This Ordeal possibility takes the hero to a junction of betrayal, abandonment, or disappointment. It's a crisis of faith in the arena of love.

Every archetype has both a bright, positive side and a dark, negative side. The dark side of love is the mask of hate, recrimination, outrage, and rejection. This is the face of Medea as she kills her own children, the mask of Medusa herself, ringed with poison snakes of blame and guilt.

A crisis may come when a shapeshifting lover suddenly shows another side, leaving the hero feeling bitterly betrayed and dead to the idea of love. This is a favorite Hitchcock device. After a tender love scene in *North by Northwest*, Cary Grant's character is betrayed to the spies by Eva Marie Saint. Grant goes into his mid-movie Ordeal feeling abandoned by her. The possibility of true love that she represented now seems dead, and it makes his Ordeal, in which he's almost gunned down by a crop-dusting plane in a cornfield, all the more lonely.

NEGATIVE ANIMUS OR ANIMA

Sometimes in the journey of our lives we confront negative projections of the anima or animus. This can be a person who attracts us but isn't good for us, or a bitchy or bastardly part of ourselves that suddenly asserts itself like Mr. Hyde taking over from Dr. Jekyll. Such a confrontation can be a life-threatening Ordeal in a relationship or in a person's development. The hero of *Fatal Attraction* finds that a casual lover can turn into a lethal force if crossed or rejected. An ideal partner can turn into the Boston Strangler or a loving father can become a killer as in *The Shining*. The wicked stepmothers and queens of the Grimms' fairy tales were, in the original versions, mothers whose love turned deadly.

GOING PSYCHO

One of the most disturbing and subversive uses of the Supreme Ordeal is in Alfred Hitchcock's *Psycho*. The audience is made to identify and sympathize with Marion (Janet Leigh), even though she is an embezzler on the run. Through the first half of Act Two, there is no one else to identify with except the drippy innkeeper, Norman Bates (Anthony Perkins), and no audience wants to identify with him — he's weird. In a conventional film, the hero always survives the Ordeal and lives to see the villain defeated in the climax. It's unimaginable that a star like Janet Leigh, an immortal heroine of the screen, will be sacrificed at the midpoint. But Hitchcock does the unthinkable and kills our hero halfway through the story. This is one Ordeal that is final for the hero. No reprieve, no resurrection, no curtain call for Marion.

The effect is shattering. You get that odd feeling of being a disembodied ghost, floating around the frame as you watch Marion's blood pour down the drain. Who to identify with? Who to be? Soon it's clear: Hitchcock is giving you no one to identify with but Norman. Reluctantly we enter Norman's mind, see the story through his eyes, and even begin to root for him as our new hero. At first we're supposed to think Norman is covering up for his insane mother, but later we discover Norman himself was the killer. We have been walking around in the skin of a psycho. Only a master like Hitchcock can pull off such a defiance of the rules about heroes, death, and Ordeals.

FACING THE GREATEST FEAR

The Ordeal can be defined as the moment the hero faces his greatest fear. For most people this is death, but in many stories it's just whatever the hero is most afraid of: facing up to a phobia, challenging a rival, or roughing out a storm or a political crisis. Indiana Jones inevitably must come face-to-face with what he fears most — snakes.

Of the many fears faced by heroes, the greatest dramatic power seems to come from the fear of standing up to a parent or authority figure. The family scene is the core of most serious drama, and a confrontation with a parent figure can provide a strong Ordeal.

STANDING UP TO A PARENT

In *Red River* Montgomery Clift's character, Matthew Garth, faces this fear halfway through the story when he tries to take away control of a cattle drive from his foster-father, Tom Dunson (John Wayne), who has become a formidable Shadow. Dunson started the story as hero and Mentor, but traded those masks for that of a tyrant in the Approach phase. He's turned into a demented god, wounded, drunk, and cruel: an abusive father to his men, carrying duty too far. When Matt challenges his Mentor and role model, he is facing his greatest fear in an Ordeal.

Dunson decrees he will play god and hang men who broke the laws of his little world. Matt stands up to him at the risk of being shot himself. Dunson, the Lord Death rising from his throne, draws to kill him; but Matt's Allies, earned in the Testing phase, step in and blow the gun out of Dunson's hand. Matt's power as a hero is now such that he doesn't need to lift a finger against his opponent. His will alone is strong enough to defeat death. In effect he dethrones Dunson and becomes king of the cattle drive himself, leaving his foster-father with nothing but a horse and a canteen. In stories like this, facing the greatest fear is depicted as youth standing up to the older generation.

YOUTH VERSUS AGE

The challenging of the older generation by the younger is a timeless drama, and the Supreme Ordeal of standing up to a forbidding parent is as old as Adam and Eve, Oedipus, or King Lear. This ageless conflict provides much of the power of playwriting. The play *On Golden Pond* deals with a daughter's frantic effort to please her father, and its Ordeals are the daughter standing up to the father, and the father experiencing his own mortality.

This generational drama is sometimes played out on a world stage. The Chinese dissident students who took over Tiananmen Square and blocked the tanks with their bodies were challenging the status quo imposed by their parents and grandparents.

Fairy-tale struggles with wolves and witches may be ways of expressing conflicts with parents. The witches are the dark aspect of the mother; the wolves, ogres, or giants the dark aspect of the father. Dragons and other monsters can be the Shadow side of a parent or a generation that has held on too long. Campbell spoke of the dragon as a Western symbol of a tyrant who has held fast to a kingdom or a family until all the life has been squeezed out of it.

The conflict between youth and age can be expressed internally as well as in external battles between children and parents. The smoldering combat that ignites in the Ordeal may be an inner struggle between an old, comfortable, well-defended personality structure and a new one that is weak, unformed, but eager to be born. But the new Self can't be born until the old one dies or at least steps aside to leave more room on the center stage.

In rare cases an Ordeal can be the occasion for a healing of deep wounds between a hero and a parent. Campbell calls this possibility "Atonement with the Father." Sometimes a hero, by surviving an Ordeal or by daring to challenge the authority of a parental figure, will win the parent's approval and the seeming conflicts between them will be resolved.

DEATH OF THE EGO

The Ordeal in myths signifies the death of the ego. The hero is now fully part of the cosmos, dead to the old, limited vision of things and reborn into a new consciousness of connections. The old boundaries of the Self have been transcended or annihilated. In some sense the hero has become a god with the divine ability to soar above the normal limits of death and see the broader view of the connectedness of all things. The Greeks called this a moment of **apotheosis**, a step up from enthusiasm where you merely have the god in you. In a state of apotheosis you *are* the god. Tasting death lets you sit in God's chair for a while.

The hero facing an Ordeal has moved her center from the ego to the Self, to the more godlike part of her. There may also be a movement from Self to group as a hero accepts more responsibility than just looking out for herself. A hero risks individual life for the sake of the larger collective life and wins the right to be called "hero."

THE WIZARD OF OZ

Dorothy and friends, trapped by the Wicked Witch and her Threshold Guardian army, now face their Supreme Ordeal. The Witch is enraged at them for having penetrated her Inmost Cave and stolen her greatest treasure, the Ruby Slippers. She descends on the foursome and threatens to kill them one by one, saving Dorothy until last.

The threat of death makes the stakes of the scene clear. The audience now knows it's going to be a battle between forces of life and death.

The Witch begins with the Scarecrow. She lights her broomstick and uses it as a torch to set him on fire. His straw blazes up and it looks like all is lost. Every child in the audience believes the Scarecrow is doomed and feels the horror of death with him.

Dorothy operates on instinct and does the only thing she can think of to save her friend: She grabs up a bucket of water and splashes it all over the Scarecrow. It puts out the fire, but it also wets down the Witch. Dorothy had no intention of killing the Witch, didn't even realize water would make her melt, but has killed her just the same. Death was in the room, and Dorothy merely deflected it onto another victim.

But the Witch does not just go "poof" and disappear. Her death is protracted, agonizing, and pathetic. "Oh, my beautiful wickedness! What a world, what a world!" By the time it's over you feel sorry for the Witch, and have had a real taste of death.

Our heroes have gone face-to-face with death and can walk away to tell about it. After a moment of being stunned, they are elated. They go on to reap the consequences of defying death, in the next step: Reward, or Seizing the Sword.

QUESTIONING THE JOURNEY

1. What is the Ordeal in *The Silence of the Lambs*? *The Prince of Tides*? *Pretty Woman*?

2. What is the Ordeal in your story? Does your story truly have a villain? Or is there simply an antagonist?

3. In what way is the villain or antagonist the hero's Shadow?

4. Is the villain's power channeled through partners or underlings? What special functions do these parts perform?

5. Can the villain also be a Shapeshifter or Trickster? What other archetypes might a villain manifest?

6. In what way does your hero face death in the Ordeal? What is your hero's greatest fear?

REWARD

STAGE NINE: REWARD

"We came, we saw, we kicked its ass."
— from *Ghostbusters*, screenplay by
Dan Aykroyd and Harold Ramis

With the crisis of the Ordeal passed, heroes now experience the consequences of surviving death. With the dragon that dwelt in the Inmost Cave slain or vanquished, they seize the sword of victory and lay claim to their **Reward.** Triumph may be fleeting but for now they savor its pleasures.

We Seekers look at one another with growing smiles. We've won the right to be called heroes. For the sake of the Home Tribe we faced death, tasted it, and yet lived. From the depths of terror we suddenly shoot up to victory. It's time to fill our empty bellies and raise our voices around the campfire to sing of our deeds. Old wounds and grievances are forgotten. The story of our journey is already being woven.

You pull apart from the rest, strangely quiet. In the leaping shadows you remember those who didn't make it, and you notice something. You're different. You've changed. Part of you has died and something new has been born. You and the world will never seem the same. This too is part of the Reward for facing death.

Encountering death is a big event and it will surely have consequences. There will almost always be some period of time in which the hero is recognized or rewarded for having survived death or a great ordeal. A great many possibilities are generated by living through a crisis, and Reward, the aftermath of the Ordeal, has many shapes and purposes.

CELEBRATION

When hunters have survived death and brought down their game, it's natural to want to celebrate. Energy has been exhausted in the struggle, and needs to be replenished. Heroes may have the equivalent of a party or barbecue at this stage in which they cook and consume some of the fruits of victory. The heroes of *The Odyssey* always offered a sacrifice and had a meal to give thanks and celebrate after surviving some ordeal at sea. Strength is needed for the return to the upper world, so time is given for rest, recuperation, and refueling. After the buffalo hunt (a Supreme Ordeal and brush with death) in *Dances with Wolves,* Dunbar and the tribe celebrate with a buffalo barbecue in which his Reward for saving a young man from death is greater acceptance by the Lakota.

CAMPFIRE SCENES

Many stories seem to have campfire-type scenes in this region, where the hero and companions gather around a fire or its equivalent to review the recent events. It's also an opportunity for jokes and boasting. There is understandable relief at having survived death. Hunters and fishermen, pilots and navigators, soldiers and explorers all like to exaggerate their accomplishments. At the barbecue in *Dances with Wolves,* Dunbar is forced to retell the story of the buffalo hunt many times.

There may be conflict over the campfire, fighting over spoils. Dunbar gets into an argument over his hat, which has been picked up by a Sioux warrior after Dunbar dropped it during the buffalo hunt.

A campfire scene may also be a chance for reminiscence or nostalgia. Having crossed the abyss of life and death, nothing will ever be the same. Heroes sometimes turn back and remember aloud what got them to this point. A loner hero might recall the events or people who influenced him, or speak about the unwritten code by which he runs his life.

These scenes serve important functions for the audience. They allow us to catch our breath after an exciting battle or ordeal. The characters might recap the story so far, giving us a chance to review the story and get a glimpse of how they perceive it. In *Red River,* Matthew Garth reviews the plot for a newcomer to the story, Tess (Joanne Dru), in a campfire scene. He reveals his feelings about his foster-father and gives the audience a perspective on the complex, epic story.

In these quiet moments of reflection or intimacy we get to know the characters better. A memorable example is the scene in *Jaws* in which Robert Shaw's character, Quint, tells about his horrible World War II experiences with sharks in the Pacific. The men compare scars and sing a drinking song. It's a "getting-to-know-you" scene, built on the intimacy that comes from having survived an Ordeal together.

In Walt Disney's classic animated features such as *Pinocchio* or *Peter Pan,* the pace is usually frantic, but Disney was careful to slow them down from time to time and get in close on the characters in an emotional moment. These quieter or more lyric passages are important for making a connection with the audience.

LOVE SCENES

The aftermath of a Supreme Ordeal may be an opportunity for a love scene. Heroes don't really become heroes until the crisis; until then they are just trainees. They don't really deserve to be loved until they have shown their willingness to sacrifice. At this point a true hero has earned a love scene, or a "sacred marriage" of some kind. The *Red River* campfire scene described above is also a highly effective love scene.

In the thriller *Arabesque,* Gregory Peck and Sophia Loren, having survived an Ordeal together, are bonded in a love scene. She is a bewildering Shapeshifter who has told him a string of lies, but he has seen through to her essential core of goodness, and now trusts her.

The romantic waltz in *Beauty and the Beast* is the Beast's Reward for having survived an Ordeal with the townspeople and Belle's Reward for having seen past the Beast's monstrous appearance.

TAKING POSSESSION

One of the essential aspects of this step is the hero taking possession of whatever she came seeking. Treasure hunters take the gold, spies snatch the secret, pirates plunder the captured ship, an uncertain hero seizes her self-respect, a slave seizes control of his own destiny. A transaction has been made — the hero has risked death or sacrificed life, and now gets something in exchange. The Norse god Odin, in his Supreme Ordeal, gives up an eye and hangs on the World-Tree for nine days and nights. His Reward is the knowledge of all things and the ability to read the sacred runes.

SEIZING THE SWORD

I also call this unit of the journey **Seizing the Sword** because often it's an active movement of the hero who aggressively takes possession of whatever was being sought in the Special World. Sometimes a reward like love is given. But more frequently the hero takes possession of a treasure or even steals it, like James Bond taking the Lektor, a Soviet translating device, in *From Russia with Love.*

A moment of taking possession follows the death-and-rebirth crisis in *King Kong*. A transformation had occurred in the monster ape during the Approach phase. King Kong shifted from being Fay Wray's abductor to being her protector, fighting off a tyrannosaur on the way to his Inmost Cave. By the time he reaches the Supreme Ordeal, defending her in a battle to the death with a giant serpent, he has become a full-fledged hero. Now he takes possession of his Reward. Like any good hero, he gets the girl.

In a tender but erotic scene, he takes her out onto the "balcony" of his cave and examines her, cradled in his enormous palm. He pulls off her clothes, strip by strip, sniffing her perfume curiously. He tickles her with his finger. The love scene is interrupted by another dinosaur threat, but it was definitely a Reward moment, a payback for having faced death head-on during the crisis.

The idea of a hero Seizing the Sword comes from memories of stories in which heroes battle dragons and take their treasure. Among the treasures there may be a magic sword, perhaps the sword of the hero's father, broken or stolen by the dragon in previous battles. The image of the sword, as portrayed in the Tarot deck's suit of swords, is a symbol of the hero's will, forged in fire and quenched in blood, broken and remade, hammered and folded, hardened, sharpened, and focused to a point like the light-sabers of *Star Wars.*

But a sword is only one of many images for what is being seized by the hero at this step. Campbell's term for it is "The Ultimate Boon." Another concept is the Holy Grail, an ancient and mysterious symbol for all the unattainable things of the soul that knights and heroes quest after. A rose or a jewel may be the treasure in another story. The wily Monkey King of Chinese legends is seeking the sacred Buddhist sutras that have been taken to Tibet.

ELIXIR THEFT

Some heroes purchase the treasure in effect, buying it with their lives or the willingness to risk life. But other heroes steal the magic thing at the heart of the story. The prize is not always given, even if it has been paid for or earned. It must be taken. Campbell calls this motif "elixir theft."

Elixir means a medium or vehicle for medicine. It could be a harmless sweet liquid or powder to which other medicine is added. Administered alone or mixed with other useless chemicals, it might still work by what's known as the "placebo effect." Studies have shown that some people get better on a placebo, a substance with no medicinal value, even when they know it's just a sugar pill — testimony to the power of suggestion.

An elixir can also be a medicine that heals every ill, a magical substance that restores life. In alchemy the elixir is one of the steps towards the philosopher's stone which can transmute metals, create life, and transcend death. This ability to overcome the forces of death is the real Elixir most heroes seek.

The hero is often required to steal the Elixir. It is the secret of life and death, and much too valuable to be given up lightly. Heroes may turn Trickster or thief to make off with the treasure, like Prometheus stealing fire from the gods for mankind, or Adam and Eve tasting the apple. This theft may intoxicate the hero for a time, but there is often a heavy price to pay later.

INITIATION

Heroes emerge from their Ordeals to be recognized as special and different, part of a select few who have outwitted death. The Immortals of ancient Greece were a very exclusive club. Only the gods and a smattering of lucky humans were exempt from death, and only those humans who had done something remarkable or pleasing to the gods would be granted admittance by Zeus. Among these were Hercules, Andromeda, and Aesculapius.

Battlefield promotions and knighthood are ways of recognizing that heroes have passed an ordeal and entered a smaller group of special survivors. Joseph Campbell's overall name for what we are calling Act Two is "Initiation," a new beginning in a new rank. The hero after facing death is really a new creature. A woman who has gone through the life-threatening territory of childbirth belongs to a different order of being. She has been initiated into the company of motherhood, a select sorority.

Initiation into secret societies, sororities, or fraternities means that you are privy to certain secrets and sworn never to reveal them. You pass tests to prove your worthiness. You may be put through a ritual death-and-rebirth Ordeal and may be given a new name and rank to signify you are a newborn being.

NEW PERCEPTIONS

Heroes may find that surviving death grants new powers or better perceptions. In the previous chapter we spoke of death's ability to sharpen the perception of life. This is beautifully captured in the northern tale of Sigurd the dragon-killer. Sigurd's Supreme Ordeal is to slay a dragon named Fafnir. A drop of the dragon's blood happens to fall on Sigurd's tongue. He has truly tasted death, and for this is granted new powers of perception. He can understand the language of the birds, and hears two of them warning him that his Mentor, the dwarf Regin, plans to kill him. He is saved from a second deadly danger because of his newfound power, the Reward for surviving death. New knowledge may be the sword that the hero seizes.

SEEING THROUGH DECEPTION

A hero may be granted a new insight or understanding of a mystery as her Reward. She may see through a deception. If she has been dealing with a shapeshifting partner, she may see through his disguises and perceive the reality for the first time. Seizing the Sword can be a moment of clarity.

CLAIRVOYANCE

After transcending death, a hero may even become clairvoyant or telepathic, sharing in the power of the immortal gods. Clairvoyant means simply "seeing clearly." A hero who has faced death is more aware of the connectedness of things, more intuitive. In *Arabesque,* after the love scene between Gregory Peck and Sophia Loren, the lovers are trying to figure out a secret code in ancient hieroglyphics. Peck suddenly realizes, with his newfound perceptive ability, that what the spies are after is not the code but a microfilm dot on the piece of paper. Surviving death has given him new power of insight. The realization is so exciting that it propels the movie into Act Three.

SELF-REALIZATION

Insight might be of a deeper type. Heroes can sometimes experience a profound **self-realization** after tricking death. They see who they are and how they fit into the scheme of things. They see the ways they've been foolish or stubborn. The scales fall from their eyes and the illusion of their lives is replaced with clarity and truth. Maybe it doesn't last long, but for a moment heroes see themselves clearly.

EPIPHANY

Others may see the hero more clearly, too. Others may see in their changed behavior signs that they have been reborn and share in the immortality of gods. This is sometimes called a moment of **epiphany**: an abrupt realization of divinity. The Feast of the Epiphany, observed in the Catholic Church on January 6, celebrates the moment when the Magi, three Wise Old Men, first realized the divinity of the newborn Christ. One of the Rewards of surviving death is that others can see that heroes have changed. Young people coming back from a war or from an ordeal like basic training seem different — more mature, self-confident, and serious, and worthy of a little more respect. There is a chain of divine experience: from enthusiasm, being visited by a god, to apotheosis, becoming a god, to epiphany, being recognized as a god.

Heroes themselves may experience epiphany. A hero may realize suddenly, after a moment of Supreme Ordeal, that he is the son of a god or a king, a chosen one with special powers. Epiphany is a moment of realizing you are a divine and sacred being, connected to all things.

James Joyce expanded the meaning of the word epiphany, using it to mean a sudden perception of the essence of something, seeing to the core of a person, idea, or thing. Heroes sometimes experience a sudden understanding of the nature of things after passing through an Ordeal. Surviving death gives meaning to life and sharpens perceptions.

DISTORTIONS

In other stories the conquest of death may lead to some distortions of perception. Heroes may suffer from an inflation of the ego. In other words, they get a swelled head. They might turn cocky or arrogant. Perhaps they abuse the power and privilege of being a reborn hero. Their self-esteem sometimes grows too large and distorts their perception of their real value.

Heroes may be tainted by the very death or evil they came to fight. Soldiers fighting to preserve civilization may fall into the barbarism of war. Cops or detectives battling criminals often cross the line and use illegal or immoral means, becoming as bad as the criminals themselves. Heroes can enter the mental world of their opponents and get stuck there, like the detective in *Manhunter* who risks his soul to enter the twisted mind of a serial killer.

Bloodshed and murder are powerful forces and may intoxicate or poison a hero. Peter O'Toole as Lawrence of Arabia shows us a man who, after the Ordeal of the battle of Aqaba, is horrified to discover that he loves killing.

Another error heroes may make at this point is simply to underestimate the significance of the Supreme Ordeal. Someone hit by the hammer of change may deny that anything has happened. Denial after an encounter with death is one of the natural stages of grief and recovery described by Dr. Elisabeth Kubler-Ross. Anger is another. Heroes may just let off some steam after the Ordeal, expressing justifiable resentment over having been made to face death.

Heroes may also overestimate their own importance or prowess after a duel with death. But they may soon find out that they were just lucky the first time, and will have other encounters with danger that will teach them their limits.

THE WIZARD OF OZ

The immediate aftermath of the Ordeal in The Wizard of Oz *is an act of Seizing. Instead of a sword, it's the burnt broomstick of the Wicked Witch that Dorothy takes possession of. Actually she's much too well mannered to just grab it; she politely asks for it from the fearsome guards who have now fallen to their knees to show their loyalty to her. Dorothy had good reason to fear they would turn on her after the Witch's death. But in fact the guards are glad the Witch is dead, for now they are free of her awful slavery. Another Reward of surviving death is that Threshold Guardians may be completely won over to the hero's side. The guards give her the broomstick gladly.*

Dorothy and companions return swiftly to the Wizard's throne room where she lays the broom before the ferocious floating Head. She has fulfilled her bargain with the Wizard, and completed the seemingly impossible task. Now she and her friends claim their heroes' Reward.

But to their surprise, the Wizard balks at paying up. He gets furious and argumentative. He is like an old personality structure or a parent that knows it must yield to a maturing offspring but is reluctant to let go, putting up one last fight.

It's then that the little dog Toto fulfills his purpose in the story. His animal intuition and curiosity got Dorothy in trouble in the first place, when he dug in Miss Gulch's flower bed. Now they are the instrument of salvation. As Toto noses around behind the throne, he discovers a meek little old man behind a curtain, controlling the monstrous illusion of Oz, the great and powerful. This man, not the bellowing head, is the real Wizard of Oz.

This is a typical post-ordeal realization or moment of insight. The heroes see, through the eyes of the intuitive, curious Toto, that behind the illusion of the mightiest organization is a human being with emotions that can be reached. (This scene has always seemed to me a metaphor for Hollywood, which tries very hard to be scary and awesome, but which is made up of ordinary people with fears and flaws.)

At first the Wizard professes to be unable to help them, but with encouragement he provides Elixirs for Dorothy's helpers: a diploma for the Scarecrow, a medal of valor for the Lion, and a windup heart for the Tin Woodsman. There is a

tone of satire about this scene. It seems to be saying: These Elixirs are placebos, meaningless symbols that men give each other. Many people with degrees, medals, or testimonials have done nothing to earn them. Those who have not survived death can take the Elixir all day long but it still won't help them.
The true all-healing Elixir is the achievement of inner change, but the scene acknowledges that it's important to get outward recognition as well. As a surrogate parent for the lot of them, the Wizard is granting them the ultimate boon of a father's approval, a Reward that few people get. Heart, brains, and courage are inside them and always were, but the physical objects serve as a reminder.

Now the Wizard turns to Dorothy and says sadly there is nothing he can do for her. He was blown to Oz in a balloon from the Nebraska state fair, and has no idea how to get back home himself. He's right — only Dorothy can grant herself the self - acceptance to "get home," that is, be happy inside herself wherever she is. But he agrees to try and orders a big hot-air balloon to be built by the citizens of Oz. The heroes have seized everything except the elusive prize of Home, which must be sought in Act Three.

Facing death has life-changing consequences which heroes experience by Seizing the Sword, but after experiencing their Reward fully, heroes must turn back to the quest. There are more Ordeals ahead, and it's time to pack up and face them, on the next stage of the Hero's Journey: The Road Back.

QUESTIONING THE JOURNEY

1. What is the modern equivalent of a campfire scene in *Thelma & Louise*? *Sister Act*? *Ghost*?

2. What do the heroes of your stories learn by observing death? By causing death? By experiencing death?

3. What do the heroes of your story take possession of after facing death or their greatest fears? What is the aftermath, the consequence, of the major event of Act Two? Have your heroes absorbed any negative qualities from the Shadow or villain?

4. Does the story change direction? Is a new goal or agenda revealed in the Reward phase?

5. Is the aftermath of the Ordeal in your story an opportunity for a love scene?

6. Do your heroes realize they have changed? Is there self-examination or realization of wider consciousness? Have they learned to deal with their inner flaws?

THE ROAD BACK

STAGE TEN:
THE ROAD BACK

"Easy is the descent to the Lower World; but, to retrace your steps and to escape to the upper air — this is the task, this the toil."
— The Sibyl to Aeneas in *The Aeneid*

Once the lessons and Rewards of the great Ordeal have been celebrated and absorbed, heroes face a choice: whether to remain in the Special World or begin the journey home to the Ordinary World. Although the Special World may have its charms, few heroes elect to stay. Most take **The Road Back**, returning to the starting point or continuing on the journey to a totally new locale or ultimate destination.

This is a time when the story's energy, which may have ebbed a little in the quiet moments of Seizing the Sword, is now revved up again. If we look at the Hero's Journey as a circle with the beginning at the top, we are still down in the basement and it will take some push to get us back up into the light.

> *Wake up, Seekers! Shake off the effects of our feast and celebration and remember why we came out here in the first place! People back home are starving and it's urgent, now that we've recovered from the ordeal, to load up our backpacks with food and treasure and head for home. Besides, there's no telling what dangers still lurk on the edge of the hunting grounds. You pause at the edge of camp to look back. They'll never believe this back home. How to tell them? Something bright on the ground catches your eye. You bend to pick it up — a beautiful smooth stone with an inner glow. Suddenly a dark shape darts out at you, all fangs. Run! Run for your life!*

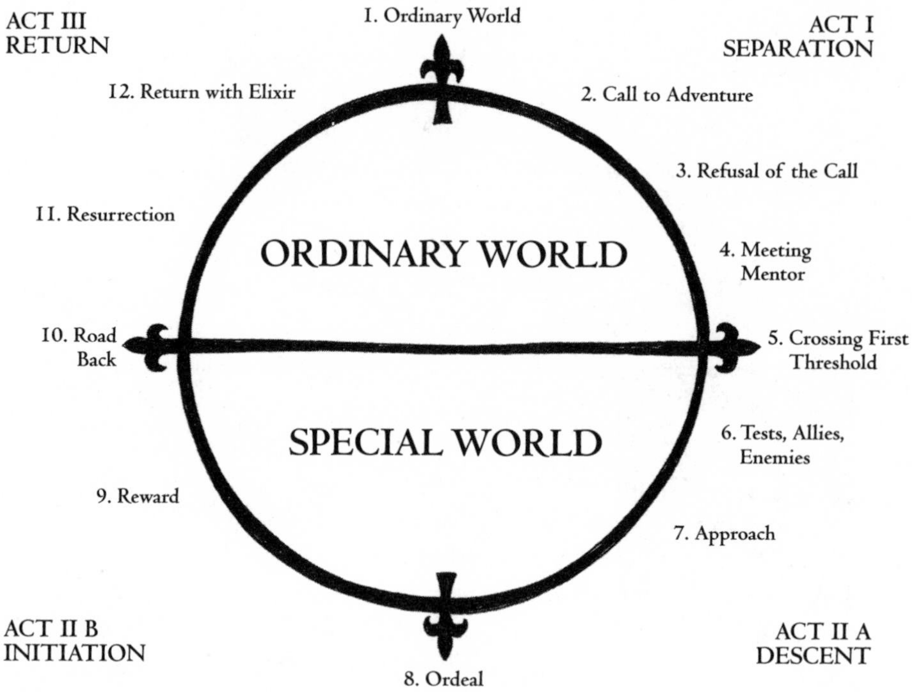
ACT III
RETURN
1. Ordinary World
ACT I
SEPARATION
12. Return with Elixir
2. Call to Adventure
3. Refusal of the Call
11. Resurrection
ORDINARY WORLD
4. Meeting
Mentor
10. Road
Back
5. Crossing First
Threshold
SPECIAL WORLD
6. Tests, Allies,
Enemies
9. Reward
7. Approach
ACT II B
INITIATION
ACT II A
DESCENT
8. Ordeal

In psychological terms this stage represents the resolve of the hero to return to the Ordinary World and implement the lessons learned in the Special World. This can be far from easy. The hero has reason to fear that the wisdom and magic of the Ordeal may evaporate in the harsh light of common day. No one may believe the hero's miraculous escape from death. The adventures may be rationalized away by skeptics. But most heroes determine to try. Like the Boddhisattvas of Buddhist belief, they have seen the eternal plan but return to the world of the living to tell others about it and share the elixir they have won.

MOTIVATION

The Road Back marks a time when heroes rededicate themselves to the adventure. A plateau of comfort has been reached and heroes must be pried off that plateau, either by their own inner resolve or by an external force.

Inner resolve might be represented by a scene of a tired commander rallying dispirited troops after a battle, or a parent pulling a family together after a death or tragedy. An external force might be an alarm going off, a clock ticking, or a renewed threat by a villain. The heroes may be reminded of the ultimate goal of the adventure.

The Road Back is a turning point, another threshold crossing which marks the passage from Act Two to Act Three. Like crossing the First Threshold, it may cause a change in the aim of the story. A story about achieving some goal becomes a story of escape; a focus on physical danger shifts to emotional risks. The propellant that boosts the story out of the depths of the Special World may be a new development or piece of information that drastically redirects the story. In effect, The Road Back causes the third act. It can be another moment of crisis that sets the hero on a new and final road of trials.

The rocket fuel may be fear of retaliation or pursuit. Often heroes are motivated to hit The Road Back when the forces they have defied in the Ordeal now rally and strike back at them. If the elixir was stolen from the central forces rather than given freely, there may be dangerous repercussions.

RETALIATION

An important lesson of martial arts is **Finish your opponent.** Heroes often learn that villains or Shadows who are not completely defeated in the crisis can rise up stronger than before. The ogre or villain that the hero confronted in the Ordeal may pull himself together and strike a counter-blow. A parent who has been challenged for dominance in the family may get over the initial shock and unleash a devastating retaliation. A martial arts opponent knocked off balance may recover his center and deliver a surprise attack. In the Tiananmen Square incident, the Chinese government rallied after several days of confusion to launch a crushing response that drove the students and their Goddess of Liberty from the Square.

One of the most vivid examples of this retaliatory movement in films is in *Red River,* when Tom Dunson has been toppled from his throne by his foster-son, Matthew Garth, in a central Supreme Ordeal. In the Reward stage, while Matt and his men are celebrating in the town where they've sold the cattle, Dunson is busy recruiting a small army of gunmen. In The Road Back phase, he comes riding after Matt with the force of a railroad train and the stated intention of killing his adopted son. What had been a story of overcoming obstacles on a cattle drive now becomes a story of a parent stalking his child to get revenge.

The peculiar force of this passage is carried in John Wayne's physical acting. He lurches toward the showdown with Montgomery Clift like a zombie, with the unstoppable energy of a machine, flicking cattle out of his path and shrugging off a bullet from a secondary character who tries to deflect him from his intent. He is the living image of the angry parental energy that can be roused by challenging a Shadow.

The psychological meaning of such counterattacks is that neuroses, flaws, habits, desires, or addictions we have challenged may retreat for a time, but can rebound in a last-ditch defense or a desperate attack before being vanquished forever. Neuroses have a powerful life force of their own and will strike back when threatened. Addicts who have made a first effort at recovery may fall off the wagon with a vengeance as their addiction fights back for its life.

Retaliation can take other forms. If you're hunting bear or killing dragons, you may find that the monster you killed in the Ordeal has a mate who comes chasing after you. A villain's lieutenant may survive him to pursue you, or you may find you have only killed an underling in the Ordeal. There may be a bigger Mr. Big who wants revenge for the loss of his servant.

An avenging force may strike a costly blow to the hero's fortunes, wounding him or killing one of his cohorts. This is when Expendable

Friends come in handy. The villain might also steal back the elixir or kidnap one of the hero's friends in retaliation. This could lead to a rescue or chase, or both.

CHASE SCENES

In many cases heroes leave the Special World only because they are running for their lives. Chases may occur in any part of the story, but the end of Act Two is one of the most popular places. Chases are useful for torquing up a story's energy. Audiences may get sleepy at this point, and you have to wake them up with some action or conflict. In the theatre, this stage is called "racing for the curtain," a time when you want to pick up the pace and build momentum for the finish.

Chases are a favorite element of movies, and they figure prominently in literature, art, and mythology as well. The most famous chase in classical mythology is Apollo's pursuit of the shy nymph Daphne, who begged her father, a river god, to transform her into a laurel tree. Transformation is often an important aspect of chases and escapes. Modern heroes may simply assume a disguise in order to escape a tight situation. In a psychological drama, a hero may have to escape a pursuing inner demon by changing behavior or undergoing inner transformation.

MAGIC FLIGHT

Fairy tales often include a chase that involves a whimsical transformation of objects, known as the **magic flight** motif. In a typical story a little girl escapes from the clutches of a witch with the help of gifts from animals she's been kind to. The girl throws down the gifts one by one in the witch's path and they magically transform into barriers that delay the witch. A comb becomes a thick forest that slows the witch while she gobbles it up. A scarf becomes a wide river which she has to drink.

Joseph Campbell gives several illustrations of magical flights, and suggests the motif stands for a hero's attempts to stall the avenging forces in any way possible, by throwing down "protective interpretations, principles, symbols, rationalizations, anything [to] delay and absorb" their power.

What the hero throws down in a chase may also represent a sacrifice, the leaving behind of something of value. The little girl of the fairy tales may find it hard to part with the lovely scarf or comb given by the animals.

Heroes of movie adventures sometimes have to decide what's really important, and toss money out the window to slow their pursuers and save their lives. Campbell cites the extreme example of Medea. Escaping with Jason from her father, she had Jason cut up her own brother and toss his pieces into the sea to delay the pursuit.

CHASE VARIATIONS: PURSUIT BY ADMIRERS

It's most common for heroes to be chased by villains, but there are other possibilities. An unusual variant of the chase is pursuit by admirers, for example in *Shane*, at the beginning of Act Three. Shane has been out on the farm trying to stay away from gunfighting, but now the brutality of the villains in the town draws him back. He tells the little farm boy (Brandon De Wilde) to stay behind, but the boy follows him at a distance. Behind the boy follows the boy's dog, who has also been told to stay home. The point is made that this kid is as faithful to Shane as a dog. It's a chase scene with a twist: Rather than hero fleeing villain, hero is being pursued by his admirer.

VILLAIN ESCAPE

Another chase scene variant is the pursuit of an escaped villain. A Shadow captured and controlled in the Ordeal escapes at this stage and becomes more dangerous than before. Hannibal "The Cannibal" Lecter in *The Silence of the Lambs*, feeling betrayed by FBI agent Clarice, escapes and begins to kill again. King Kong, taken to New York to be displayed in chains, escapes and goes on a rampage. Countless movie and TV Westerns depict a villain trying to make a getaway, then being ridden down and tackled by the hero prior to a final fistfight or gun duel. Such scenes were a staple of the Roy Rogers and Lone Ranger serials and TV shows.

As mentioned above, villains may steal back the treasure from the hero or make off with one of his team members. This could lead to pursuit by the hero and rescue or recovery.

SETBACKS

Another twist of The Road Back may be a sudden catastrophic reversal of the hero's good fortune. Things were going well after surviving the Ordeal, but now reality sets in again. Heroes may encounter setbacks that seem to doom the adventure. Within sight of shore the ship may spring a leak. For a moment, after great risk, effort, and sacrifice, it may look like all is lost.

This moment in the story, the climax of Act Two, may be the Delayed Crisis spoken of earlier. It could be the moment of greatest tension in Act Two and should set the story on the final path to resolution in Act Three.

The Road Back at the end of Act Two may be a brief moment or an elaborate sequence of events. Almost every story needs a moment to acknowledge the hero's resolve to finish, and provide her with necessary motivation to return home with the elixir despite the temptations of the Special World and the trials that remain ahead.

THE WIZARD OF OZ

The Wizard has prepared a hot-air balloon with which he hopes to take Dorothy on The Road Back to Kansas. The people of Oz gather to see them off with a brass band. However, it's seldom that easy. Toto, seeing a cat in the arms of a woman in the crowd, runs after it, and Dorothy runs after Toto. In the confusion, the balloon wobbles off with the Wizard aboard and Dorothy is left behind, apparently stuck in the Special World. Many heroes have tried to return using familiar means — old crutches and dependencies. But they find the old ways as artificial and difficult to control as the Wizard's hot-air balloon. Dorothy, guided by her instincts (the dog) knows deep down that this is not the way for her. Yet she is ready to take The Road Back, and keeps looking for the proper branching of the path.

Heroes gather up what they have learned, gained, stolen, or been granted in the Special World. They set themselves a new goal, to escape, find further adventure, or return home. But before any of those goals are achieved, there is another test to pass, the final exam of the journey, Resurrection.

QUESTIONING THE JOURNEY

1. What is The Road Back in *A League of Their Own*? *Awakenings*? *Unforgiven*? *Terminator 2*? From the writer's point of view, what are the advantages and disadvantages of heroes being ejected or chased from the Special World? Of leaving voluntarily?

2. What have you learned or gained from confronting death, defeat, or danger? Did you feel heroic? How can you apply your feelings to your writing, to the reactions of your characters?

3. How do your heroes rededicate themselves to the quest?

4. What is The Road Back in your story? Is it returning to your starting place? Setting a new destination? Adjusting to a new life in the Special World?

5. Find the Act Two/Act Three turning points in three current feature films. Are these single moments or extended sequences?

6. Is there an element of pursuit or acceleration in these sections? In The Road Back section of your own story?

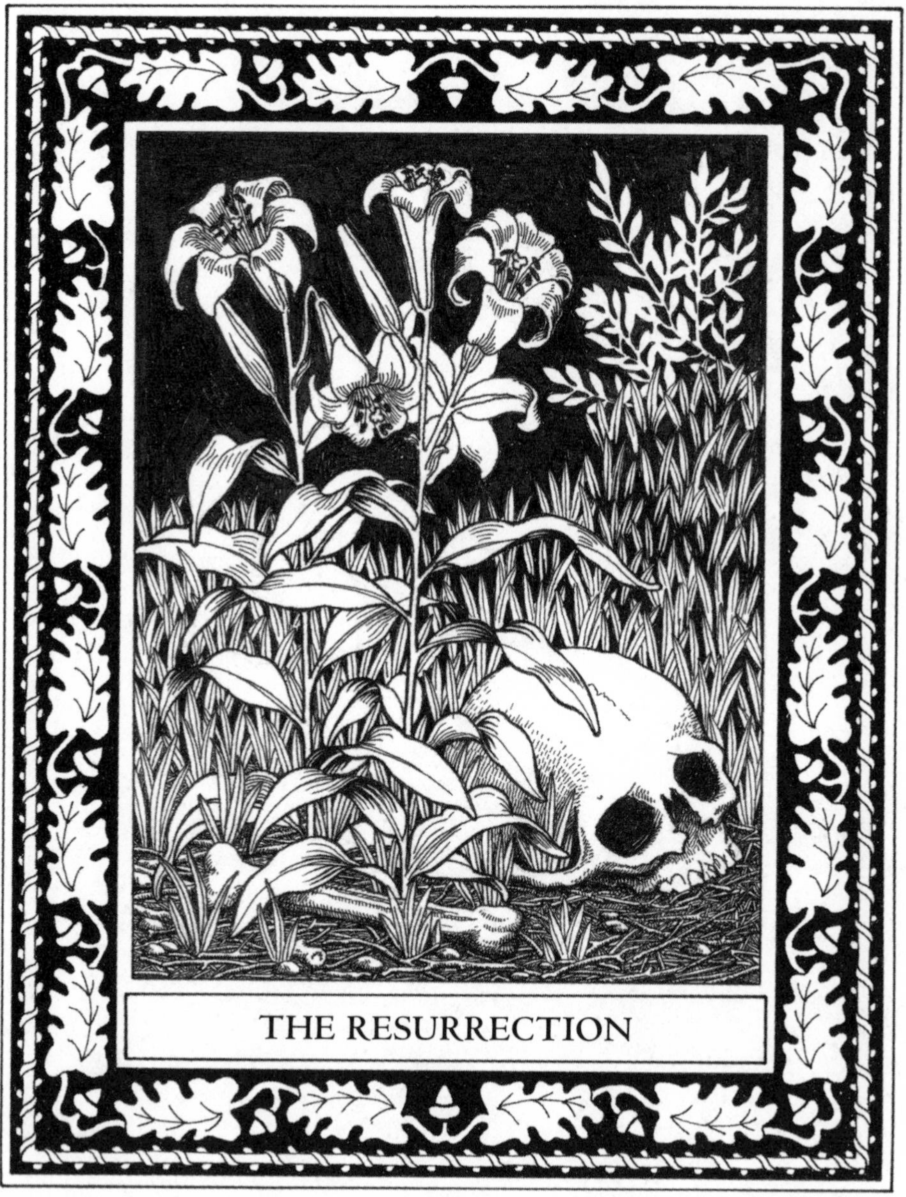

THE RESURRECTION

Stage Eleven: THE RESURRECTION

"What can I do, old man? I'm dead, aren't I?"
— from *The Third Man* by Graham Greene

Now comes one of the trickiest and most challenging passages for the hero and the writer. For a story to feel complete, the audience needs to experience an additional moment of death and rebirth, similar to the Supreme Ordeal but subtly different. This is the **climax** (not the crisis), the last and most dangerous meeting with death. Heroes have to undergo a final purging and purification before reentering the Ordinary World. Once more they must change. The trick for writers is to show the change in their characters, by behavior or appearance rather than by just talking about it. Writers must find ways to demonstrate that their heroes have been through a **Resurrection**.

We weary Seekers shuffle back towards the village. Look! The smoke of the Home Tribe fires! Pick up the pace! But wait — the shaman appears to stop us from charging back in. You have been to the land of Death, he says, and you look like death itself, covered in blood, carrying the torn flesh and hide of your game. If you march back into the village without purifying and cleansing yourselves, you may bring death back with you. You must undergo one final sacrifice before rejoining the tribe. Your warrior self must die so you can be reborn as an innocent into the group. The trick is to keep the wisdom of the Ordeal, while getting rid of its bad effects. After all we've been through, fellow Seekers, we must face one more trial, maybe the hardest one yet.

A NEW PERSONALITY

A new self must be created for a new world. Just as heroes had to shed their old selves to enter the Special World, they now must shed the personality of the journey and build a new one that is suitable for return to the Ordinary World. It should reflect the best parts of the old selves and the lessons learned along the way. In the Western *Barbarossa,* Gary Busey's farmboy character goes through a final ordeal from which he is reborn as the new Barbarossa, having incorporated the lessons of his Mentor, Willie Nelson, along the way. John Wayne emerges from the ordeal of death in *Fort Apache* and incorporates some of the dress and attitudes of his antagonist, Henry Fonda.

CLEANSING

One function of Resurrection is to cleanse heroes of the smell of death, yet help them retain the lessons of the ordeal. The lack of public ceremonies and counseling for returning Vietnam War veterans may have contributed to the terrible problems these soldiers have had in reintegrating with society. So-called primitive societies seem better prepared to handle the return of heroes. They provide rituals to purge the blood and death from hunters and warriors so they can become peaceful members of society again.

Returning hunters may be quarantined safely away from the tribe for a period of time. To reintegrate hunters and warriors into the tribe, shamans use rituals that mimic the effects of death or even take the participants to death's door. The hunters or warriors may be buried alive for a period of time or confined in a cave or sweat lodge, symbolically growing in the womb of the earth. Then they are raised up (Resurrected) and welcomed as newborn members of the tribe.

Sacred architecture aims to create this feeling of Resurrection, by confining worshippers in a narrow dark hall or tunnel, like a birth canal, before bringing them out into an open well-lit area, with a corresponding lift of relief. Baptism by immersion in a stream is a ritual designed to give the Resurrection feeling, both cleansing the sinner and reviving him from symbolic death by drowning.

TWO GREAT ORDEALS

Why do so many stories seem to have two climaxes or death-and-rebirth ordeals, one near the middle and another just before the end of the story? The college semester metaphor suggests the reason. The central crisis or Supreme Ordeal is like a midterm exam; the Resurrection is the final exam. Heroes must be tested one last time to see if they retained the learning from the Supreme Ordeal of Act Two.

To learn something in a Special World is one thing; to bring the knowledge home as applied wisdom is quite another. Students can cram for a test but the Resurrection stage represents a field trial of a hero's new skills, in the real world. It's both a reminder of death and a test of the hero's learning. Was the hero sincere about change? Will she backslide or fail, be defeated by neuroses or a Shadow at the eleventh hour? Will the dire predictions made about hero Joan Wilder in Act One of *Romancing the Stone* ("You're not up to this, Joan, and you know it") turn out to be true?

PHYSICAL ORDEAL

At the simplest level, the Resurrection may just be a hero facing death one last time in an ordeal, battle, or showdown. It's often the final, decisive confrontation with the villain or Shadow.

But the difference between this and previous meetings with death is that the danger is usually on the broadest scale of the entire story. The threat is not just to the hero, but to the whole world. In other words, the stakes are at their highest.

The James Bond movies often climax with 007 battling the villains and then racing against time and impossible odds to disarm some Doomsday device, such as the atomic bomb at the climax of *Goldfinger*. Millions of lives are at stake. Hero, audience, and world are taken right to the brink of death one more time before Bond (or his Ally Felix Leiter) manages to yank the right wire and save us all from destruction.

THE ACTIVE HERO

It seems obvious that the hero should be the one to act in this climactic moment. But many writers make the mistake of having the hero rescued from death by a timely intervention from an Ally — the equivalent of the cavalry coming to save the day. Heroes can get surprise assistance, but it's best for the hero to be the one to perform the decisive action; to deliver the death blow to fear or the Shadow; to be active rather than passive, at this of all times.

SHOWDOWNS

In Westerns, crime fiction, and many action films, the Resurrection is expressed as the biggest confrontation and battle of the story, the **showdown** or shootout. A showdown pits hero and villains in an ultimate contest with the highest possible stakes, life and death. It's the classic gunfight of the Western, the swordfight of the swashbuckler, or the last acrobatic battle of a martial arts movie. It may even be a courtroom showdown or an emotional "shootout" in a domestic drama.

The showdown is a distinct dramatic form with its own rules and conventions. The operatic climaxes of the Sergio Leone "spaghetti Westerns" exaggerate the elements of the conventional showdown: the dramatic music; the opposing forces marching towards each other in some kind of arena (the town street, a corral, a cemetery, the villain's hideout); the closeups of guns, hands, and eyes poised for the decisive moment; the sense that time stands still. Gun duels are almost mandatory in Westerns from *Stagecoach* to *High Noon* to *My Darling Clementine*. The so-called Gunfight at the O.K. Corral in 1881 was a brutal shootout that has become part of the myth of the American West and has spurred more film versions than any other.

Duels to the death form the climaxes of swashbucklers such as *Robin Hood: Prince of Thieves, The Seahawk, Scaramouche,* and *The Flame and the Arrow;* knights battle to the death in *Ivanhoe, Excalibur,* and *Knights of the Round Table.* Duels or shootouts are not fully satisfying unless the hero is taken right to the edge of death. The hero must clearly be fighting for his life. The playful quality of earlier skirmishes is probably gone now. He may be wounded or he may slip and lose his balance. He may actually seem to die, just as in the Supreme Ordeal.

DEATH AND REBIRTH OF TRAGIC HEROES

Conventionally heroes survive this brush with death and are Resurrected. Often it is the villains who die or are defeated, but some tragic heroes actually die at this point, like the doomed heroes of *They Died with Their*

Boots On, The Sand Pebbles, Charge of the Light Brigade, or *Glory*. Robert Shaw's character, Quint, is killed at this point in *Jaws*. However, all these doomed or tragic heroes are Resurrected in the sense that they usually live on in the memory of the survivors, those for whom they gave their lives. The audience survives, and remembers the lessons a tragic hero can teach us.

In *Butch Cassidy and the Sundance Kid* the heroes are cornered in an adobe building, surrounded and outnumbered. They run out to face death in a climax that is delayed to the final seconds of the film. The chances are good they're going to die in a hail of bullets, but they'll go down fighting and are granted immortality by a final freeze-frame, which makes them live on in our memories. In *The Wild Bunch* the heroes are elaborately killed, but their energy lives on in a gun which is picked up by another adventurer who we know will carry on in their wild style.

CHOICE

Another possibility for a Resurrection moment may be a climactic choice among options that indicates whether or not the hero has truly learned the lesson of change. A difficult choice tests a hero's values: Will he choose in accordance with his old, flawed ways, or will the choice reflect the new person he's become? In *Witness,* policeman John Book comes to a final showdown with his ultimate enemy, a crooked police official. The Amish people watch to see if Book will follow the violent code of his Ordinary World or the peaceful way he has learned in their Special World. He makes a clear choice not to engage in the expected shootout. Instead he puts down his gun, leaving the villain armed, and stands with the silent Amish. Like them, he is a witness. The villain can't shoot when there are so many witnesses. The old John Book would have shot it out with his opponent, but the new man chooses not to. Here is the test that proves he's learned his lesson and is a new man, Resurrected.

ROMANTIC CHOICE

The Resurrection choice may be in the arena of love. Stories like *The Graduate* or *It Happened One Night* take heroes to the altar at the climax, where a choice of spouses must be made. *Sophie's Choice* is about the impossible choice of a mother who is told by the Nazis to pick which of her two children will die.

CLIMAX

The Resurrection usually marks the climax of the drama. **Climax** is a Greek word meaning "a ladder." For us storytellers it has come to mean an explosive moment, the highest peak in energy, or the last big event in a work. It may be the physical showdown or final battle, but it can also be expressed as a difficult choice, sexual climax, musical crescendo, or highly emotional but decisive confrontation.

THE QUIET CLIMAX

The climax need not be the most explosive, dramatic, loud, or dangerous moment of the story. There is such a thing as a **quiet climax**; a gentle cresting of a wave of emotion. A quiet climax can give a sense that all the conflicts have been harmoniously resolved, and all the tensions converted into feelings of pleasure and peace. After a hero has experienced the death of a loved one, there may be a quiet climax of acceptance or understanding. The knots of tension created in the body of the story come untied, perhaps after a gentle tug from a final realization.

ROLLING CLIMAXES

Stories may need more than one climax, or a series of **rolling climaxes**. Individual subplots may require separate climaxes. The Resurrection stage is another nerve ganglion of the story, a checkpoint through which all the threads of the story have to pass. Rebirth and cleansing may have to be experienced on more than one level.

The hero may experience a climax on different levels of awareness in succession, such as mind, body, and emotion. A hero might go through a climax of mental change or decision which triggers a physical climax or showdown in the material world. This could be followed by an emotional or spiritual climax as the hero's behavior and feelings change.

Gunga Din combines effective physical and emotional climaxes in succession. Cary Grant and his two English sergeant pals have been badly wounded, leaving the water carrier Gunga Din, once a clown, to act as the hero and warn the British army of an ambush. Although wounded himself, Gunga Din climbs to the top of a golden tower to blow a bugle call. The army is warned and many lives are saved in an action scene which is the story's physical climax, but Din himself is shot from the tower and falls to his death. However, his death is not in vain. He is recognized as a hero by his comrades and is Resurrected. In a final emotional climax the Colonel reads a poem which Rudyard Kipling has written in Din's honor. Superimposed on the scene is Din's spirit, dressed in full army uniform and grinning as he salutes, Resurrected and transformed.

Of course, a well-made story can bring all levels — mind, body, and spirit — to climax in the same moment. When a hero takes a decisive action, her whole world can be changed at once.

CATHARSIS

A climax should provide the feeling of **catharsis.** This Greek word actually means "vomiting up" or "purging," but in English has come to mean a purifying emotional release, or an emotional breakthrough. Greek drama was constructed with the intent of triggering a vomiting-up of emotions by the audience, a purging of the poisons of daily life. Just as they took purgatives to empty and cleanse their digestive systems from time to time, the Greeks at regular times of the year would go to the theatre to get rid of ill feeling. Laughter, tears, and shudders of terror are the triggers that bring about this healthy cleansing, this catharsis.

In psychoanalysis, catharsis is a technique of relieving anxiety or depression by bringing unconscious material to the surface. The same is true, in a way, of storytelling. The climax you are trying to trigger in your hero and audience is the moment when they are the most conscious, when they have reached the highest point on a ladder of awareness. You are trying to raise the consciousness of both the hero and the participating audience. A catharsis can bring about a sudden expansion of awareness, a peak experience of higher consciousness.

A catharsis can be combined with a simple physical showdown, for a satisfying emotional effect. In *Red River,* Tom Dunson and Matthew Garth come together for an explosive fight to the death. At first Garth won't fight. He is determined not to be provoked into abandoning his principles. Dunson hammers at him until Garth is forced to fight back to save his own life. They commence a titanic battle and it looks for all the world as if one or both of them must be killed. They crash into a wagon loaded with domestic goods — calico, pots and pans — and destroy it, suggesting the death of hope for building home, family, or society on the frontier.

But a new energy enters the scene: Tess, an independent woman who has come to love Matthew Garth. She stops the fight with a gunshot to get their attention. In an emotional climax — a genuine catharsis — she spews up all her feelings about the two men, and convinces them that their fight is foolish, because they really love each other. She has changed a deadly physical showdown into an emotional catharsis, a moment of highest awareness.

A Resurrection showdown is resolved by an emotional catharsis.

Catharsis works best through physical expression of emotions such as laughter and crying. Sentimental stories can bring an audience to a catharsis of tears by pushing their emotions to a climax. The death of a beloved character, like Mr. Chips or the doomed young woman in *Love Story,* may be the climactic moment. Such characters are inevitably "resurrected" in the hearts and memories of those who loved them.

Laughter is one of the strongest channels of catharsis. A comedy should crest with a gag or a series of gags that create a virtual explosion of laughter, jokes that relieve tension, purge sour emotions, and allow us a shared experience. The classic Warner Bros. and Disney short cartoons are constructed to reach a climax of laughter, a crescendo of absurdity, in only six minutes. Full-length comedies have to be carefully structured to build to a climax of laughter that releases all the boxed-in emotions of the audience.

CHARACTER ARC

A catharsis is the logical climax of a hero's **character arc.** This is a term used to describe the gradual stages of change in a character: the phases and turning points of growth. A common flaw in stories is that writers make heroes grow or change, but do so abruptly, in a single leap because of a single incident. Someone criticizes them or they realize a flaw, and they immediately correct it; or they have an overnight conversion because of some shock and are totally changed at one stroke. This does happen once in a while in life, but more commonly people change by degrees, growing in gradual stages from bigotry to tolerance, from cowardice to courage, from hate to love. Here is a typical character arc compared with the Hero's Journey model.

CHARACTER ARC	HERO'S JOURNEY
1) limited awareness of a problem	Ordinary World
2) increased awareness	Call to Adventure
3) reluctance to change	Refusal
4) overcoming reluctance	Meeting with the Mentor
5) committing to change	Crossing the Threshold
6) experimenting with first change	Tests, Allies, Enemies
7) preparing for big change	Approach to Inmost Cave
8) attempting big change	Ordeal
9) consequences of the attempt (improvements and setbacks)	Reward (Seizing the Sword)
10) rededication to change	The Road Back
11) final attempt at big change	Resurrection
12) final mastery of the problem	Return with the Elixir

The stages of the Hero's Journey are a good guide to the steps needed to create a realistic character arc.

THE CHARACTER ARC

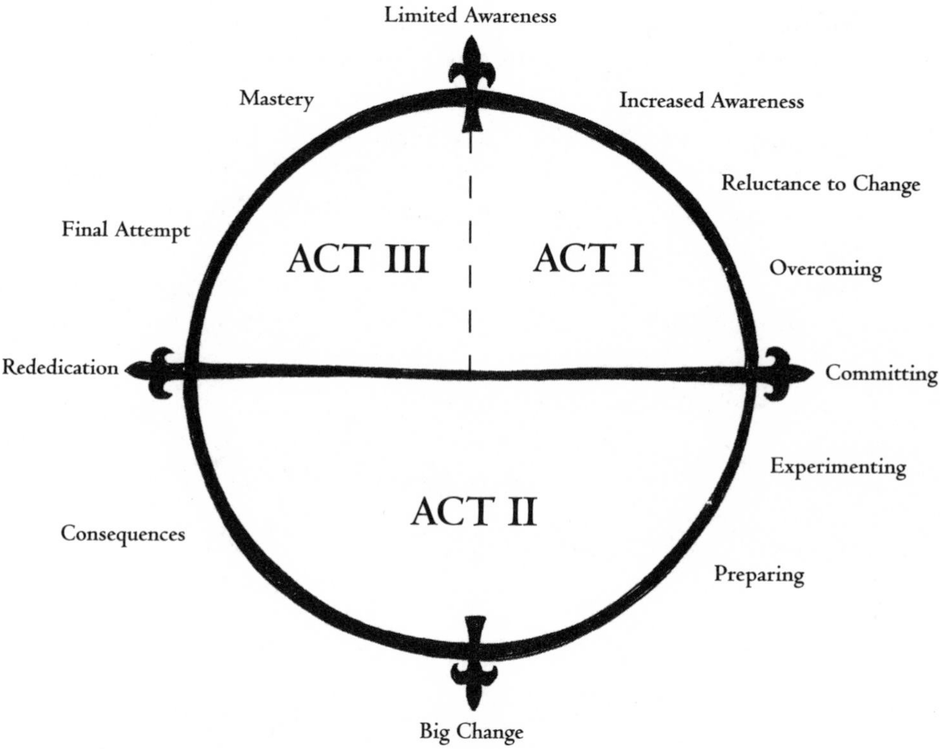

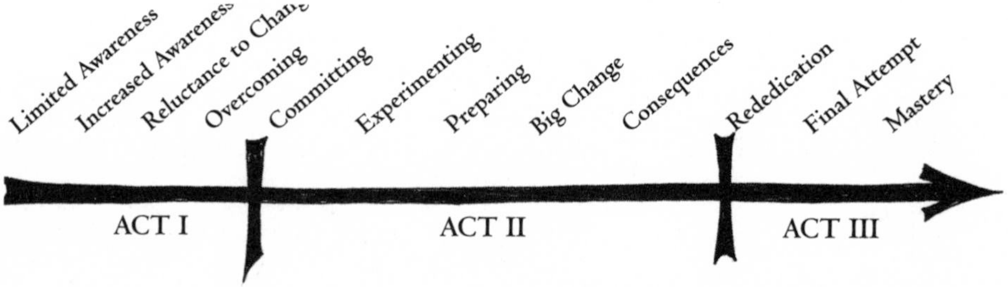

LAST CHANCE

The Resurrection is the hero's final attempt to make major change in attitude or behavior. A hero may backslide at this point, making those around think he's let them down. Hope for that character is temporarily dead, but can be resurrected if he changes his mind. The selfish loner Han Solo in *Star Wars* turns his back on the final attempt to crack the Death Star, but shows up at the last minute, showing that he has finally changed and is now willing to risk his life for a good cause.

WATCH YOUR STEP

The Resurrection can be a potential misstep for a returning hero who may be walking a narrow sword-bridge from one world to the next. Hitchcock often uses heights at this point in a story to stand for the potential failure to return from the Special World alive. In *North by Northwest,* Cary Grant's and Eva Marie Saint's characters end up hanging from the stone portraits on Mount Rushmore, keeping the audience in suspense about their ultimate fates until the last possible moment. The climaxes of Hitchcock's *Vertigo, Saboteur,* and *To Catch a Thief* all take heroes to high places for a final struggle between life and death.

Sometimes great drama comes from heroes dropping the ball at the last moment just before reaching their goal. The heroes of *Quest for Fire* come back to their people with the elixir of flame, but at the threshold of their world, the fire goes out, dropped into the water by accident. This apparent death of all hope is the final test for the hero, the leader of the quest. He reassures the people, for he knows the secret of fire; he has seen the more advanced tribe using a special stick to make fire at his Ordeal. However, when he tries to copy their technique, he finds he has forgotten the trick. Again hope seems dead.

But just then his "wife," a woman he met on the adventure and a member of the more advanced tribe, steps in and gives it a try. The men are not too happy about this, being shown up by a woman and a foreigner at that. However, only she knows the secret (spitting on your hands before using the fire-stick). She succeeds, fire blooms, and the possibility of life returns to the tribe. In fact the tribe itself has passed a final test by learning that the combined knowledge of men and women is needed to survive. A stumble at the final threshold has led to Resurrection and enlightenment.

The misstep for a hero might not be a physical event, but a moral or emotional stumble at the threshold of return. In *Notorious* there are both physical and emotional tests in the closing moments. Alicia Hueberman (Ingrid Bergman) is in grave physical danger from being poisoned by the Nazis, while Devlin (Cary Grant) is in danger of losing his soul if he doesn't rescue her from the clutches of the enemy where his own devotion to duty has placed her.

THE FALSE CLAIMANT

A common Resurrection moment in fairy tales involves a last-minute threat to a hero who has gone on a quest to achieve impossible tasks. As he stakes his claim on the princess or the kingdom, a pretender or **false claimant** suddenly steps forward questioning the hero's credentials or claiming that he, not the hero, achieved the impossible. For a moment it looks like the hero's hopes are dead. To be reborn, the hero must provide proof that he is the true claimant, perhaps by showing the ears and tail of the dragon he slew, perhaps by besting the pretender (the Shadow) in a contest.

PROOF

Providing proof is a major function of the Resurrection stage. Kids like to bring back souvenirs from summer vacations, partly to remind them of the trips, but also to prove to the other kids that they really visited these exotic locales. Not being believed is a perennial problem of travelers to other worlds.

A common fairy-tale motif is that proof brought back from the magic world tends to evaporate. A sack full of gold coins won from the fairies will be opened in the Ordinary World and be found to contain nothing but wet leaves, leading other people to believe the traveler was just sleeping off a drunk in the woods. Yet the traveler knows the experience was real. This motif signifies that spiritual and emotional experiences in a special world are hard to explain to others. They have to go there for themselves. Special World experiences may evaporate if we have not truly made them part of our daily lives. The real treasure from traveling is not the souvenirs, but lasting inner change and learning.

SACRIFICE

Resurrection often calls for a **sacrifice** by the hero. Something must be surrendered, such as an old habit or belief. Something must be given back, like the libation the Greeks used to pour to the gods before drinking. Something must be shared for the good of the group.

In *Terminator 2* the shapeshifting villain is destroyed in a physical climax, but the story brings the audience to a higher emotional climax when the robot hero, the Terminator (Arnold Schwarzenegger), must sacrifice himself to keep from causing future violence. In another sense, the boy John Connor is the hero at this point and must sacrifice part of himself, his Mentor/father figure, by allowing the Terminator to leap to his death. A similar self-sacrificial climax is found in *Alien 3,* when Ripley (Sigourney Weaver), knowing she has a monster growing inside her, gives herself up to destruction for the good of the group. The classic sacrifice in literature is found in Charles Dickens' *A Tale of Two Cities,* where a man gives his life on the guillotine to save another man's life.

Sacrifice comes from Latin words meaning "making holy." Heroes are often required to sanctify a story by making a sacrifice, perhaps by giving up or giving back something of themselves. Sometimes the sacrifice is the death of members of the group. Luke Skywalker, at the climax of *Star Wars,* sees many of his comrades killed in the effort to destroy the Death Star. Luke also gives up part of his personality: his dependence on machines. With Obi Wan's voice in his head, he decides to "Trust the Force," and learns to trust human instinct rather than machinery.

Luke undergoes another personal sacrifice at the climax of the second film in the series, *The Empire Strikes Back.* Here he is escaping from the Emperor and loses a hand in the getaway. In repayment, he gains new control over the Force in the third film of the trilogy, *Return of the Jedi.*

INCORPORATION

Resurrection is an opportunity for a hero to show he has absorbed, or incorporated, every lesson from every character. Incorporation literally means he has made the lessons of the road part of his body. An ideal climax would test everything he's learned, and allow him to show that he has absorbed the Mentor, Shapeshifter, Shadow, Guardians, and Allies along the way. By the time the heroes of *City Slickers* endure their climax, they can apply everything they've learned from a variety of Mentors and antagonists.

CHANGE

The higher dramatic purpose of Resurrection is to give an outward sign that the hero has really changed. The old Self must be proven to be completely dead, and the new Self immune to temptations and addictions that trapped the old form.

The trick for writers is to make the change visible in appearance or action. It's not enough to have people around a hero notice that she's changed; it's not enough to have her talk about change. The audience must be able to see it in her dress, behavior, attitude, and actions.

Romancing the Stone has a well-developed sense of Resurrection that is realized in visual terms. At the action climax of the film, Joan Wilder and Jack Colton unite to defeat the villains, rescue her sister, and reclaim the treasure. But Jack immediately pulls away, putting Joan's romantic plot line in jeopardy. Perfection through a man was within her grasp, but it's snatched away at the last minute. Jack gives her a farewell kiss and tells her she always had what it takes to be a hero, but ultimately he follows money rather than his heart. Colton goes after the emerald, which has been swallowed by an alligator. He dives off a high wall, leaving Joan romantically bereaved and unsatisfied. The action plot has ended in triumph, but the emotional plot appears to be a tragedy. In effect, Joan's hope of emotional completion is dead.

From the shot of Joan looking out over the parapet there is a slow dissolve to a matching shot of her Resurrected self in a New York office a few months later. Her agent is reading Joan's latest manuscript, based on her real-life adventures. It's apparent from every choice on the screen that Joan Wilder has changed, that in some way she has hit bottom, died, and been emotionally reborn. The manuscript has brought the hard-hearted agent to tears. She pronounces it by far Joan's best book, and notes that it was completed very quickly. The Ordeals of the Special World have made Joan a better writer, and she looks better as well, more "together" than we've ever seen her.

At the end of the scene, Joan is put through a final emotional test. The agent refers to the conclusion of the book, which unlike Joan's real life, ends with the hero and heroine united. She leans in close and, in her forceful way, calls Joan "a world-class hopeless romantic."

Joan could have caved in here, perhaps crying about the sad reality that she didn't get her man. Or she could have agreed with the agent's assessment of her as hopeless. The old Joan might have cracked. But she doesn't. Joan passes this emotional test with her answer. She gently but firmly disagrees, saying, "No, a hopeful romantic." Her look tells us she is still in some pain, but that she really is all right. She has learned to love herself regardless of whether or not some man loves her, and she has the self-confidence she lacked before. Later, on the street, she is able to brush off men who would have intimidated her before. She has been through a Resurrection. She has changed, in appearance and action, in ways you can see on the screen and feel in your heart.

THE WIZARD OF OZ

The Wizard of Oz *is not as visual as* Romancing the Stone *in its depiction of how the hero has changed, and yet there is rebirth and learning, expressed in words. The Resurrection for Dorothy is recovering from the apparent death of her hopes when the Wizard accidentally floated off in the balloon. Just when it looks as though Dorothy will never achieve her goal of returning home, there is another appearance by the Good Witch, representing the positive anima that connects us to home and family. She tells Dorothy she had the power to return home all along. She didn't tell Dorothy because "She wouldn't have believed me. She had to learn it for herself."*

The Tin Woodsman asks bluntly, "What have you learned, Dorothy?" She replies that she's learned to look for her "heart's desire" in her "own back yard." Like Joan Wilder, Dorothy has learned that happiness and completion are within her, but this verbal expression of change is not as effective as the visual and behavioral changes you can see on the screen in the Resurrection scene of Romancing the Stone. *Nevertheless, Dorothy has learned something and can now step up to the last threshold of all.*

Resurrection is the hero's final exam, her chance to show what she has learned. Heroes are totally purged by final sacrifice or deeper experience of the mysteries of life and death. Some don't make it past this dangerous point, but those who survive go on to close the circle of the Hero's Journey when they Return with the Elixir.

QUESTIONING THE JOURNEY

1. What is the Resurrection in *King Kong*? *Gone with the Wind*? *The Silence of the Lambs*? *Death Becomes Her*?

2. What negative characteristics has your hero picked up along the way? What flaws were there from the beginning that still need to be corrected? What flaws do you want to preserve, uncorrected? Which are necessary parts of your hero's nature?

3. What final ordeal of death and rebirth does your hero go through? What aspect of your hero is Resurrected?

4. Is there a need for a physical showdown in your story? Is your hero active at the critical moment?

5. Examine the character arc of your hero. Is it a realistic growth of gradual changes? Is the final change in your character visible in her actions or appearance?

6. Who learns anything in a tragedy where the hero dies, where the hero didn't learn his lessons?

RETURN WITH THE ELIXIR

Stage Twelve: RETURN WITH THE ELIXIR

"No, Aunt Em, this was a real truly live place. And I remember some of it wasn't very nice. But most of it was beautiful. But just the same all I kept saying to everybody was 'I want to go home.'"
— from *The Wizard of Oz*

Having survived all the ordeals, having lived through death, heroes return to their starting place, go home, or continue the journey. But they always proceed with a sense that they are commencing a new life, one that will be forever different because of the road just traveled. If they are true heroes, they **Return with the Elixir** from the Special World; bringing something to share with others, or something with the power to heal a wounded land.

We Seekers come home at last, purged, purified, and bearing the fruits of our journey. We share out the nourishment and treasure among the Home Tribe, with many a good story about how they were won. A circle has been closed, you can feel it. You can see that our struggles on the Road of Heroes have brought new life to our land. There will be other adventures, but this one is complete, and as it ends it brings deep healing, wellness, and wholeness to our world. The Seekers have come Home.

RETURN

Quest for Fire has a wonderful Return sequence that shows how storytelling probably began, with hunter/gatherers struggling to relate their adventures in the outer world. The film's heroes enjoy the fruits of their quest at a barbecue around a campfire. The Trickster clown of the hunting party now becomes the storyteller, acting out an adventure from the Tests phase, complete with sound effects and a funny mimed impression of a mammoth Threshold Guardian they met on the quest. A wounded hunter laughs as his injuries are tended: in film language, a declaration of the healing power of stories. Returning with the Elixir means implementing change in your daily life and using the lessons of adventure to heal your wounds.

DENOUEMENT

Another name for the Return is *denouement*, a French word meaning "untying" or "unknotting." (*noue* means knot). A story is like a weaving in which the lives of the characters are interwoven into a coherent design. The plot lines are knotted together to create conflict and tension, and usually it's desirable to release the tension and resolve the conflicts by untying these knots. We also speak of "tying up the loose ends" of a story in a denouement. Whether tying up or untying, these phrases point to the idea that a story is a weaving and that it must be finished properly or it will seem tangled or ragged. That's why it's important in the Return to deal with subplots and all the issues and questions you've raised in the story. It's all right for a Return to raise new questions — in fact that may be highly desirable — but all the old questions should be addressed or at least restated. Usually writers strive to create a feeling of closing the circle on all these storylines and themes.

TWO STORY FORMS

There are two branches to the end of the Hero's Journey. The more conventional way of ending a story, greatly preferred in Western culture and American movies in particular, is the **circular** form in which there is a sense of closure and completion. The other way, more popular in Asia and in Australian and European movies, is the **open-ended** approach in which there is a sense of unanswered questions, ambiguities, and unresolved conflicts. Heroes may have grown in awareness in both forms, but in the open-ended form their problems may not be tied up so neatly.

THE CIRCULAR STORY FORM

The most popular story design seems to be the **circular** or **closed form**, in which the narrative returns to its starting point. In this structure you might bring the hero literally full circle back to the location or world where she started. Perhaps the Return is circular in a visual or metaphoric way, with a replay of an initial image, or the repetition of a line of dialogue or situation from Act One. This is one way of tying up loose ends and making a story feel complete. The image or phrases may have acquired a new meaning now that the hero has completed the journey. The original statement of the theme may be re-evaluated at the Return. Many musical compositions return to an initial theme to rephrase it at the ending.

Having your hero Return to her starting point or remember how she started allows you to draw a comparison for the audience. It gives a measure of how far your hero has come, how she's changed, and how her old world looks different now. To give this circular feeling of completion and comparison, writers will sometimes put their heroes through an experience at the Return that was difficult or impossible for them at the beginning, so the audience can see how they have changed. In *Ghost,* the hero was unable to say "I love you" in his Ordinary World. But at the Return, having died and passed many tests in the land of death, he is able to say these all-important words so that his still-living wife can hear them.

In *Ordinary People,* the young hero Conrad is so depressed in his Ordinary World that he can't eat the French toast his mother makes for him. It's an outward sign of his inner problem, his inability to accept love because he hates himself for surviving his brother. In the Return, having passed through several death-and-rebirth ordeals, he goes to apologize to his girlfriend for acting like a jerk. When she asks him to come inside for some breakfast, this time he finds he has an appetite. His ability to eat is an outward sign of his inner change. This actual change in behavior is more dramatically effective than Conrad just saying he feels different, or someone else noticing that he's grown and remarking on it. It communicates change on the symbolic level, and affects the audience indirectly but more powerfully than a blatant statement. In a subtle way it gives a sense that a phase of his life is over, that a circle has been closed, and a new one is about to begin.

ACHIEVEMENT OF PERFECTION

The "happy endings" of Hollywood films link them with the world of fairy tales, which are often about the achievement of perfection. Fairy tales frequently end with a statement of perfection, like "and they lived happily ever after". Fairy tales bring the shattered family back into balance, back to completion.

Weddings are a popular way to end stories. Marriage is a new beginning, the end of an old life of being single and the beginning of a new life as part of a new unit. New beginnings are perfect and unspoiled in their ideal form.

Striking up a new relationship is another way to show a new beginning at the end of a story. In *Casablanca,* Humphrey Bogart makes a difficult Resurrection sacrifice, giving up the chance to be with the woman he loves. His reward, the Elixir he brings away from the experience, is his new alliance with Claude Rains. As he says, in one of the most famous tag lines in the history of the movies, "Louie, I think this is the beginning of a beautiful friendship."

THE OPEN-ENDED STORY FORM

Storytellers have thought of many ways to create a circular feeling of completion or closure, basically by addressing the dramatic questions raised in Act One. However, once in a while a few loose ends are desirable. Some storytellers prefer an **open-ended** Return. In the open-ended point of view, the storytelling goes on after the story is over; it continues in the minds and hearts of the audience, in the conversations and even arguments people have in coffee shops after seeing a movie or reading a book.

Writers of the open-ended persuasion prefer to leave moral conclusions for the reader or viewer. Some questions have no answers, some have many. Some stories end not by answering questions or solving riddles, but by posing new questions that resonate in the audience long after the story is over.

Hollywood films are often criticized for pat, fairy-tale endings in which all problems are solved and the cultural assumptions of the audience are left undisturbed. By contrast the open-ended approach views the world as an ambiguous, imperfect place. For more sophisticated stories with a hard or realistic edge, the open-ended form may be more appropriate.

FUNCTIONS OF THE RETURN

Like the journey's other stages, Return with the Elixir can perform many functions, but there is something special about being the last element in the journey. Return is similar to Reward in some ways. Both follow a moment of death and rebirth and both may depict consequences of surviving death. Some functions of Seizing the Sword may also appear in the Return, such as taking possession, celebrating, sacred marriage, campfire scenes, self-realization, vengeance, or retaliation. But Return is your last chance to touch the emotions of the audience. It must finish your story so that it satisfies or provokes your audience as you intended. It bears special weight because of its unique position at the end of the work, and it's also a place of pitfalls for writers and their heroes.

SURPRISE

A Return can fall flat if everything is resolved too neatly or just as expected. A good Return should untie the plot threads but with a certain amount of surprise. It should be done with a little taste of the unexpected, a sudden revelation. The Greeks and Romans often built a "recognition" scene into the endings of their plays and novels. A young man and woman, raised as shepherds, discover to everyone's surprise they are prince and princess, promised to each other in marriage long ago. In the tragic mode, Oedipus discovers the man he killed in the Ordeal was his father and the woman he joined with in sacred marriage was his own mother. Here the recognition is cause for horror rather than joy.

The Return may have a twist to it. This is another case of misdirection: You lead the audience to believe one thing, and then reveal at the last moment a quite different reality. *No Way Out* flips you a totally different perception of the hero in the last ten seconds of the film. *Basic Instinct* makes you suspect Sharon Stone's character of murder for the first two acts, convinces you she is innocent in the climax, then leaps back to doubt again in an unexpected final shot.

There is usually an ironic or cynical tone to such Returns, as if they mean to say, "Ha, fooled ya!" You are caught foolishly thinking that human beings are decent or that good does triumph over evil. A less sardonic version of a twist Return can be found in the work of writers like O. Henry, who sometimes used the twist to show the positive side of human nature, as in his short story "The Gift of the Magi." A poor young husband and wife make sacrifices to surprise each other with Christmas presents. They discover that the husband has sold his valuable watch to buy his wife a clip for her beautiful long hair, and the wife has cut off and sold her lovely locks to buy him a fob for his beloved watch. The gifts and sacrifices cancel each other out but the couple is left with a treasure of love.

REWARD AND PUNISHMENT

A specialized job of Return is to hand out final rewards and punishments. It's part of restoring balance to the world of the story, giving a sense of completion. It's like getting your grades after final exams. Villains should earn their ultimate fate by their evil deeds and they should not get off too easily. Audiences hate that. Punishment should fit the crime and have the quality of **poetic justice**. In other words, the way the villain dies or gets his just comeuppance should directly relate to his sins.

Heroes should get what's coming to them as well. Too many movie heroes get rewards they haven't really earned. The reward should be proportionate to the sacrifice they have offered. You don't get immortality for being nice. Also if heroes have failed to learn a lesson, they may be penalized for it in the Return.

Of course, if your dramatic point of view is that life isn't fair and you feel justice is a rare thing in this world, then by all means reflect this in the way rewards and punishments are dealt out in the Return.

THE ELIXIR

The real key to the final stage of the Hero's Journey is the **Elixir**. What does the hero bring back with her from the Special World to share upon her Return? Whether it's shared within the community or with the audience, bringing back the Elixir is the hero's final test. It proves she's been there, it serves as an example for others, and it shows above all that death can be overcome. The Elixir may even have the power to restore life in the Ordinary World.

Like everything else in the Hero's Journey, returning with the Elixir can be literal or metaphoric. The Elixir may be an actual substance or medicine brought back to save an endangered community (a feature of several "Star Trek" TV plots and the object of the quest in *Medicine Man*).

It may be literal treasure wrested from the Special World and shared within a group of adventurers. More figuratively, it may be any of the things that drive people to undertake adventure: money, fame, power, love, peace, happiness, success, health, knowledge, or having a good story to tell. The best Elixirs are those that bring hero and audience greater awareness. In *The Treasure of the Sierra Madre,* the physical treasure of gold is revealed to be worthless dust, and the real Elixir is the wisdom to live a long and peaceful life.

In the tales of King Arthur, the Grail is the Elixir that, once shared, heals the wounded land. The Fisher King can rest easy again. If Percival and the knights had kept the Grail for themselves, there would have been no healing.

If a traveler doesn't bring back something to share, he's not a hero, he's a heel, selfish and unenlightened. He hasn't learned his lesson. He hasn't grown. Returning with the Elixir is the last test of the hero, which shows if he's mature enough to share the fruits of his quest.

THE ELIXIR OF LOVE

Love is, of course, one of the most powerful and popular Elixirs. It can be a reward the hero doesn't win until after a final sacrifice. In *Romancing the Stone* Joan Wilder has surrendered her old fantasies about men and said goodbye to her old, uncertain personality. The payoff for her is that unexpectedly, Jack Colton comes for her after all, miraculously transporting a romantic sailboat to her New York neighborhood to sweep her away. He has transmuted the Elixir he was after — the precious emerald — into another form, love. Joan gets her reward of romance, but she has earned it by learning that she could live without it.

THE WORLD IS CHANGED

Another aspect of the Elixir is that the wisdom which heroes bring back with them may be so powerful that it forces change not only in them, but also those around them. The whole world is altered and the consequences spread far. There is a beautiful image for this in *Excalibur*. When Percival brings the Grail back to the ailing Arthur, the King revives and rides out with his knights again. They are so filled with new life that flowers burst into bloom at their passing. They are a living Elixir, whose mere presence renews nature.

THE ELIXIR OF RESPONSIBILITY

A common and powerful Elixir is for heroes to take wider responsibility at the Return, giving up their loner status for a place of leadership or service within a group. Families and relationships get started, cities are founded. The hero's center has moved from the ego to the Self, and sometimes expands to include the group. Mad Max, the loner hero of George Miller's *Road Warrior* and *Mad Max: Beyond the Thunderdome,* forsakes his solitude to become Mentor and foster-father to a race of orphaned children. The Elixir is his skill at survival and his recollection of the old world before the apocalypse, which he passes on to the orphans.

THE ELIXIR OF TRAGEDY

In the tragic mode, heroes die or are defeated, brought down by their tragic flaws. Yet there is learning and an Elixir brought back from the experience. Who learns? The audience, for they see the errors of the tragic hero and the consequences of error. They learn, if they are wise, what mistakes to avoid, and this is the Elixir that they bring away from the experience.

SADDER BUT WISER

Sometimes the Elixir is heroes taking a rueful look back at their wrong turns on the path. A feeling of closure is created by a hero acknowledging that he is **sadder but wiser** for having gone through the experience. The Elixir he bears away is bitter medicine, but it may keep him from making the same error again, and his pain serves as fair warning to the audience not to choose that path. The heroes of *Risky Business* and *White Men Can't Jump* have been down a road of learning that mixed pain and pleasure. They ultimately lose the prize of love, must Return without the woman of their dreams, and have to console themselves with the Elixir of experience. These stories create a feeling that the account is closed and the heroes are being presented with the final balance.

SADDER BUT NO WISER

A "sadder but wiser" hero is acknowledging that he's been a fool, which is the first step to recovery. The worse kind of fool is the one who doesn't get it. Either he never sees the error or he goes through the motions but has not really learned his lesson. Even after enduring terrible ordeals, he slides back to the same behavior that got him in trouble in the first place. He is **sadder but no wiser.** This is another kind of circular closure.

In this style of Return, a roguish or foolish character seems to have grown and changed. Perhaps he is a clown or Trickster, like Bob Hope in the Crosby-Hope pictures or Eddie Murphy in *48 Hours* or *Trading Places,* who swears he has learned his lesson. However, in the end he fumbles the Elixir and returns to an original error. He may fall back to his original, irrepressible attitude, closing the circle and dooming himself to repeat the adventure.

For this is the penalty of failing to return with the Elixir: **The hero, or someone else, is doomed to repeat the Ordeals until the lesson is learned or the Elixir is brought home to share.**

EPILOGUE

Just as some stories may have a prologue that precedes the main action, there may also be a need for an **epilogue** that follows the bulk of the story. An epilogue or postscript on rare occasions can serve to complete the story, by projecting ahead to some future time to show how the characters turned out. *Terms of Endearment* has an epilogue that shows the characters a year after the main story has ended. The feeling communicated is that even though there is sadness and death, life goes on. *Look Who's Talking* has an epilogue that shows the birth of the baby hero's little sister nine months after the main plot has been resolved. Stories that show a group of characters at a formative or critical period, like *American Graffiti* or war movies such as *Glory* or *The Dirty Dozen,* may end with a short segment that tells how the characters died, progressed in life, or were remembered. *A League of Their Own* has an extensive epilogue in which an aging woman ballplayer, having remembered her career in flashback for the main body of the film, visits the Baseball Hall of Fame and sees many of her teammates. The fates of the players are revealed and the surviving women, now in their sixties, stage a game to show that they still know how to play ball. Their spirit is the Elixir that revives the hero and the audience.

These have been a few of the purposes and functions of Return. There are also pitfalls to avoid in Returning with the Elixir.

PITFALLS OF THE RETURN

It's easy to blow it in the Return. Many stories fall apart in the final moments. The Return is too abrupt, prolonged, unfocused, unsurprising, or unsatisfying. The mood or chain of thought the author has created just evaporates and the whole effort is wasted. The Return may also be too ambiguous. Many people faulted the twist ending of *Basic Instinct* for failing to resolve uncertainty about a woman's guilt.

UNRESOLVED SUBPLOTS

Another pitfall is that writers fail to bring all the elements together at the Return. It's common for writers today to leave subplot threads dangling. Perhaps in the hurry to finish and deal with the main characters, the fates of secondary characters and ideas are forgotten about, even though they may be extremely interesting to the audience. Older films tend to be more complete and satisfying because the creators took time to work out every subplot. Character actors could be counted on to do their bit somewhere at the beginning, the middle, and the end. A rule of thumb: **Subplots should have at least three "beats" or scenes distributed throughout the story, one in each act.** All the subplots should be acknowledged or resolved in the Return. Each character should come away with some variety of Elixir or learning.

TOO MANY ENDINGS

On the other hand, the Return should not seem labored or repetitive. Another good rule of thumb for the Return phase is to operate on the KISS system, that is: **Keep It Simple, Stupid.** Many stories fail because they have too many endings. The audience senses the story is over but the writer, perhaps unable to choose the right ending, tries several. This tends to frustrate an audience, dissipating the energy the writer has created. People want to know the story's definitively over so they can quickly get up and leave the theater or finish the book with a powerful charge of emotion. An overly ambitious film like *Lord Jim*, trying to take on a dense novel, can exhaust an audience with climaxes and endings that seem to go on forever.

An extreme example of keeping it simple might be the karate match that forms the climax of *The Karate Kid.* When the last kick is delivered and the hero wins, the credits roll immediately in a burst of final theme music. There is almost no denouement. We know the kid is bearing the Elixir of lessons learned well in his training.

ABRUPT ENDINGS

A Return can seem too abrupt, giving the sense the writer has quit too soon after the climax. A story tends to feel incomplete unless a certain emotional space is devoted to bidding farewell to the characters and drawing some conclusions. An abrupt Return is like someone hanging up the phone without saying goodbye, or a pilot bailing out without bringing the plane in for a landing.

FOCUS

A Return may feel out of focus if the dramatic questions, raised in Act One and tested in Act Two, are not answered now. Writers may have failed to pose the right questions in the first place. Without realizing it, a writer may have shifted the theme. A tale that started out as a love story may have turned into an exposé of government corruption. The writer has lost the thread. The story will not seem focused unless the circle is closed by Returning to the original themes.

PUNCTUATION

The final function of Return is to conclude the story decisively. The story should end with the emotional equivalent of a punctuation mark. A story, like a sentence, can end in only four ways: with a period, an exclamation point, a question mark, or an ellipsis (the three or four little dots that indicate your thoughts have just trailed off vaguely. Example: Do you want to go now, or...).

The needs of your story and your attitude may dictate ending with the feeling of a period, an image or line of dialogue flatly making a declarative statement: "Life goes on." "Love conquers all." "Good triumphs over evil." "That's the way life is." "There's no place like home."

An ending can give the effect of an exclamation point if the intent of the work is to stir action or create alarm. Science fiction and horror films may end on a note of "We are not alone!" or "Repent or perish!" Stories of social awareness may end with a passionate tone of "Never again!" or "Rise up and throw off chains of oppression!" or "Something must be done!"

In a more open-ended approach to structure, you may want to end with the effect of a question mark, and the feeling that uncertainties remain. The final image may pose a question such as "Will the hero Return with the Elixir or will it be forgotten?" An open-ended story may also trail off with the feeling of an ellipsis. Unspoken questions may linger in the air or conflicts may remain unresolved with endings that suggest doubt or ambiguity: "The hero can't decide between two women, and therefore..." or "Love and art are irreconcilable, so..." or "Life goes on... and on... and on..." or "She proved she's not a killer, but..."

One way or another, the very ending of a story should announce that it's all over — like the Warner Bros. cartoon signature line "That's all, folks." Oral storytellers, in addition to using formulas like "...and they lived happily ever after," will sometimes end folktales with a ritual statement like "I'm done, that's that, and who'll ease my dry throat with a drink?" Sometimes a final image, such as the hero riding off into the sunset, can sum up the story's theme in a visual metaphor and let the audience know it's over. The final image of *Unforgiven,* a shot of Clint Eastwood's character leaving his wife's grave and returning to his house, signals the end of the journey and sums up the story's theme.

These are only a few of the features of Return with the Elixir. As we come full circle, let's leave a little opening for the unknown, the unexpected, the unexplored.

THE WIZARD OF OZ

Dorothy's Return begins with saying goodbye to her Allies and acknowledging the Elixirs of love, courage, and common sense she has gained from them. Then, tapping her heels and chanting "There's no place like home," she wishes herself back to Kansas where she started.

Back home in the Ordinary World, back to black and white, Dorothy wakes up in bed with a compress on her head. The Return is ambiguous: Was the trip to Oz "real," or was it the dream of a girl with a concussion? In story terms, however, it doesn't matter; the journey was real to Dorothy.

She recognizes the people around her as characters from Oz. But her perceptions of them have changed as a result of her experience in the Special World. She remembers that some of it was horrible, some beautiful, but she focuses on what she's learned — there's no place like home.

Dorothy's declaration that she will never leave home again is not meant to be taken literally. It's not this little frame house in Kansas to which she refers, but her own soul. She is a fully integrated person in possession of her best qualities, in control of the worst, and in touch with the positive forms of masculine and feminine energy within her. She has incorporated every lesson she has learned from every being along the road. She is finally happy in her own skin and will feel at home no matter where she is. The Elixir she brings back is this new idea of home, a new concept of her Self.

And so the Hero's Journey ends, or at least rests for a while, for the journey of life and the adventure of story never really end. The hero and the audience bring back the Elixir from the current adventure, but the quest to integrate the lessons goes on. It's for each of us to say what the Elixir is — wisdom, experience, money, love, fame, or the thrill of a lifetime. But a good story, like a good journey, leaves us with an Elixir that changes us, makes us more aware, more alive, more human, more whole, more a part of everything that is. The circle of the Hero's Journey is complete.

QUESTIONING THE JOURNEY

1. What is the Elixir of *Basic Instinct*? *Big*? *City Slickers*? *Fatal Attraction*? *Dances with Wolves*?

2. What is the Elixir your hero brings back from the experience? Is it kept to herself or is it shared?

3. Does your story go on too long after the main event or climax is over? What would be the effect of simply cutting it off after the climax? How much denouement do you need to satisfy the audience?

4. In what ways has the hero gradually taken more responsibility in the course of the story? Is the Return a point of taking greatest responsibility?

5. Who is the hero of the story now? Has your story changed heroes, or have characters risen to be heroes? Who turned out to be a disappointment? Are there any surprises in the final outcome?

6. Is your story worth telling? Has enough been learned to make the effort worthwhile?

7. Where are you in your own Hero's Journey? What is the Elixir you hope to bring back?

LOOKING BACK ON THE JOURNEY

EPILOGUE: LOOKING BACK ON THE JOURNEY

"I've had a hell of a lot of fun, and I've enjoyed every minute of it."
— Errol Flynn

Now that we have come to the end of the Road of Heroes, it may be useful to examine how this model works in some representative film stories. I have chosen *Titanic, Pulp Fiction, The Lion King,* and *The Full Monty* as movies that made creative, entertaining use of the Hero's Journey archetypes and structures. I also want to say a few words about the *Star Wars* saga, which has been much a part of the development of the Hero's Journey idea.

Analyzing these films and tracing the Hero's Journey in them has been a rewarding exercise, revealing some story flaws but also surprising levels of meaning and poetic connection. I strongly recommend you try this for yourself on a movie, novel or story of your own. This material pays back a rich reward when you apply it to a story or a life situation. However, before presenting these analyzes, a few warnings and guidelines are in order.

CAVEAT, SCRIPTOR

First, Caveat Scriptor! (Let the writer beware!) **The Hero's Journey model is a guideline.** It's not a cookbook recipe or a mathematical formula to be applied rigidly to every story. To be effective, a story doesn't have to concur with this or any other school, paradigm, or method of analysis.

The ultimate measure of a story's success or excellence is not its compliance with any established patterns, but its lasting popularity and effect on the audience. To force a story to conform to a structural model is putting the cart before the horse.

It's possible to write good stories that don't exhibit every feature of the Hero's Journey; in fact, it's better if they don't. People love to see familiar conventions and expectations defied creatively. A story can break all the "rules" and yet still touch universal human emotions.

FORM FOLLOWS FUNCTION

Remember: The needs of the story dictate its structure. Form follows function. Your beliefs and priorities, along with the characters, themes, style, tone, and mood you are trying to get across, will determine the shape and design of the plot. Structure will also be influenced by the audience, and the time and place in which the story is being told.

The forms of stories change with the needs of the audience. New story types with different rhythms will continue to be created. For instance, thanks to television and MTV styles of cutting, the attention span of the world audience is shorter these days and its sophistication is greater than ever before. Writers can build faster-moving stories and can assume the audience will be able to handle twists and shortcuts in familiar structures.

New terms are being created every day and new observations about story are being made every time one is written. The Hero's Journey is only a guideline, a starting point for hammering out your own story language and rules of thumb.

CHOOSE YOUR METAPHOR

The pattern of the Hero's Journey is but one metaphor for what goes on in a story or a human life. I have used hunting, college classes, and human sexual response as metaphors to help explain the pattern I see in story, but these are far from the only possibilities. Work out a different metaphor or several of them, if it helps you understand storytelling better. You might find it useful to compare a story to a baseball game, with nine innings instead of twelve stages, and terms like "Seventh-Inning Stretch" instead of Seizing the Sword. You might decide the process of sailing a boat, baking bread, rafting a river, driving a car, or carving a statue makes a more meaningful comparison to telling a story. Sometimes a combination of metaphors is needed to illuminate different facets of the human journey.

The stages, terms, and ideas of the Hero's Journey can be used as a design template for stories, or as a means of troubleshooting a story so long as you don't follow these guidelines too rigidly. It's probably best to acquaint yourself with the Hero's Journey ideas and then forget about them as you sit down to write. If you get lost, refer to the metaphor as you would check a map on a journey. But don't mistake the map for the journey. You don't drive with a map pasted to your windshield. You consult it before setting out or when you get disoriented. The joy of a journey is not reading or following a map, but exploring unknown places and wandering off the map now and then. It's only by getting creatively lost, beyond the boundaries of tradition, that new discoveries can be made.

DESIGN TEMPLATE

You may want to experiment with the Hero's Journey as an outline for plotting a new story or troubleshooting one in the works. In Disney Animation we have used the Hero's Journey model to tighten up storylines, pinpoint problems, and lay out structures. Hundreds of writers have told me they plotted their screenplays, romance novels, or TV sitcom episodes using the Hero's Journey and the guidance of mythology.

Some people begin to plot a movie or novel by writing the twelve stages of the journey on twelve index cards. If you already know some of the major scenes and turning points, write these down where you think they match up with the twelve stages. In this way you begin to map out your story by filling in the gaps in your knowledge of the characters and what happens to them. Use the ideas of the Hero's Journey to ask questions about your characters: What are the Ordinary and Special Worlds for these people? What is my hero's Call to Adventure? How is fear expressed in Refusal? Is it overcome by Meeting with a Mentor? What is the First Threshold my hero has to cross? And so on. Before long the gaps fill and you can progress to chart Hero's Journeys for all the characters and subplots until the complete design is worked out.

You may find that a certain scene matches with the function of one of the stages, but it comes at what seems to be the "wrong" point in the Hero's Journey model. In your story a Mentor might be needed to present a Call and Refusal in Act Two or Three instead of Act One, as the Hero's Journey model appears to indicate. Don't worry about this — put in the scene wherever it seems right to you. The model only shows the most likely place for an event to occur.

Any element of the Hero's Journey can appear at any point in a story. *Dances with Wolves* begins with a hero's Ordeal or Resurrection that you usually expect to see at the midpoint or end of a Hero's Journey, and yet the story works. All stories are composed of elements of the Hero's Journey, but the units can be arranged in almost any order to serve the needs of your particular story.

This is why you use index cards rather than writing the stages on a single sheet of paper. You can move the cards around to situate scenes as needed, and you can add more cards in case a movement like Call and Refusal needs to be repeated a number of times (as was the case with *Titanic*).

You may find that as you visualize your story, you will think of some scenes that don't seem to match any particular stage of the journey. You may have to invent your own terminology or metaphors to cover this category of scenes, as well as tailoring the Hero's Journey terminology to suit your own picture of the universe.

DEMONSTRATION OF THE IDEA

Now let's look at four very different films to demonstrate how the motifs of the Hero's Journey keep being re-created with new combinations of the old patterns.

DROWNING IN LOVE

A Hero's Journey Analysis of James Cameron's *Titanic*

When the great ocean liner Titanic, on its maiden voyage from Liverpool to New York, scraped against an iceberg and sank on the evening of

April 14, 1912, a story of extraordinary emotional impact began to form. Stunned news reports flashed around the world, telling of over fifteen hundred people lost, more than half the souls aboard the supposedly unsinkable luxury liner. Then came the individual stories of cowardice and courage, arrogant selfishness and noble self-sacrifice. The threads were bound together into one great epic which, with its powerful elements of terror, tragedy, and death, was retold for succeeding generations in the form of books, articles, documentaries, feature films, stage plays, and even a musical or two. The Titanic disaster became part of Western popular culture, a subject of abiding fascination like the Pyramids, UFOs, or Arthurian romance.

Then, after eighty-five years of Titanic stories, an unusual coalition of two Hollywood studios, Paramount and 20th Century Fox, offered the public yet another version — James Cameron's *Titanic*. Not only did this one top all the other Titanic-related movies in its production values and opulence, it was also the most expensive movie ever made, costing more than two hundred million dollars to produce and many millions more to advertise and distribute. Director and writer James Cameron's vision, requiring the pooled financial resources of two studios, was so colossal that many observers predicted the same fate for the movie as the ship. This new movie was sure to sink, possibly taking the studios and their top executives down with it. No matter how popular it would be, no matter how fantastically well-executed were the special effects, such an arrogantly enormous production could not possibly recoup its costs.

After all, said the critics who specialize in reviewing movies before they are made, it had so many strikes against it. First, everyone knows how the story turns out. They dance, they hit the iceberg, they die. That vital element of surprise, of not knowing what happens next, would be lacking.

Second, it was a period piece, set in the obscure time before World War I, and everyone knows period pieces are expensive and often unpopular because they are not "relevant" to modern audiences. Third, the structure of the script was considered as flawed as the design of the Titanic, forcing audiences to endure an hour and half of melodrama, the length of a normal movie, before delivering the iceberg and the action. It had a tragic ending, which is usually death at the box office. At over three hours long, it was almost twice the ideal picture length from the point of view of theatre owners, who could schedule fewer screenings per day. And finally, its featured players were not considered big stars at that time.

Twentieth Century Fox executives, who had put up most of the money in return for the international distribution rights, had particular cause to worry. The Titanic story was familiar in the U.S. and the U.K., but not in Asia and other foreign markets. Would the vital international audiences turn out for a costume drama about a long-ago shipwreck?

Well, they did, in unprecedented numbers, and repeatedly. To the amazement of everyone, including the filmmakers, audiences around the world embraced *Titanic* on a scale as huge as the ship itself. Its fantastic costs were recouped within two months, ensuring that Fox and Paramount would reap immense profits. It remained number one at the box office around the world for more than 16 weeks. A sweep of the Academy Awards, with the film pulling down fourteen nominations and eleven Oscars, including best picture and best director, provided another boost in revenue. The soundtrack hit number one on the charts and perched there for four months.

Titanic fever extended far beyond attending the movie or listening to the music. We live in a collecting society, where the ancient urge to own little pieces of a story can be indulged on a fantastic scale. In the same impulse that caused Neolithic people to carve bone models of their favorite goddess or totem animal, the contemporary movie audience wanted to own a piece of the *Titanic* experience.

They bought models of the ship, books about the movie, movies about the movie, and movie props such as lifeboats, deck chairs, and china offered in luxury catalogs. Some even went so far as to sign up for an expensive ride to the bottom of the sea in a high-tech submarine, to actually visit the wreck of the great ship and the somber graveyard of its passengers.

As the film continued to be the number-one box office attraction for four months, people began to wonder what was going on. What was fueling this unusual response to a mere movie?

QUANTUM MOVIE EVENTS

Certain films, because of surprising box office success or memorable content, become permanent monuments on the cultural landscape. *Titanic*, like *Star Wars*, *Easy Rider*, *Close Encounters*, and *Independence Day*, has become such a monument. Movies of this type are quantum events, breaking through old shells and boundaries, flinging the idea of a movie to a whole new level. These quantum-event films capture something that resonates in many, many people. They must express some nearly universal emotion or satisfy a widely shared wish. What was the universal wish that *Titanic* granted?

Naturally, I'm inclined to think the movie succeeded because it satisfies the universal wish for meaning, and that it does so through extensive use of Hero's Journey motifs and concepts. As James Cameron said, in a letter to the Los Angeles Times, March 28, 1998, *Titanic* "intentionally incorporates universals of human experience and emotion that are timeless — and familiar because they reflect our basic emotional fabric. By dealing in archetypes, the film touches people in all cultures and of all ages."

These archetypal patterns turn a chaotic event like the sinking of an ocean liner into a coherent design that asks questions and provides opinions about how life should be lived.

As a story on an epic scale, *Titanic* indulges the luxury of a leisurely storytelling pace, taking its time to set up an elaborate framing device which has a complete Hero's Journey structure of its own. In this plotline, parallel to the central story of the Titanic's passengers, at least two Hero's Journeys are unfolded: one of a scientist-adventurer seeking a physical treasure, the other of an old woman returning to the scene of a great disaster to relive a grand passion. A possible third Hero's Journey is that of the audience, traveling into the Titanic world to learn the dead ship's lessons.

Like many movies, *Titanic* is "bookended" by an outer tale, set in modern day, that serves several important story functions. First, by using actual documentary footage of the Titanic wreck on the bottom of the sea, it reminds us that this is more than a made-up story — it's a dramatization of a real event. The wreck of the ship and the mournful, homely relics of its human passengers bring out one of the most powerful elements in the production — that this could happen, this did happen, and it happened to people like us.

Second, by introducing the character of Old Rose, the bookend device connects this story of another time with our own day, and reminds us that the Titanic disaster was not so long ago, within the span of one human life. Old Rose dramatizes the fact that there are many people alive today who remember the Titanic, and a few who actually survived it.

Third, the framing device creates mystery — who is this elderly woman who claims to be a Titanic survivor, and what happened to the jewel the explorer is so eager to get? Did Rose find love and did her lover survive? These question marks are hooks that engage the audience's attention and create suspense even though we know the general outcome of the Titanic story.

Titanic begins by introducing us to one **HERO** of this mini-story, the very contemporary figure of Brock Lovett, the scientist/businessman/explorer who can't quite decide how to present himself to the public. His **ORDINARY WORLD** is that of a showman trying to raise money for his expensive scientific adventures. His **OUTER PROBLEM** is trying to find a treasure, a diamond thought to have been lost on the Titanic; his **INNER PROBLEM** is trying to find an authentic voice and a better system of values.

The figure of the scientist-explorer is common enough to have become an archetype, expressed as Sir Arthur Conan Doyle's creation, Professor Challenger; Allan Quartermain of *King Solomon's Mines*; the explorer-showman Carl Denning of *King Kong*, and the contemporary Indiana Jones. These fictional characters are reflections of real adventuring archaeologists and researchers like Howard Carter, Heinrich Schlieman, Roy Chapman Andrews, and Jacques Cousteau. Robert Ballard, the scientist-adventurer-businessman who actually found the wreck of the Titanic, is one model for Lovett in the movie, and actually went through his own Hero's Journey in choosing how to regard the ship. At first he came as a kind of scientific conqueror, but gradually was moved deeply by the human tragedy and decided the wreck site was a sacred place that should be left undisturbed as a memorial to those who died on the ship.

In this plot thread, the young scientist is following a prime directive: find the treasure. But through the magic of the old woman's story, a tale that occupies the body of the film, the explorer is transformed from a money-driven capitalist to a true explorer of the heart, who comes to understand that there are more important treasures in life than jewels and money.

THE OBJECT OF THE QUEST

What is the Holy Grail Lovett seeks in his quest? It's a diamond called "The Heart of the Ocean," a name that links the theme of love with the setting of the film. The jewel is a true MacGuffin — something small and concrete to focus the audience's attention and symbolize the hopes and aspirations of the characters. A diamond is a symbol of perfection, of the immortal, eternal power of the gods. Its facets, with their mathematical precision, are physical proof of the grand design, of the creative hand and mind of the gods. Like the gods, certain substances, such as gold, silver, and jewels, seem to be immortal. Where flesh and bone, leaf and tree, even copper and steel, corrode away, jewels remain, untouched, unchanged. They miraculously survive the crushing power of the bottom of the sea in perfect condition. Jewels and precious metals have always been used, along with incense, perfumes, beautiful flowers, and divine music, to connect religious and dramatic presentations to the world of the gods. They are little pieces of heaven, islands of perfection in an imperfect world, "doors of perception" giving a glimpse of Paradise. "The Heart of the Ocean" is a symbol for the idealized notions of love and honor that the movie reveres.

Lovett ransacks the ship with his remote-controlled robot but doesn't find the bit of heaven he's seeking, at least not in the way he anticipated. Opening the safe he's retrieved, he finds rotted pulp that was once money and a miraculously preserved drawing of a beautiful young woman, wearing nothing but the diamond he is looking for. Lovett makes a CNN broadcast that is a CALL heard by Old Rose and her granddaughter Lizzy Calvert.

Old Rose's **ORDINARY WORLD** is that of an elderly but active artist living in Ojai, California. She is a **HERO** in her own drama, bringing her long life to a climax and conclusion, but she also serves as a **MENTOR** for Lovett and the audience, guiding us through the special world of the Titanic and teaching a higher system of values. Her **OUTER PROBLEM** is how to get across the Titanic experience; her **INNER PROBLEM** is dredging up these strong memories that for a long time have been swimming in her unconscious. She issues her own **CALL** to Lovett, claiming to be the woman in the drawing he has found, and asserting that she knows something about the diamond. After some **REFUSAL** to accept her story, he accepts and brings her out to his research vessel, where she begins to tell her story of the Titanic's first and last days at sea.

MAIN STORY — ORDINARY WORLD

Now the movie leaves the framing device to fully enter the main story and the world of the Titanic. We see the ship in her new-minted glory for the first time. The bustling dock is the **ORDINARY WORLD** stage on which the main protagonists or **HEROES,** young Rose and Jack, are introduced. Rose gets an elaborate **ENTRANCE** as one of the beautiful possessions in the entourage of Cal Hockley, her fiancé and the **SHADOW** or villain of the piece, a sneering "heavy" straight out of a Victorian melodrama. We also meet the sub-villain, Hockley's henchman Lovejoy, who executes Cal's arrogant wishes.

Our first sight of Rose is her hand in a delicate white glove, emerging from the motorcar. The hands of the lovers, twining and separating, will become a continuing visual thread. She is elegantly dressed but feels a prisoner, as Old Rose tells us in voice-over. She is a **HERO** on a journey, but at this moment wears the mask of the **VICTIM** archetype, a damsel in distress, beautiful but powerless.

Cal represents the arrogance and bigotry of his class and also the dark, Shadow side of manhood and marriage. He is at one extreme of a **POLARITY**, representing repression and tyranny, with Jack as his polar opposite representing liberation and love. Although the Titanic is a great feat of the imagination, built by honest laboring men, it has deep, fatal flaws, the fault of arrogant men like Cal. He has bought into and identified with the hubristic aspects of the Titanic, believing fully that it is unsinkable because it was created by men of Cal's exalted class, by "gentlemen." He claims that "not even God himself could sink her." In the world of myth, a statement like that is sure to bring down the wrath of the gods, who listen carefully and punish swiftly.

Rose's mother, Ruth DeWitt Bukater, is another **SHADOW** figure, representing the dark side of femininity, the repressive, smothering potential of motherhood, a witchy, scheming queen like Medea or Clytemnestra.

Rose has received a dark **CALL TO ADVENTURE**, being manipulated into marrying a man she doesn't love. As Rose **CROSSES THE THRESHOLD** of the gangway with her mother and Cal it is a kind of royal procession, but Rose experiences it as a march to slavery, and the Titanic as a slave ship taking her to captivity in America. She doesn't quite **REFUSE THE CALL** but is certainly a reluctant hero.

Now we meet the second principal **HERO**, Jack, who with his **ALLY**, the young Italian immigrant Fabrizio, is gambling, risking everything on fate or chance. A clock is ticking, setting up a **MOTIF** of time running out, of the general shortness and preciousness of life. Jack's **ORDINARY WORLD** is that of drifting and adventure, trusting to luck and his own skills and gifts. The **CALL TO ADVENTURE** comes, on one level, as he wins the card game and a pair of third-class tickets on the Titanic. He shows no **RELUCTANCE** or fear at this level — he's not the reluctant kind of hero. However, the **IRONY** is thick as he declares himself and Fabrizio to be "the luckiest sons-of-bitches alive." If he knew what awaits him, he might have cause to be afraid.

Jack is a slightly superhuman figure who doesn't appear to have major flaws, but he will have an **INNER PROBLEM**, trying to find and win the love of his life. If he has a flaw, it's that he's a little too cocky and arrogant, which later worsens his problems with Cal and Lovejoy. His **OUTER PROBLEM** or challenge is first to climb into society and then to survive the disaster. He is something of a **CATALYST HERO**, one who is already fully developed and who doesn't change much, but who spends his energy in helping others to change. He is also a **TRICKSTER HERO**, using deceit and disguise to penetrate the enemy's defenses. In the end he makes the ultimate heroic **SACRIFICE**, giving his life to save the woman he loves.

Together Jack and Rose form a pair of **POLAR OPPOSITES**, male and female, poor and rich, but also express the great oppositional forces of Flight and Restriction. Jack stands for freedom, no boundaries, not accepting the limits imposed by society, an Icarus daring to fly above his station. At the beginning of the film Rose is aligned, against her will, with the opposite force of Restriction, bound by society's conventions, by the force of her mother's grasping will, by her promise to marry Cal Hockley, the dark prince of society. She is a Persephone being dragged down to the underworld. Cal, like Pluto, the god of the underworld who kidnapped Persephone, obsesses about money and is harsh and judging. Pluto was the god of wealth and one of the official judges of the dead. Persephone's lover in the underworld was Adonis, a phenomenally beautiful youth. Like Adonis, Jack comes to Rose in her dark imprisonment and reminds her of the joys of life.

Rose's **INNER PROBLEM** will be to break away from her **ORDINARY WORLD**, to re-align herself with the freedom and ability to fly that Jack embodies. Her **OUTER PROBLEM** will be sheer survival so she can implement what she's learned in a long, happy life.

Titanic elaborately explores the function of **MENTOR**, with a number of characters wearing the mask at different times. In addition to Old Rose, Molly Brown does the **MENTOR** job, guiding Jack through the **SPECIAL WORLD** of First Class and, like a fairy godmother, providing him with a proper costume so he can pass as a gentleman.

Captain Smith is supposed to be a **MENTOR** for the entire voyage, a leader and the king of this little world. But he is a fatally flawed king, arrogant and complacent, overconfident on the triumphal final voyage of his career.

Jack wears the mask of **MENTOR** for Rose, teaching her how to enjoy life and be free. He fulfills the fantasy of many a young woman by freely offering the gift of commitment. From nothing but a glance he decides he can't abandon her, for "I'm involved now." Later, when the ship goes down, he gives her the vital knowledge of how to survive by staying out of the water as long as possible and swimming away from the suction of the sinking ship.

Another **MENTOR** to Rose is Thomas Andrews, the architect of the ship. She wins his respect by her intelligent questions about the Titanic, and he rewards her by telling her how she can find Jack when he is trapped below decks. In this he is a Daedalus to Rose's Ariadne. Daedalus was the architect of the deadly Labyrinth, and gave its secrets to the young princess Ariadne so she could rescue her love, Theseus, who ventured into the Labyrinth to battle a monster that represented the dark side of her family.

CROSSING THE THRESHOLD in *Titanic* is celebrated with an elaborate sequence depicting the ship "stretching her legs." This movement climaxes with Jack and Fabrizio on the bow of the ship, and Jack exulting, "I'm king of the world!" Jack and Rose have other Thresholds to cross — each entering the other's world and both entering a Special World of love and danger.

TESTS, ALLIES, and **ENEMIES** play out in conflicts between Jack and Rose and the forces of Restriction. Jack and Rose connect and become **ALLIES** when she tries to kill herself by jumping off the ship.

He **RESCUES** her and wins an invitation to dine with Rose and Cal in First Class. He enters that **SPECIAL WORLD** with the help of **MENTOR** Molly Brown, and is **TESTED** severely at the dinner by the taunting of his **ENEMIES**, Cal and Rose's mother. He passes these tests and stands up to their ridicule, delivering his credo, an expression of the movie's theme: Life's a gift, learn to take it as it comes, make each day count. He wins Rose's greater respect and guarantees further clashes with Cal.

Rose's **TEST** comes a little later when Jack, promising to show her a "real party," guides her into the **SPECIAL WORLD** of Third Class. In a sequence of wild music, dancing, and drinking, Rose is initiated into the world of Dionysus, the god of intoxication, passion, and ecstasy. It's a test of her society girl standards — will she be offended by the earthy, brawling orgy? She passes the test by outdoing the immigrants with her drinking, smoking, and dancing.

The stage of **APPROACH** is expressed in the lovers' tentative romantic dance with each other, including the lyrical moment when Jack positions Rose at the bow of the ship, making her its figurehead, teaching her how to fly, how to balance between life and death. If he is king of the world, now she is queen.

Rose makes a deeper **APPROACH** when she asks Jack to draw her picture, trustingly exposing her naked self to him. This is a **TEST** for Jack which he passes by acting like a gentleman and a professional artist, enjoying the erotic moment but not taking advantage of her vulnerability.

THRESHOLD GUARDIANS abound as the lovers draw near to the Inmost Cave and the beginning of an elaborate, multi-leveled **ORDEAL**. Dozens of White Star Line stewards stand guard at doors, elevators, and gates, and a squadron of them, like a pack of hunting dogs, is sent by Cal to seek out the lovers. Jack and Rose, fleeing from Restriction, find themselves deep in the hold where they face an **ORDEAL** on the level of intimacy. They climb into the Inmost Cave of the luxury motorcar and join as lovers. In the "little death" of orgasm Rose's hand streaks the window glass, looking like the hand of a drowning victim, drowning in love. By crossing this great threshold, they have died to the old life and are reborn in the new.

The death-bringing **ORDEAL** for the Titanic comes moments later when the ship hits the iceberg, the mute, inexorable force of Nemesis, that spirit sent by the gods to punish prideful mortals. The death of the ship and of hundreds of passengers occupies the next major movement of the drama.

Jack and Rose harvest some **REWARD** from their death-and-rebirth experience. They are bonded, supporting each other in the struggle to survive. This is tested when Rose is given a chance to escape in a lifeboat. Sensing that Cal will abandon Jack to die, Rose fights her way back onto the ship to share her fate with Jack's.

THE ROAD BACK is the battle for survival, which includes a classic **CHASE** as Cal, impatient for the ship to do its work, tries to hasten Jack and Rose's death with bullets. The other characters face life-and-death tests, some choosing to die with honor, others to live at all costs, and some, like Lovejoy, dying despite their most ignoble efforts to survive. Act Two concludes with Jack and Rose balancing on the stern rail and riding the ship as it plunges toward the bottom.

RESURRECTION commences as Jack and Rose fight to preserve the warmth of life in the frozen sea. Finding that the bit of floating wreckage they cling to will support only one person's weight, Jack puts Rose's life ahead of his in a classic **HERO'S SACRIFICE**. He has already lived a full life and has experienced perfect happiness with her. She is relatively new to freedom and life, and he charges her to live richly and fully enough for both of them. He lets go of life, confident of being **RESURRECTED** in her heart, in her memories.

Rose herself goes to the edge of death, but is **RESURRECTED** as the lone lifeboat searches for survivors in the sea of dead faces. In a final **TEST** of all she has learned from Jack, she summons the strength to swim to get a whistle from a dead officer's lips, calling for rescue. With that Old Rose concludes her story, returning us to the framing device in modern day and counting the toll of the Titanic's dead.

The robot sub leaves the wreck in peace and silence. On the research ship, Lovett tosses away the cigar he had saved to celebrate finding the diamond, a little **SACRIFICE** of an old personality trait. He admits to Rose's granddaughter that he spent three years thinking of the Titanic but never really got its message. He has been **TRANSFORMED** by the **ORDEAL**, and his **REWARDS** are his insight and the sympathy of

Rose's granddaughter. Is there a glimmer of romance, a chance to fully live out the truncated love of Jack and Rose in another generation? He has not found the physical treasure he came seeking, but has he, like Jack, found a greater treasure in the new world of emotion?

Old Rose goes to the railing of the research ship, echoing her flying scene at the bow with Jack. She even climbs up on the railing as she did so long ago. In a final moment of **SUSPENSE** we don't know her intention — will she jump, joining Jack in the sea at last, like a belated Juliet joining her Romeo in death? But instead she pulls out the diamond and in a quick flash we see young Rose finding it in her pocket beneath the Statue of Liberty, an **ELIXIR** rewarded for survival. With a little cry of final dramatic **CLIMAX**, Old Rose releases it into the water where, like Jack, it spirals down into mystery, a last **SACRIFICE** that says her experience and memories are more important than any physical possession. This is the **ELIXIR**, the healing message the movie means to send the audience home with.

Dissolve now to Old Rose falling asleep, surrounded by photos of her long, full life. Here, after **FINAL ORDEAL**, is **FINAL REWARD**, fulfillment of Jack's prophecies — Rose is an adventuress, a pilot, an actress, riding horses by a California pier, having babies, living a life for both of them, part of the **ELIXIR** she brought back. The dark wounds of her family history have been healed.

Rose dreams, and in that **SPECIAL WORLD** the Titanic and its passengers live again, **RESURRECTED** by the power of the unconscious. Through Rose's eyes, we pass the **THRESHOLD GUARDIANS** of the White Star Line one last time, entering the heaven of First Class where all the good folk live eternally. (The villains are conspicuously absent, no doubt bobbing in a frigid, wet hell.) Jack stands at his old place by the clock, a supernatural being conquering time. He extends his hand, they touch again, they kiss, and the ship's company applaud this final **SACRED MARRIAGE**. Camera up to the ceiling dome, the vault of heaven, and its white purity fills the screen. Rose has her **ELIXIR**.

THE END

Titanic is certainly not a perfect movie, and there are boatloads of critics to point out its flaws — a certain bluntness in the writing: a tendency to end scenes with crude, obvious utterances like "Shit!", "Oh, shit!", and

"I'll be God damned!" For a while at the beginning the movie seems to have Tourette's Syndrome. There is a sense of pandering to the modern audience in an exaggerated attempt to make the story "relevant" with contemporary dialogue and acting styles; and there is a one-dimensional quality to some characters, especially the sneering, unshaded villains.

Although well played by Billy Zane, Cal in the screenplay is one of the weakest parts of the design, and would have been a more effective rival if he were more seductive, a better match for Rose, real competition for Jack, and not such an obvious monster. Then it would have been a real contest, not a one-sided match between the most attractive young man in the universe and a leering, abusive cad with a bag of money in one hand and a pistol in the other.

The chase scene in which Cal is shooting at Jack and Rose while the Titanic is sinking strikes some people as absurd dramatic overkill and takes them out of the movie. Perhaps it serves a story purpose — Cameron may have felt he needed his heroes to endure one more round in the belly of the Titanic and used Cal to drive them there — but another device, such as needing to go back in to rescue someone, could have achieved the same effect.

Maybe this round of ordeals isn't needed at all. The movie would benefit from cutting and this sequence of underwater tension seems repetitive after they've already burst through so many gates. The whole sequence seems to be structured to build up to a climactic shot in which Jack and Rose run from a wall of water — an iconic tableau of their struggle with the force of death. However, this shot is one of the least effective illusions in the movie, for the actors' faces are queasily pasted onto the stuntpeople's bodies by some electronic magic which has not quite been perfected. The whole sequence could be cut or trimmed — there's enough tension, already.

However, we are here not to bury Caesar, but to analyze him — how does Cameron succeed, what outweighs the flaws in his design?

A GREAT STORY

First, the fate of the Titanic and its passengers is a great epic story in its own right, and has worked its fascination since the day the ship went down. A dramatization of the Titanic disaster, only recently unearthed in a film vault, was produced by a German company within weeks of the tragedy. It was only the first of many documentaries and feature films, not to mention countless books and articles, about the disaster. Like the tragic, fairy-tale story of Princess Diana, the events around the sinking of the Titanic fall into dramatic patterns that harmonize with deep, archetypal images, shared and understood by everyone.

SYMBOLISM OF "TITANIC"

From its archaic, archetypal name on down, the Titanic is laden with symbolism and meaning. The ship's name is a choice that reveals much about the psychology of its builders. In the movie, Rose asks Bruce Ismay, the businessman behind the Titanic project, why he chose that name. He replies that he wanted a name to evoke great magnitude, moving Rose to comment on the Freudian overtones of male preoccupation with size.

However the movie doesn't address the mythological origins of the word "titanic," which were certainly known to the classics-trained English gentlemen who chose that name. It refers to the immense Titans, giant predecessors and deadly enemies of the gods. The Titans were fundamental forces from the beginning of time — greedy, rude, and ruthless — and the gods had to fight a great battle to defeat them and imprison them under the earth before they spoiled and looted everything. When the press of the time called first-class passengers like Astor and Guggenheim "Titans of industry and capital," they were indicating more than the gigantic size of their empires.

A few years before the Titanic was built, German archaeologists unearthed a Hellenistic temple called the Pergamon Altar that depicted in dramatic relief the battle between the gods and the Giants, recalling an earlier epic struggle with the gods' age-old enemies, the Titans. This monument is virtually a storyboard in stone for what would be a great special-effects movie. The builders of the Titanic, who probably had seen pictures of these reliefs, chose to identify themselves and their clients not with the gods but with their ancient enemies, the Titans. They were truly challenging the gods by this choice. Many people felt, even before the ship sailed, that the builders were tempting fate to give the ship such a grandiose name. Even worse was to claim that it was unsinkable. That was a foolish blasphemy, challenging the almighty power of God. A superstitious aura surrounds the Titanic, something like the curse of King Tut's tomb, a belief that the builders called down the wrath of God by their arrogance and pride.

The story of the Titanic resonates with an old literary concept, The Ship of Fools. Storytellers created this satirical form around the time of Columbus' first voyage to the New World. One of the first expressions was Sebastian Brant's narrative poem, "Das Narrenschiff," printed only two years after Columbus first successfully crossed the Atlantic. It tells of a ship's passengers bound for Narragonia, the land of fools, and is a scathing depiction of the follies of its time. It was widely translated and adapted into books and plays.

The Ship of Fools is an allegory, a story in which all the conditions of life and levels of society are lampooned savagely in the situation of a boatful of pathetic passengers. It is a sardonic tale, harshly depicting the flaws in the people and social systems of its time.

Titanic goes in for broad-brush social criticism as well, portraying the rich and powerful as foolish monsters, and the poor as their noble but helpless victims. The exceptions are Jack, who is poor but not helpless, and Molly Brown, who is rich but not monstrous. She is the nouveau riche American who rose from the same level as Jack and who may represent the healthy side of the American immigrant experience — ambitious, climbing the social ladder, but also big-hearted, egalitarian, generous, and fair. *Titanic* is more hopeful, less cynical than The Ship of Fools, suggesting that a few can transcend their foolishness and victimization to live full, meaningful lives.

The irony of "The Ship of Fools" was derived from the point of view, the audience's knowledge that the struggles of the passengers are meaningless and foolish because they are all trapped and doomed anyway. *Titanic* has some of that ironic feeling as Jack and Fabrizio exult in their good fortune at winning tickets on a ship that we know will sink. Irony goes with the territory in a story about a ship that we know is fated to destruction.

The idea of The Ship of Fools is summed up in the old phrase "We're all in the same boat." It shows that despite our foolish attention to superficial differences of birth, wealth, and status we are all trapped by the absolutes of life, all alike in being subject to inevitable forces like gravity, fate, death, and taxes.

A ship isolated at sea on a long journey becomes a convenient symbol of the human condition, of the soul's lonely passage through life. The isolation of the Titanic in the North Atlantic makes her a little world, a microcosm, a nearly perfect model of the society of her time, in which the two thousand people on board represent all the millions alive at that time.

Like the ship itself, the scale of this story is epic, larger than life, big enough to tell the story of a whole culture, in this case of the whole Western world at that time. This vast story is made comprehensible and digestible by selecting the lives and deaths of a few who represent qualities and polarities present to some degree in all members of the culture.

Like its epic predecessors, the Iliad, the Odyssey, the Aeneid, the Arthurian romances, or the Ring Cycle of Wagner, *Titanic* tells part of a vast story, the bridging of two worlds, the Old World and the New. Within these enormous supertales are hundreds of substories and epic cycles, each with its own dramatic structure and completeness. No single work can tell all the threads, but the individual story can communicate the sense, the dramatic facts, of the entire situation. *Titanic* has been criticized for not dramatizing this or that substory — the Carpathia's race to the scene, the stories of the Astors and Guggenheims, the difficulties of the telegrapher in getting out distress calls, etc. But no film could tell all the substories. Storytellers of the future can choose other incidents and personalities to highlight. It will take the combined output of many artists to fully tell the tale of the Titanic, just as it has taken Homer, Sophocles, Euripides, Strauss, Kazantzakis, Hallmark Productions, Classic Comics, and thousands of other artists to fully tell the epic story of the Odyssey, itself only one of dozens of epic cycles in the superstory of the Trojan War.

As a story about the rapid crossing of the Atlantic, *Titanic* symbolizes this century's preoccupation with speedy travel and increasing global consciousness. It speaks of centuries of European culture passing to America, of the waves of immigrants filling the American continents, lured by the seductive promise of freedom. In the film the Statue of Liberty is a recurring symbol of the immigrant dream, a lighthouse beckoning the newcomer. Poor doomed Fabrizio pretends he can see her all the way from Cherbourg.

The Statue of Liberty, a gift from the people of France to the people of America, is a colossal example of the ancient practice of sending statues of gods and goddesses from a founding city to its colonies to connect them by a psychic thread, a religious tie. France and the United States went through revolutions at the same time and are linked by their devotion to liberty, one of many cultural links between New World and Old.

The context of *Titanic's* release has to be taken into account in evaluating its success. It came out at a time when we were becoming more aware of a global society and links between Europe and America. Shocks like the Gulf War, the collapse of the Berlin Wall, and the fall of Communism in Russia joined with unpredictably shifting worldwide weather patterns to make a time of uncertainty when the ship of life seems fragile. We were two years away from the end of the century and in a mood to look back at the beginnings.

The stage was set for the new Titanic movie by the discovery a few years before of the wreck's location on the ocean floor. The finding of the ship was a major triumph of science and a powerful psychological moment. For centuries it has been impossible to find ships lost at such depths. The Titanic being buried in the sea for so long, then found again, makes a strong symbol of our surprising power to recover lost memories from the subconscious. It is a godlike thing to be able to go down and see the Titanic, and a true Hero's Journey to recover lost treasure from the subconscious.

The discovery led to the fantasy of raising the Titanic, as described in Clive Cussler's novel, *Raise the Titanic,* but soon the fantasy became a real possibility. The experts agree it is feasible to raise the pieces of the ship, and many artifacts have been brought up, but for the moment the consensus is that it's better to leave the wreck where it lies as a monument to its victims. The spectacular drama of seeing live TV of the wreck with its poignant human remains helped provide the right climate for releasing another Titanic movie.

Much has been made of the inclusion of a young love story as a factor in *Titanic's* great popularity. It was a kind of Romeo and Juliet plot device, an easily relatable tale of young people from warring factions falling in love.

Romance is the genre Cameron has chosen to present the Titanic story, and by making that choice he opens the story invitingly to women. He could have chosen other genres, telling the Titanic story as a mystery, a detective story, a treasure hunt, or even as a comedy. At times it is all of those things, but the primary theme and design principle is romantic love, and the structure is that of a romance. For that choice he gains a clear-cut formula with a high degree of audience identification — a triangular relationship in which a woman must be saved from domination by a cruel older man through the intervention of a younger rescuer.

This triangulated relationship is a familiar pattern in romance novels and in the country of film noir and hard-boiled fiction. It provides the three-cornered stage for conflict, jealousy, rivalry, betrayal, revenge, and rescue just as do the stories of Guinevere, Lancelot, and King Arthur, the romance novels where the heroine must choose between two men, and the film noir motif of the young woman who must choose between Mr. Big and the young drifter or detective.

Leonardo DiCaprio plays the drifter corner of the triangle in *Titanic*. The secret of his remarkable attractive powers may be that he projects the archetypal mask of the sensitive young man, displaying both masculine action and feminine sensitivity. He is well suited to play Jack, a Peter Pan, a puer aeternas (eternal youth) who remains forever young by his beautiful, sacrificial death. Rose is another Wendy, a girl in bedclothes running around a ship dodging an evil Captain Hook while the eternal youth teaches her how to fly and how to embrace life. The iceberg and the ticking of the clock fulfill the same archetypal purpose as the crocodile which has swallowed a clock in *Peter Pan*. They are projections of the Shadow, the unconscious force that threatens to destroy us, sooner or later, if we don't acknowledge it.

Further back in our mythic past, Jack's slight, youthful persona resonates with David, the giant-killer, and especially with doomed young gods like Adonis and Balder, who die tragically young. Jack is also a twin with Dionysus, the god of revelry, passion, intoxication, who appeals to the wild side of women, who drives them wild. The drunken dance in the lower depths of steerage, in which Rose is drenched head to foot in beer, is a true Dionysian revel and her initiation into those ancient mysteries, with Jack as her initiator.

Jack is a **HERO**, but of a specialized type, a **CATALYST** hero, a **WANDERER** who is not greatly changed by the story but who triggers change in the other characters. Jack is an ethereal, otherworldly creation who leaves no trace except in Rose's heart. There's no record of him being aboard the Titanic and he left no legacy, not even a silver bullet, unless you count Old Rose's memories. One character, Bodine, Lovett's sidekick and a kind of **THRESHOLD GUARDIAN** to Old Rose, even suggests that the whole thing could have been her romantic invention, a story too good to be true. Like all travelers to the other world, Rose has to be taken on faith.

The character of young Rose is a manifestation of the "damsel in distress" archetype. As such she is a sister of Sleeping Beauty and Snow White, princesses caught between life and death and wakened by a kiss; the Twelve Dancing Princesses rescued from enchantment by a young man who makes himself invisible to follow them into their world; Psyche in love with the mysterious young flying god Cupid (Eros); Persephone kidnapped to an underworld hell by a cruel king; Helen of Troy snatched away from her brutal husband by a sensuous young admirer; and Ariadne rescued from a bad marriage by the passionate, artistic god Dionysus.

Women struggle with the "damsel in distress" archetype because it perpetuates patterns of domination and submission, and can encourage a passive, victimized attitude. However, it is an easy archetype to identify and empathize with, representing the feelings of anyone who has felt powerless, trapped, or imprisoned. The "woman in jeopardy" is a staple of movie and TV plots because it creates instant identification and sympathy and raises the emotional involvement of the audience. In *Titanic* the audience can both feel sorry for Rose in her imprisonment and enjoy seeing her become free and active as she tears away the "damsel in distress" mask and grows into the role of Hero.

There may be another factor in the movie's particular appeal to women. *Titanic* is a special-effects movie that does not scream science fiction, war, or macho male adventure. It offers a spectacle that does not exclude or ignore the interests of women, and is given human scale with an emotional melodrama dealing with issues of love and fidelity.

For men as well as women, *Titanic* fulfills another contract with the audience, providing an unparalleled opportunity for **COMPARISON**. The movie offers examples of human behavior in a set of dire, extreme circumstances against which viewers can measure themselves. People can enjoy speculating, from the safety of their seats, on how they would act in a similar situation. How would I have handled the challenge of the Titanic? Would I face death with honor and courage, or would I panic and act with selfish frenzy? Would I fight for life or would I sacrifice my place in the lifeboat so women and children could go first?

The movie has the fascination of a train wreck or a highway smashup. It's natural to contemplate and compare when we see such a disaster, to measure our own luck against that of the victims. We watch with compassion but also with relief that we are not among the suffering.

We seek lessons and make conclusions about fate and honor from what we see.

People describe certain movies as spectacular, but forget that the word comes from the ancient Roman spectacles, which were ritual dramas, combats, races, games, and contests enacted in the arenas and amphitheaters throughout the empire. In those days the most thrilling (and expensive) form of entertainment was the "Naumachiae," the staging of great sea battles, in which the arena would be flooded and the spectators treated to the sight of ships ramming each other and capsizing, of sailors and doomed passengers drowning.

Titanic is a spectacle in this tradition. Lives were certainly sacrificed to the effort to put on this show, and the movie itself presents a feast of death, the deaths of fifteen hundred people being re-enacted for our entertainment and edification. There is still something compelling about the spectacle of death on such a massive scale, like the gladiatorial combats and ritual sacrifices of the ancient world. A vast amount of life force is being released all at once, and in an almost ghoulish way we feast on it. At the sight of people hurtling from a great height to smash against various machinery our eyes grow big, as if we are drinking in the sight of death. We study the sea of frozen faces for signs of how they died and how it will be for us.

Titanic plays on fears that have a high degree of identification for the audience — the universal fear of heights, fear of being trapped and imprisoned, fear of drowning in a bottomless sea, fear of fire and explosion, fear of loneliness and isolation.

The movie offers an imaginable horror. It could happen to anyone. Since it provides a complete spectrum of the society of its time, any viewer can find an identity there, as a well-off member of the ruling class, as a worker, as an immigrant, as a dreamer, as a lover. And we can appreciate the truth that certain inexorable forces — nature, death, physics, fate, accident — affect all of us, across the spectrum without exception. For a while the human story is reduced to one archetype — the Victim.

Titanic is a coherent design in part because it observes the unities of time, place, and theme. The confinement of the central story to the time from the Titanic's sailing to her death concentrates the dramatic energy. This concentration intensifies in the second half of the film which follows the surging events in real time, moment by moment. Confining the action to one place, the world of the ship alone at sea, makes it into a microcosm of life. It is an island of life in a dead sea, just as this island Earth is adrift in an ocean of space. And the ideas and arguments of *Titanic* are woven into a coherent design by concentrating on a single theme — that love liberates us and transcends death.

Cameron casts his arms wide in beckoning the audience to identify with his story. There's room enough on that ship for all of us. We can all identify with touches like the Turk who, while the boat sinks, frantically tries to read a corridor sign with a Turkish-English dictionary. We are all strangers somewhere. We're all in the same boat.

The movie is cast to appeal to a broad range of age groups. The young have the youthful love story to relate to, the old are invited to identify with Old Rose, who is still lively and active, and the baby-boomer generation is represented by the scientist-explorer and Rose's granddaughter.

The movie is not quite universal in that you don't see black or Asian faces. Certainly the slave experience is mentioned as a metaphor of Rose's emotional captivity, although here is where metaphor breaks down — Rose's pampered life is hardly the same as the Middle Passage in the bowels of the Amistad. However, the symbols of *Titanic* seem broad enough that almost everyone around the world can find something of themselves in it.

Where Cameron is most successful is as a visual and emotional poet. *Titanic* is a tapestry, a weaving of plots and threads. He finds poetry in braiding together the big story and the little story. He articulates connections very well, connections between the little story of Lovett and the big story of Old Rose's colorful life, between the little story of Jack and Rose and the big story of the Titanic, which is in turn part of the bigger story of the 20th century.

He organizes all this connection by finding a **SYMBOL** to concentrate and focus it, the narrow eye of a needle to pass all the threads through. "The Heart of the Ocean," connecting in its name the threads of romance and the sea, is a metaphor tying together all the plot lines, making them into a coherent design. (Cameron uses a wedding band to similar purpose in *The Abyss*.)

The jewel has a European pedigree, was once a crown jewel of the ill-fated Louis XVI, and makes a good symbol of the treasure of European experience and wisdom, art and beauty, but also class warfare and bloodshed.

Old Rose's action of tossing away the diamond at the end is a powerful poetic image that brings all the plot threads together for a real **DENOUEMENT**, an untying of all the knots and a smooth finish for all the plot threads. Lovett doesn't get the treasure but has a shot at love, Cal is thwarted and doesn't get Rose's heart or the diamond, Old Rose has kept her secret and now returns it to the sea. It was something private between her and Jack, hers to withhold all these years, hers to give back now.

The audience feels the material value of the stone — it's still a shock to see something worth so much money tossed away — but by that shock the whole experience of *Titanic* is concentrated into a symbol of fading memory. The emotions, the unconscious materials stirred up by the movie can recede to their proper place, though the memory will linger. As the stone spins away, we see how the filmmaker wants us to regard the Titanic. Let it remain where it is, a mystery and a monument to the human tragedy.

Old Rose, like every hero returning from a journey to the unconscious, had a choice to face. Do I scream and shout about my elixir, try to exploit it or evangelize about it? Or do I simply go about the business of my life, letting what I have learned radiate out from me and inevitably change, revive, rejuvenate those around me, and then the whole world? Do I choose an outer or an inner path to express my elixir? Obviously, Rose took the latter path, containing and internalizing the treasure from the special world, a poetic lesson taught by the Celtic tales, where heroes who come back and brag about their adventures in the Underworld find nothing but seaweed where they thought they'd collected fairy treasure. But the rare one, like Rose, keeps the fairies' secrets and lives a long and happy life.

James Cameron honors his Celtic ancestors with the folk music that plays below decks and whenever emotion surges. It makes a strong contrast with the courtly European dance and church music played in first class, and contributes to the poetic feeling. This is the epic telling of the Titanic by a Celtic bard, accompanied by pipes and harps as in days of yore.

This is supported by visual poetry and structural connectedness like the serpentine braiding of a Celtic graphic design. Simple polarities, bow and stern, above decks and below, first class and third, light and dark, give strong symmetrical axes for an almost mathematical composition. Cameron's design offers a number of poetic metaphors — the boat as a model of the world, the diamond as a symbol of value and love, the clock as a symbol of fleeting time, the angel statue on the main staircase as an image of Rose's innocence. In the broad strokes of a pop song, the movie provides metaphors against which the audience can compare themselves, a set of tools for interpreting their own lives.

Finally, **CATHARSIS** is the elixir this movie provides, the healthy purging of emotions that Aristotle identified and that audiences still want above anything. People rewarded this story for giving them the rare chance to feel something. We are well defended against emotion, and the movie hammers away with shocking effects and strong sentiments until even the most jaded and guarded must feel some reaction, some release of tension. Shots of panicking passengers fighting for lifeboat spaces, of Jack and Rose battling to survive, and of terrified victims falling to their horrid deaths bring the tension to an almost unbearable pitch, and yet there must be something rewarding and satisfying about this, for people stayed in their seats and many returned for multiple viewings. They couldn't get enough of the emotions released by this film. It gives the chance for a shudder of horror and a good cry, valuable sensations in any age.

The audience witnessing this spectacle goes through an ordeal along with the characters. Joseph Campbell used to say that the purpose of ritual is to wear you out, to grind down your defenses so that you fall open to the transcendent experience. Wearing you out seems to be part of *Titanic's* strategy, making you feel something of what the passengers felt by immersing you in the Titanic world for so long.

In this cynical, jaded time, it takes courage to be so nakedly emotional, for both the filmmaker and the audience. Movies like *Titanic, The English Patient, Braveheart, Dances with Wolves,* and *Glory* are taking a big risk in being sentimental on a grand scale. The darkness of the theatre offers the audience some protection — they can cry silently and few will witness their emotional vulnerability. But the filmmakers must expose emotions in public, under the full light of a cynical society, and deserve some respect for this act of courage.

IN THE WAKE OF *TITANIC*

What will be the long-term effect of *Titanic* on the movie industry? Its success shows that the big gamble sometimes pays off. Big production values generally do pay off in the long run — even *Cleopatra*, the film that nearly sank 20th Century Fox in the 1960s, eventually made back its production costs and is now a jewel in the company crown. *Titanic* turned a profit quickly, and its success will undoubtedly encourage others to spend big in hopes of hitting the same kind of jackpot.

In the short run, however, some executives responded by setting tight limits on their budgets. Although the Fox and Paramount executives had won the gamble, they didn't enjoy the suspenseful period before the film opened, and they didn't want to sweat like that again. Of course they reserve the option of making *Titanic*-sized exceptions now and then if all the key executives in the company are agreed that it's worth the risk on a specific project.

In all likelihood, other films will be made on the scale of *Titanic* and even greater quantum levels will be reached. There will always be an audience for spectacle, especially when it moves many of us emotionally. On the other hand, small-budget films at the opposite end of the spectrum can be more profitable in relation to their cost. The major Hollywood studios are learning from the example of independent filmmakers, developing lower-budget films for carefully targeted, specialized audiences, to keep profit flowing while they gamble on the big ones.

It's likely also that filmmakers will be influenced by Cameron's choice to build his script around a young love story, which is widely regarded as a significant factor in the film's success. It's becoming a rule of thumb in Hollywood that an expensive period piece has a better chance if it features a romantic melodrama, preferably with young lovers to make it inviting for the core of the moviegoing audience.

Some critics worry that the weaknesses of the script will become institutionalized because *Titanic* made so much money, and that future writers will be forced to "dumb down" their scripts to appeal to the mass audience needed to offset the big budgets. That would certainly be nothing new; studios and producers have always argued for broader appeal in expensive productions. But maybe there's another scenario, in which audiences thirst for more sophistication and reward filmmakers who try harder to make their stories both more intelligent and more emotionally universal.

SYNERGY

James Cameron has spoken of a certain synergy that operated with *Titanic,* a combination of elements that somehow adds up to more than the sum of its parts. Just as certain combinations of chemical elements sometimes produce unexpected powers and capacities, so the elements of acting, sets, costumes, music, effects, story, context, the needs of the audience, and the skills of the artists combined into a mysterious, organic whole which has an emotional and transformative power greater than the sum of the individual parts.

Part of that synergy is the use of the motifs and archetypes of the Hero's Journey, such as tests, crossings, ordeals, suspense, death, rebirth, rescues, escapes, chases, sacred marriages, etc. These devices give the audience reference points in the long story and contribute to making it a coherent design, directed to maximum cathartic effect. In the tradition of the Hero's Journey, *Titanic* explores death but makes the case for the full embrace of life.

Ultimately the success of the film is a mystery — a secret compact between the audience and the story. Like the men in the mini-sub we can shine some light on this mystery, but in the end we must simply withdraw and wonder.

THE LION KING AND OTHER PROBLEMS

In the summer of 1992 I was asked by the executives at Disney Feature Animation to review story materials on a project called "King of the Jungle." It came to be known as *The Lion King* and eventually turned into the most successful animated film Disney had done so far, but at the time it was just another opportunity to use the tools of the Hero's Journey on story problems.

As I drove to "animation country" in an anonymous industrial district of Glendale, California, I recalled what I knew of the project so far. This was an unusual undertaking, a departure from the Disney tradition of adapting popular children's literature or classics. For the first time it was an original story idea, cooked up by Jeffrey Katzenberg and his team of young animators on the company jet. They were on a flight back from New York where they had just previewed their latest work, *Beauty and the Beast.*

Katzenberg, a recent and enthusiastic convert to animation, engaged the animators in a discussion of the moment when they first felt the stirrings of adulthood. He related his own moment of feeling he had become a man, and they all realized it was an interesting thing to make a movie about. They began discussing formats and settings that could support such a story, and eventually hit on the idea of doing it entirely in the world of African animals. Disney had not done an exclusively animal-driven animated feature since *Bambi* in 1942, so it seemed fresh and also could play on the public's fondness for nature shows. It would avoid some of the problems of animating humans. To animate a human character you have to represent a particular ethnic group and choose certain hair and skin colors, which may prevent audience members with different features from fully identifying with the character. Much of this limitation is swept away with the use of animals, where human concerns about race and genetics are less relevant.

A father-and-son story was developed by borrowing inspiration from *Hamlet*. Katzenberg liked to bolster animation stories with plot elements from several sources so that a treatment for *The Odyssey* or *Huckleberry Finn* might be woven together with themes and structure from *It Happened One Night* or *48 Hours*. *The Lion King* had elements of *Bambi* but was made richer and more complex by weaving in some *Hamlet* plot elements. These included a jealous uncle who bumps off the hero's father and unjustly assumes the throne, and an unready young hero who gradually gathers his will and strikes back.

One of my first assignments, after having read the "King of the Jungle" treatment, was to read *Hamlet* carefully and draw out elements we could use in our script. I did a Hero's Journey analysis of the *Hamlet* plot to illustrate its turning points and movements, and then listed many of its memorable lines which the writers could use to playfully evoke the Shakespearean connection. The Disney animated films were conceived to work for all levels of the audience, with physical gags for the youngest kids, irreverent verbal wit and action for teenagers, and sophisticated inside jokes for the adults. Some of Shakespeare entered the script, especially through the character of Scar, the villain, voiced by the English actor Jeremy Irons. He delivered twisted Hamlet references in droll and ironic fashion, with a knowing wink to the grown-up audience.

Arriving at the Disney animation complex, I entered the special world of what would become *The Lion King*. Every animator's cubicle was plastered with photos and drawings of African life and several of the staff had made photo safari trips to Africa to gather inspiration. Storyboards were set up in the theatre and I sat down with the animators and designers to see the latest presentation by the directors, Rob Minkoff and Roger Ailers.

Here was an opportunity to test some of the Hero's Journey ideas on a major project. I was one of literally hundreds of people giving their opinions on the story, but for a moment I had a chance to influence the final product by my reactions and arguments. I took notes as the animators unfolded the story that was to become *The Lion King.*

To the rhythms of "The Circle of Life," the African animals gather to honor the birth of a young lion, Simba, whose father is Mufasa, ruler of the region around Pride Rock. One guest at the gathering is a strange old baboon, Rafiki, who is chased away by the King's advisor, a fussy bird named Zazu. Simba grows into a sassy young cub who sings "I Just Can't Wait to be King." Disobeying his father, he sneaks off to explore the spooky Elephant's Graveyard with his young lioness playmate Nala, and there they are terrorized by two comically scary Jackals, servants of Mufasa's jealous brother Scar. Mufasa rescues them but sternly rebukes Simba for disobeying him.

Simba is just beginning to learn the lessons of kingship from his father when Mufasa is cruelly killed in an antelope stampede, thanks to Scar's underhanded trickery. Scar makes Simba think he caused his own father's death, and Simba, fearing Scar will kill him, escapes across the desert like Hamlet leaving the court of Denmark after his uncle killed his father.

In Act Two, a guilt-wracked Simba comes to the SPECIAL WORLD of a lush jungle area where he meets two funny sidekicks, fast-talking meerkat Timon and tubby warthog Pumbaa, the Rosencrantz and Guildenstern of the piece. To get his mind off his guilt, they teach him the take-it-easy philosophy of "Hakuna Matata" and show him how they live on the jungle's never-ending banquet of bugs. Simba grows into a powerful teen-aged lion and one day has a violent encounter with another lion who was menacing Pumbaa. However it turns out to be Nala, who has grown into a beautiful and powerful young lioness. Their love blossoms in a romantic duet. But Nala is on a mission. She tells him how Scar has tyrannized Pride Rock, enslaved the animals, and tried to take her as his mate. She pleads with him to return and take his rightful place as king. Haunted by his guilt and unsure of his strength, Simba hesitates. Like many heroes, he isn't eager to leave the pleasures of the SPECIAL WORLD. But his father's spirit appears (like the ghost of Hamlet's father in Act One of "Hamlet") and urges him to face his destiny.

In Act Three, Simba shakes off his guilt, returns to Pride Rock, and confronts Scar. A fierce battle breaks out. Simba's "manhood" and right to be king are put to the ultimate test. Simba's ALLIES come to his aid, and Scar falls from power with a touch of poetic justice, echoing the way he allowed Mufasa to fall to his death. Simba takes his father's place and "The Circle of Life" continues.

As the presentation concluded, it wasn't difficult to see the Hero's Journey elements in *The Lion King*. Simba is a classic hero whose **ORDINARY WORLD** is that of privilege and the knowledge that he will one day be king. His first **CALL** is his father's demand that he grow up and face the responsibilities of kingship. Earning the right to rule the land as king is a metaphor for adulthood in many fables and fairy tales. His cockiness and disobedience constitute a **REFUSAL OF THE CALL**. He receives other **CALLS** — the temptation to explore the forbidden zone, a call of childhood romance from Nala, and most drastically, the death of his father that calls him to enter a new phase of life in which he has to run away to survive.

Simba has many **MENTORS** throughout the story. His father is his first great teacher, showing him the path of kingship and the Circle of Life, but he also learns diplomacy and statecraft from Zazu and something of the magical side of life from Rafiki. In Act Two his **MENTORS** are Timon and Pumbaa, teaching him their Hakuna Matata lifestyle. At the end of Act Two, Nala comes to teach him about love and responsibility, and his father's spirit is a supernatural **MENTOR** encouraging him to face his destiny. In the climax, Nala, Timon, and Pumbaa become his **ALLIES** against Scar. Nala is also a kind of **SHAPESHIFTER** from Simba's point of view, changing drastically from a playful cub into a sleek, powerful she-lion, presenting him a face of love but also demanding that he do something to save his domain.

The energy of the **SHADOW** is manifested in Scar and his underlings, the Jackals. Scar represents the dark side of kingship, totalitarian and compassionless. He can be read as a harsh model of adulthood, in which the early wounds dished out by life have become excuses for jealousy, cynicism, sarcasm, and a victim complex that turns into tyranny when the lifelong victim finally gets power. He is the dark possibilities in our hero, Simba. If Simba doesn't shake off his guilt and take responsibility, he could turn out the same way, a rogue male living bitterly on the fringes, waiting for a weakness to exploit. The Jackals are a lower form of life than the lions, living by scavenging rather than by noble hunting. They are bullies who readily follow the tyrant because they enjoy tormenting his subjects and lording it over them.

Rafiki, the crazy baboon witch doctor, was one of the most interesting characters in the script, combining elements of a **MENTOR** and a **TRICKSTER**. In early versions, I felt his function was not clear. He was played for comedy, as a loony fellow who came around to make magical noises but who commanded no respect. The king regarded him as a nuisance and Zazu, the king's bird advisor, shooed him away when he approached the baby Simba. He had little to do in the script after the first scene, and appeared mostly for comic relief, more **TRICKSTER** than **MENTOR**.

In the meeting that followed the storyboard presentation, I suggested taking him a little more seriously as a **MENTOR**. Perhaps Zazu was still suspicious and would try to run him off, but the more wise and compassionate Mufasa would let him approach the child. I had the impulse to accentuate the ritualistic aspects of the moment, referring to the rituals of baptism and christening, or the coronation ceremonies in which a new king or queen is anointed on the forehead with holy oil. Rafiki would bless the baby lion, perhaps with berry juice or some substance from the jungle. One of the animators said Rafiki already carried a stick with strange gourds tied to it, and came up with the idea of Rafiki cracking open one of the gourds in a mysterious gesture and marking the lion cub with a colorful liquid.

I thought, too, of the presentation rituals in various religions, in which the holy books, images, and artifacts are held up for veneration. I remembered that the Catholic churches I grew up with had stained-glass windows strategically placed to create stunning effects when beams of colored light fell on the altar. It occurred to me that when Rafiki held up the baby lion to show the assembled animals, a beam of sunlight from the clouds could strike the cub, giving the divine stamp of approval to the specialness of this child and to Mufasa's royal line. There was an almost audible crackle of energy in the room at that moment. The image came into several minds at once and I experienced the *frisson*, the shiver down

The Mentor marks the Hero as a chosen leader.

the back that always tells me when an idea expresses the truth of the story.

One hotly-argued issue at this stage was the matter of Mufasa's death. Some of the animators felt that the graphic depiction of the death of a parent (even an animal parent) was too intense. In the storyboards, Mufasa is trampled to death in an antelope stampede and the young Simba is shown approaching, nudging, and sniffing the corpse, looking for signs of life but finally understanding that his father is dead. Some felt this was too strong for young children.

Others replied that Disney has always shown the dark, tragic, and brutal side of life, and that though the company has often been criticized for it, such scenes are part of the Disney tradition, from the death of Bambi's mother to the death of Old Yeller, the family hound in a movie of the same name. Walt weathered a squall of controversy around Old Yeller's death, and later came to feel that killing off a beloved character was a breach of his contract with the audience. When the question came up on the animated adaptation of *The Jungle Book,* Walt insisted, "The bear lives!"

In the end, it was decided that *The Lion King* would confront death directly, and the scene was shot as originally boarded. The arguments that prevailed were that the movie was striving for the realism of a nature documentary, that the audience was used to seeing realistic treatments of animal violence, and that we were making a movie for the entire spectrum of the audience, not just for infants who might be traumatized by the scene. I agreed with this choice, feeling that it was true to the animal world we were trying to depict, but was somewhat disappointed when the movie then strayed from realism in Act Two, with carefree comedy replacing what would have been a desperate struggle to survive.

I was bothered by one structural element in Act One — the excursion to the scary Elephant's Graveyard. Instinctively I felt that though it was a good scene, it was in the wrong place. It was a dark visit to the country of death, and it felt more appropriate as the stage for an Act Two ordeal. Act One was already heavily weighted with the death of Simba's father, and I felt the Elephant's Graveyard sequence both made the first act too long and overwhelmed it with death energy. I suggested saving the Graveyard location as an **INMOST CAVE** for an Act Two central crisis of death and rebirth, and replacing the Act One scene with some other transgression by Simba that tests his father's patience, but with a lighter, less morbid tone. This bit of advice was not taken and who can say if it would have made any difference.

I do feel, however, that the movie is weakened by the turn it takes in Act Two. The almost photographic realism of the Act One animal scenes is replaced with a more old-fashioned Disney cartoon style, especially the comic rendering of Timon and Pumbaa. Simba is a growing carnivore and there is nothing realistic about him subsisting on a diet of bugs. I feel the movie missed a big chance to follow through on the promise of the first act with a realistic series of **TESTS**, leading to a life-threatening **ORDEAL** near the midpoint. Someone should have been teaching Simba real survival skills, how to stalk his prey, how to hunt, how to fight for what is his. I offered a range of possibilities. Timon and Pumbaa could teach him, he could meet another lion to teach him survival skills, or Rafiki could appear to carry on the teaching of Mufasa. I advocated creating a scene where Simba is truly tested, a real **ORDEAL** in which he discovers his mature power in a battle with a crocodile, a water buffalo, a leopard, or some other formidable foe.

The development of Simba from a scared little cub into a jaunty teen-aged lion is handled too quickly, in my opinion, with a few quick dissolves of him growing older as he crosses a log bridge. A montage of scenes of him learning to hunt, first comically and then with greater assurance, would have been more effective storytelling. Timon and

Pumbaa add much-needed comic relief to the story, but fail to dramatize the stages of Simba's development, the individual lessons that he has to learn. They teach him how to kick back and enjoy life, but they don't give him what he really needs. The lessons learned in Act Two (be laid back, relax, enjoy life, don't stress out, be scoundrelly and a little gross, recognize love when you find it) don't prepare Simba for the **ORDEAL** he must ultimately face.

Meanwhile I felt there was more work for Rafiki to do in this story. I wanted him to be more like Merlin, an experienced wise man who had perhaps been the king's counselor at one time, who pretends to be crazy so he can appear harmless to the usurper, and who is charged with looking after the young prince as he grows up in obscurity, training him for the moment when he's ready to take his rightful throne. I advocated weaving him into Act Two as a **MENTOR** who accompanies Simba into the **SPECIAL WORLD** and does a **MENTOR'S** function — giving the hero something needed to complete the journey and outface death. Rafiki was needed to teach real survival lessons that Timon and Pumbaa failed to impart. I envisioned Rafiki showing up soon after Simba arrived in the **SPECIAL WORLD**, and that he would guide Simba through a series of escalating tests that prepared him for his ultimate showdown with Scar. Of course Timon and Pumbaa would still be there as welcome comic relief.

The character of Rafiki grew significantly through the rest of the development process. The animators ended up making him a true **MENTOR**, a gruff Zen master who gives Simba tough advice and hard knocks, but also the gift of inspiration, guiding him to the vision of his father's spirit. He wasn't as active or present as I would have liked, although a couple of brief scenes were added in the first half of Act Two. Rafiki witnesses the devastation of Pride Rock by Scar and, thinking Simba is dead, sadly smears a drawing of him on a cave wall. Later, Rafiki's shamanic powers tell him that Simba is still alive and, after adding an adult lion's mane to the rock drawing, he sets out to summon the young hero to his destiny.

Rafiki really comes into action at the end of Act Two as he takes Simba on a vision quest that has elements of a **CALL** and **REFUSAL**, and an **ORDEAL** in which Simba has an encounter with death (the ghost of his father) and wins a **REWARD** in the form of enhanced self-confidence and determination.

The encounter with the father's ghost is another borrowing from "Hamlet," although in Shakespeare the young hero encounters his father's ghost in Act One. It made for a powerful scene in *The Lion King,* although one that small children sometimes find confusing. When I saw the film I heard children in the audience ask their parents questions like "Wasn't he dead before?" and "Is he back alive again?" The appearance of the ghostly father is dramatic and emotionally moving, but it plays mostly on the verbal and intellectual level. Simba gets encouraging advice, but the lessons are not dramatized as tests. The teaching of Rafiki is more satisfyingly concrete and physical — the baboon shaman raps him on the head to teach him a lesson about putting his mistakes in the past.

At the time of the storyboard presentation, the details of Simba's return to Pride Rock had not been worked out. We discussed many options. Simba could leave the **SPECIAL WORLD** with Nala, Timon, and Pumbaa, agreeing to face Scar together. Simba and Nala could go together, after having a parting of the ways with Timon and Pumbaa, who might show up later having had a change of heart. The final decision was to have Simba go off alone during the night, leaving Nala, Timon, and Pumbaa to wake up and find him gone the next morning. Rafiki tells them Simba has gone to take his rightful place, and they hurry to join him.

Act Three marches swiftly to the climactic battle, although it feels somewhat weighted down by Simba's lingering guilt over his belief that he caused his father's death. Scar dredges it up again, hoping to turn the lions against Simba by getting him to admit his responsibility for his father's death. I felt the writers played too heavily on this note, making the story seem turgid and overly melodramatic, and turning Simba into an angst-ridden modern protagonist, more appropriate to a novel than to an animated film about animals. However, it does provide a **RESURRECTION** moment in which Simba passes a final test by accepting responsibility for his father's death instead of running from it.

The Lion King can be faulted for giving center stage to the male characters and relatively little energy to the females. Nala is fairly well developed but Simba's mother is underutilized and passive. She could have been more significant in training Simba in Act One and resisting Scar in Act Two. This imbalance is addressed in Julie Taymore's stage version of *The Lion King,* which gives more weight and action to female characters, and which makes Rafiki a female shaman.

There was considerable suspense around the release of *The Lion King*. None of us in the production knew how the film would play for the audience. The Disney animated films had been climbing in popularity with *The Little Mermaid* and *Beauty and the Beast*, and many wondered if *The Lion King* would fail to top them. To everyone's relief, it performed even better, becoming the most successful animated film to date, and the most profitable motion picture in history. Why? Partly because people were delighted by the animation of the animals and the exuberant, African-flavored music, but also thanks to the universal power of the Hero's Journey patterns in its story. The challenge of growing up and claiming your rightful place in the world is a classic Hero's Journey motif that naturally struck something deep in many people. The familiar rhythms of the Journey were not the only principles guiding *The Lion King* — in fact, at times, they were outweighed by other concerns like low comedy and sheer fun — but I can say that this is one case where they were applied consciously to make the work more accessible to a broad audience and more dramatically satisfying.

HEROIC JOURNEYS IN *PULP FICTION*

with reference to the screenplay
by Quentin Tarantino, *from stories*
by Tarantino *and* Roger Roberts Avary

For the past few years, the film that young people were most interested in talking about was *Pulp Fiction*. They wanted to know how on earth the structure of the Hero's Journey could be found in that film. Its defiance of the conventions of structure, content, framing, dialogue, and editing intrigued them. They enjoyed its passionate intensity and sardonic humor. Some people were offended by its vulgarity and flashes of violence, but most admired the film for proving that unorthodox subject matter and uncompromising style can be both entertaining and highly successful. However, despite its innovative qualities, *Pulp Fiction* can be interpreted with the reliable old tools of the mythic Hero's Journey. Seen this way, the film in fact presents at least three distinct journeys for three different heroes; Vincent, Jules, and Butch.

THE POST-MODERN MIRROR

Young people may have responded to *Pulp Fiction* because it reflects the post-modern artistic sensibility they grew up with. Post-modernism is the result of a world blown apart, fragmented into millions of pieces by a century of war, social disruption, and rapid technological change. The doors of perception have been shattered by machines and the frantic pace of electronification. Young people now come to awareness in a high-intensity bombardment of random images and brief story segments torn from all the previous styles of art and literature. The bits may have an internal consistency and obey some rules of the old story world, but they assault the consciousness of the young in no apparent order.

Young people perceive the world as reflections in a shattered mirror, whether they channel-surf to cut up the stories themselves or have the stories chopped up for them by MTV-style editing. They are accustomed to juggling story lines, time periods, and genres at staggering speed. Because of the archival nature of television, constantly churning images and eras, post-modern kids live in a stew of styles. The young can costume themselves in fashions ranging from '60s hippie to heavy metal headbanger, from cowboy to surf dude, from gangsta to grunger to preppie. They master the idioms and attitudes of all these options and more. On their interactive, multi-media computers, they are comfortable with randomly sampling bits of entertainment and information without concern for the old world's notions of time and sequence.

Pulp Fiction reflects the postmodern condition in both style and content. Postmodernism is most apparent in its unusual structure, which disregards the conventional cinema's respect for linear time. The sequences appear to have been sliced up with a samurai sword and thrown in the air, although in fact the order of scenes has been carefully chosen to develop a coherent theme and produce a definite emotional effect. The signs of postmodernism are also present in the film's content. The nightclub where Vincent and Mia dance is a perfect postmodern microcosm. Contemporary characters find themselves in an environment peopled by icons of former eras — Marilyn Monroe, James Dean, Elvis Presley, Jayne Mansfield, Ed Sullivan, Buddy Holly, Dean Martin, and Jerry Lewis. Most of these people are dead, but they eerily live on through their immortal images. Vincent and Mia perform novelty dances from the 1960s to music that hasn't been heard in movies for thirty years. *Pulp Fiction* is part of the pop-culture jet stream, flowing easily out of the current collective unconscious, charged with images and sounds from previous eras.

RELATIVITY AND WORLD CULTURE

Pulp Fiction is postmodern also in its sense of cultural relativity. Although the film is set in America, it is shot through with a sense of worldwide culture and a global viewpoint. The characters are constantly comparing one culture to another, one set of standards to another. Jules and Vincent discuss the peculiar way American fast food is named and consumed in other countries, and marvel at drug laws in other lands. Butch, the American boxer, compares notes with a South American woman cabdriver on personal names in different cultures — her Spanish name is poetic and meaningful, while in America, he says, our names don't mean anything. This consciousness of other cultures may have contributed to the film's worldwide popularity.

The characters in *Pulp Fiction* are engaged in debate about value systems, reflecting the postmodern sense that no single code of ethics is adequate anymore. Jules and Vincent argue the moral significance of foot massage and the cosmic importance of a pattern of bullet holes. Where Vincent sees a meaningless accident requiring no response, Jules sees a divine miracle demanding a complete change of behavior. In the postmodern universe, everything is relative, and moral values are the most relative of all. Although the audience has seen Jules as a cold-blooded killer, he can seem like a hero compared with those around him. The story appears to say that Western society's narrow value judgments about morality are outdated. In the new world, each person must select his or her own moral code, argue it fiercely, and live or die by it.

THE ETERNAL TRIANGLE IN *PULP FICTION*

One of the pop-culture streams tapped by *Pulp Fiction* is the tradition of film noir and its sources in the hard-boiled fiction of 1930s and '40s pulp magazines. Like *Titanic,* the film employs the powerful archetype of the Eternal Triangle. The Mr. Big of *Pulp Fiction* is Marsellus Wallace, mysterious crime boss; the Young Woman is Mia, Marsellus' wife; and Vincent is the Young Man, who as usual finds himself attracted to the Young

Woman, testing their loyalty to Mr. Big. Vincent passes through this ordeal without betraying Mr. Big, like a Grail-questing knight refusing to yield to grievous bodily temptation. But, as we shall see, in another arena, another branch of his Hero's Journey, Vincent fails a more spiritual test.

"PROLOGUE"

AN ORDINARY WORLD

In *Pulp Fiction's* opening segment, titled "Prologue," two young people sit talking in a "normal Denny's, Spires-like coffee shop in Los Angeles." What could be more ordinary than this world? However, it turns out this young man (Pumpkin) and woman (Honey Bunny) are discussing the pros and cons of various forms of armed robbery. It's a different kind of **ORDINARY WORLD**, an underworld of low-level criminals, a world most of us would rather not think about. It's too horrifying to consider that all around us are legions of dull-witted crooks waiting for their chance to rob us or kill us, perhaps sitting right across from us in our favorite '50s coffee shop.

Pumpkin's first words are characteristic of a **REFUSAL** — "No, forget it, it's too risky. I'm through doin' that shit." Apparently Honey Bunny has just issued a **CALL** by proposing they rob another liquor store, their line of crime until now (their **ORDINARY WORLD**). While demeaning Asians and Jews who run liquor stores, the English-accented Pumpkin talks himself and Honey Bunny into robbing the restaurant, where there are no security guards or cameras, and where the employees have no need to play hero. He evokes a **MENTOR** of sorts, referring to the story of a bank robbery in which the robbers used terror and trickery to seize control. Working each other into a frenzy, Pumpkin and his daffy girlfriend **CROSS THE THRESHOLD**, waving their guns, bringing the possibility of instant death into play. Then with a swirl of retro surfer music, we are thrown into the main titles and the body of the movie.

This opening sequence exercises the cinematic rule of "Disorientation leads to suggestibility." You don't know if these punks are the heroes of the story or, as it turns out, mere bookends. The filmmaker's intention is to leave you a bit disoriented and guessing about their importance. You're also left guessing about the fate of these hotheads and the people in the restaurant.

VINCENT AND JULES

Now for the first time, we see our two protagonists, Vincent Vega and Jules Winnfield, driving in a big American car. They, too, are in their **ORDINARY WORLD** having a mundane conversation about the subtle differences in fast-food menus and customs in the countries of Europe. Vincent has spent some time in Europe where things are different — a Big Mac is called Le Big Mac in France, and the rules about drugs in Amsterdam are different. He has been to a **SPECIAL WORLD** and has the experienced air of a hero reliving a previous adventure.

Vincent and Jules stop at an apartment building and take guns from the trunk of their car. The feeling is that this is just another day at the office for them, a routine job in their Ordinary World.

As they approach the apartment to perform their mission, the conversation turns to Mia (a **SHAPESHIFTER**), wife of their criminal boss Marsellus Wallace (Mr. Big). This is the first note of a **CALL TO ADVENTURE** for Vincent, who has been put in the difficult position of being asked by Marsellus to escort his wife on a date while he's in Florida. The danger of this Call is made clear (a form of **REFUSAL**) in the complex philosophical discussion about foot massage. Jules points out that a Samoan gangster named Antwan Rockamora was thrown off his balcony into a greenhouse just for giving Mia a foot rub. Jules thinks the punishment was out of proportion to the crime, but Vincent understands very well that a foot massage could be a sensual experience and could get you killed. Nonetheless he has accepted the Call and will be Mia's escort. He promises not to get in trouble with Mia and denies that it will even be a real date, but Jules is skeptical.

After a long pause at the door, they **CROSS A THRESHOLD**, entering the apartment of Three Young Guys "obviously in over their heads." They have something which Marsellus Wallace wants, and apparently they have tried to stiff him in a deal for the contents of a mysterious briefcase. Jules, menacingly standing over the leader, Brett, intimidates him by eating his fast food and questioning him about what restaurant he bought it from. It's not a Wendy's or McDonald's hamburger, it's a Big Kahuna burger. Kahuna is Hawaiian magic, so it suggests big magic coming. Certainly there is magic in the briefcase, whose glowing contents hypnotize Vincent when he opens it to check on them. What's in the briefcase? It doesn't matter because it's just a MacGuffin, and in keeping with the Hitchcock tradition, Tarantino never bothers to say what it really is. It's enough that it's something of importance to the characters, something worth the risk of dying for. It's a Holy Grail or a Golden Fleece, a symbol of all the desires that draw heroes into quests.

Confronting the terrified young men, Vincent and Jules are **HERALDS** bringing a fatal **CALL**, acting at this moment as the allies of Death, the servants of the **SHADOW**. They are agents of Nemesis, the goddess of retribution, who brings punishment on those who offend the order of the gods. The god in this case is Marsellus Wallace. Brett and Roger have offended Mr. Big by trying to cheat him in the deal for the briefcase.

Jules makes his power manifest by shooting Roger without provocation. Before executing Brett, Jules performs a ritual, reciting the Bible passage from Ezekiel 25:17 which is his trademark:

"The path of the righteous man is beset on all sides by the iniquities of the selfish and the tyranny of evil men. Blessed is he who, in the name of charity and good will, shepherds the weak through the valley of darkness, for he is truly his brother's keeper and the finder of lost children. And I will strike down upon thee with great vengeance and furious anger those who attempt to poison and destroy my brother. And you will know my name is the Lord when I lay my vengeance upon you."

This, in effect, is a statement of the theme of the movie, a complex statement that can be interpreted many ways. On this reading, Jules seems to identify with only part of the message, the part about "great vengeance and furious anger," for he and Vincent empty their guns into Brett when the speech is done.

Then a miracle occurs. While Jules' friend Marvin, who has been there all along, mutters in a corner, a Fourth Young Man bursts out of the bathroom, firing away at Jules and Vincent with a heavy handgun. The miracle is that the bullets seem to have no effect. The Young Man is blown off his feet by return fire from Jules and Vincent.

This sequence establishes the Ordinary World for the protagonists of this thread of the story. They are enforcers for a powerful gangster, a notch or two above the level of the two kids in the coffee shop, but not far above. They are trying to work out an ethical system between them, and are concerned about the limits of honor and duty. The twin heroes are traveling down the same road so far, but their paths are about to split because of their differing reactions to the miracle that has just occurred.

"VINCENT VEGA AND MARSELLUS WALLACE'S WIFE"

A title card now establishes that the prologue or framing device is over and the first of the pulp fiction short stories is about to begin. But before bringing Vincent and Mia together, the storytellers introduce two new characters, Marsellus Wallace and Butch Coolidge, projecting ahead to Butch's story thread. Marsellus, described as sounding like "a cross between a gangster and a king," sits talking to Butch, a knocked-around prizefighter. In Butch's Hero's Journey, he is in his **ORDINARY WORLD**, getting a dark **CALL** to throw a fight.

Marsellus is both **HERALD** and **MENTOR**, godlike, seen only from behind, possessed of a **MENTOR'S** wisdom and a definite philosophy of life. Perhaps significantly, he has a Band-Aid on the back of his neck. Was he simply cut while shaving his perfectly bald head, or does the Band-Aid cover something more sinister — like the alien brain implants from the 1950s classic *Invaders From Mars*? Like the glowing contents of the briefcase, it poses a puzzle which the moviemakers decline to solve.

Marsellus counsels Butch to swallow his pride and give up his shot at being featherweight champion of the world in return for the sure thing. Butch doesn't hesitate before accepting his Call to throw the fight. He takes the money unhesitatingly. He seems to be accepting the Call, but in fact, as we later learn, he is planning to **REFUSE** this particular Call, intending instead to win the fight and collect big money by betting on himself.

Vincent and Jules enter with the briefcase, but are dressed quite differently than in the previous scene. They wear T-shirts and shorts, which look a little out of place in the bar. Later we'll see that several days have passed since we last saw Vincent and Jules, and that they have been through several major **ORDEALS**.

Vincent clashes with Butch, mocking him as a washed-up palooka, in a confrontation typical of the **TESTS, ALLIES, ENEMIES** phase. Vincent throws a challenge, which Butch refuses to rise to. The chance encounter with Butch is a **TEST** which shows a flaw in Vincent, a lack of respect for his elders. He should know that Butch is an experienced hero, a potential **MENTOR** who could teach him a few things, but instead he makes fun of him. Butch's **REFUSAL** to rise to this challenge shows that he is mature and careful. He sees that Vincent is a friend of Marsellus and wisely decides to let it ride — for now. However, a potential **ALLY** has been turned into an **ENEMY** by Vincent's arrogance.

The thread now follows Vincent, who has previously received the **CALL** to take Mia on a date. In keeping with the criminal underworld theme, Vincent approaches his own kind of **MENTOR** — his drug dealer, Lance — before **CROSSING THE THRESHOLD** to deal with Mia. The Mentor's lair is an old house in Echo Park. This Mentor, like a shaman equipping a hunter with magic potions and healing herbs, presents an array of heroin options for Vincent's selection. Vincent pays top dollar for the strongest stuff.

Vincent shoots up and cruises over in a blissful daze to pick up Mia. Here is another of Vincent's flaws — he is weakened by his drug addiction. Vincent **CROSSES A THRESHOLD** as he enters Marsellus' house. He passes by strange metal sculptures, like **THRESHOLD GUARDIANS** from some primeval culture. There's a sense that the gods are watching.

Inside, Mia operates in the godlike realm of Mr. Big, playing with Marsellus' toys. Like Mr. Big in many noir movies, she watches from a hidden upper room, manipulating Vincent by remote control with her disembodied voice. The rules are different in this **SPECIAL WORLD**. In Vincent's **ORDINARY WORLD**, he and his gun are the absolute rulers. Here, a barefoot woman holds the power of life and death. She calls the tune and selects the theme music for the evening.

Moving further into the **SPECIAL WORLD**, Vincent takes Mia to the strange '50s cafe for a **TESTS, ALLIES, ENEMIES** scene. Jackrabbit Slim's is a model of the postmodern world, in which images of the recent past are continually chopped up, recycled, and harnessed to new tasks. Legendary faces like Marilyn Monroe, Elvis, and Buddy Holly are reduced to waiting tables and delivering hamburgers.

In a typical Hero's Journey Stage Six bar scene, Mia and Vincent **TEST** each other out. Menu choices assume great importance as clues to character. Phallic cigarettes are rolled and ignited. They get the measure of one another through cool but probing dialogue. Vincent boldly tests Mia by asking about her relationship with the fellow who was thrown out the window. He passes her **TESTS** by asking diplomatically, without assuming she was in the wrong. They become **ALLIES**.

They are linked in another way, revealed when Mia gets up to "powder her nose," in fact, to snort cocaine. Like Vincent she is weakened by her addiction and it will lead to her **ORDEAL**.

The cue to enter the dance contest is an **APPROACH**, moving them a step closer to the life-and-death matter of sex. From the way they groove together on the dance floor, it's clear they would have fantastic sex. Their dance moves and hand gestures reflect the **SHAPESHIFTER** archetype, as they try out various masks and identities in the **APPROACH** to love.

Vincent and Mia return to her house to face a **SUPREME ORDEAL.** Mia is looking very seductive, and Vincent retires to the bathroom to steel himself. He talks to his image in the mirror, convincing himself not to have sex with Mia. In this area, at least, he passes an important **TEST**, remaining loyal to his boss despite strong temptation. His motivation may not be so noble — he knows Marsellus will probably find out and kill him if he does fool around with Mia — but he passes the **TEST** nonetheless.

Meanwhile Mia finds Vincent's heroin in his coat, and mistaking it for cocaine, snorts it greedily and passes out. Vincent finds her with blood running from her nose and panics. Here Vincent is not just facing Mia's death, but also his own — for he will surely be killed if Mia dies. It was his heroin, his weakness, that caused the problem, along with Mia's lust for sensation.

Vincent races to his Mentor's house (**THE ROAD BACK**) where a frantic search for a medical book, a marker pen, and a huge adrenaline needle commences. Vincent digs deep for the hero's courage to plunge the needle into Mia's heart. In a weird reversal of the classic scene from vampire movies, driving a stake into her heart is actually the way to bring her abruptly back to life, a **RESURRECTION.** Vincent, like Sir Lancelot, has the godlike power to bring someone back from the land of the dead.

Vincent returns Mia to her house (**RETURN WITH THE ELIXIR**) where, pale and wan, she gives him a kind of **ELIXIR**, a feeble joke from the TV pilot she appeared in. They part with another **ELIXIR**, a sense of friendship and mutual respect arising from sharing an **ORDEAL** together. They promise each other they won't tell Marsellus what happened. You get the feeling that if anything ever happened to Marsellus Wallace, these two would probably get together.

BUTCH'S STORY

The story now switches to another thread, the Hero's Journey of Butch, the boxer. It takes us back to Butch's early **ORDINARY WORLD**, a scene from his childhood in suburbia, where he watches a Speed Racer cartoon on TV in 1972.

A CALL TO ADVENTURE is issued by a **HERALD** or **MENTOR**, Captain Koons, the Air Force officer who brings the gold watch that belonged to his father and forefathers. In a long monologue Koons describes the watch's tradition of being carried by American soldiers in Butch's family. He relates the ORDEAL that he and Butch's father endured in the Vietnamese prison camp. The watch becomes an emblem of manly tradition that connects it to symbols like the magic swords that heroes inherited from their fathers. However, we're brought crashing back to reality with the earthy detail of where Butch's father hid the watch for five years, and Captain Koons used a similar hiding place for two years after Butch's father died. Fulfilling the **DONOR** function of a **MENTOR**, the officer gives the watch to Butch.

We're then thrown back to the present where we see Butch getting another **CALL** — this time his manager calling him into the ring for the fight he's supposed to throw.

"THE GOLD WATCH"

A title card now makes it clear we are taking up a major thread of another Hero's Journey. We find out, through the radio that plays in the taxicab outside, that instead of throwing the fight as agreed with Marsellus, Butch has won the fight and killed the other boxer. He has refused Marsellus' **CALL**, but has answered other calls — the **CALL** of his own spirit to fight well, and the **CALL** of temptation to cheat Marsellus and collect a lot of money.

Butch **CROSSES A THRESHOLD** as he leaps from a window into a dumpster. He boards the cab and begins stripping off the attributes of a prizefighter, leaving this part of his life behind. In a **TESTS, ALLIES, ENEMIES** scene, his attitude is probed through his conversation with Esmerelda Villalobos, the woman cabdriver from Colombia. She explains her name has a beautiful, poetic meaning ("Esmerelda of the Wolves"), and Butch says his name, like most American names, doesn't mean anything. Again the note of cultural relativity is sounded. She is morbidly curious about what it feels like to kill a man. Instead of horrifying her, it seems to turn her on. Everything is relative. Butch himself offers a rationalization for having killed the other boxer. If he was a better fighter, he'd be alive. He makes an **ALLY** of her and wins her promise to tell the police she never saw him.

By his actions he has made **ENEMIES** of Marsellus Wallace and his crew. We see Marsellus sending his minions to hunt down Butch, all the way to Indo-China if necessary.

In an **APPROACH** phase, Butch makes a phone call to check on his winnings. He goes to his French girlfriend, Fabienne, at a motel and they make plans to skip the country once he's collected his money. Their flirtatious talk, characteristic of intimate **APPROACH** scenes, seems to be more of the seemingly banal chatter that marks the early scenes between Vincent and Jules. It has the same sense of cultural relativity and differing value systems. Here the distinctions are along gender lines, as the girlfriend tries to make Butch understand her precise attitude about potbellies on women. They make love and the night ends with a false sense that all will be well.

A new and immediate **CALL TO ADVENTURE** is sounded the next morning as Butch discovers she has failed to retrieve his father's watch from his apartment. Without consulting any Mentors, he overcomes his fear of being caught by Marsellus and goes to get the watch. Driving to his apartment, he is **CROSSING THE THRESHOLD** into a **SPECIAL WORLD** of increased danger.

After a careful **APPROACH** to his apartment, Butch takes possession of the watch, **SEIZING THE SWORD**. However, he encounters a **THRESHOLD GUARDIAN** sent by Marsellus to kill him. It's Vincent, who has been reading a book in the bathroom (the comic spy thriller *Modesty Blaise* by Peter O'Donnell). Foolishly, in a fatal, tragic mistake, Vincent has underestimated his opponent, and has left his gun sitting on the kitchen counter. Butch hears the toilet flush, grabs the gun, and kills Vincent. It's a near-death **ORDEAL** for Butch, but it's the tragic **CLIMAX** for Vincent, who has been brought down by one of his flaws — his disrespect for his elders. He is punished with true poetic justice, and in a humiliating way, being caught gunless while exiting the toilet. We don't know it yet, but Vincent also appears to be paying the price for having denied a miracle — the miracle of escaping the bullets of the Fourth Young Man in the earlier scene. His death at this point seems like divine punishment for having refused to acknowledge divine intervention.

With the **REWARD** of the watch in his pocket, Butch hits **THE ROAD BACK**, trying to get to his girlfriend. On the way, he literally runs into his **SHADOW**, Marsellus, ramming him with the car when he sees Marsellus crossing the street. However, Butch is also injured and dazed when his car collides with another car, a quick **REVERSAL**. Marsellus, appearing dead to a bystander, comes back to life (**RESURRECTION**) and staggers towards Butch with a gun.

Butch wobbles into the "Mason-Dixon Gunshop" and Marsellus follows him (a **CHASE** typical of **THE ROAD BACK**). Butch punches Marsellus and is about to kill him when he's stopped by the gunshop owner, Maynard, who is armed with a shotgun.

Butch and Marsellus don't realize they've stumbled into an **INMOST CAVE** more sinister than anything they have encountered, an underworld beneath the underworld in which they live. Maynard knocks out Butch and summons his brother Zed, like him, a **SHADOW** projection of the worst aspects of white American male culture. Marsellus and Butch wake up, chained and gagged with S&M gear, in the still deeper cave of the dungeon beneath the store.

Zed brings up a leather-clad creature, The Gimp, from a still deeper pit beneath the floor. Whether he is their retarded brother or a poor victim driven mad by their torture, The Gimp suggests the horrors that await Marsellus and Butch. Marsellus is chosen to be the first victim of the evil brothers' sadistic attention, and is taken into a room once occupied by another victim, Russell. There is a sense in this adventure that others have gone before and have not won their round with death.

Butch hears the sounds of the two brothers raping Marsellus, a terrible **ORDEAL** that brings death to Marsellus' manhood. (In these scenes, again, is a sense of relativity. No matter how harshly we may have judged Marsellus and Butch for their behavior, there are still worse villains and lower circles of hell. Marsellus and Butch look like villains or **SHADOWS** from society's point of view, but compared to the denizens of the gunshop they are **HEROES**.)

Butch sees an opportunity and escapes, punching out The Gimp, who falls limp and hangs himself on his leash. Butch escapes upstairs and actually has his hand on the door, ready to leave, but has a crisis of conscience. He decides to make a true hero's **SACRIFICE**, risking his life by returning to rescue Marsellus, even though he knows Marsellus wants to kill him for not throwing the fight. He selects a samurai sword from the many weapons at hand (literally **SEIZING THE SWORD**), and descends once again into the **INMOST CAVE** for his ultimate **ORDEAL.**

Butch kills Maynard, and Marsellus grabs a shotgun, shooting Zed in the groin. Marsellus is free, having rebounded from almost certain death, a **RESURRECTION.** Butch's heroic action balances the moral books for Butch's killing of the other boxer. Marsellus is **TRANSFORMED** by the experience, and grants a **BOON** to Butch, sparing his life and allowing him to escape so long as he promises not to tell anyone what happened, and to stay away from Los Angeles. Then he calls upon a **MENTOR**, Mr. Wolf, for help in cleaning up the situation.

Butch **SEIZES A SWORD**, so to speak, taking the motorcycle that belonged to one of the monstrous bikers. On this steed the hero takes **THE ROAD BACK** to collect his fair lady. Although he may not be able to collect the **ELIXIR** of the gambling money, the hero has been rewarded with a greater **ELIXIR** of life. He rides off with Fabienne on the motorcycle, which bears the significant name of "Grace," an **ELIXIR** granted to those who make the right moral choices on the Hero's Journey.

"THE BONNIE SITUATION"

Now the thread of Vincent and Jules is picked up again at the moment when Jules recites his Bible passage in the apartment of the Young Men, and we hear the scripture for a second time. The Young Man bursts out shooting at them, clearly a death-dealing **ORDEAL.** By rights they should be dead, but somehow they survive and the bullets pock the wall all around them.

The two young men react quite differently to their brush with death. Vincent dismisses it as a lucky break or coincidence, but Jules has an **APOTHEOSIS.** He is deeply moved and recognizes it as a miracle, an act of God, a sign which requires a change in attitude. Their reaction is a kind of **TEST**, one which Vincent appears to fail and Jules appears to pass with flying colors. Jules wins a **REWARD** from the experience, a greater spiritual awareness, but Vincent gets nothing out of it.

(The fact that we have already seen Butch kill Vincent makes this scene a kind of **RESURRECTION** for Vincent; we have seen him die, but now we see him alive again. This is another manifestation of the fractured postmodern time sense, which says the notion of linear time is an arbitrary convention.)

On the **ROAD BACK** from this death-and-rebirth moment, Vincent makes a deadly error, again due to his flaw of lack of respect. He has insufficient respect for the tools of death, and waving the gun around in the car, accidentally puts a bullet through the head of their accomplice Marvin in the backseat.

Jules recognizes that this must be cleaned up and drives to the house of his friend and **ALLY**, Jimmy Dimmick, played by Quentin Tarantino. He appears to be a middle-class fellow whose connection to the criminal world is never specified. He is worried about the moral wrath of his wife, Bonnie, who will soon be returning home from the night shift. (Here the filmmaker is creating contrast between the criminal underworld and the bourgeois world in which most of us live. The joke is that they are more afraid of Bonnie's irritation than of the danger of the law coming down on them for manslaughter.)

Jules and Vincent try to clean themselves up, but are only partially successful. Jules scolds Vincent for getting blood all over the guest towels, another sign that Vincent is careless and disrespectful, traits which we know will get him killed. He is in danger of turning another **ALLY**, Jimmy, into an **ENEMY**.

Jules calls Marsellus for help, and he in turn summons a **MENTOR** and **ALLY** in the form of Winston Wolf, played by Harvey Keitel. His name links him with Esmerelda Villalobos, Esmerelda of the Wolves, an Ally in another thread of the story. They fulfill some of the same functions performed by Animal Helpers in many folktales.

Wolf appears to be a specialist in problem solving, experienced at getting rid of inconvenient evidence. He arrives at supernatural speed and takes charge of the problem, issuing orders authoritatively. However, once again Vincent is disrespectful of his elders, and balks at being ordered around. Wolf handles it with humor but also unquestionable authority, making it clear that Vincent should not make an **ENEMY** of his **ALLY**.

Wolf supervises as Vincent and Jules cleanse the bloody car. The whole sequence is a protracted **RESURRECTION** for the young men, in which they and their vehicle are purified before the **RETURN**. Meanwhile Jimmy has to make a **SACRIFICE**, surrendering sheets and towels for the cleanup, but Wolf promptly compensates him with a **REWARD** of money for new furniture.

Then, acting precisely like a shaman putting warriors through a cleansing ordeal of **RESURRECTION**, Wolf orders Vincent and Jules to strip off their bloody clothes. He makes Jimmy hose them down with icy water as they soap themselves clean of the blood. Next Jimmy issues them new clothing, significantly, boyish shorts and T-shirts. They look like schoolboys or college kids instead of tough gangsters. Like returning hunters, they have been put through a death-and-rebirth ritual that makes them innocent children again. Now they can re-enter the **ORDINARY WORLD** cleansed of the death they have faced and dealt with. Throughout, they have hung onto the mysterious briefcase, an **ELIXIR** which they brought back from the **ORDEAL** in the yuppie apartment.

Wolf escorts them to an auto graveyard where the body and the car will be disposed of. He says farewell and goes off with his young girlfriend Raquel, daughter of the junkyard owner, showing how an experienced Mentor enjoys his **ELIXIR**, won through "correct" behavior by the rules of this movie's universe. He compliments Jules for showing respect to his elders, a sign of character.

"EPILOGUE"

Finally, the narrative returns to the original scene in the diner for the Epilogue, the last word on the subject. While Pumpkin and Honey Bunny plan their stickup, Jules and Vincent review what has happened. Vincent, typically, tries to dismiss it, but Jules insists they have seen a miracle today. He resolves to live his life differently from now on, "walking the Earth" like Cain in the TV series "Kung Fu." This seems to mean wandering about doing good and seeking peace rather than living a criminal life. He has truly been through a moral **RESURRECTION** and transformation. Vincent doesn't value any of this and gets up to go to the bathroom, the same action that ultimately gets him killed.

As a final **TEST** of Jules' resolve, Pumpkin and Honey Bunny start screaming and waving their guns around. Pumpkin tries to seize the **ELIXIR** of the mystery briefcase, opening it and falling under its spell, but Jules gets the drop on him. (Pumpkin's attempt echoes the fairy-tale motif of the False Claimant, who appears just as the hero is ready to claim his reward.)

Jules talks calmly but intensely to Pumpkin and Honey Bunny. He makes a deal with Pumpkin, giving him money from his wallet in return for leaving the briefcase alone. It's a final moment in which we are balanced between life and death. Jules recites his Bible passage for a third time, although on this reading it has a totally different meaning for him. Where before he identified with the wrathful face of God, dealing death to the unrighteous, now he identifies with the hand of mercy and justice, trying to be the blessed one "who, in the name of charity and good will, shepherds the weak through the valley of darkness." He has moved his center from thoughtless killing to a new level of heroic action, from which he can use his warrior skills for good. He is able to defuse the potentially deadly situation and walks away with the **ELIXIR** in hand. A **SHOWDOWN** which would normally leave at least one person dead has been handled with finesse and grace worthy of Mr. Wolf. Jules has grown from being a **SHADOW**, a ruthless killer, to being a true **HERO**. Pumpkin and Honey Bunny walk away with the **ELIXIR** of their lives, which they won by making the right decision and keeping cool under Jules' orders. If they are smart, they will move up the ladder of souls and prepare for adventures on the level of Jules and Vincent.

Vincent and Jules walk away with the **ELIXIR**-filled briefcase. The tale is "over," although we know that in linear time, there is still much of the story ahead. Vincent and Jules will now deliver the briefcase to Marsellus at the bar, Vincent will show disrespect for Butch and will undergo his **ORDEAL** with Mia, Butch will not throw the fight and will kill Vincent before surviving his **ORDEAL** with Marsellus. The real ending, if these events are rearranged in linear sequence, is the moment when Butch and his girlfriend ride off on the motorcycle.

The theme of *Pulp Fiction* seems to be the testing of men by ordeals. Different characters react differently to their respective confrontations with Death. Despite the relativistic tone of the film, the storytellers do seem to have a moral point of view. They sit in God's chair, dealing out the punishment of death for Vincent, who offends against the moral code of the movie, and rewarding Jules and Butch with life for making the right choices in the scheme of the film. In this the filmmakers, despite the appearance of unconventionality, are quite conventional, following a moral code as strict as that in a John Ford or Alfred Hitchcock movie.

The most interesting case is that of Vincent, who faces ordeals in two completely different arenas, with different results. In the arena of love and loyalty, on his date with Mia, he behaves with chivalry and courage, like a knight of old, and for this he is rewarded by brief survival. But in the arena of respect for Higher Powers and for his more experienced elders, he fails, and is swiftly punished. Once again a relativistic note is sounded, suggesting that mastery over one area of life doesn't necessarily mean mastery of all aspects.

The interwoven Hero's Journeys of Vincent, Jules, and Butch present a full spectrum of heroic possibilities, encompassing the dramatic, the tragic, the comic, and the transcendent. Like Joseph Campbell's definition of myth, *Pulp Fiction* is a "shapeshifting yet marvelously constant story... with a challengingly persistent suggestion of more remaining to be experienced than will ever be known or told."

THE FULL MONTY

At the opposite end of the spectrum from *Titanic* is a little film that Fox produced at the same time through its Searchlight division. As a work in the iconoclastic independent film spirit, it makes a good contrast with the old-time Hollywood epic scale of *Titanic*, and yet both films exhibit the signposts of the Hero's Journey. *The Full Monty* expresses it on a more intimate scale but the elements loom large in it nonetheless.

The Full Monty tells the comic adventures of a group of men whose **ORDINARY WORLD** is the ailing steel town of Sheffield. The men are different from one another, gay and straight, fat and thin, divided by social class and race, and yet they are united by the new conditions of their society. In the old days, sketched by a hilariously upbeat promotional film from the 1960s, Sheffield was a booming industrial center where the men were in charge, earning the wages and heading the households. Now the world has been stood on its head. The mills have been closed, the men are out of work, and it's a service economy in which the women are more likely to be the breadwinners.

Gaz is the principal protagonist, a boyish man whose immaturity isolates him from his ex-wife and son. His **OUTER PROBLEM** is to scrape together some money, his **INNER** challenge is to earn his son's respect and to learn to respect himself. He gets his **CALL TO ADVENTURE** when he sees his ex-wife and her girlfriends exercising their freedom by taking in a male strip show. He conceives the idea of raising money by staging a strip show of his own, recruiting a chorus line from the rejected men of Sheffield.

There are many **REFUSALS** from his skeptical friends and associates, who are not eager to expose themselves. These men, like all men, have many secrets to protect and conceal. Gaz doesn't want the other men to know he's done jail time. His overweight friend Dave hides his lack of sex drive, which leads his wife to think he's having an affair. Gerald, Gaz's former boss at the steel mill, has kept secret from his wife the fact that he lost his job months ago. Lomper, the mill security officer, has hidden the fact that he's gay, perhaps even concealing it from himself. Guy is a fellow who can't dance, but makes up for it by revealing a secret — he has the fullest monty of them all. His willing self-exposure sets an example for the men who will all be slowly unveiling themselves throughout the movie. Horse is the best dancer of the lot and becomes a kind of **MENTOR** to the rest, along with Gerald, who has been taking ballroom dancing lessons with his wife. But even Horse has a secret — the reason for his name — and this one is never revealed.

Gaz's steadfast **MENTOR** in his quest is his son Nathan, a Wise Young Man who voices an emotional wish early in the story, "Why can't we do normal things once in a while?" He keeps Gaz honest and on the track, and at the end gives him the courage to face the ultimate exposure, the final test of his commitment to something.

Gaz **CROSSES THE FIRST THRESHOLD** when he holds an audition for his male strip show. He turns an **ENEMY** into an **ALLY**, recruiting his old supervisor who initially wanted nothing to do with the project. The men slowly reveal themselves and experiment with the **SPECIAL WORLD** of trusting each other and allowing themselves to be honest and vulnerable.

Their **APPROACH** is a phase of preparation and rehearsal, in which they learn more about themselves. An encounter with Death marks the central **ORDEAL**, when Dave has severe doubts and wants to quit the enterprise, and Lomper's mother dies. In addition the men are arrested for indecent exposure when their dress rehearsal is captured on a plant security camera. It looks like they're finished. But this is quickly followed by **REWARD**, a phase in which Gaz gets reassurance that word of his show is spreading; the arrest has been good for their publicity. Lomper and Guy also reap a reward, discovering that they care for each other as they run from the police.

In another thread of the plot, Dave faces an **ORDEAL** of honesty, revealing to his wife the true reason for his lack of sexual interest. His **REWARD** is the knowledge that she loves him anyway, which gives him courage to rejoin the strip show. On **THE ROAD BACK**, he joins the men in the final preparations for the big act.

The hall fills with rowdy women. The **RESURRECTION** is enacted when Gaz gets cold feet at the thought of exposing himself, not only to women, but to a few men who have slipped into the hall. His involvement with the group seems to die for a few moments as the other men go on stage without him. But his son encourages him to go on and he is **REBORN** with a late entry into the strip act, passing the final test of commitment and honesty. The men reveal themselves totally, **RETURNING WITH THE ELIXIR** of self-knowledge, cooperation, understanding, and self-respect. They have found a new way to be men in the new society.

The Full Monty connected with audiences because of its infectious good humor and its upbeat music and dance, which combined effectively with the realistic settings and believable, down-to-earth characters. It is a "feel-good" movie that communicates a sense that the filmmakers like people and believe that though they are complex and troubled, they are basically good and are capable of change. The audience has the identification and satisfaction of cheering for the underdogs. The film has a visual inventiveness that employs many poetic touches like the image of Dave and Gaz stranded in a canal on a sinking abandoned car as Gaz's practical son Nathan scampers away on the bank. Meanwhile the multilayered plot, telling little stories about six men and a boy, is organized into a coherent dramatic experience by the use of Hero's Journey motifs and devices. By their actions within this framework, these ordinary men are transformed into heroes for the edification and enjoyment of the audience. And because of the universal recognition of the Hero's Journey pattern, audiences around the world could find something of themselves in this story.

STAR WARS

Before closing the book on the permutations of the Hero's Journey in popular films, I have to acknowledge the lasting impact of the *Star Wars* series. The first *Star Wars* film, now re-titled *Star Wars Episode IV: A New Hope*, was released in 1977 as I was just beginning to digest the ideas of Joseph Campbell, and was a stunning confirmation of the power of the mythic patterns I had found there. Here was a fully developed expression of his concept of the Hero's Journey, exactly as Campbell described. It helped me work out the theory and test my own ideas, and it quickly became one of those quantum movie events, breaking records and setting a higher standard for what a movie could be.

As I began to teach "mythic structure," the film provided a convenient, widely seen example to demonstrate the movements and principles of the Hero's Journey, in which the function of the parts were simple, clear, and vivid. It entered the language of pop culture, providing useful metaphors, symbols, and phrases that expressed how we all felt about good and evil, technology and faith. It spawned a billion-dollar industry of sequels, prequels, ancillaries, franchises, and a whole universe of toys, games, and collectibles. Entire generations have grown up under its influence, and it has inspired countless artists to think big and pursue their dreams of creativity. It filled the same function for millions that the old myths did, giving standards for comparison, providing metaphors and meaning, inspiring people to stretch beyond their earthly bounds.

If the *Star Wars* movie of 1977 had been a one-shot cinema event, its cultural impact would still have been considerable, but its influence was tripled by the continuation of the series with *Episode V: The Empire Strikes Back* (1980) and *Episode VI: Return of the Jedi* (1983). Series creator George Lucas had always planned a vast canvas on the scale of Wagner's *Ring* cycle, an epic tale that might take a dozen movies to tell in full. For the following sixteen years fans wondered if Lucas would ever fulfill the promise of more films, extending the saga into the past and possibly into the future. In what is known as "the Expanded Universe," various side-plots and back-stories were developed in comic books, novels, cartoon series, and TV specials, but it was only in 1999 that Lucas returned to the film series, eventually producing three "prequel" films that told the story of the generation before Luke Skywalker and Princess Leia, and revealed the events and character flaws that led to the development of Darth Vader, the series' supreme embodiment of evil.

The master plan for organizing this huge canvas of six feature films seems to reflect a polarized view of the universe and of the hero myth itself, allowing full exploration of the dark and light possibilities of the heroic model. The films released in the 1970s and '80s represent the positively charged, optimistic view of heroism, in which the young hero Luke Skywalker is severely tempted by power and rage but ends up triumphant and morally balanced, an example of what Campbell calls "the Master of Two Worlds." The dramatic intention is quite different in the three prequel films (*The Phantom Menace*/1999, *Attack of the Clones*/2002, *Revenge of the Sith*/2005). Though sprinkled with moments of lightness and humor, the overall tone is dark and tragic, showing the destruction of a human spirit by fatal flaws of anger, pride, and ambition.

A mythic theme that seems to run through all the films is a fascination with the emotional territory between fathers and sons. The impact of positive male role models, surrogate fathers and mentors like Obi Wan Kenobi, Yoda, Qui-Gon Jinn, Luke's Uncle Owen, and Mace Windu is emphasized, but the series is as much interested in the effect of absent or distant fathers and negative role models on a young man's developing personality.

The first three films released portray Luke Skywalker's quest to discover the identity of his father and his struggle with the dark tendencies in his own nature. *Episode IV*, the film released in 1977, more or less follows an Arthurian model, with the young nobleman raised in humble surroundings, unaware of his true nature, and watched over by a Merlin-like figure (Obi-Wan) who gives him a powerful weapon that belonged to his father, a light saber similar to Arthur's sword Excalibur.

In the next two films, Luke will discover more of his parentage and learn that Princess Leia is his twin sister. His relationships with surrogate fathers will continue to develop, losing Obi-Wan as a living influence (though his ghostly presence continues to guide Luke) and gaining a new father figure in Yoda. As he learns to master the Force he is tempted by the dark side, represented by the villainous Darth Vader, who eventually reveals himself as Luke's true father. Like many a hero before him, Luke must confront the fact that his father was not perfect, and that he has some of the same dangerous tendencies that made his father a tyrant and a monster. In this section the plot somewhat resembles the Wagnerian scenario of Siegfried, the young hero who must re-forge a broken sword that represents the failure of the previous generation.

Luke passes a major Resurrection test in *Episode VI: Return of the Jedi,* when he has the opportunity and the motivation to kill his father, for Lord Vader is threatening to turn Luke's sister Princess Leia to the dark side of the Force. Luke spares his father's life, signifying his choice to uphold the positive side of the Force. The evil Emperor who has manipulated Darth Vader and is a kind of evil father figure for him now begins to destroy Luke with powerful lightning bolts. Moved by the sight of his son's impending death, Vader reverses polarity and goes over to the light side of the Force, throwing the Emperor to his death. Vader, dying himself from the struggle with the Emperor, asks Luke to remove his helmet, revealing the fragile human beneath the mask of technology. He seeks forgiveness and his son grants it. Luke, though wounded, dismembered, and sorely tempted by his own dark potential, ends up as a positively charged hero, able to use his powers responsibly for the good of all. He is even able to forgive the fact that his own father chopped off his arm and tried to kill him. One of the final images of *Episode VI,* theoretically the absolute end of the series, is that of the ghost of Darth Vader, redeemed and forgiven, standing benevolent watch over his son alongside the ghosts of Obi-Wan and Yoda, a trinity of father figures.

Sixteen years after the release of *Episode VI,* Lucas returned to his unfinished canvas to fill in the first three episodes, detailing the ascendancy of Luke's father, the young Jedi knight Anakin Skywalker, and his corruption into the totally evil Darth Vader. Continuing his exploration of father-son or mentor-student relationships, in *Episode I: The Phantom Menace* (1999), Lucas begins with a young Obi-Wan training under his wise master, Qui-Gon Jinn. Qui-Gon and a galactic princess, Padmé Amidala, find a brilliant, strong-willed nine-year-old boy, Anakin Skywalker, who is a slave on the desert planet of Tatooine where his son Luke Skywalker will later be raised. The boy, unnaturally skilled in mechanics and piloting, seems to be the fulfillment of a Jedi prophecy that a "Chosen One" will bring balance to the Force. But already the seeds of evil are present in the child, who has a quick temper and is difficult to control. Only Yoda seems to notice something is wrong with the boy, and warns that pride and anger may come to dominate in him.

Interestingly in a story about fathers and sons, the boy Anakin has no father in the conventional sense. Like many mythic heroes of the past, his birth was almost miraculous, an "immaculate conception," for his mother was impregnated not by a human father but by mysterious microscopic life forms called "midi-chloridians" that the Jedi believe are channels for the Force. An important element in the moral compass of the *Star Wars* series is how humans will make the transition from purely organic creatures into beings of the future enhanced or modified by technology and machines. There are warnings implied throughout the series that though the technological possibilities are marvelous, we must be careful not to get out of balance, and yield too much of our humanity to the chemical and mechanical possibilities that will come our way in the future. The fact that Anakin has no natural father leads him to be alternately seeking and rebelling against father figures, and helps explain how he is able to become the monstrous, more-than-half-machine that is Darth Vader.

The complex chronology of the films places the watcher of the prequels in a curious position. On the one hand, young Anakin seems to be doing the archetypal job of the hero, as the primary active character and someone whose fate we should care about. But it's very difficult to identify fully with a character who we know will turn out to be a science fiction equivalent of Hitler or Genghis Khan, even if we know he will be ultimately redeemed. Though the prequel films performed extremely well at the box office, the dramatic experience of watching them was necessarily muted by the knowledge that their principal hero is fated to be a despicable villain. Many people watched the prequel films with a certain detachment, unable to get behind the hero's struggles as they had with Luke Skywalker's in *Episodes IV-VI.*

Some of the audience's need to identify with positively charged characters was transferred from Anakin to other members of the cast in the three prequel films, such as Qui-Gon Jinn, Obi-Wan, Queen Padmé Amidala, and others. Nevertheless a certain chilliness hangs over the prequel films, part of the artistic risk that Lucas took in attempting such a large and complex composition. Anakin's story grows darker as the films progress. In *Episode II: Attack of the Clones,* his special status as a genius allows him to fall prey to pride and arrogance. His mixed feelings about father figures leads him to rebel against positive role models like Obi-Wan and Yoda and to seek the twisted counsel of negative father possibilities like Senator Palpatine/Darth Sidious.

That most human element, love, is awakened in the young Anakin by his secret romance and marriage with Princess Amidala. However, his capacity to love becomes distorted by the death of his mother at the hand of Tusken raiders. In a sequence that recalls the Western movie universe of John Ford's *The Searchers,* Anakin finds his mother horribly tortured by the savages and overreacts to her death, unleashing a tide of bloody revenge that makes him almost unredeemable in an audience's eyes.

In *Episode III: Revenge of the Sith,* Anakin becomes obsessed with the fear of losing that which he loves, Princess Amidala, and is haunted by prophetic dreams of her dying in childbirth. He is thus easy prey for the temptations of Senator Palpatine, who holds out the promise of an elixir that can rescue loved ones from death. Anakin makes further bad choices, preventing positive Jedi mentor Mace Windu from killing Palpatine and allowing Palpatine to kill Windu. When Amidala pleads with him to leave public life, Anakin errs again, choosing to remain at the center of things in the vain hope of overthrowing Palpatine someday.

Paradoxically, Anakin nearly causes that which he fears the most, Amidala's death, by almost strangling her when he suspects she has betrayed him to Obi-Wan. She dies of a broken heart after giving birth to the future Luke and Leia. Anakin's descent into monsterhood is completed in a final duel with Obi-Wan, who cuts off both his arms and one leg, leaving him to roll near the scorching lava of a volcano. Palpatine, now revealed to be the evil schemer Darth Sidious, rescues Anakin and uses machines to turn him into the less-than-human creature we know as Darth Vader. In this dark and tragic climax, the only ray of hope is that the infants Luke and Leia are sent to be raised by surrogate parents, Luke going to his aunt and uncle on Tatooine and Leia being raised by a noble family, the Organas, on the planet Alderaan.

Audiences and critics had mixed reactions to the three prequel films, ranging from strong criticism of comic elements like the character of Jar-Jar Binks to expressions of disappointment that Lucas seemed to have lost some of the bright, cheerful spirit of episodes IV-VI. One possible explanation for the markedly different tone of the prequels is that Lucas was in a different stage of his life when he returned to his youthful creation. In making the first three films in the '70s and '80s, Lucas had only a short walk backwards to reach his childhood, and was firmly in touch with the optimism and hopefulness of youth. The road back to innocence was a lot longer by 1999, and his perspective was no longer that of a young rogue filmmaker, but that of a responsible parent and head of a huge network of companies. Although in *Episode I* Lucas was dealing with the early childhood of his protagonist, Anakin Skywalker, the boy genius in the film sounds more like a world-weary adult.

Though Lucas has said he has completed his original vision with the six feature films, the universe he founded continues to be developed in countless novels, comics, animation series, and games. It has a definite life of its own, quite apart from the intentions of its creator, and it has been embellished by original contributions from fans who feel they own it. And we are entitled to wonder if someday, perhaps in a universe far, far away, one version of the original scheme will ever be realized, one that called not only for three prequel films, but also three sequels, presumably *Episodes VII, VIII,* and *IX,* that might deal with the further adventures of Luke, Leia, and Han Solo, and perhaps their descendants or students. It would be interesting to see, in that hypothetical universe, how the perspective of the creator might mellow, perhaps producing a tone completely different from those of the first six films, in a future where humans will have to make ever more difficult choices about the Force and the god-like possibilities of technology. Having explored idealized goodness in the first three films, and the roots of evil in the prequels, Lucas and his successors might find a synthesis in a future triad of films that finally brings a balance to the Force.

In 2001 I participated in the making of a documentary film, *A Galaxy Far, Far Away,* looking into the "*Stars Wars* phenomenon" that was cresting in the public imagination because of the revival of the series. The film took a light-hearted view of the curious obsessions of *Star Wars* fans and the importance of the movies in their lives. Given that fathers and sons are so significant in the films, it's not surprising that a major conclusion of the filmmakers was that the *Star Wars* saga is one of the few cultural events that unites generations, making strong bonds between fathers and sons. Many young men interviewed for the documentary reported that the *Star Wars* films were among the few movies that fathers and sons could watch together, and that they had become an important part of family memories. Despite their occasional flaws and missteps, the films collectively are an impressive achievement of the mythic imagination, continuing the epic tradition and proving that abundant energy still surges in the motifs of the Hero's Journey.

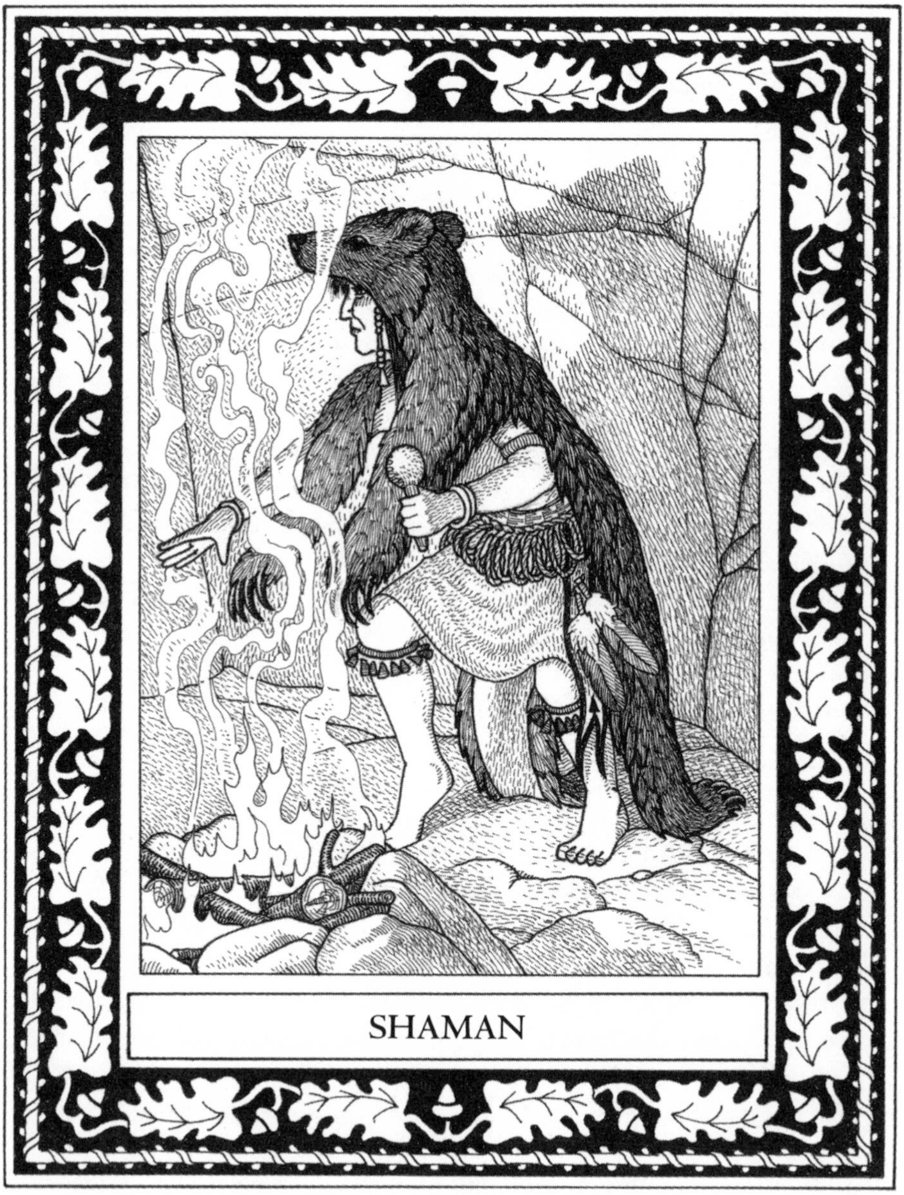
SHAMAN

THE WRITER'S JOURNEY

The beauty of the Hero's Journey model is that it not only describes a pattern in myths and fairy tales, but it's also an accurate map of the territory one must travel to become a writer or, for that matter, a human being.

The Hero's Journey and the Writer's Journey are one and the same. Anyone setting out to write a story soon encounters all the tests, trials, ordeals, joys, and rewards of the Hero's Journey. We meet all of its Shadows, Shapeshifters, Mentors, Tricksters, and Threshold Guardians in the interior landscape. Writing is an often perilous journey inward to probe the depths of one's soul and bring back the Elixir of experience — a good story. Low self-esteem or confusion about goals may be the Shadows that chill our work, an editor or one's own judgmental side may be the Threshold Guardians that seem to block our way. Accidents, computer problems, and difficulties with time and discipline may torment and taunt us like Tricksters. Unrealistic dreams of success or distractions may be the Shapeshifters who tempt, confuse, and dazzle us. Deadlines, editorial decisions, or the struggle to sell our work may be the Tests and Ordeals from which we seem to die but are Resurrected to write again.

But take hope, for writing is magic. Even the simplest act of writing is almost supernatural, on the borderline with telepathy. Just think: We can make a few abstract marks on a piece of paper in a certain order and someone a world away and a thousand years from now can know our deepest thoughts. The boundaries of space and time and even the limitations of death can be transcended.

Many cultures believed the letters of their alphabets were far more than just symbols for communication, recording transactions, or recalling history. They believed letters were powerful magical symbols that could be used to cast spells and predict the future. The Norse runes and the Hebrew alphabet are simple letters for spelling words, but also deep symbols of cosmic significance.

This magical sense is preserved in our word for teaching children how to manipulate letters to make words: spelling. When you "spell" a word correctly, you are in effect casting a spell, charging these abstract, arbitrary symbols with meaning and power. We say "Sticks and stones may break my bones, but words can never hurt me," but this is manifestly untrue. We know that words have power to hurt or heal. The simple words of a letter, telegram, or phone call can strike you like a hammer blow. They're just words — marks on paper or vibrations of air — but mere words such as "Guilty," "Ready, aim, fire!" "I do," or "We'd like to buy your screenplay" can bind us, condemn us, or bring us joy. They can hurt or heal us with their magic power.

The healing power of words is their most magical aspect. Writers, like the shamans or medicine men and women of ancient cultures, have the potential to be healers.

WRITERS AND SHAMANS

Shamans have been called "the wounded healers." Like writers, they are special people set apart from the rest by their dreams, visions, or unique experiences. Shamans, like many writers, are prepared for their work by enduring terrible ordeals. They may have a dangerous illness or fall from a cliff and have nearly every bone broken. They are chewed by a lion or mauled by a bear. They are taken apart and put back together again in a new way. In a sense they have died and been reborn, and this experience gives them special powers. Many writers come to their craft only after they have been shattered by life in some way.

Often those chosen to be shamans are identified by special dreams or visions, in which the gods or spirits take them away to other worlds where they undergo terrible ordeals. They are laid out on a table to have all their bones removed and broken. Before their eyes, their bones and organs are split, cooked, and reassembled in a new order. They are tuned to a new frequency like radio receivers. As shamans, they are now able to receive messages from other worlds.

They return to their tribes with new powers. They have the ability to travel to other worlds and bring back stories, metaphors, or myths that guide, heal, and give meaning to life. They listen to the confusing, mysterious dreams of their people and give them back in the form of stories that provide guidelines for right living.

We writers share in the godlike power of the shamans. We not only travel to other worlds but create them out of space and time. When we write, we truly travel to these worlds of our imagination. Anyone who has tried to write seriously knows this is why we need solitude and concentration. We are actually traveling to another time and place.

As writers we travel to other worlds not as mere daydreamers, but as shamans with the magic power to bottle up those worlds and bring them back in the form of stories for others to share. Our stories have the power to heal, to make the world new again, to give people metaphors by which they can better understand their own lives.

When we writers apply the ancient tools of the archetypes and the Hero's Journey to modern stories, we stand on the shoulders of the mythmakers and shamans of old. When we try to heal our people with the wisdom of myth, we are the modern shamans. We ask the same ageless, childlike questions presented by the myths: Who am I? Where did I come from? What happens when I die? What does it mean? Where do I fit in? Where am I bound on my own Hero's Journey?

APPENDICES

STORIES ARE ALIVE

STORIES ARE ALIVE

"All the works of man have their origin in creative fantasy. What right have we then to depreciate imagination?"
— Jung

"Pleased to meet you, hope you guess my name,
But what's puzzling you is the nature of my game."
— The Rolling Stones
"Sympathy for the Devil"

Proposition: Stories are alive and conscious and respond to human emotions.

At one point when the Disney company was remaking itself in the 1980s, I was called upon to review the major fairy tales of world cultures, looking for potential animation subjects on the order of Walt Disney's colorful interpretations of European folk stories, like "Snow White" and "Cinderella" from the Brothers Grimm and "The Sleeping Beauty" from Perrault's collection of French fairy tales. It was a chance to reopen the mental laboratory to study old friends from my childhood that Walt Disney had not gotten around to tackling, like Rapunzel and Rumpelstiltskin. It was also a great opportunity for me to sample many kinds of stories from different cultures, identifying similarities and differences and extracting storytelling principles from this broad sample.

In the course of my adult wanderings through what is normally considered children's literature, I came to a few firm conclusions about stories, these powerful and mysterious creations of the human mind. For instance, I came to believe that *stories have healing power,* that they can help us deal with difficult emotional situations by giving us examples of human behavior, perhaps similar in some way to the struggles we are going through at some stage of life, and which might inspire us to try a different strategy for living. I believe *stories have survival value* for the human species and that they were a big step in human evolution, allowing us to think metaphorically and to pass down the accumulated wisdom of the race in story form. I believe *stories are metaphors* by which people measure and adjust their own lives by comparing them to those of the characters. I believe the basic metaphor of most stories is that of the journey, and that *good stories show at least two journeys, outer and inner*: an outer journey in which the hero tries to do something difficult or get something, and an inner journey in which the hero faces some crisis of the spirit or test of character that leads to transformation. I believe *stories are orientation devices*, functioning like compasses and maps to allow us to feel oriented, centered, connected, more conscious, more aware of our identities and responsibilities and our relationship to the rest of the world.

But of all my beliefs about stories, one that has been particularly useful in the business of developing commercial stories for the movies is the idea that *stories are somehow alive, conscious, and responsive to human emotions and wishes.*

I have always suspected that stories are alive. They seem to be conscious and purposeful. Like living beings, stories have an agenda, something on their minds. They want something from you. They want to wake you up, to make you more conscious and more alive. They want to teach you a lesson disguised as entertainment. Under the guise of amusement, stories want to edify you, build up your character just a little by showing a moral situation, a struggle, and an outcome. They seek to change you in some small way, to make you just a bit more human by comparing your behavior to that of the characters.

The living, conscious, intentional quality of stories is here and there revealed in familiar fairy tales, like the one the Brothers Grimm collected called "Rumpelstiltskin," the tale of the little man with his power to spin straw into gold and a mysterious desire to own a human child. The story is found in many cultures where the little man is known by strange and funny names like Bulleribasius (Sweden), Tittelintuure (Finland), Praseidimio (Italy), Repelsteelije (Holland), and Grigrigredinmenufretin (France).

This was one of the stories that posed challenging questions in the mental laboratory of my earliest childhood. Who was this little man, where did he get his powers, and why did he want that human child? What was the lesson the girl in the story was supposed to learn? Later in life, as I returned to contemplate that story as part of my work for Walt Disney animation, many of those mysteries remained, but the deep wisdom of the folk tale helped me understand that stories are alive, that they actively respond to wishes, desires, and strong emotions in the characters, and that they are compelled to provide experiences that teach us some lesson in life.

THE STORY OF RUMPELSTILTSKIN

The well-known tale begins with a lovely young girl in a dangerous situation, an archetypal damsel in distress. She is the daughter of a miller who brags to the king that his daughter is so talented, she can even spin straw into gold. The king, a literal-minded fellow, says "That's the kind of talent I like!" and locks her in a room in his castle containing only a spinning wheel and piles of straw, warning that he's going to have her killed in the morning if she doesn't spin the straw into gold as her daddy promised.

The girl doesn't know what to do and begins to weep. At once the door opens and a little man, or "manikin" as the tale says, comes in, asking her why she is crying so. Apparently he has been attracted by her strong emotions, as faerie folk are said to be. When she explains her predicament he says he can spin straw into gold, no problem, and asks what she can give him if he does the job for her. She hands over her necklace and he at once sits down and spins the straw, whir, whir, whir, into shining gold wire on a spool.

In the morning the little man has vanished. The king is very pleased with the gold, but being greedy, locks the girl into a bigger room with more straw, and again demands that she spin it all into gold by dawn. If not, she will die. All alone in the room that night, the girl feels hopeless and weeps once more. As if summoned again by her emotions, the little man appears a second time. This time she offers him a ring from her finger to get out of her predicament. Whir, whir, whir, straw is spun into gold.

The king finds bigger spools of gold wire in place of straw the next morning and is delighted, but again is greedy and locks the girl in the biggest room in the palace, stuffed to the ceiling with straw. If she can turn it all into gold by dawn he will marry her, but if not, she will die.

The girl's weeping in the locked room attracts the little man for a third time, but now she has nothing left to give him. So he asks her, "If you become queen, will you give me your first-born child?"

Thinking nothing of the future, the girl agrees. Whir, whir, whir, the mountain of straw is spun into gold. The king collects his gold and marries the girl as promised. A year goes by and the girl, now a queen, has a beautiful child.

One day the little man comes and claims the child as his reward for saving her life. Horrified, the young queen offers him all the riches of the realm, but the little man refuses, saying "Something alive is dearer to me than all the treasures in the world." The girl laments and cries so much that the manikin relents a little for, as we have seen, he is very sensitive to human emotions. He strikes a new bargain with her. If she can guess his name within three days, she will get to keep the child. But she will never guess it, he says confidently, for he has a very unusual name.

The queen stays up all night thinking of every name she's ever heard and sends out messengers far and wide to assemble lists of unusual names. When the manikin comes to see her the first day, she tries out all these names but none is right. On the second day she sends out more messengers to the distant corners of the kingdom to collect weird names, but again the little man's name is not among them and he goes away laughing, sure he will get to keep the child.

On the third day the queen's most faithful, far-traveling messenger reports that he's struck pay dirt. In his wanderings he didn't uncover any new names, but far away, atop a mountain, he did come across a little house, in front of which a fire was blazing, and around it was dancing a ridiculous little man. The messenger heard him shout a rhyme that revealed his name was Rumpelstiltskin.

The little man appears once more in the queen's room, sure she will be unable to guess his absurd name. But after two bad guesses ("Conrad?" "Harry?"), she gets it right — Rumpelstiltskin! The tale ends abruptly as the little man, crying out that the devil must have told her his name, stamps his right foot so furiously that it goes through the floor and sticks deep in the earth. With his two hands he seizes the other foot and literally tears himself in two!

A fitting end for one who has connived to take a human child from its mother. Or is it?

Who is this strange little man with his supernatural powers to enter locked rooms and spin straw into gold? Although the tale only calls him a "little man" or "manikin," he is clearly one of the faerie people of worldwide folklore, perhaps an elf or a gnome. The oral storytellers may have avoided calling him what he is because the faerie folk are notoriously touchy about their names and identities. But it is likely that any hearer of this tale in medieval times would instantly recognize the little man as a supernatural creature from the faerie world. Like other denizens of that world he appears when he wants to and only to certain people. Like them, he is interested in human children and attracted by strong human emotions.

From early times people have associated the faerie folk with a certain sadness, perhaps because they lack some things that human beings take for granted. According to one theory, they are unable to conceive their own young and are therefore fascinated by human children, sometimes kidnapping them in the night, as Shakespeare's faerie queen Titania snatched an Indian princeling as her darling toy in *A Midsummer Night's Dream.* Sometimes the faeries steal children from their cradles and replace them with blocks of wood or soul-less replica children called changelings.

The faeries' ability to feel emotions may be different from ours, for they seem to be curious about our emotional outbursts, and are in fact attracted to them. It's as if they exist in a parallel dimension but are summoned into our world by strong human emotions, as demons and angels supposedly can be summoned by ritual ceremonies and prayers intended to focus emotional energy. Some authorities hold that faeries do not know simple human emotions like love or grief but are intensely curious to know what they are missing.

Re-experiencing the story of "Rumpelstiltskin" as an adult, I was struck by how instantaneously the girl's tears of despair summoned the little man. Implied in the girl's weeping is a cry for help, a wish. If given words, it might be "Please, get me out of this!" It appears the inhabitants of the faerie world are attracted to human emotions especially when they are focused into wishes. In this case, the wish is to get out of a desperate, hopeless situation. In the fairy-tale logic of cause and effect, the girl's shedding of tears is a positive action that generates a positive result. By crying, she acknowledges her powerlessness and sends out a signal to the world of spirits that surrounds us. "Isn't there someone with the magical powers my father claimed for me, who can get me out of this uncomfortable spot?" And the story hears, and responds by sending a messenger, a supernatural creature who has the power to grant her unspoken wish to escape.

However, as always, there's a catch. The price for getting out of her trouble is very high, escalating from material treasures, like a necklace or a ring, to life itself. But the girl isn't thinking about that right now. Having a child is a remote possibility. When she gets to that point, maybe she can work something out or maybe the little man will just go away. Whatever the risk, she'll agree to it to get out of that room and out of danger from the king's wrath. Her wish to escape, expressed by a strong burst of emotion, has called the little man and the adventure into being.

THE POWER OF WISHING

I began to realize that wishing may be an underlying principle of storytelling. The hero is almost always discovered in a difficult or uncomfortable situation, very often making a wish to escape or to change the conditions. The wish is often verbalized and is clearly stated in the first act of many movies. In *The Wizard of Oz,* Dorothy's song "Somewhere over the Rainbow" is a wish to escape to a land where troubles are far behind her. In *Lost in Translation,* Scarlett Johansson's character expresses the theme of the movie in a line in the first act where she says to Bill Murray's character, meeting in a Japanese hotel bar, "I wish I could sleep," symbolizing a wish for spiritual and emotional peace.

The expression of a wish, even a frivolous one, near the beginning of a story has an important function of *orientation* for the audience. It gives a story a strong throughline or what is called a "desire line," organizing the forces in and around the hero to achieve a clear goal, even if that goal may later be re-examined and re-defined. It automatically generates a strong polarization of the story, generating a conflict between those forces helping the hero achieve her goal, and those trying to prevent it.

If the wish is not expressed by one of the characters, it may be implied by the character's dire situation. Audience members making strong identification with a character in trouble will make the wish themselves, desiring the hero to be happy, triumphant, or free, and getting themselves in alignment with the forces polarizing the story.

Spoken or not, the story hears the wish, seemingly attracted by the intense emotion contained in it. Carl Jung had a motto carved above his door, "Vocatus atque non vocatus, deus aderit," which loosely translated means "Summoned or not, the god will come." In other words, when the emotional conditions are right, when the need is great, there is an inner cry for change, a spoken or unspoken wish that calls the story and the adventure into being.

The story's response to the human wish is often to send a messenger, sometimes a magical little man like Rumpelstiltskin, but always some kind of agent who leads the hero into a special kind of experience we call an adventure — a sequence of challenges that teach the hero, and the audience, a lesson. The story provides villains, rivals, and allies to challenge or aid the hero and impart the lessons that are on the story's agenda. The story sets up moral dilemmas that test the hero's beliefs and character, and we are invited to measure our own behavior against that of the players in the drama.

The adventure has a special quality of the unexpected. The story is tricky. It acts in the roundabout, indirect, slightly mischievous way of the faerie folk who are its frequent agents, providing the hero with a series of unexpected obstacles that challenge the way the person has been doing business. It usually grants the hero's wish but in an unexpected way, a way that teaches the hero a lesson about life. Many of life's teachings can be boiled down to "Be careful what you wish for," which is a lesson taught by countless science-fiction and fantasy stories as well as love stories and stories of ambition.

WANTS vs. NEEDS

Through the triggering device of wishes, stories seem to like arranging events so that the hero is forced to evolve to a higher level of awareness. Often the hero wishes for something that she or he desperately *wants* at that moment, but the story teaches the hero to look beyond, to what he or she really *needs*. A hero may think she *wants* to win a competition or find a treasure, but in fact the story shows that she needs to learn some moral or emotional lesson: how to be a team player, how to be more flexible and forgiving, how to stand up for herself. In the course of granting the initial wish, the story provides hair-raising, life-threatening incidents that challenge the hero to correct some flaw in his or her character.

By imposing obstacles to the hero in achieving the goal, the story may appear to be hostile to the hero's well-being. The intention of the story may seem to be to take something away from the hero (like life itself!), but in fact the real aim of the story is benevolent, to teach the hero the needed moral lesson, to fill in a missing piece in the hero's personality or understanding of the world.

The lesson is presented in a particular, ritualized way, reflecting a more universal principle we might call "Not Only... But Also" (NOBA). NOBA is a rhetorical device, a way of presenting information that can be found in "fortune-telling" systems like the I Ching and the Tarot. Not Only... But Also means: Here is a truth that you know perfectly well, but there is another dimension to this truth of which you may not be aware. A story might be telling you, through the actions of a character, that not only are your habits holding you back but also if you keep going in this direction your habits will destroy you. Or it might be telling you that not only are you beset with difficulties, but also these very difficulties will be the means to your ultimate victory.

In Lajos Egri's famous example from "the Scottish play," the premise is that Macbeth's ruthless ambition inevitably leads to his destruction. But Macbeth doesn't see it that way, not at first. He thinks only that ruthless ambition leads to power, to being king. But the story, summoned into life in response to Macbeth's thirst for power, teaches him a lesson in NOBA form. Ambition leads not only to being king, but also to Macbeth's destruction.

The words "but" and "however," as lawyers know, are very useful for setting terms and conditions, and can be powerful tools of rhetoric and storytelling. A story is like a long sentence or a paragraph, with a subject, the hero; an object, the hero's goal; and a verb, the emotional state or physical action of the hero. "So and so wants something and does something to get it." The NOBA concept introduces the word "but" or "however" into that sentence. Now it's "So and so wants something and does something to get it, but there are unexpected consequences, forcing so and so to adapt or change in order to survive."

The aim of good storytelling is to get the audience to make the wish along with the hero. Stories do this through the process of "identification," by making the hero sympathetic, the victim of a misfortune or an understandable error of judgment. Good storytellers invite audiences to invest themselves in the fate of the characters by making them likeable or giving them universal drives, desires, and human weaknesses. Ideally, what happens to the hero is happening, on some emotional level of connection, to the audience. The story and the hero are not the only active agents in the drama. The members of the audience are also agents in the play, emotionally involved, actively wishing for the hero to win, learn the lesson, survive, and thrive. They identify with heroes in a threatened position where it appears their wishes may not be granted and their real needs may not be met.

The wishes of heroes are a strong point of identification for many people, since we all have wishes and desires that we secretly cherish. In fact, that's one of the main reasons we go to movies and watch TV and read novels — to have our wishes granted. Storytellers are, most of the time, in the wish-granting business. The Disney empire built its entire corporate identity around the belief in wishing, from its theme song "When You Wish Upon a Star" to the wish-granting fairy godmothers of *Sleeping Beauty* and *Cinderella*, to the genie who grants three wishes in *Aladdin*. Hollywood executives and best-selling novelists aim to know the secret wishes of their audiences and fulfill them. Popular stories of recent years have granted widely held wishes to walk with the dinosaurs, trod the soil of alien planets, seek high adventure in mythic realms or in times gone by, and outpace the boundaries of space, time, and death itself. So-called "reality television" grants wishes on a nightly basis, bestowing on ordinary people the thrill of being seen by millions and having a shot at stardom or riches. Politicians and advertisers play on the wishes of the public, promising to grant security, peace of mind, or comfort. A good technique of Hollywood pitching is to begin by asking "Did you ever wish you could —" (fly, be invisible, go back in time to fix your mistakes, etc.), connecting up the desires of the story's hero with a strong wish that a lot of people might have.

THE WISHES OF THE AUDIENCE

It pays to think about what audience members wish for themselves and the heroes in stories. As writers we play a tricky game with our readers and viewers. We evoke a strong wish through our characters, then spend most of the story frustrating the wish, making it seem that the characters will never get what they want or need. Usually, in the end, we grant those wishes, and show how they are achieved by struggle, by overcoming obstacles, and by reconsidering them, with the desire sometimes shifting from what the hero thinks she wants to what she really needs.

We thwart the deep wishes of the audience at our peril. Movies that deny the wishes of the audience to see the heroes ultimately happy or fulfilled may not perform well at the box office. The audience will inwardly cheer for poetic justice — the hero receiving rewards proportionate to his struggle, the villain receiving punishment equivalent to the suffering he has inflicted on others. If that sense of poetic justice is violated, if the rewards and punishments and lessons don't match up to our wishes for the characters, we sense something is wrong with the story, and go away unsatisfied.

We have wishes for our villains as well as our heroes. I remember my mother, an astute critic of popular movies and books, muttering under her breath phrases like "I hope he dies a horrible death," when a villain had done something particularly heinous to one of her heroes on the screen. If the movie didn't deliver a poetically appropriate fate for the villain, she was disappointed and that movie went down in her books as a bad one.

Once in a while, the strategy of thwarting the audience's desires is effective, to challenge the assumptions of the watchers, to reflect a harsh view of reality, or to depict a tragic, doomed situation as a kind of warning to the audience. For example, in the novel and movie *Remains of the Day*, the butler to the family of a British lord spends his entire life failing to connect emotionally with other people. His wish, we might say, is to have a sense of tight control over his personal life, one area where he does not compromise. This masks a deeper desire, the need to make an emotional and physical connection with another human being. The audience forms a strong wish for him to be happy, to seize an opportunity for intimacy that comes his way late in life. But, true to his tragic character, he doesn't take the chance for change, and the movie ends with the feeling that though he has gotten what he wants (privacy and control), he will never get what he needs, or what we wish for him and ourselves. It plays as a cautionary tale, a warning to us — if we don't take up the opportunities that life offers us, we could end up frustrated and alone. In this case, our wish to see the character happy is superseded by our need to realize that we could end up in the same sad situation if we don't open up to opportunities to love.

The focus on wishing that gives life to many tales is but one of the verbs that activate the emotional mechanisms of story. Wishes must be translated into action, dreams must be made real, or else the story, and perhaps a person's life, will stagnate, stuck in an unrealistic, endless fantasy of daydreaming. Wishing is important, for it is the first step in a pyramid of mental states, the yearning of a seed to grow into something great. It forms the initial intention of a story, or the beginning of a new phase of someone's life. "Be careful what you wish for" applies in a multitude of cases, as stories show us over and over that a wish is a powerful act of the imagination. The idea is constantly affirmed in stories that human imagination is extremely powerful, especially when focused into a wish, but that it is difficult to control. The wish and the imagination work together to create a mental image of the desired thing, person, situation, or outcome, so vivid that it calls the adventure into being, and launches the hero in the direction of seeing how the wish will actually be fulfilled, usually in an unsuspected and challenging way. The image may be faint and hazy in the beginning, or detailed but highly idealized and unrealistic, a fantasy of the future uninformed by real experience.

But for a story or a person's life to move along it is necessary to pierce the bubble of fantasy, and to convert wishing into something else — doing, the next step of the pyramid. The essence of movies is the director's command, "Action." Do something, actors. The root of the word "actor" is "do-er," someone who does something. Dreams and wishes must be tested in the crucible of reality, in action, by doing.

PROGRESSING FROM WISHING TO WILLING

Encountering conflicts and obstacles can force characters to evolve to a yet higher level on the pyramid of emotions, that of willing, which is quite a different mental state than mere wishing. Martial arts and classic philosophies teach people to develop a strong will, so that wishes can be transformed into actions, so that even when distracted or set back by obstacles, the developing personality can return quickly to the center line of its intention. Will is a wish concentrated and focused into a firm intention to achieve a goal step by step. Wishes can evaporate at the first setback but the will endures.

Willing is a kind of filter, separating those who only wish from those who actually take responsibility for improving themselves and pay the price of real change. With a focused will, a character can take the blows and setbacks that life hands out. Martial arts strengthen the will, as stories do, by delivering a series of blows and falls that toughen the student. Challenging and stressful situations are repeatedly introduced so that the developing person becomes more resilient, accustomed to conflict and opposition, and determined to overcome any obstacle.

Like making a wish, making an act of the will calls forces into motion. A strong act of will sends out signals to the world. Here is someone who wants something and is willing to pay a high price to get it. All sorts of allies and opponents will be summoned by such a declaration, each with its lesson to teach.

Like wishing, the will must be managed. A will for power can be dangerous, and an overly strong will can overpower and victimize weaker ones. But the development of a strong will, outgrowing the stage of simple wishing, is a necessary stage of human development.

There is a connection between needs and willing. Both evolve from the idea of wishing or wanting. Once you progress beyond wishing to knowing what your needs truly are, you can focus your vague wishes into much more concentrated acts of the will. All the levels of your being can be aligned in the direction of achieving a clear and realistic goal. The girl in "Rumpelstiltskin" starts as a passive victim, just crying her eyes out and sitting alone in a room wishing to be anywhere but there. When she is a little older and realizes she needs to protect the life of her child, she develops a will and applies it again and again until she accomplishes her goal.

The language of movies and fantasy, particularly that of the Disney variety, tends to show us the magical power of wishing but often stops short at that point, leaving the other steps of the pyramid unsaid but implied. Often fantasies are dedicated solely to exploring the mechanisms of wishing, developing the "Be careful what you wish for" concept to show that wishes might have to be refined or re-stated to adjust to reality, without necessarily evolving into the more powerful and focused mental state of willing an outcome. Sometimes an entire story remains in the wish mode by ending not with the development of a strong will, but the forming of a new wish, simply transferring unfocused desire from one object to the next.

Wishing and willing can be selfish mental states, and there are undoubtedly other possible steps higher on the pyramid of human emotional development, which might include learning to love, learning to have compassion for other beings, or in a few highly spiritual stories, learning to transcend human desires entirely to merge with a higher form of consciousness. But it's clear that wishing and its more evolved form, willing, are important tools for storytellers and necessary stages of everyone's development. Wishing in particular seems to invite a story to come to life and consciousness, launching an adventure that may teach us valuable lessons in survival.

And what about poor Rumpelstiltskin, tearing himself in two because he can't have the child he wants for unknown purposes? The outcome of the story doesn't seem fair. True, he has tried to kidnap a child from its mother, but what if he has a right to the child? The Queen has a bad record of motherhood, having bartered her child's life for her freedom, and the presumed father, the King, would make a menacing role model for a child, having threatened to behead his future wife. For all we know, the little man might have made a better parent to the child than either of them. Rumpelstiltskin loses the child because the young Queen is able to meet his seemingly impossible conditions, but what if he has a right to custody of the child, and not because of the deal he made with her that night? After all, what is there to do in an empty room for three nights when all the straw has been spun into gold?

QUESTIONS

1. Have you noticed examples of characters making wishes early in stories? Give an example and tell how the wish was granted (or not) by the story.

2. What has been the role of wishing in your life? Have you learned to be careful what you wish for? Is there a story in that experience?

3. What are your short-term and long-term wishes, and how can you convert them into will and action? How would that work for characters in your story?
4. Can you think of examples of a story providing an unexpected answer to a character's wish? Write a story around the idea of someone wishing for something.

5. Are there wishes expressed or implied in other classic fairy tales and myths? How are the wishes granted or denied? Write a modern version of a fairy tale or myth and use the concept of wishing.

6. Read a myth, view a movie, read a book and analyze what universal wishes the story satisfies. What human wishes are expressed in your story?

7. Are there such things as fate or destiny? What do these terms mean to you? Do they have a role any more in modern life?

8. Brainstorm around the concept of wishing. Write the word in the center of a blank page and then around it write all the things you have wished for or are now wishing for in the future. See if some patterns emerge. Are your wishes realistic? What happens when your wishes are granted? What is keeping you from granting your own wishes? Apply the same exercise to a character. What is he or she wishing for? How do they convert wishing into will to achieve their goals?

POLARITY

POLARITY

"Students achieving Oneness will move on to Twoness."
— Woody Allen

A persistent feature of the Hero's Journey is that its stories tend to be *polarized* like two essential forces of nature, electricity and magnetism. Like them, stories create energy or exert force through polarities that organize the elements present into opposing camps with contrasting properties and orientations. *Polarity* is an essential principle of storytelling, governed by a few simple rules but capable of generating infinite conflict, complexity, and audience involvement.

A story needs a sense of oneness — unity — to feel like a satisfying and complete expression. It needs a single theme — a spine — something to unite it into a coherent work. But a story also needs a level of two-ness, a dimension of duality, to create tension and the possibility of movement. As soon as you choose a single thought or character to unite your story, you have automatically generated its polar opposite, a contrary concept or antagonistic character, and therefore a duality or polarized system that conducts energy between the two parties. Unity begets duality; the existence of one implies the possibility of two.

As soon as you imagine two points in space, you have generated a line of force between them and the potential for interaction, communication, deal-making, movement, emotion, and conflict.

If your story is about the single quality of trust, the possibility of suspicion immediately arises. Suspicion is necessary to test and challenge the concept of trust. If your main character wants something, there must be someone who doesn't want her to get it, who brings out hidden qualities in your hero by opposing her. If not, there's no story. We enjoy stories that are polarized by a struggle between two strong characters, like *The African Queen* or *Driving Miss Daisy*, but we are also entertained by stories polarized by great principles of living that tug the characters in two directions at once, so they are torn between duty and love, for example, or between revenge and forgiveness. Many a show-business tale like *The Buddy Holly Story* is polarized by loyalty and ambition; loyalty to the group that the hero grew up with versus the demands of ambition that require ditching those people when the hero moves to a new level of success.

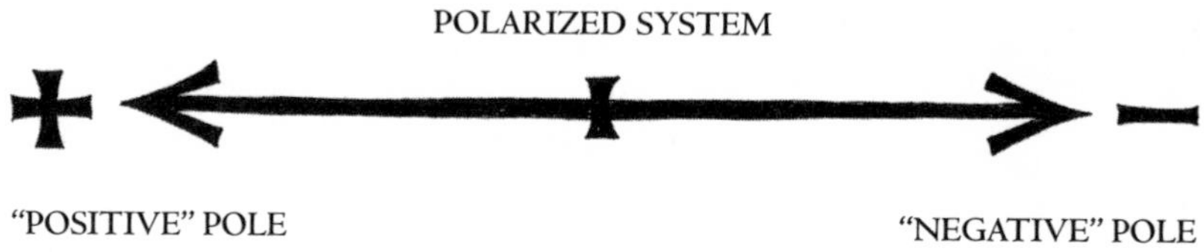

Every aspect of the Hero's Journey is polarized along at least two lines, the inner and outer dimensions and the positive and negative possibilities for each element. These polarities create potential for contrast, challenge, conflict, and learning. As the polarized nature of magnetic fields can be used to generate electrical energy, polarity in a story seems to be an engine that generates tension and movement in the characters and a stirring of emotions in the audience.

We live in a polarized universe, both as a physical fact all around us and as a deeply ingrained mental habit. On the physical level we are ruled by the very real polarities of day and night, up and down, earth and space, inside and outside. Our bodies are polarized, with limbs and organs distributed to the left and right sides, and a brain whose left and right sides have quite different responsibilities. We are polarized as a species, coming in two basic models, male and female. Polarized categories like age and youth or life and death are realities that no one can ignore.

The Universe itself seems to be polarized into systems like matter and energy, matter and anti-matter, atoms that carry plus or minus charges, positive or negative poles in magnetism and electricity. Our entire galaxy is polarized, a spinning disk of stars, dust, and gases that has definite north and south poles and its own polarized magnetic field. And of course the whole world of modern computer technology has been generated from a simple binary system, 0 and 1, a polarized off-on switch which apparently can yield infinite computing power from one little polarity.

Polarity is an equally pervasive force as a habit of thinking. We often act as if all questions have a right or wrong answer, all statements are either true or false, people are either good or bad, normal or abnormal. Either a thing is real or it isn't. Either you are with me or against me. Sometimes these categories are useful, but they can also be limiting and may not adequately represent reality. Polarization is a powerful force in politics and rhetoric, allowing leaders and propagandists to mobilize anger and passion by artificially dividing the world into "us" and "them" categories, a simplification of the world that makes it easier to deal with, but ignores many intermediate or alternative points of view.

However, polarity is a real phenomenon in human relationships and an important engine of conflict in storytelling. Characters in relationships strongly tend to become polarized as part of their process of growing and learning through conflict. Polarity follows certain rules, and good storytellers instinctively exploit them for their dramatic potential.

THE RULES OF POLARITY

1. Opposites Attract

The first rule of polarity is that opposites attract. A story is in some ways like a magnet with its mysterious, invisible power of attraction. Two magnets, properly aligned, with the south pole of one pointed at the north pole of the other, will strongly attract each other, just as two contrasting characters can be drawn powerfully to one another. The clash of their differences attracts and holds an audience's attention.

Two lovers, friends, or allies may be attracted to one another because they complete one other, perhaps clashing at first because they possess contrasting qualities, but discovering that each needs something the other has. Unconsciously, people may seek out those whose strengths and weaknesses balance weak and strong qualities in themselves.

Hero and villain may be locked together in a struggle, drawn together by circumstances but operating in strongly contrasting, polarized ways that show the whole range of possible human responses to a stressful situation. Nations may be drawn into polarized conflicts because of radically opposed ways of perceiving reality.

2. Polarized Conflict Attracts the Audience

A polarized relationship naturally generates conflict as the characters at two contrasting extremes explore and challenge each other's boundaries, concepts of the world, and strategies for living. We find this endlessly fascinating. Conflict, like magnetic energy, is attractive, automatically drawing the attention of the spectator. As a magnet or a magnetized object has the power to attract certain metals like iron and nickel, so a polarized, conflict-filled human situation attracts and focuses the attention of an audience or a reader.

3. Polarity Creates Suspense

Polarity generates not only struggle but also suspense about the outcome. Which world-view will triumph in the end? Which character will dominate? Who will survive? Who's right? Who will win, who will lose? What are the consequences when a hero chooses one side or the other of a polarity? A polarized system attracts our attention initially because we all perceive that our lives are sawed back and forth by similar contradictions and conflicts, tugging us in many directions at once along multiple lines of polarity, such as man and wife, parent and child, employee and boss, individual and society. We continue to watch with interest to see how the polarized situations will turn out, looking for clues about how to handle these challenges in our own lives.

4. Polarity Can Reverse Itself

When the conflict heats up after several rounds of conflict between the two sides in a polarized drama, the forces that draw two people together may reverse themselves, changing from a force of attraction to a force of repulsion. Two magnets that have been stuck together will fly apart if one of them is flipped so that its polarity is reversed. A moment before, they had been so strongly attracted to each other that it was difficult to pull them apart, and the next moment it's almost impossible to force them together, so strong is the force of repulsion.

Among the curious properties of electrical and magnetic fields is the fact that the polarity of these systems can abruptly reverse itself. The direction the energy is flowing in alternating current electrical systems flips back and forth from positive to negative fifty or sixty times a second, while the magnetic fields of heavenly bodies reverse polarity infrequently but on some mysterious timetable. For reasons that are poorly understood, the giant magnetic field of the sun reverses its polarity every eleven years or so, generating immense storms of radiation that wash over the earth like invisible tsunamis and disrupt communications and electronics worldwide. Scientists believe the magnetic field of the Earth has flipped poles many times over thousands of years, presumably making magnets and compasses point south for much of the lifetime of the planet. Reversals of polarity on this giant scale seem to be part of the life cycle of stars and planets, like a gigantic heartbeat.

Such reversals are also part of the life cycle of a story. They may be temporary, quick reversals of attraction or power within a scene, or they may be major hinges or turning points of a story. Within a scene, a quick change of polarity might happen because one of the lovers gets a new piece of information that reverses his or her attitude, say from trust to mistrust, or from physical attraction to disgust. The piece of information might turn out to be false, only temporarily challenging the attraction of opposites, but it creates tension along the line of energy that connects the two characters, and that tension makes good drama.

5. Reversals of Fortune

Reversal of polarity in a story can be the abrupt overturning of a character's fortune, a change of luck or circumstances that switches the prevailing conditions from negative to positive or vice versa. Good stories have at least three or four of these reversals for the main character, some have many, and some are even constructed so that they produce reversals of fortune in every scene. In fact, that might be a good minimum requirement for a scene — that it produce at least one reversal of fortune for someone on some level of the story. A shift in power, the underdog standing up to the bully, the fates dealing a blow to the victorious athlete, a lucky break or a sudden setback, all these are reversals of polarity that punctuate a story and give a sense of dynamic movement. The moments of reversal can be thrilling and memorable, like the scene of *Norma Rae* standing up in the factory to organize the workers.

ARISTOTLE'S CONCEPT OF REVERSAL

Aristotle in his *Poetics* describes the essential dramatic device of the reversal. He calls it *peripateia,* which refers to the "Peripatos" or covered walkway of Aristotle's Lyceum where he used to walk and talk with his students, developing ideas as they strolled back and forth. Perhaps he used the structure to demonstrate his logic, building up an argument forcefully as they traversed the colonnade in one direction, then demolishing it just as thoroughly on the reverse trip.

Aristotle says the sudden reversal of a situation for the protagonist can produce the desirable emotions of pity and terror in the audience; pity for someone who suffers undeserved misfortune, and terror when it happens to someone like us. A story captures our emotions by putting someone a little like us in a threatening situation that reverses the hero's fortunes a number of times. Think of the reversals of fortune in movies like *Papillon, Shakespeare in Love,* or *The Far Side of the World,* with the sympathetic characters alternating between moments of freedom or triumph and periods of danger, disappointment, and defeat.

Reversals of fortune in the life of a hero are inevitable and they make for good entertainment, holding our attention as we watch to see what will happen next, and wonder if the positive or negative energies will dominate at the end of the story. Even if we know the outcome, as in the movie *Titanic,* we enjoy watching how the contest plays out and how the characters react to the ups and downs dealt out by fate or the playwright. In a well-constructed story these repeated reversals accumulate power, adding up to the emotional impact that Aristotle claimed was the point of it all: *catharsis,* an explosive and physical release of emotion, be it tears of pity, shudders of terror, or bursts of laughter. The reversals, like drumbeats, impact our emotions, triggering reactions in the organs of our bodies. By Aristotle's theory, these drumbeats were supposed to accumulate tension in the bodies of the audience members until the biggest beat of all, at the climax of the play, released a pleasurable shudder of emotion that was believed to cleanse the spirit of poisonous thoughts and feelings. Stories retain their power to release cathartic emotions which is still a profound human need.

CATASTROPHIC REVERSAL

Since the beginning of Greek drama in Aristotle's day, the name for the biggest reversal in a character's fortunes has been "catastrophe." "Kata-" means "over" or "down" in Greek and "strophe" is "turn" or "twist", thus a catastrophe is an overturning or down-twisting. "Strophe" may also refer to a strap or a strip of leather or a length of plant fiber that could be woven into a basket, and is the parent of our words for strip, stripe, strap, and strop. It suggests that a play is a kind of weaving in which the strands of the plot, the fortunes of the various characters, interlock and crisscross, typically with the fortunes of the antagonist going up when the luck of the hero is going down and vice versa. A strophe in a classical Greek drama was a turning movement across the stage by part of the chorus, which recited a critical line of text to accompany the move. This was balanced by an opposite turn by another part of the chorus reciting an answering line of text, called the anti-strophe. It made the drama into a kind of polarized dance with the movements and phrases representing contradicting threads of thought or emotion within the society. We speak of "turning points" in stories and these are usually examples of reversal, with the biggest one, the catastrophe, coming just before the end of a classically constructed drama, and having, we hope, the cathartic effect that Aristotle recommended.

6. RECOGNITION

In the ancient world a favorite device for bringing about an emotionally charged reversal was a recognition scene, in which the disguised identity or secret relationship of a character is revealed, and the fortunes of the characters are reversed. These are scenes where long-lost lovers are united, where cruel tyrants realize they are about to execute their own sons, where the masked superheroes are unveiled, where the Prince puts the glass slipper on Cinderella's foot and realizes she's the girl of his dreams. A mainstay of Robin Hood movies is a scene where King Richard, who has been creeping around England in disguise to see what's been going on in his absence, throws off his outer robe to reveal the rampant lions on his surcoat. Robin and all his men instantly recognize him as the King, falling to their knees in reverent awe. It represents a moment in the story when the tide decisively has turned.

A recognition scene makes a good climactic reversal when a character has been going around in disguise, like *Tootsie* or *Mrs. Doubtfire.* Often it represents the catastrophe of unmasking that the hero has dreaded but it also is the opportunity for emotional honesty and self-acceptance. That the apparent disaster turns out to be the means of dramatic fulfillment makes for a double reversal.

7. Romantic Reversals

A kind of current, like magnetic current or electric current, flows through the invisible lines that connect characters in stories and people in relationships. We feel a certain flow of energy with some people and want to be with them, and we can sense when the flow of energy is strangled, blocked, reversed, or completely cut off. We know when there is "good chemistry" or a "spark" between two actors in a romance, two buddies in a comedy, or two rivals in an adventure, and are disappointed when there isn't enough current flowing in a relationship. We feel something when the polarity of a friendship or romance reverses itself, flipping from a strong force of attraction to one of repulsion.

In stories of romance the two lovers may go through several cycles of reversal, alternating between attraction and repulsion or trust and suspicion, as in Hitchcock's romantic spy thrillers *North by Northwest* and *Notorious,* or movies like *Body Heat, Casino, Fatal Attraction,* etc. The romance may begin with attraction, based on noticing superficially similar tastes or sensing that the other person can supply the elements missing from one's personality. We perversely enjoy watching the reversal of this situation, as the lovers inevitably discover their partners are quite different than they first appeared and are temporarily driven apart. After several reversals of attraction and repulsion, the lovers usually end up in alignment, the forces within them lined up in harmonious energy that promotes their connectedness, unless of course you are portraying a tragic, doomed love affair.

On the other hand a love story might begin with initial repulsion and mistrust, which will gradually reverse itself to attraction as the lovers overcome their differences and discover common ground, although there may be several reversals of polarity and episodes of attraction and repulsion along the way.

8. Polarity and the Character Arc

One of the dependable polarized plot forms is the genre of buddy comedy/adventure, in which two mismatched heroes go through a two-tiered adventure together. On one level, the outer dimension, they are cops, spies, or ordinary people battling some external enemy, creating a polarized struggle between good and evil. But on another level, an inner or emotional dimension, they are in a polarized relationship with one another, usually turning on a sharp contrast in their lifestyles, philosophies, or background. They may want the same overall, external goal, but they go about it in wildly contrasting ways, generating conflict, drama, suspense, and humor through polarity. Examples include *Trading Places,* the *Lethal Weapon* series, *Zoolander*, the *Rush Hour* movies, etc.

These stories became formulaic in the 1980s and '90s, where I read a lot of them that studios like Disney and Fox were considering. However predictable they became, they were a fascinating laboratory for studying the myriad ways that writers deal with the kind of story they call a "two-hander," one that has two protagonists or heroes but in a polarized, antagonistic relationship with another.

The first written story we know of, the epic of Gilgamesh, is the prototype for all polarized buddy adventures to follow. A playboy king, Gilgamesh, is so out of control that his people pray to the gods to send someone to distract him. They send him a real challenge in the form of a huge wild man of the forest, Enkidu. They battle at first, become good friends, battle monsters together, and fully explore the polarity of two different kinds of manhood. The adventure takes a tragic and more noble turn at the death of Enkidu, which sends Gilgamesh on a spiritual quest for the elusive secret of immortality.

A polarized relationship, be it a friendship, partnership, alliance, or romance, allows for a full exploration of character as the two people, representing opposite ends of a spectrum of behavior, find their standards and habits intensely challenged by energy that is just the opposite of theirs, perhaps outgoing where theirs is shy and private, or highly organized where their lives are chaotic. Here is a partial list of possible polarities within a relationship. Entire stories could be built around each of these pairs of opposites. I'm sure you can think of many more.

Sloppy	*vs.*	neat
Brave	*vs.*	cowardly
Feminine	*vs.*	masculine
Open	*vs.*	closed
Suspicious	*vs.*	trusting
Optimistic	*vs.*	pessimistic
Planned	*vs.*	spontaneous
Passive	*vs.*	active
Low-key	*vs.*	dramatic
Talkative	*vs.*	taciturn
Living in the past	*vs.*	forward-looking
Conservative	*vs.*	liberal
Underhanded	*vs.*	principled
Honest	*vs.*	dishonest
Literal	*vs.*	poetic
Clumsy	*vs.*	graceful
Lucky	*vs.*	unlucky
Calculated	*vs.*	intuitive
Introvert	*vs.*	extrovert
Happy	*vs.*	sad
Materialistic	*vs.*	spiritual
Polite	*vs.*	rude
Controlling	*vs.*	impulsive
Sacred	*vs.*	profane
Nature	*vs.*	nurture

THE DOCTRINE OF CHANGE

A polarized relationship of opposites may temporarily reach a state of equilibrium or balance, but most polarized systems don't stay balanced for very long. Energy is always flowing, creating change. One side of the polarity exerts force on the other. When a situation is extremely polarized, when the two sides have been driven out to their most extreme positions, there is a tendency for the polarity to reverse itself. According to the ancient Chinese philosophy of the I Ching, the doctrine of changes, things are always in the process of flowing into their opposites. Extreme idealists can turn into cynics, passionate lovers into cold-hearted haters. Abject cowards have the sleeping potential to become heroes, and many saints began as great sinners. This eternally changing feature of reality is described by the Taoist symbol of Yin and Yang, the two comma shapes flowing into one another, each with the seed of its opposite deep in its center.

The more polarized a system is, the more likely it is to reverse its polarity. This can happen little by little, in graduated stages, or it can come about catastrophically and all at once. Under the stimulus of conflict with a polarized opposite, a character will begin to oscillate, to swing like a pendulum, further away from the opposite at times, closer at other times. If the stimulus is continued to a certain tipping point, the character may flip polarity, and become temporarily aligned with the opposite pole.

The shy person, impacted repeatedly by an outgoing person, will retreat and advance, but if the stimulus continues, he or she will make a comical or dramatic reversal to experiment with the unfamiliar experience of being confident and highly social. Movies like *The Nutty Professor* or *As Good as It Gets* use this technique to explore the extremes of behavior and show us characters gradually and then drastically reversing their polarity.

The reversal may be almost imperceptible at first, trickling bit by bit like grains of sand in an hourglass. For example, in the classic screwball comedy *Topper,* a man who has been rigid, disciplined, and meek his entire life enters into a polarized relationship with two playful ghosts, the Kirbys, who are loose, free, and rebellious. At first Cosmo Topper is driven to even greater rigidity to counteract the wild energy of the Kirbys. But this extreme position is unnatural and inherently unstable. Under continued challenge from the Kirbys, Topper experiments tentatively with the free, loose behavior of his polar opposites, then retreats to comfortable rigidity, repeating the process several times until reaching a tipping point where he can no longer resist, and gives himself over completely to their madcap strategy for living, totally reversing his polarity. In the end, he reverts to something like his old, meek behavior, but now has access to his freer side and is happier for it.

Sometimes, however, the reversal of polarity happens early in the story and all at once, in a catastrophic collapse of the effort to maintain an extreme, polarized position. In *Fargo,* William Macy's character topples a lifetime of following the rules by reversing polarity to become the planner of a kidnapping that goes disastrously awry. *Liar, Liar* shows us a man who has lied to everyone and kidded himself his entire life suddenly forced to tell the truth in all circumstances thanks to the powerful birthday wish of his sincere and honest son. In both cases we see the characters torn between their old polar positions and catastrophic new conditions that place them abruptly at the opposite end of the spectrum.

9. THE OTHER END OF THE SPECTRUM

When a character goes through a reversal of polarity, what happens to his or her partner in the polarized relationship? Some of these partners exist only to catalyze change in a main character, and will not change much themselves. The Kirbys in *Topper* aren't going to suddenly turn into spineless weaklings like Cosmo Topper had been. But they may shift their point of view a little, realizing they've been too hard on him or that their meddling has caused him problems that they have to solve. When a character reverses polarity, the laws of polarity suggest that there be some reciprocal movement from the character or force at the opposite pole.

When Character A makes a seismic polarity shift, Character Z at the other end of the spectrum in the relationship may also take a little vacation from his or her comfort zone, or may be driven to a complete reversal himself. It can become uncomfortably crowded at one pole if both people in the relationship are suddenly expressing the same kind of energy.

If Character Z has been habitually lazy, and has come to depend on a habitually energetic Character A to do all the work, it can be alarming when the energetic A suddenly decides to experiment with laziness. No one is left to do the work. and Z, who is lazy by nature, may be forced into the unfamiliar role of the worker, with potentially comic results. In movies like *Trading Places,* characters get to walk in each other's shoes, experiencing unfamiliar worlds, undergoing temporary reversals, and experimenting with unfamiliar behavior. *Analyze This* is built around two characters reversing polarity in opposite directions, as Robert De Niro's gangster character discovers his softer side and the habitually soft psychiatrist played by Billy Crystal is forced to act like a tough guy to survive.

10. GOING TO EXTREMES

Experimenting with any polarized system involves going to the extremes. Comedy or tragedy may result as people who have habitually leaned to one side of a polarity not only experiment with the unaccustomed opposite quality, but take it to the limit. Those who have been shy take new-found confidence too far, becoming obnoxious instead of suave or self-assured. They overcompensate, missing the point of balance. They may then retreat to the opposite extreme of sullenness or some other exaggerated form of their original behavior. Eventually, through a series of such pendulum swings they may learn a new way to behave, somewhere in the middle ground.

Learning how to handle any quality is a process of finding the boundaries by experimentation. In many polarized relationships, one person is more experienced and has already made a fool of himself in long-ago experiments, so now he knows precisely how to handle women, cards, guns, cars, or money. To the inexperienced person it's all new, so we get to watch him or her making the beginner's hilarious mistakes.

Often there is a reciprocal area where the experienced person is weak, and is forced to make a comical effort to master the unaccustomed quality, such as politeness, sincerity, or compassion. However, the more experienced person will likely not have as far to travel in his or her path of learning as the inexperienced person.

11. REVERSAL OF THE REVERSAL

In effect the characters are learning from each other, shocked into it by contact with someone who is a polar opposite in one or more dimensions of behavior. They reverse polarity in order to experiment with behavior that is outside of their normal comfort zone. However, rarely is this the end of the story. There is usually at least one more reversal, as the characters recover from the temporary insanity imposed by the story and return to their true natures. It is a very strong rule in drama, and in life, that people remain true to their basic natures. They change, and their change is essential for drama, but typically they only change a little, taking a single step towards integrating a forgotten or rejected quality into their natures.

Having learned something useful by their first reversal, they may retreat to the pole that represents their true nature, but they end up in a little different place from where they started. This is realistic character change, an incremental movement rather than a total 180-degree reversal. Complete and permanent reversals of polarity are rare in stories and in life.

If a story has done its work, the character has experimented with something unfamiliar, realized that some special quality was lacking, and incorporated some aspect of that quality into his or her life. He or she returns to their general comfort zone, but to a more nearly balanced position nearer the center, not polarized to either extreme.

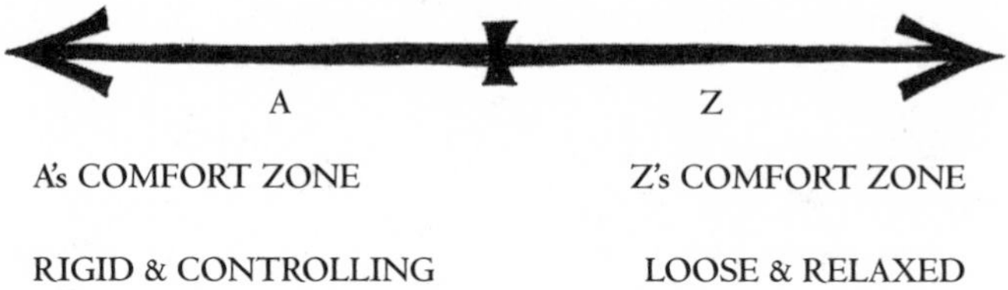

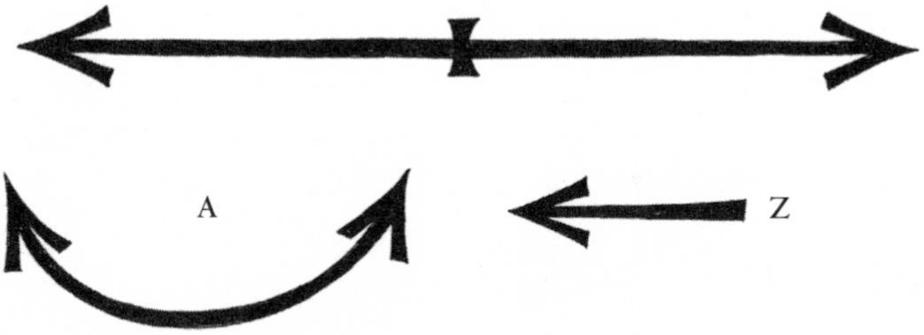

UNDER PRESSURE FROM Z, A BEGINS TO OSCILLATE, EXPERIMENTING WITH EXTREMES OF BEHAVIOR.

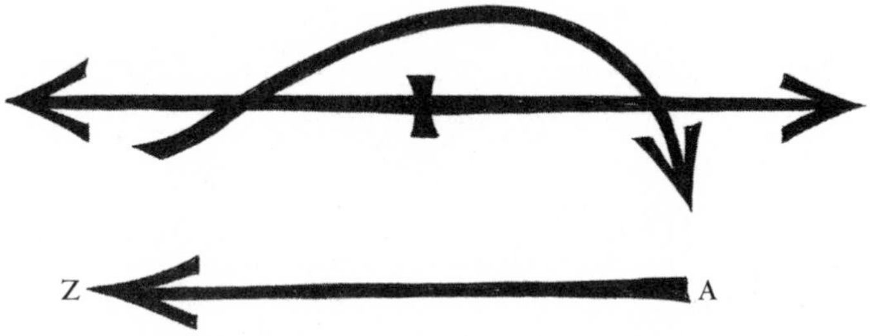

A EXPERIENCES TEMPORARY REVERSAL OF POLARITY, PUSHING Z TOWARDS OPPOSITE POLE.

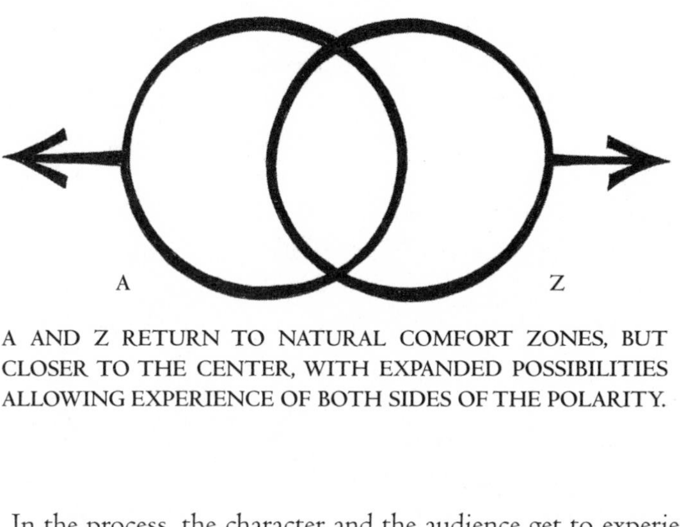

A AND Z RETURN TO NATURAL COMFORT ZONES, BUT CLOSER TO THE CENTER, WITH EXPANDED POSSIBILITIES ALLOWING EXPERIENCE OF BOTH SIDES OF THE POLARITY.

In the process, the character and the audience get to experience all points along the spectrum, both the extremes and a range of positions in between. In most cases it's not desirable or realistic to end up exactly in the middle of the two positions. Most stories end with the characters back more or less on the side of the polarity where they started, but several steps closer to the center and the opposite side. The characters' range of possible behavior now avoids the extreme positions and overlaps a little into the territory of the opposite side, producing a more balanced personality that leaves room for the formerly unexpressed quality. This is a good place to end up, because from this position the character can retreat to his or her old comfort zone if threatened, but still reach across to experience something of the opposite side.

In the Chinese system known as the Book of Changes, this is considered a more stable state, more desirable than extreme polarization. In a throw of three coins, two heads and a tail or two tails and a head symbolizes a stable, more balanced and realistic situation, whereas a throw of three heads or three tails represents a situation that is too polarized, too much of one thing, and must certainly collapse or reverse polarity soon, becoming its opposite.

Any character who begins at an extreme or is driven to it is ripe for a process of polarity reversal.

12. POLARITY SEEKS RESOLUTION

Sometimes the two big ideas or life-ways that have been polarized throughout a story will seek resolution by converting into something else, a third way that resolves the contradiction between the two elements.

The classic Western *Red River* shows two ways of living sharply polarized in the form of the older and younger men played by John Wayne (Tom Dunson) and Montgomery Clift (Matthew Garth). Dunson is brave but bull-headed, masculinity taken to its most macho extreme, while Garth's softer style is radically different, merciful where Dunson is ruthless. It is an almost Biblical polarity, like the difference between the wrathful, jealous Old Testament God and the gentle, compassionate Son of God depicted in the New Testament. Their struggle turns deadly, with Dunson swearing he will hunt down and kill Garth, who has been like a son to him. They fight at the climax and it looks like the polarity can only be resolved by the death of one party or the other, but this tragic fate is avoided by the intervention of pure female energy. The young woman played by Joanne Dru (Tess Millay) breaks up the fight with a gunshot and reminds the men that "anyone can see you two love each other." The men realize she's right and stop fighting. Dunson declares he'll change his cattle brand to reflect his acceptance of Garth, and the polarity is resolved. The two opposing styles of living are resolved into a third way, one that balances Dunson's extreme masculinity with feminine emotion and compassion. It makes dramatic sense, for it was Dunson's rejection of the feminine side in the early part of the film that set the whole plot in motion, when Dunson refused to take his lady love along with him on his journey to Texas.

We could say the protagonist's point of view or style of living is the thesis of the story. The anti-thesis is the antagonist's opposing viewpoint and style. The synthesis is whatever resolves the polarized conflict at the end. It may be a restatement of the protagonist's wishes or world-view, incorporating new learning or strength gained from the clash with the antagonist. It may be a radical new approach to life that the hero finds, or it may be a return to the hero's original position, but even then it will always be shifted a little by the polarized struggle the hero has been through. Typically heroes learn something from their polar opposites and incorporate this into their new pattern of behavior.

The resolution of some polarized stories could be the realization that the polarization itself was false, based on a misunderstanding, or that it was totally unnecessary if the seemingly opposed parties had simply communicated better in the beginning. Polarized romantic comedies can be built entirely around misunderstandings to show the difficulty of male-female communication, but might end with the lovers realizing they had been saying the same thing all along.

13. POLARIZED UNIVERSES

Polarity is a meta-pattern, a system that operates at all levels in stories, from large-scale clashes of cultures to intimate human relationships, all the way down to polarities within individuals. On the big scale a story can show a polarized clash between two cultures, generations, world-views, or philosophies of life. Ancient myths were polarized by eternal struggles between gods and giants or between primordial elements like fire and ice. Most Westerns put the hero into a town or a situation that is sharply polarized between pairs of opposing forces: Indians vs. the cavalry, cattle barons vs. immigrant farmers, ex-Confederates vs. ex-Yankees, etc. Film noir and the genre of "cops-and-robbers" split the world into polarized levels, the sun-lit upper world of law-abiding society and the shadowed Underworld of the criminals. The movie *Titanic* is polarized between the worlds of upper and lower decks, representing the classes of society and the conflict between desire for control and desire for freedom. The *Terminator* and *Matrix* movies are polarized between humans and machines, the *Star Wars* movies between dark and light sides of the Force. *Platoon* is polarized by a young soldier's choice between brutal and humane ways of going through a war, represented by two older men with contrasting approaches to survival.

14. INNER POLARITY

A story can be built around the polarities that sometimes exist within a person, as explored in stories and movies like *Dr. Jekyll and Mr. Hyde* and *Fight Club*. *Psycho* shows us a man who has internalized the feminine side of his dead mother, and half the time speaks in her voice. Stories like these externalize and make visible the usually unseen dualities of personality.

There is no better dramatization of a polarized inner struggle than the chilling scene in *The Lord of the Rings: The Two Towers,* where Gollum alternates between the good and evil sides of his own personality. The good side is what remains of his original identity as an innocent hobbit, Smeagol, and it resists temptation heroically, remembering the kindness and humanity shown by his master, Frodo. But eventually the wheedling, crafty, evil side that has degenerated into Gollum triumphs with fierce hate and jealousy, reversing the power balance within the character. The polarity of the character had been aligned towards hope for Gollum's salvation; now it is aligned to the certainty that he will betray the hobbits in his greed to have the Ring. Polarity was used here to show an inner struggle in a divided self.

15. AGON

Around the globe, people have imagined the creation of the world as a polarized situation. God divides light from darkness and the heavens from the earth. Primordial gods wrestled monsters of chaos in the earliest stories of creation, and the earliest dramas were religious rituals re-enacting these polarized struggles. In the ancient world, where abstract qualities such as luck, love, war, and victory were personified, humanized, and worshipped as gods, the potent force of polarity was recognized in the person of the Greek god Agon, the force of struggle and conflict, ruling over athletic events and contests of all kinds, even legal disputes, for agon also means a judgment. In an athletic event or a courtroom, a judgment is being made about who is the best or who is right.

Agon was pictured as a young athlete carrying a pair of jumping weights called "halteres" in his hands. The weights gave the jumper an extra boost on long jumps and may have been a symbol of some quality associated with Agon, perhaps an extra edge he gave to the athlete who prayed and offered sacrifice to him. There was an altar of sacrifice dedicated to Agon at

Olympia, where the Olympic games were held. Not much is known about Agon or his "backstory" but he may have been part of a family of Zeus's children who were responsible for other qualities that had roles to play in the lives of athletes, such as speed, victory, competitive spirit, and even chaos.

The spirit of Agon is imbedded in the polarized terms "protagonist" and "antagonist". We cheer for the protagonist in the struggle or contest, and we wish for the defeat of the antagonist.

The English word "agony" derives from agon and signifies that the process of struggle is sometimes painful and arduous. The word is sometimes used as one pole of a polarized expression, as in the title *The Agony and the Ecstasy* or the phrase from TV coverage of the Olympic Games, "the thrill of victory, the agony of defeat." These phrases describe the dramatic emotional extremes that a polarized agon can generate. To antagonize someone is to create an agon or conflict with that person where none existed before.

AGON: THE ARGUMENT OF THE PLAY

In ancient Greek drama, the "agon" was a formal debate between two characters in which their contrasting views of a current public issue were presented, judged by a chorus. We could still find use for the word to describe the main philosophical debate or clash of lifestyles in a play, novel, or film script. Movies like *Wall Street* and *A Few Good Men* and TV shows like *The West Wing* dramatize an agon, a kind of debate about a current social issue.

MODERN-DAY PUBLIC *AGON*

An "agon" among the Greeks and Romans also meant a formal competition to determine who was best at a given skill such as singing, composing plays or music, delivering speeches, etc. As in our modern star system of awards, prizes were given for the best performances of the year. These "agonic" competitions were organized like our sports leagues, with local and regional competitions leading to a national contest held at a great yearly festival in the capital. We still have a strong need to arrange this kind of agon each year to determine which team or performer is the best in the region, the country, and the world. Each stage of our athletic system pits pairs of teams and individuals against each other, recreating the polarized agon time after time until there are only two teams or people left for the final contest. Agon thrives in the eternally popular game shows and competitive "reality" programs of the day.

THE PERSONAL *AGON*

At the personal level, an agon was any challenge that pitted one side of a person's makeup against another. For example, the mind is always trying to master the lazy tendencies of the body. The struggle of the artist with her work is an agon, pitting her will to bring creativity into form against all the forces that make it difficult. Or the agon can be a person's struggle with some external condition that makes life challenging, such as a birth defect, an accident, or an injustice.

All the entertainment of the ancient world was based on the polarizing principle of the agon, and it seems to have an almost magnetic affect on us even today, in our sports, in politics, and in entertainment.

16. Polarity Gives Orientation

Magnets are widely used for purposes of orientation. A magnetic compass automatically orientates itself to point north, and from this we can determine south, east, west and all points in between. Polarity in a story serves a similar function, giving the audience orientation about the characters and situation, from the simplest level of white hats and black hats to represent good guys and bad guys, to the most sophisticated psychological dramas. Polarity lets us know who has the power and suggests how it might shift. It signals us who we are to be aligned with in the story and helps us understand how all the characters and situations are aligned with one force or the other.

Most of the time, you have to play fair with the audience and not make it difficult for them to get their bearings in a story. A polarized town, family, or society, a polarized agon between contrasting opponents, a polarized personality about to reverse itself, all these can help the audience determine what is up and down, right and wrong, in this story. They can quickly align themselves for or against characters depending on their choices about the polarized condition in the story. The writer can then start sending positive or negative energy into the scenes, bringing temporary victory or defeat to the characters until the final resolution.

Of course, some stories deal precisely with the grey areas, the kinds of characters and situations that are remarkable and interesting because they aren't obviously polarized. Some artists don't want to take sides or push their characters into simplistic categories. There is room for this artistic approach, but polarities will still naturally arise simply from having two characters in the same room at the same time.

CONCLUSION

As noted, polarities are useful tools in stories and are a practical way of organizing reality, but they can be misused to oversimplify situations that may actually be quite complex. Audiences are sophisticated these days and while they enjoy stories that are strongly polarized, they enjoy them more when they are also nuanced with small shadings and contradictions that make stories and characters seem realistic, even when dealing in worlds of pure fantasy. Like any technique, polarization in a story can be heavy-handed and too obvious. Polarization without shading or the possibility of change would quickly become boring, just two people shouting at each other. The fun is in seeing a tiny seed of the opposite quality coming to life in a polarized character or situation. It may only come to life for an instant, showing the possibility of reversal but then snatching it away forever, or it may work its way slowly until the character or situation reverses polarity dramatically.

Polarities in politics, sports, war, or relationships can divide us, but they also have the possibility of uniting us when we have been through a struggle together. An old soldier may have more in common with his former enemies than he does with his grandchildren. Polarized family feuds will sometimes dissolve when after many years neither party can remember what all the fighting was about.

Polarities in stories form a conceptual framework with which to organize ideas and energy, building up positive and negative charges around selected characters, words, and concepts. They may serve a survival function for us in dramatizing useful distinctions about behavior, and in identifying patterns in human relationships. They serve an essential dramatic function by stirring us up, triggering emotional involvement and physical reactions in the organs of our bodies. Words on a page, actors on a stage, images on a screen can pull us this way and that until we have a small but potentially significant emotional release, for when we laugh at the characters in a funny movie, we are laughing in part at ourselves. When we cry over the fate of the characters in a tragedy or a romance, we cry in part for ourselves. When we shudder in terror at the latest horror film or novel, we shudder for ourselves. We sense our part in the great polarities, spirit and matter, male and female, life and death, good and evil, and we find healthy release in stories that explore their workings.

QUESTIONS

1. "To be or not to be, that is the question." Shakespeare uses many dualities and polarities in his plays and sonnets, using twins, pairs of lovers, and contrasting ideas such as the relationship of Prince Hal and Sir John Falstaff in *Henry IV* parts one and two, where they are flip sides of the same coin of knighthood, Prince Hal representing honor and Sir John dishonor. Read a Shakespeare play and see how many polarities you can find in it. What is the effect of these polarities on the reader or audience?

2. Review a movie such as *Pulp Fiction* or *The Fellowship of the Ring* from the *Lord of the Rings* trilogy. How many dualities and polarized relationships can you detect? Do they add to the dramatic experience or are they just repetitious?

3. Compile your own list of polarities. Pick one at random and see if you can generate characters and a story from it.

4. "Agon" means contest or struggle but also can be a central challenge in someone's life, perhaps something temporary that comes up, or it could the one great thing he or she must wrestle with throughout life. What is the agon in your life, at the moment and over the long run? What is the agon of your character?

5. Agon can also be used to describe the central debate or issue of a drama. In this sense, what is the agon or main argument of your play, movie script, computer game, short story, or novel? What qualities are being contrasted, and what are the arguments for each side?

6. Here is the list of pairs of polarized opposites from this chapter. Can you think of a movie or story that uses each polarity as a plot device?

Sloppy	*vs.*	neat
Brave	*vs.*	cowardly
Feminine	*vs.*	masculine
Open	*vs.*	closed
Suspicious	*vs.*	trusting
Optimistic	*vs.*	pessimistic
Planned	*vs.*	spontaneous
Passive	*vs.*	active
Low-key	*vs.*	dramatic
Living in the past	*vs.*	forward-looking
Conservative	*vs.*	liberal
Underhanded	*vs.*	principled
Honest	*vs.*	dishonest
Literal	*vs.*	poetic
Clumsy	*vs.*	graceful
Lucky	*vs.*	unlucky
Calculated	*vs.*	intuitive
Introvert	*vs.*	extrovert
Happy	*vs.*	sad
Materialistic	*vs.*	spiritual
Polite	*vs.*	rude
Controlling	*vs.*	impulsive
Sacred	*vs.*	profane
Nature	*vs.*	nurture

7. What are the polarities in your family? If your town was the location of a Western, how would a stranger riding into town find it polarized? How does polarity operate at the national level?

8. Have you ever experienced a reversal of polarity in your own life or in someone around you? Describe this and how it made you feel.

9. How do polarities work in a half-hour TV show? Watch an episode of a show and identify the polarities and moments of reversal.

10. Look at two of your favorite teams or athletes competing for a championship. What are their contrasting qualities, their strengths and weaknesses? How does the winner exploit these polarities?

CATHARSIS

CATHARSIS

"We're going to stimulate some action,
We're gonna get some satisfaction.
We're gonna find out what it is all about,
After midnight, we're gonna let it all hang out."
— J. J. Cale, "After Midnight"

Several times in this book we have used the word catharsis, referring to a concept found in the works of Aristotle, one of his terms that has survived to become part of the general theory of drama and narrative. It is a critical concept, the point of drama according to Aristotle, and its roots go back to the beginnings of language, art, and ritual.

We have little chance of ever knowing for sure what Aristotle meant by catharsis. His work has come down to us in shreds. Less than half of what he wrote survives and most of that comes from rotted, jumbled manuscripts found under a building. Scholars disagree vigorously about what Aristotle meant by catharsis and there is even a theory that the word was inserted into the *Poetics* by an over-eager copyist at a place where the text was garbled, because Aristotle had promised in an earlier book that he would eventually get around to defining catharsis.

Whatever it meant to Aristotle, the word has come to mean something to us: a sudden release of emotions that can be brought about by good entertainment, great art, or probing for psychological insight. Its roots are deep in our spirits and in the history of our species. If we look back a little into the origins of drama, we might find that catharsis has always been a desired effect and in fact is the mainspring of the dramatic experience.

To find the origins of drama, narrative, art, religion, and philosophy we have to cast our minds back to the time when human beings were in their earliest stages of development. Through a few miracles of preservation, we have windows into the soul of those times, through the marvelous cave paintings and sculptures that have survived from as early as forty thousand years ago. We know from these breathtaking, life-like rendering of animals and hunters that the people of those times made pilgrimages deep into the belly of the earth, and must have performed some rituals in which they played the parts of the animals they hunted or the forces of nature that they perceived around them. Through these rituals, the beginnings of storytelling and drama, they must have tried to master or appease these powers. Joseph Campbell recognized one figure from the cave paintings with his antlered costume as a shaman, a go-between, embodying the spirit of the animals his people depended on for life.

A physical catharsis or emotional reaction is hard to avoid when going into a deep cave, even today. If you go as they went, long ago, with only fitful candles to light your way down the narrow tunnels, you can't help but feel the weight of the earth and imagine the forces and beings that might be lurking there in the endless darkness just outside the glow of your flame. There is still a sense of wonder when coming out into a big cavern deep in the earth, especially when its walls are painted with huge animals that seem to leap across the ceiling in the flickering candle light. It would be a perfect stage to initiate young people into the mysteries of the tribe, its deepest beliefs, the essence of its compact with nature.

I can testify to the still-impressive power of a candle in a dark place to animate things. It is the cheapest but most effective of special effects. I was visiting Hamlet's castle at Elsinore, or Helsingør as the Danes call it, on a tip of Denmark, facing Sweden across a short expanse of water. In the frigid crypts of the castle is kept a brooding statue of Denmark's version of King Arthur or El Cid, shown as a rugged Viking sitting on his throne with a drawn sword across his knees. He is Holger Danske, Ogier the Dane, one of Charlemagne's paladins and Denmark's legendary protector in time of need. Troops of Danish schoolchildren and tourists are marched past the statue to stand shivering before it, marveling at the illusion of life, for at the feet of the statue is a candle, or rather these days an electric imitation of a candle, a small flickering light. In the otherwise darkened crypt, so like a cave, the erratic light casts a nervous glow over the statue's features, and shadows dance and shift on the chamber walls. In an eerie way that makes the hair stand up on your arms and the back of your neck, the stone image seems to your eyes and your Stone Age nervous system to be distinctly alive. You could swear the Viking chieftain is asleep but breathing, about to wake up and surge off his pedestal at any moment. It makes a convincing theatrical illusion that the country's eternal fighting spirit is slumbering but ready to return to action when needed. No doubt the ancient people felt the same awe as flickering torches and oil lamps made the giant horses and bison gallop across the cave walls.

A feature of some commercial cave tours in the modern world is to turn off the electric lights at some point so the visitors can get a sense of the pure blackness of the lightless cave. Perhaps our ancestors used a similar dramatic technique in their cave rituals, putting out the oil lamps and torches so the young initiates could experience the deep dark. For some it would be terrifying, for others, soul-expanding, and some might be visited with visions that made them feel connected to the animals or the powers that made the world. Perhaps the paintings are memorials of those visions, amended and painted over by successive generations of initiates.

Emerging from a cave is another hazardous passage, climaxed with the feeling of relief upon emerging into sunlight and open space once again. For some there is a feeling of transformation, of having died in some sense down there, or having come very close to death and other eternal forces, and now coming to new life on the surface.

Ancient people undoubtedly had other places that served a similar function of enhancing dramatic experiences and evoking a religious feeling, such as intimate groves of trees, natural amphitheatres, isolated mountain tops like Mt. Olympus, sacred wells and fountains, or arrangements of monumental stones. Trees could be planted in rows or in circles to create spaces that enhanced a group feeling of awe and connection with greater forces. In those spaces rituals were performed that tried to link the world of people to the world of the gods. People played the parts of gods, heroes, and monsters to enact the drama of creation and the stories of the ancestors. The first plays may have been the texts of these rituals, recited at first by a chorus but with actors gradually taking the parts of individual characters.

As humans made the transition from nomadic hunting to the settled life of farmers in societies like those of Egypt, Mesopotamia, and the Indus Valley, drama found different theatres of expression and dramatic forms, with a new emphasis on time and the vast calendar of the stars.

On the fertile, muddy plains on the banks of great rivers, people built civilizations that needed dramatic rituals to bring order, unity, and a shared sense of purpose to a large population. By communal effort they fashioned river mud into bricks and built huge temple mounds that were like artificial mountains, connecting their society to the heavens and providing a stairway to the world of the gods.

These temple pyramids or ziggurats also served as spectacular backdrops for highly theatrical presentations designed to evoke a healthy religious feeling in a whole population.

These religious spectacles were staged with exquisite precision to a calendar set by a giant celestial clock, the movement of the sun, moon, and stars across the sky. Lives were short but people accumulated thousands of years of observations that could be passed down by various forms of notation. They paid particularly close attention to the exact turning points of the year, the spring and fall equinoxes and the summer and winter solstices, the four points marking the change of season. The great festivals of the year were held at these times, with a greater festival marking the beginning of the New Year.

Their interest in the cycles of time was practical, a life and death matter. A delay of as little as a few days in planting or harvesting could mean that a crop would fail and there would be nothing to eat through the winter, dooming most to die. Even in earlier times the hunters knew that the movements of the animals and the fruiting of the trees follow the celestial calendar.

The dramatic meat of these seasonal turning point festivals was the staging of an elaborate adventure, in which the king or the statues of the gods "disappeared," supposedly having been kidnapped, stolen away, or killed and dismembered by dark forces of chaos. The whole society pretended to mourn them, giving up the pleasures of life for a period of time in sympathy with the kidnapped or dead gods or king.

In some versions of seasonal festivals in ancient Babylon, the statues of the gods were actually removed from the temples and buried in the desert or destroyed. Later in the festival they would be returned to their rightful positions or replaced with new ones, triggering great relief and celebration by the people.

Sir James Frazer in *The Golden Bough* persuasively makes the case that many societies pass through an early stage where the office of king is a temporary job, held only for a set period of time, perhaps just one year. In the most primal of these societies the old king is either executed or must fight a ritual combat with the new candidate. The sacrificial death of the old king cleans the slate and pays for the mistakes of the past year. Gradually, popular or very powerful kings managed to extend their rule but the tradition of sacrificing the old king ran very deep and was often represented symbolically in the customs, traditions, and ritual pageants of the mound-building cultures. The literal sacrifice of the king and his replacement with a successor was replaced by a mythological death and rebirth, like that of Osiris. The king was identified with the god who had died and come back to life again, and acted out his death, dismemberment, and rebirth in dramatic rituals rather than by actually dying.

The scholar Theodore Gaster described four types of ritual in the ancient world of the Near East that followed one another in a seasonal sequence of Mortification, Purgation, Invigoration, and Jubilation, all related to the death and rebirth of the god or king. Sometimes all four elements could be combined in an elaborate ritual drama that involved all the members of society as actors in the play, whose stage was the whole city, and whose subject was the death and rebirth of the god-king. Gaster says ancient ritual drama was of two types, rituals of *kenosis* or emptying, and rituals of *plerosis* or filling. Mortification and Purgation emptied the body and mind, cleansing and purifying them while giving a taste of death, and Invigoration and Jubilation rituals filled and satisfied the people while re-invoking the principle of life.

Performing these rituals at the seasonal turning points was a symbolic but also practical way of allowing the whole society to cool down after a strenuous season of work. As we now grant ourselves frequent holidays to punctuate the year and break our work into manageable, bearable spans of time, so did our ancestors sensibly stop the drumbeat of the work routine from time to time, but very consciously and purposefully.

In the Mortification and Purgation phases they shut down as many of life's systems as possible, using mourning for the absent gods or king as a pretext to give a rest to all commerce, labor, lawsuits, etc. Shops, warehouses, and factories were closed. The hearth fires that burned in every home were put out, and the great fire that burned eternally in the temple was extinguished too. Even the processes of the body were shut down, and people fasted, stopped talking, and gave up life's pleasures to become more quiet and contemplative for a few hours. It was considered a time out, time outside of time, a grinding down of the giant clock, and in some calendars the festival days were not given numbers or names, signifying that this was sacred turning point time, not subject to the ordinary daily rhythms.

Mortification meant bringing the body near the point of death by fasting, but also denying oneself any of the little pleasures of the body. They believed the body needed to be humbled or mortified from time to time, so it knows the mind is the master. The absence of things that were normally taken for granted created a renewed appreciation for them. It also focused the minds of the people and reminded them of the possibility of death that was always near.

Lamentation was an important part of the ritual at this point. People were supposed to meditate sympathetically on the death of the hero-god-king until the tears ran down their faces. Special songs were composed with the aim of triggering the emotions of grief and sorrow. The dramatic form of tragedy was developed from the rituals, chants, and dances of mourning that tried to evoke sympathy for the suffering god or king. Tragedy comes from the word "tragos" or goat, because goats were often used as sacrificial stand-ins for the yearly sacrifice of the king.

The Purgation phase of seasonal rituals was marked by cleansing the body and the environment as much as possible. People would bathe and anoint themselves with oil to symbolize the shedding of an old skin from the previous season. Houses and temples would be cleansed with water and fumigated. Bells and gongs would be rung to chase out unclean spirits. Fireworks have been used in China for centuries for this purpose.

Purgation was both metaphorical and literal in these ancient societies. Mentally and metaphorically, people were supposed to purge themselves of sour feelings, resentments, jealousies, and so on. But they were also supposed to cleanse the body of impurities by fasting and even by inducing vomiting.

Catharsis was a medical term in Aristotle's time for the natural processes by which the body eliminates poisons and wastes. It comes from the word "katharos" which means pure, so a catharsis is a purification, but it can also be a purgation, a vomiting up or violent expelling of impurities. Sneezing is a cathartic reaction to rid the nasal passages of impurities.

In the *Poetics,* Aristotle used the term "catharsis of the emotions" as a metaphor, comparing the emotional effect of a drama with the way the body rids itself of toxins and impurities. The Greeks and other ancient peoples knew that life is hard, involving many unpleasant compromises and the eating of much crow. Emotional impurities and poisons build up in the body just as physical ones do, and can have catastrophic effects if not purged at regular intervals. They believed that people who get no emotional release from art, music, sports, dance, or drama inevitably will be overcome by poisonous feelings that will surface as aggression, hostility, perversion, or madness, all things dangerous to the society. Therefore they institutionalized purging and purification of mind and body with seasonal festivals that artificially induced catharsis on a quarterly schedule. Drama was a sacred thing, not available for daily consumption, and confined only to the important turning points of the year.

The fasting and purging created a condition of extreme dramatic suggestibility in the population. It was then that the whole society gathered in the squares and streets of the city-state to witness a spectacular dramatization of some great event in the mythic history of the culture. The people were not a passive audience, but took an active part in the dramatic presentation. The city itself with its gates, processional avenues, and towering temples became the stage set for an enormous collective re-enactment of creation, a great battle between gods of order and chaos, or the death and rebirth of the god-king.

The Greeks adopted the general patterns of these seasonal dramatic rituals and made them part of their yearly calendar of religious festivals, built around the doings of gods like Apollo and Dionysos. The great Greek tragedies and comedies evolved slowly from ritual re-enactments and recitations of poems about the gods and heroes, and originally were conceived as religious ceremonies, sacramental acts designed to have a beneficial effect on the spirit. The magnificent outdoor theatres of ancient Greece were originally built as temples dedicated to the god Dionysos, one of the dying and rising gods. The plays enacted there were intended as the dramatic climax to vast religious pageants, and they were carefully designed to bring about the emotional effect that Aristotle called catharsis, a feeling of pity and fear evoked by watching the unfolding fate of a hero. The hero of a Greek tragedy was a stand-in for the old god-king, undergoing a sacrificial death on behalf of all the members of the society, and bringing about a catharsis in the members of the audience through sympathy with his or her sufferings.

In Athens, along with dramatic rituals honoring Apollo and Dionysos, seasonal festivals were organized around the myth of Demeter and Kore (Persephone), a primal mother and daughter who once ruled over an endless summer of abundance. Their story tells how the seasons began, and its festivals are timed to coincide with the seasonal rhythms of planting, tending, harvesting, and surviving the winter. Their drama's Call to Adventure was the kidnapping of Persephone by Hades, lord of the Underworld. The rituals re-enacted her kidnapping in October, at the Thesmophoria, three days of festivals exclusively for women. This was the emptying, introducing the time of Mortification and Purgation.

In the myth, Demeter's grief at the disappearance of her daughter brings about a terrible season in which the earth lies barren as the goddess of the harvest neglects her duties in order to mourn and search for her daughter. Demeter becomes the hero of an epic quest, playing many roles as she seeks out her daughter in the Underworld and induces the gods to make a deal with Hades to allow Persephone to return to the world of light and life, at least for part of the year.

Kore/Persephone's return was celebrated at festivals called the Lesser Eleusinia in February, marking the return of spring.

Every five years, the Greater Eleusinia, the greatest festival in the Greek calendar, was held in September. Some of the carvings from the pediment of the Parthenon depict these jubilant ceremonies, when the young horsemen of Athens would fetch the sacred objects from the temple of Demeter and march them to a special shrine, the Eleusinion, at the base of the Acropolis. The story of Demeter and Kore was acted out in secret ceremonies of great emotional impact for a select group of initiates, using all the effects of lighting, music, dance, ritual, and staging to bring about the desired catharsis.

Nowadays we may use the term catharsis more broadly to mean any kind of emotional release or breakthrough. Catharsis was adopted by the psychological community to describe a therapeutic process in which repressed thoughts, fears, emotions, or memories are deliberately brought to consciousness, triggering an emotional release or breakthrough that is supposed to relieve anxiety and relax tension. Movies and stories as well as art and music can have a role to play in triggering a psychologically healthy cathartic reaction.

THE CATHARSIS OF COMEDY

In the classical Greek system, it was recognized that balance is needed in a dramatic presentation or else it can be overwhelming and exhausting. They added comedies to the ritual line-up to relieve the emotional intensity of the tearful tragedies with some cathartic laughter for contrast.

Comedy belongs to the "plerosis" or filling up portion of the ritual cycle. Once emptying and purging have been fully experienced, it's time to fill up again with something healthy, tasty, and life-affirming that stimulates Invigoration and Jubilation.

The word comedy comes from "komos" which means "the revels," a wild party or orgy. Rituals of Invigoration in very ancient times involved a big feast in which eating, drinking, and all kinds of merriment were encouraged, to make a vivid contrast with the somber tone of the Mortification and Purgation rituals that preceded it. One aspect of comedy is the stirring up of sexual urges. Greek comedy often dealt with power struggles between men and women and celebrated sexuality with exaggerated costumes and situations. Freud considered that there was a strong linkage between laughter and sexuality, and of course sex is a natural catharsis that relieves tension.

The Greeks thought two or three heavy doses of tragedy would do a good job of mortifying and purging you, and a dose of comedy was just the right finish to a ritual cycle, sending you back into the next season of the year refreshed, psychologically cleansed and reborn, and cheerful. As they used to say in vaudeville, "Always leave 'em laughing."

RETURN OF THE LIGHT

A feature of the seasonal rituals in ancient times was the re-lighting of the sacred fire in a central temple, symbolic of the victory of life over death. The flame would then be passed from person to person, carrying home candles or small oil lamps from which the individual hearth fires could be re-lit to Invigorate the culture. The hearth fire would be used to cook a feast that was consumed as part of the Jubilation that concluded the seasonal cycle.

Some of these rituals survive in various ways around the world today. I witnessed one remnant at a Greek Orthodox Easter service in New York City. Part of the Lenten observations is to cover the beautiful painted statues and icons with purple cloths and put out the candles for a time, symbolically evoking grief and lamentation over Christ's suffering, death, and burial. Then, at a moment symbolizing the Resurrection, a large Paschal candle is lit in the darkened church. In the Greek Orthodox church in New York, the congregants had brought along small candles which they lit from the big one. At the end of the service they exited the church, but the ritual went on as the families walked home or got into their cars, carefully shielding the flames from the wind, preserving the light of the new season to kindle their own symbolic hearth fires in their homes, just as people used to do thousands of years ago. In similar ceremonies in Jerusalem, Greek pilgrims will even carry home the sacred flames on specially chartered airplanes.

When we deal in drama or narrative today, we are building on forty thousand years of tradition and experience. Humans have always sought orientation and emotional release through drama. Although our entertainment is more evenly distributed throughout the year, we still partake of some of the seasonal ritual effect. New shows on television are typically launched in September, time of the fall equinox. Going to movies with family at holiday times or watching particular holiday films like *It's a Wonderful Life* each year is an emotional tradition for many people. Certain kinds of movies seem to be associated with specific seasons. In general we like love stories and sport stories in the spring and summer, while more thoughtful dramas tend to be released in fall and winter. The winter solstice, roughly coinciding with the Christmas and New Year's holidays, is a good time to release big fantasy pictures, especially those that comprise trilogies that can be run over successive year-end holidays. Summer is the time for the blockbusters and action pictures.

THE POWER OF THE SEASONS

We are not so conscious of the seasons these days since we are somewhat insulated from their effects, and most of us no longer live by the rhythms of planting and harvesting. However, the seasons still have their power over us, affecting our lives and our moods in ways both obvious and subtle. The seasons of the year and seasonal holidays can be useful to the writer, providing natural turning points, a measure of the passage of time, and distinct emotional associations. The passage of a single season makes an effective time frame for a movie (*That Championship Season, Summer Catch*) or a story's four-movement structure could be built around the passage of the seasons (*The Four Seasons*). A change of seasons in a story can signify a change in the hero's fortunes or mood. A story could be built around a character who is disastrously out of synch with the rhythm of the seasons.

In your writing, remember that the purpose of everything you're doing is to bring about some kind of emotional reaction in your reader or viewer. It may not always be the full-blown explosive reaction of catharsis, but it should have its effect on the organs of the body, stimulating them through repeated blows of conflict and setback for your hero. You are always raising and lowering the tension, pumping energy into your story and characters until some kind of emotional release is inevitable, in the form of laughter, tears, shudders, or a warm glow of understanding. People still need catharsis, and a good story is one of the most reliable and entertaining ways of bringing it about.

QUESTIONS

1. What role do holidays and the seasons play in your life? What role in your stories? Do you associate the holidays with emotional catharsis? Do your characters?

2. What happens if you resist or ignore the rhythms of the seasons? What happens if you don't participate in the seasonal rituals of your culture?

3. How is the seasonal cycle of catharsis played out in the world of sports? Do we get more catharsis from playing athletic games or from watching them?

4. Why are competitive reality shows and talent contests so popular? What is the catharsis that they provide?

5. What is the effect of experiencing a dramatic catharsis in a group? How is watching a movie or play in a packed theatre different from reading a book, playing a computer game alone, or watching television at home? Which do you prefer, and why?

6. Has reading a book or watching a movie, play, or sporting event ever triggered a feeling like catharsis in you? Describe that experience and try to make the reader feel it too.

7. What was your most memorable holiday experience? Could that experience be material for a short story, a one-act play, or a short film script? Would a character in it experience a catharsis?

8. What role does fashion play in the seasonal cycle? Are we manipulated by the fashion industry or is it natural to wear different colors and fabrics for each season?

9. What seasonal rituals are still practiced in your community? Do any of them use dramatic effects to create catharsis? What feelings are stirred by these rituals?

10. Where are movies going in their search for situations that will trigger some kind of emotional or physical reaction? Is it harder to stimulate people today, and what will moviemakers and storytellers of the future use to bring about catharsis?

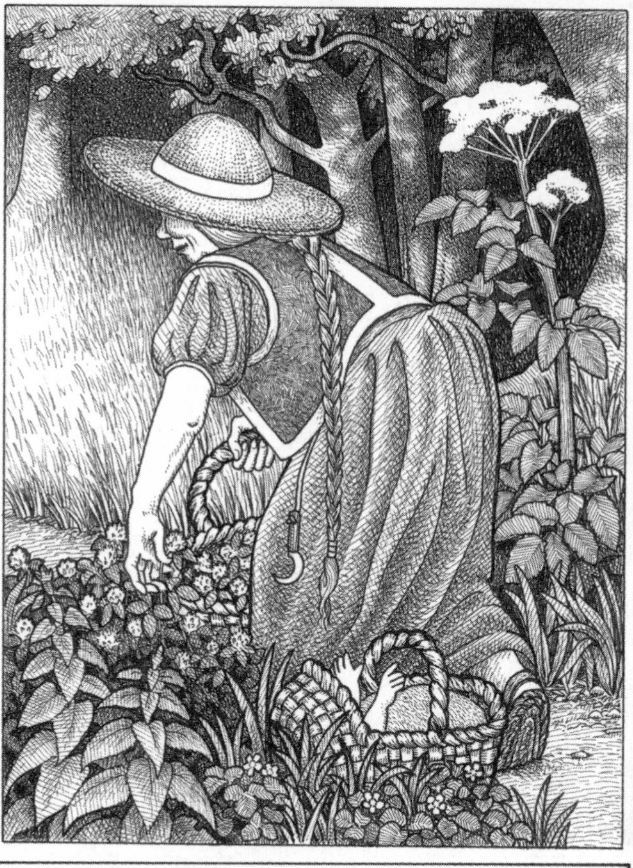

THE WISDOM OF THE BODY

THE WISDOM OF THE BODY

"There is more wisdom in your body than in your deepest philosophy."
— Friedrich Nietzsche

Although we use our minds to process and interpret stories, much is going on throughout the rest of the body as we interact with a narrative. We react to art and to stories about our fellow creatures with the organs of our body. In fact the whole body is involved, skin, nerves, blood, bones, and organs.

Joseph Campbell pointed out that the archetypes speak to us directly through the organs, as if we were programmed to respond chemically to certain symbolic stimuli. For example, big-eyed infants of any species trigger a reaction of sympathy and protectiveness, or cause us to say things like "How cute!" Puss-in-Boots from the *Shrek* movies knows how to exploit this deep emotional trigger by making his eyes huge when he wants sympathy. Emotions are complex processes, but on one level they are simple chemical reactions to stimuli in our environment, a fact that storytellers have always used to get their emotional effects.

Certain images or tableaux have an automatic emotional impact on us, felt in the organs of our bodies. A tableau is a figure or several figures in a setting, enacting some primal scene that either affects us intuitively, on an almost animal level, or that has become charged with emotion because of long tradition. The Last Supper, images of the Madonna and child, and the Pietà depicting Christ's mother cradling her dead son's body are all emotionally loaded religious tableaux. Similar images with equal force existed in earlier cultures, like the Egyptian goddess Hathor nursing her child or Isis tenderly assembling the scattered pieces of her dismembered husband Osiris. Images of beings in conflict, people in combat or gods and heroes wrestling with monsters, cause tension in our stomachs as we identify with one or another of the combatants. Images of protective or generous spirits (kindly grandmothers, angels, Santa Claus) give us a warm feeling of comfort. Representations of sympathetic characters in physical torment evoke a physical response, as in graphic medieval art depicting the Crucifixion and the martyrdoms of various saints like St. Sebastian who was shot full of arrows.

Classical Greek drama used startling visceral effects on stage, like Oedipus appearing with his eyes torn out, to elicit a strong reaction in the bodies of the beholders. The language of Greek plays could be bold and brutal, hammering at the audience with vivid word choices that suggested violent blows and the spilling of blood. Often a bloody act was committed off-stage, but described with stomach-wrenching detail, or the shocking evidence was displayed in the form of blood-soaked clothing or actors portraying corpses.

The Romans took this to extremes in their version of Greek theatre which became more degenerate and cruel as the Empire stumbled to its death. Symbolic or simulated acts of violence were replaced by real ones, with condemned criminals suffering the fate of the fictional characters, literally bleeding and dying on stage to amuse the Roman public. Gladiators stepped into plays to enact mythological combats and actually fought to the death in the theatres.

In the late 1700s, the puppet character of Guignol was imported from Lyons to Paris, where his brash, violent nature gave birth to a whole wave of plays known as Grand Guignol, whose object was to provide thrills of terror and shudders of horror with the realistic depiction of torture, beheadings, dismemberments, and other insults to the human body.

Observers of the first impact of moving pictures on the public remarked on the realism and physical power of the images on the screen, causing audiences to jump back when a train approached or flinch when a gun was pointed at them for the first time in *The Great Train Robbery*.

In the 1950s and '60s, Alfred Hitchcock was known for provoking physical reactions in his audiences, and he was a master organist, playing the viscera like a mighty Wurlitzer in tension-filled movies like *Psycho, The Birds,* and *Vertigo,* but he was not alone, for all good directors know instinctively how to use their tools to make us feel something, physically and emotionally. They employ everything in the toolbox — story, characters, editing, lighting, costumes, music, set design, action, special effects, and psychology — to bring about physical responses such as holding the breath in suspense, gasping in response to surprises, and exhaling in relaxation when the on-screen tension is released. In fact, the secret of drama may come down to control of the audience's breathing, for through the breath all the other organs of the body can be regulated.

In the 1970s the special effects–laden movies of Irwin Allen (*Poseidon Adventure, The Towering Inferno*) were heralded, and sometimes condemned, as a new wave of visceral entertainment, playing to the body rather than the mind. With the arrival of the modern special effects masters of the Spielberg and Lucas generation, movies were able to seduce the eye and the other organs of the body ever more convincingly.

Along the way there have been many experiments to enhance the physical effects of entertainment and drama, from the burning of incense at Greek rituals to modern technical marvels like 3D, IMAX, and mechanized seats that vibrate in time to on-screen machine-gun fire. In Roman theatres and stadia, the presence of gods could be suggested by sprays of perfumed vapor and showers of fragrant flower petals. In the 1950s experiments were done with 3D, "smell-o-vision," and "Percepto," an effect in theatres specially rigged for William Castle's unique effort, *The Tingler.* Seats were wired with buzzers that made them vibrate at supposedly shocking moments on screen, where a creature was depicted attaching itself to people's spines.

THE BODY AS A GUIDE TO CRITIQUING

It's not easy to critique your own writing work or that of others. It can be hard to articulate what's wrong, how the story made you feel, what was lacking. Sometimes the best way to measure a story's effect and diagnose its problems is to ask "How did it make me feel — in the organs of my body? Did I feel anything physical at all, or was I just having mental processes that didn't much involve anything but the brain? Did it make my blood run cold? Did it make my toes curl with horror or delight? Did it make my nervous system alert as if the dangers the hero faces were actually threatening me?" If not, there may be something missing, an appeal to the body, a physical threat, an emotional tension.

As a professional evaluator of stories I became keenly attuned to the emotional and physical effects a manuscript could have on me. I came to depend on the wisdom of the body to determine the quality of the story. If it was bad and boring, my body would grow leaden and the pages would weigh a thousand pounds apiece. I knew it was bad if, as my eyes scanned down the page, my head kept drooping and I nodded off to sleep. The good ones, I noticed, the ones that ultimately made good movies, had the opposite effect on my body. They woke me up. The organs of my body came to life one by one. The body became alert, light, and happy, squirting fluids into the pleasure centers of the brain, "the proper pleasure" as Aristotle called it, of experiencing emotional and physical release through a well-told, cathartic tale.

As we watch a good movie or are engrossed in a good novel, we actually go into an altered state of consciousness, with a measurable change in brain waves detectable by the tools of science. Perhaps changes in the rhythm of the breath, combined with focusing the attention on the imaginary world of the story, bring about this almost hypnotic effect.

When I started critiquing screenplays and stories for a living, I soon found that what I was really reporting was how they had triggered chemical reactions in the organs of my body. The organs squirt fluids, all day long, as we react to various emotional and physical situations in our environment, and it's no different when we watch a movie or imagine scenes from a novel. When we are stressed or frightened, our adrenal glands transmit a chemical jolt through the body, sending signals to increase the heart rate and pace of breathing. When we are in shock from seeing traumatic or frightening things, our bodies send messages to shut down certain processes to preserve a core of life in an emergency.

The word "horror" derives from the Latin word for bristling and reflects the body's automatic reaction to uncanny events, things that upset the normal order. Such sights trigger a physical reaction in the skin of the arms that resembles the response to cold air. Tiny muscles cause the hairs on the arms to stand up, a reaction called "horripilation," that means "bristling hair" or hair standing on end. Horror is hair-raising. Some scientists think this may be a survival from hairier times in human history, when having your thick pelt of hair stand up when threatened would make you look bigger and scarier, as many animals will swell up or ruffle up their fur when facing threats.

A tip for designers of sensory experiences: A sudden blast of chilly air can trigger a shuddering effect in audiences, especially if they are keyed up for it by some emotional or musical manipulation. The chill can trigger the graveyard shudder of fear or a more exalted form of physical reaction, like awe, wonder, or spiritual rebirth.

The effect of shuddering, in which the muscles of the body, especially the arms and back, involuntarily ripple or spasm, is associated with other emotional effects in addition to horror. Religious awe or deep psychological insight can produce shudders that can be very pleasurable, signs of grace, endorsement from the body of the rightness of a thought. A shiver of this kind in French is called a "frisson," and I noticed the phenomenon when I concentrated hard on working out a story problem, especially when working collaboratively in open discussion with other people. In the course of trying out different ideas someone would say something that triggered a shiver of response in me. I would feel a tingle passing down my spine, almost as if thousands of small pebbles were rolling down my spinal column. It felt the way a rain stick sounds, one of those hollow wooden tubes with dried peas inside that makes a sound like falling rain. Sometimes other people would feel it too, or feel something like it, because I could see their bodies being jolted by it. The shiver ran round the room.

I learned to value those physical reactions because they were telling me I was in the presence of something true and right, something beautiful. In these story sessions, sometimes the answer to a story problem rang true, on many levels of my being, sending a subtle physical signal that elements were lining up to create a desirable emotional outcome, or that the story would now make better sense or be more realistic or funnier. It suggested to me that there is an inner grid of rightness about art and emotion, and that our bodies respond with pleasure when we make works that line up with this grid, allowing emotional energy to flow at full power like electrical current. Solutions to story problems can have a certain beauty or elegance, as theories of physics or mathematical solutions are said to be elegant. Perhaps we sense that the solution is in harmony with some universal truth, some essential reality in the universe.

Stories appeal to the organs at different levels, and there is a hierarchy, an ascending order of emotional development that is reflected in the Indian concept of the chakra system. These are imagined to be a number of invisible but very real centers of life within the body, most of them located along the spine. There are seven principal chakras, each governing a different function, ascending from the crude physical needs of the body to the highest aspirations of the soul. Chakra means ring or circle and the chakras are conceived as ring-like centers of energy near important organs. They are pictured as lotus flowers that can be open or closed depending on the person's spiritual development. They form a map of the stages of a person's growth or at least potential for growth, for few people progress past the first three levels, having to do with sheer survival, sex, and power, all below the belt line. Some are lucky enough to progress to the heart chakra and experience love. Few reach the level of the throat chakra that allows for expression of the other drives. Writers and artists may be among these. With spiritual enlightenment the sixth chakra, in the region of the "third eye," can be opened, sometimes granting psychic abilities, and for a very few saintly people, the seventh or crown chakra may flower, showering the fully awakened person with a fountain of divine grace.

These symbols can be useful in charting the development of a character, giving metaphors for the stages of change and growth. Some people don't ascend the ladder of emotional development in proper order but may skip up to open two or more chakras at different levels, with very different effects and many possible combinations. According to some modern Hindu sages, Hitler may have been very open in the power and throat chakras, making him an effective communicator who could stir the emotions and marshal power with his voice, but he was probably shut tight in most of the other chakras.

According to theory, the chakras can be stimulated in various ways and each is responsive to specific colors, smells, and especially sounds. Supposedly, unhealthy chakras can be cleansed or opened by exposure to the vibrations of gongs, bells, drums, and trumpets. In movies, big emotional breakthroughs duplicate the opening of the higher chakras, and are enhanced and emphasized by climaxes in the music and action.

In evaluating story material for the Hollywood studios, I began to think about how modern entertainment plays upon the various emotional and physical centers of the body, and observed that good stories affected me in at least two organs at once, perhaps getting my heart racing with tension while making my throat choke up with sympathy for the death of a character. I needed to tear up, choke up, freeze up, or laugh it up, and the more of those physical reactions I felt, the better the story was. Ideally perhaps, all the organs of the body should be stimulated by a good story in the course of exploring all the possibilities of an emotional situation. My motto as a story evaluator became, "If it isn't making at least two organs of my body squirt fluids, it's no good."

Catharsis, discussed elsewhere in this volume, is the biggest emotional and physical trigger of them all. We may get it in small doses from almost every drama or story we see, but the big catharsis, a whole-body emotional and physical spasm that cleans out your entire system of toxins or triggers a complete change of orientation, is pretty rare. You wouldn't want to go through that disruption every day, for a catharsis usually means a radical reorganization of priorities and belief systems. But it does still happen now and then, when the story and the listener are lined up just right, and it's the thing that makes so many people want to go into show business and the arts. They've felt it. In the presence of work that is beautiful and true, honest and real, something smashes you like a hammer striking glass and allows you to suddenly put your own experience into proper new perspective. You might have experienced that deep shudder of realization, a moment of profound connection with your family, your country, your humanity, with the divine, or the things you believe in. A story, once in a great while, can touch us at the deepest level, giving us a new view of the world or a new reason to live, perhaps when we are ready for that particular story to speak its truth to us. No wonder some people want to be artists and storytellers, to participate in that mystery, and create the possibility of that experience for others.

QUESTIONS

1. What sensations do you get in watching a powerful dramatic experience or a moving performance by a singer or other artist?

2. Think of a story that you particularly enjoyed or that meant something to you. How did it affect the organs of your body?

3. What symbols or tableaux are particularly moving or meaningful to you? How would you describe your feelings so someone else could experience what you felt?

4. How has your body reacted to frightening or life-threatening situations? Write a short story or short film script capturing this experience.

5. Watch a scary movie and observe how the filmmaker manipulates your breathing with editing, suspense, musical rhythms, color, etc.

6. What kind of scene stirs up the most emotion or the strongest physical reaction for you? Write a series of scenes aiming to evoke specific emotional or physical reactions — to bring a shiver down the back, to raise goose-bumps on the arms, to trigger tears or laughter.

TRUST THE PATH

TRUST THE PATH

"In the midst of life's journey I found myself in a dark wood, for the right path was lost."

So said Dante at the beginning of the *Inferno* and so I found myself at a certain passage in the journey of my life, hiking alone in the forest near Big Sur, California. I was in a dark wood, all right, and lost. I was cold, hungry, shivering, exhausted, and panicked by the thought of night closing in.

It had been a rainy winter, with storm after storm saturating the hillsides after years of drought. I felt pounded by heavy weather in my own life, and had come north to the sacred country of Big Sur to find some things I had lost: solitude, peace of mind, clarity. I felt I had failed in important areas of jobs and relationships and was confused about which way to move next. I had some decisions to make about my direction and knew instinctively that a plunge into the wilderness could give me a vision of the future to lead me out of my present confusion.

As I set out on the well-marked Forest Service trail that winds into the wild canyons of Big Sur, I noted a little sign that warned the trail was rough in spots. I expected the path to be wet and muddy in places because of the recent rains, but quickly found out I had underestimated the ferocious impact of the winter storms on the fragile hillsides. The whole mountain range was a vast sponge that was now draining slowly into the canyons, unimaginable amounts of water carving new canyons and streams. Time and again I rounded a corner to find that the trail ahead simply vanished for fifty yards because a whole hillside had washed away, trail and all, leaving a damp scar of crumbling shale and a waterfall cascading down the raw rock. The freshly exposed rock is easily broken into shards called scree that flow downhill almost as easily as water, and can be as treacherous as quicksand. I could see the trail continuing again beyond the stretch where the hillside had collapsed, and had no choice but to scramble like a crab across the shifting, slippery rock face, clinging by fingertips and toes, digging into the tumbling scree until I was back on the level surface of the broken path. It continued for a few hundred feet around a shoulder of the mountain, only to disappear again in another mudslide that had to be crossed by the finger-and-toe method.

At first this seemed exhilarating, just the kind of minor wilderness challenge that I was after. But after the third or fourth time of edging out across a sheer, unstable cliff face with muddy water streaming over me, the process began to take its toll. My arms and legs began to tremble from the unaccustomed exertion, my fingers and toes grew cramped. My core temperature dropped from repeated soakings as the cool air chilled my clothes and skin by evaporation. At times the whole hillside of yellow mud and shale seemed to be shuddering and slipping under me, flowing in a slow-motion mudslide. By the tenth crossing I was starting to get worried. The hike that was supposed to take an hour had taken three hours and there was no end in sight. I lost my footing a couple of times in the muck and barely caught myself, clinging to the crumbling rock with fingers cramped and arms shaking, knowing I would fall for hundreds of feet before I hit something solid and level.

And then, as my adventure led me around the cooler, shadow side of the mountain, I reached a vast, wet scar where a whole slab of the mountain had fallen away into a deep canyon, leaving a slanted field of jagged boulders the size of houses that would be challenging to cross. I didn't know whether to turn back or keep going. I began to measure my strength very precisely, recognizing a primal, instinctive hyper-awareness that comes when one is at the edge of death. For as I watched the sun sink into the tree-line, I felt my life energy draining, and realized I was in one of those classic California wilderness tragedy situations that you read about in the newspapers. Some fool gets himself stuck in the woods at night and falls into a canyon and breaks his neck or wanders lost for days until he starves to death. It happens all the time. Was this my turn?

With my heightened awareness I knew almost to the calorie how much energy was left in my body. I had brought little food with me, just a handful of trail mix, and had consumed that long ago, observing how the nuts and raisins instantly charged me with energy, only to send me crashing a few minutes later when I had burned them off in scrambling across the treacherous shale. How thin is the margin that preserves life. I knew that every step from now on was drawing on core reserves. I could almost see the sands in the hourglass of my life rushing inevitably down to nothing.

The question was whether to turn back or go ahead. The way ahead was uncertain. I couldn't see the trail picking up on the other side of the landslip and I knew it would be a difficult task to cross the rugged face of the scar, which was the only way to continue. It would take as much energy as I had already expended, maybe more, and there was no assurance that I would be able to find the trail again in the trees on the other side. I might just be plunging deeper into the wilderness with night coming on.

I thought about turning back and re-tracing the broken trail I had just traversed with such difficulty, but I knew with a terrible certainty that if I tried that, I would die. My hands were cramping up like claws and would be almost useless. My arms and legs were shaking and I was absolutely sure that I would fall if I tried to go back across three or four more of those muddy vertical rock faces, especially in the dark.

So I gathered my strength and continued on across the field of boulders, crawling like an ant, an insignificant dot on the flank of a mountain. I was impressed by the immense forces that had raised these rocks thousands of feet into the sky in the first place and now had torn down the mountainside. I finally made it across into the trees, winded, cold, and feeling at the end of my strength, but now there was a different problem. Where was the trail? There was no sign of it. Vague paths seemed to lead me deeper into darkness, into brambles, into impenetrable cool thickets like those surrounding cursed castles in fairy tales. I stumbled up and down the mountainside, my face and hands scratched by branches, hoping to intersect with the true path, but getting more and more hopelessly lost and frantic as night crept near. I had to get out of there. I knew it was a very bad idea to attempt to spend the night in the forest, unprepared. People die of exposure out here all the time. I noticed for the first time that air on a mountain flows at different times of day like a mass of water. Cold air seemed to be rushing downhill all around me, flooding the bottomless canyon and chilling my blood, dragging my spirits further down.

I dread that word "lost" and tried to deny it to myself, but I had to admit it. A whole host of unfamiliar sensations and thoughts came over me as I watched the shadows of the black trees march down the canyons. My heart pounded, my hands shook. The forest seemed to be speaking to me, pleading with me, calling to me. "Come," it said in a witch's voice of a million leaves rasping together. "Here is an easy end to your pain. Join us! Jump! Take a run and launch yourself off this cliff into this canyon. It will all be over in an instant. We'll take care of everything." And oddly enough, that plea sounded appealing and reasonable to some part of me, the part that was terrified, the part that just wanted this awful moment to be over.

But another sliver of my brain stepped back, and recognized that I was experiencing the common human psychological state known as panic. The Greeks, with their talent for naming things, called it panic because they believed it was a visit from the nature god Pan, goat-footed, flute-playing Pan, who can inspire mortals but also has the power to terrify them, overwhelming their senses with the awesome forces at his command, causing them to do foolish things and die.

I felt the presence too of the witches from the old European and Russian folk tales, fearsome figures who represent the dual nature of the primeval forest. The heroes of those tales learn that the witches, like the forest, can quickly break, destroy, and consume you, but, if you learn how to appease and honor them, they can also support and protect you like a kindly grandmother, hiding you from enemies and providing you food and shelter. At the moment, the forest was turning its nastiest and most seductive witchy face to me. There was something alive and evil and hungry out there, like the witch in "Hansel and Gretel" but stretched out over the whole forest. I was in big trouble.

I stopped and took a breath. That simple act brought a sudden surge of clarity and common sense to my panicked brain that was causing me to rush about like a terrified animal. I realized I had not been breathing properly, that my gasping and panting had deprived my brain of oxygen. Together with my exhaustion and the sudden chill, I was in a mild state of shock, blood rushing away from the head and extremities to preserve a core of life force and heat. I took a few deep breaths and could feel blood returning to my skull.

Instead of thrashing around pointlessly, I took in my surroundings and got in touch with something ancient and instinctive in me, a reliable inner sense of what to do in dangerous situations.

Just then, a voice came into my head, clear as sunlight. "Trust the path," it said. I truly heard this, as a spoken sentence that seemed to be coming from a deep part of me. But I smiled, scoffing at the idea. That's the problem, I said to myself. There is no path. I trusted the Forest Service trail and look where it got me. I've been looking for the path for half an hour and it's just not here. And in the larger sense, in the big picture of my life, over a period of years, I had also lost sight of the true way.

"Trust the path," said the voice again, patient and true. In that voice was a certainty that there must be a path, and that it could be relied upon to do its job.

I looked down and saw a little groove in the weeds — an ant trail. There, oblivious to my panic, ants were going about their tiny business in an endless column. With my eyes I followed the ant trail, the only path I could see.

It led me to a slightly deeper groove in the underbrush, a little trail used by field mice and other small creatures, almost a tunnel through the brambles. And soon that guided me to a broader path, a zigzagging deer trail that climbed the mountainside in easy stages. I started putting one foot in front of the other, following that trail. It led me out of the labyrinth, like Ariadne's thread leading Theseus out of the maze. In a few steps I came to a clearing, a mountain meadow were the sun was still shining. Across the meadow I found a well-maintained trail and realized I was back on an official Forest Service path, the right road, the way back.

As I walked along, calmer now, the way out of my personal confusion became clearer. "Trust the path," my voice had said, and I took that to mean "Keep marching ahead to the next stage of life. Don't try to go backwards, don't allow yourself to get paralyzed or panicked, just keep marching. Trust that your instincts are good and natural and will lead you to a happier, safer place." Then the hiking trail merged with a fire road, wide as two firetrucks, and in half an hour I was back on the highway where my blessed Volkswagen was parked. The sun was still blazing on the Western horizon, though I knew back in those canyons it was already deepest night, and I could have died there.

As I looked back at the mountains and forest that had just held me in their jaws, I realized I'd been given a gift with that phrase, Trust the Path, and I pass it on to you. It means that when you are lost and confused, you can trust the journey that you have chosen, or that has chosen you. It means others have been on the journey before you, the writer's journey, the storyteller's journey. You're not the first, you're not the last. Your experience of it is unique, your viewpoint has value, but you're also part of something, a long tradition that stretches back to the very beginnings of our race. The journey has it own wisdom, the story knows the way. Trust the journey. Trust the story. Trust the path.

As Dante says, at the beginning of the *Inferno,* "In the midst of life's journey I found myself in a dark wood, for the right path was lost." I think we're all doing that, in our various ways, finding ourselves through the journey of our writing lives. Looking for our Selves in the dark wood. I wish you luck and adventure and I hope you find yourself on your journey. Bon voyage.

FILMOGRAPHY

Adventures of Robin Hood, The
African Queen, The
After Midnight
Agony and the Ecstasy, The
Aladdin
American Graffiti
Analyze This
Anna and the King
Annie Hall
Arabesque
Arthur
As Good as It Gets
Awakenings
Back to the Future
Barbarossa
Basic Instinct
Beauty and the Beast
Beverly Hills Cop
Big
Big Chill, The
Big Sleep, The
Body Heat
Breakfast Club, The
Butch Cassidy and the Sundance Kid
Casablanca
Casino
Charade
Chinatown
Citizen Kane
City Slickers
Clash of the Titans
Close Encounters of the Third Kind
Connecticut Yankee in King Arthur's Court, A
Count of Monte Cristo, The
Dances with Wolves
Dead Again
Death Becomes Her
Dirty Dozen, The
Driving Miss Daisy
Dr. Jekyll and Mr. Hyde
Dune
E.T., The Extraterrestrial
East of Eden
Eiger Sanction, The
El Cid
Empire Strikes Back, The
Excalibur
Fantasia
Fargo
Fatal Attraction
Father of the Bride
Few Good Men, A
Field of Dreams
Fight Club
First Blood
Fisher King, The
Five Easy Pieces
Flame and the Arrow, The
Fort Apache
48 Hours
Four Seasons, The
Fried Green Tomatoes
From Russia with Love
Full Monty, The
Ghost
Ghost of Frankenstein
Great Escape, The
Great Train Robbery, The
Glory
Godfather, The
Goldfinger
Gone with the Wind
Goodbye, Mr. Chips
Goodfellas
Gorillas in the Mist
Graduate, The
Great Escape, The
Guess Who's Coming to Dinner
Gunga Din
Henry V
High Noon
Hurricane
Indiana Jones and the Last Crusade
Indiana Jones and the Temple of Doom
In-Laws, The
It Happened One Night
It's a Wonderful Life
Ivanhoe
Jaws
Jester Till
Karate Kid, The
King Kong
Lady from Shanghai, The
Last Boy Scout, The
Last of the Mohicans, The
Lawrence of Arabia
League of Their Own, A
Lethal Weapon (series)
Liar, Liar
Life and Times of Judge Roy Bean, The
Lion King, The
Look Who's Talking
Looking for Mr. Goodbar
Lord Jim
Lord of the Rings, The: The Two Towers
Lost in Translation
Love Story
Maltese Falcon, The
Manhunter
Master and Commander: The Far Side of the World
Matrix
Medicine Man
Midnight Cowboy
Moby Dick
Mommie Dearest
Mrs. Doubtfire
Mr. Smith Goes to Washington
My Darling Clementine
Norma Rae
No Way Out
North by Northwest
Notorious
Nutty Professor, The
Officer and a Gentleman, An
On Golden Pond
Ordinary People
Papillon

Peter Pan
Pinocchio
Platoon
Poseidon Adventure, The
Pretty Woman
Prime of Miss Jean Brodie, The
Prince of Tides, The
Psycho
P. S. Your Cat Is Dead
Public Enemy, The
Pulp Fiction
Quest for Fire
Raiders of the Lost Ark
Rain Man
Rebel Without a Cause
Red River
Remains of the Day
Return of the Jedi
Risky Business
Road Warrior
Robin Hood, Prince of Thieves
Rocky
Romancing the Stone
Rush Hour (series)
Sand Pebbles, The
Scarface
Sea Hawk, The
Searchers, The
Shadow of a Doubt
Shakespeare in Love
Shane
Shining, The
Silence of the Lambs, The
Sister Act
Sleeping Beauty, The
Snow White
Sophie's Choice
Stagecoach
Stand and Deliver
Star Trek (series)
Star Wars
Stranger, The
Strangers on a Train
Summer Catch
Suspicion
Terminator, The
Terminator 2: Judgment Day
Terms of Endearment
That Championship Season
Thelma & Louise
They Died with Their Boots On
Thin Red Line, The
Till Eulenspiegel
Tingler, The
Titanic
To Catch a Thief
Tootsie
Topper
Torn Curtain
Towering Inferno, The
Trading Places
Treasure of the Sierra Madre, The
Unforgiven
Vertigo
Volcano
Wall Street
White Men Can't Jump
Who Framed Roger Rabbit?
Wild Bunch, The
Wild One, The
Willow
Witness
Wizard of Oz, The
Young Guns
Zoolander

BIBLIOGRAPHY

Benet's Reader's Encyclopedia, Harper & Row 1987

Bolen, Jean Shinoda, M. D., *Goddesses in Everywoman*, Harper & Row 1985

Bolen, Jean Shinoda, M. D., *Gods in Everyman*, Harper & Row 1989

Bulfinch, Thomas, *Myths of Greece and Rome*, Penguin Books 1981

Campbell, Joseph (with Bill Moyers), *The Power of Myth*, Doubleday 1988

Campbell, Joseph, *The Hero with a Thousand Faces*, Bollingen Series/Princeton University Press 1973

Davidson, H. R. Ellis, *Gods and Myths of Northern Europe*, Penguin Books 1984

Graves, Robert, *The Greek Myths*, Penguin Books 1979

Halliwell, Leslie, *Filmgoer's Companion*, 8th Edition, Charles Scribner's Sons 1983

Homer, *The Odyssey*, transl. by E. V. Rieu, Penguin Books 1960

Johnson, Robert A., *He: Understanding Masculine Psychology*, Harper & Row 1977

Johnson, Robert A., *She: Understanding Feminine Psychology*, Harper & Row 1977

Johnson, Robert A., *We: Understanding the Psychology of Romantic Love*, Harper & Row 1983

Knight, Arthur, *The Liveliest Art*, New American Library 1957

Lattimore, Richmond, *The Iliad of Homer*, University of Chicago Press 1967

Leeming, David, *Mythology*, Newsweek Books 1976

Levinson, Daniel J., *The Seasons of a Man's Life*, Ballantine Books 1978

Luthi, Max, *The Fairytale as Art Form and Portrait of Man*, Indiana University Press 1987

Mast, Gerald, *A Short History of the Movies*, Bobbs-Merrill 1979

Murdock, Maureen, *The Heroine's Journey: Woman's Quest for Wholeness*, Shambala 1990

Pearson, Carol S., *Awakening the Heroes Within*, Harper San Francisco 1991

Propp, Vladimir, *Morphology of the Folktale*, University of Texas Press 1979

Wheelwright, Philip, *Aristotle*, The Odyssey Press 1955

SUBJECT INDEX

D

G

M

W

ABOUT THE AUTHOR

Christopher Vogler is one of Hollywood's premier
story consultants and a popular speaker on
screenwriting, movies, and myth.
He is president of Storytech, a literary
consulting firm to help writers, producers,
and studio executives shape their projects.
Storytech provides a complete range
of services including evaluation of screenplays,
novels, and concepts; detailed
development notes; and expert story analysis
for copyright litigation.
You can visit Storytech's website at:
www.thewritersjourney.com

Storytech rates and other services are available
upon request from:
vogler.christopher@gmail.com

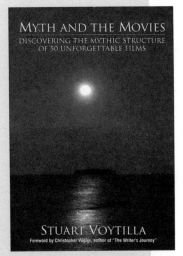

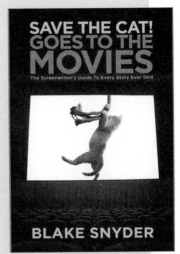

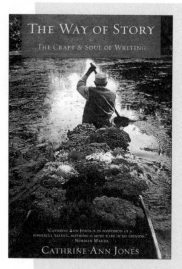

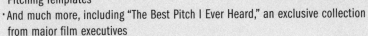

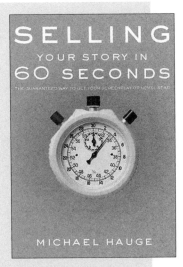

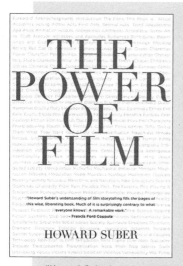

THE MYTH OF MWP

In a dark time, a light bringer came along, leading the curious and the frustrated to clarity and empowerment. It took the well-guarded secrets out of the hands of the few and made them available to all. It spread a spirit of openness and creative freedom, and built a storehouse of knowledge dedicated to the betterment of the arts.

The essence of the Michael Wiese Productions (MWP) is empowering people who have the burning desire to express themselves creatively. We help them realize their dreams by putting the tools in their hands. We demystify the sometimes secretive worlds of screenwriting, directing, acting, producing, film financing, and other media crafts.

By doing so, we hope to bring forth a realization of 'conscious media' which we define as being positively charged, emphasizing hope and affirming positive values like trust, cooperation, self-empowerment, freedom, and love. Grounded in the deep roots of myth, it aims to be healing both for those who make the art and those who encounter it. It hopes to be transformative for people, opening doors to new possibilities and pulling back veils to reveal hidden worlds.

MWP has built a storehouse of knowledge unequaled in the world, for no other publisher has so many titles on the media arts. Please visit www.mwp.com where you will find many free resources and a 25% discount on our books. Sign up and become part of the wider creative community!

Onward and upward,

Michael Wiese
Publisher/Filmmaker